ECONOMICS FOR BUSINESS DECISIONS

Economics for Business Decisions

F. Livesey

BA(Econ)
*Head of School of Economics and Business Studies,
Preston Polytechnic*

PITMAN PUBLISHING
128 Long Acre, London WC2E 9AN

A Division of Longman Group UK Limited

© Macdonald & Evans Ltd 1983

First published in Great Britain 1983
Reprinted 1987, 1989

British Library Cataloguing in Publication Data
Livesey, Frank
　Economics for business decisions
　　1. Managerial economics
　I. Title
　330'.024658　HD58.5

ISBN 0 273 02847 2

All rights reserved. No part of this publication may be reproduced, stored in a retrieval system, or transmitted, in any form or by any means, electronic, mechanical, photocopying, recording and/or otherwise without either the prior written permission of the Publishers or a licence permitting restricted copying in the United Kingdom issued by the Copyright Licensing Agency Ltd, 33-34 Alfred Place, London WC1E 7DP. This book may not be lent, resold, hired out or otherwise disposed of by way of trade in any form of binding or cover other than that in which it is published, without the prior consent of the Publishers.

Produced by Longman Group (FE) Ltd
Printed in Hong Kong

Preface

As the title suggests, this book is concerned with the application of economic analysis to business decisions. In addition to those decisions taken by economists, there are many which are taken by non-economists where the economist's approach can make a useful contribution. Central to this approach is an assessment of the costs and benefits associated with alternative uses of resources.

When organisations allocate their resources they take account of the economic environment in which they operate. Consequently we begin by discussing the economic environment in Part I.

In business, increasing attention is being given to the collection and presentation of information in quantitative form, and various methods and techniques of measurement are discussed in Part II. (Techniques using more advanced mathematics and statistics are presented in C. A. N. Morris, *Quantitative Approaches in Business Studies*, also published by Pitman Publishing. These methods relate to both the assessment of the present situation and the prediction of future situations.

In Part III a range of models of markets and of the firm are presented. A long-running controversy has surrounded the role and nature of the firm in economic models. Some economists believe that the firms should be abstract entities. Others believe that the firms should, in their objectives and behaviour, resemble—albeit in a highly simplified manner—actual firms. This controversy is reflected in Part III, where the progression is from first viewpoint in Chapter 7 to the second in Chapter 9.

Part IV focuses on the activities of actual firms, and in particular on the ways in which they formulate their long-term strategic plans.

Finally in Part V we discuss the various competitive weapons used by firms in implementing their strategy. Economists have traditionally emphasised price competition, and this is discussed in Chapters 13 and 14. Non-price competition is discussed at length in Chapter 15.

The entire manuscript was read by Michael Barnato, a business economist in a major nationalised industry, and Christopher J. Clarke, Principal in a large management consultancy practice. I am very grateful to both for their comments. I am also grateful to Liz Campbell who typed most of the manuscript, and whose productivity I sometimes found difficult to match.

1983   F.L.

Contents

Preface   v

PART I   THE ECONOMIC ENVIRONMENT

1   The Economic Environment   3

Objectives Introduction The components of final expenditure The implications of changes in expenditure The determination of national income Final expenditure, gross national product and national income A simple model of income determination Questions

2   Macro-economic Policy   14

Objectives Introduction An increase in expenditure Inter-relationships between expenditure flows Increased expenditure and the price level The consequences of inflation The challenge to Keynesianism The two approaches compared The "monetarist" experiment Questions

3   Micro-economic Policy   25

Objectives Introduction Reasons for government intervention The policies Competition policy Nationalisation Industrial policy Regional policy Manpower policy The United Kingdom and the European Economic Community Questions

PART II   MEASUREMENT IN ECONOMICS

4   The Assessment of Demand   47

Objectives Introduction Extrapolation Barometric techniques Econometric models Surveys Assessing the demand for new or modified products Market evaluation Scenario analysis Questions

5   Cost Analysis   60

Objectives Introduction The behaviour of costs as output changes with a given scale of organisation The behaviour of costs with a given scale of organisation: summary The behaviour of costs with a changing scale of organisation The behaviour of costs with a changing scale of organisation: summary Measurement of economies of scale Economies of scale, specialisation and joint ventures Additional cost concepts Changes in input prices Questions

CONTENTS

6 The Cost of Finance and Investment Appraisal   87

Objectives Introduction Sources and uses of funds: an overview Internal sources of finance External sources of finance The financing of public-sector producers The cost of funds Investment appraisal Uncertainty and investment appraisal Discounting methods of investment appraisal Other methods of investment appraisal Areas of application of investment appraisal Capital rationing and investment decisions Investment appraisal in the public sector Questions

PART III MODELS

7 Models of Markets   121

Objectives Introduction A classification of markets Perfect competition Monopoly Monopolistic competition Oligopoly Market models and the firm Questions

8 Models of the Firm   138

Objectives Introduction Firms' objectives Long-run profit maximisation Models incorporating the maximisation of other variables Equilibrium Questions

9 Price Takers and Price Makers   155

Objectives Introduction Price taking in open markets Price taking in other markets Price makers Pricing with different cost structures The co-ordination of activities Questions

PART IV STRATEGY FORMULATION

10 Corporate Strategy   179

Objectives Introduction The role of corporate strategy The strategic planning process Examining the firm's environment Evaluating the firm's strengths and weaknesses Identifying the direction of change Selection of the firm's portfolio Strategy formulation in multinational enterprises Other determinants of direct foreign investment The ownership of production facilities Patterns of control Case studies Questions

11 Market and Non-market Relationships   206

Objectives Introduction Vertical relationships Horizontal expansion Diversification External growth De-mergers Quasi-market relationships Questions

12 The Nature and Impact of Technological Change   223

Objectives Introduction Technological change and the choice of technique Technological change and new products Research and development as an investment decision Strategic objectives of research and development Portfolio selection Factors affecting the success of innovations Questions

PART V IMPLEMENTATION OF STRATEGY

13 Price and Output Decisions — 243

Objectives Introduction The determinants of basic price The firm's objectives The relationship between price and other elements of the marketing mix The relative importance of price in purchase decisions Price awareness and sensitivity of consumers Legal constraints The implementation of pricing policies Pricing in bid situations Product analysis pricing Questions

14 Subsidiary Pricing Decisions — 272

Objectives Introduction Elasticity of demand and price differentials Costs, price differentials and price discrimination The subdivision of markets The subdivision of markets by space The subdivision of markets by time The subdivision of markets by the functional role of the customer Quantity discount structures The subdivision of markets by the personal characteristics of purchasers Promotional pricing Pricing and the product life cycle Product line pricing Transfer pricing Questions

15 Non-price Competition — 301

Objectives Introduction The development and protection of markets Non-price competition and stability of demand The relative importance of alternative forms of competition Advertising The demand for advertising The supply of advertising Sales promotions Other forms of marketing communication The introduction of new products Packaging Service Credit Choice of distribution channels Market information Questions

Index — 333

PART ONE

The Economic Environment

CHAPTER ONE
The Economic Environment

OBJECTIVES

After studying this chapter the reader should be able to: explain how the level of economic activity is measured; list the major factors causing changes in the relative importance of the various forms of expenditure; understand the implications for companies of changes in expenditure; construct a simple model explaining the determination of national income.

INTRODUCTION

Business decisions are concerned with the acquisition of resources, and the transformation of these resources into goods and services to be supplied to customers of various types. Most of this book is devoted to an analysis of this process of acquiring and transforming resources, but first we discuss the environment within which this process takes place. The transformation of resources into goods and services is undertaken only because there is a demand for these goods and services, and we begin our discussion of the economic environment by examining changes in the markets for different types of product. Markets can be classified in various ways and we consider first a very broad classification, as presented in the national income accounts.

THE COMPONENTS OF FINAL EXPENDITURE

Final expenditure is composed of four major expenditure flows, four broad types of market: expenditure on consumers' goods, expenditure on investment goods, government consumption, and exports (a combination of expenditure by overseas consumers, firms and governments).

Spending has increased in all four types of market, but at different rates. Table I shows the relative importance of these four expenditure flows. Consumers' expenditure accounts for almost half of final expenditure; however its share has fallen as consumers' expenditure has risen less rapidly than total expenditure.

TABLE I. SHARE OF TOTAL FINAL EXPENDITURE

	1971 (%)	1981 (%)
Consumers' expenditure	51.2	48.8
Government consumption	14.7	17.8
Investment	15.4	11.4
Exports	18.7	21.9

Source: *Economic Trends*

Spending on investment goods has also risen at a relatively slow rate so that its share of the total has fallen. On the other hand a higher share has been achieved by government consumption and by exports. We now look at the composition of each of these four flows, beginning with the biggest, consumers' expenditure.

Consumers' expenditure

As incomes have risen over the past decade, so has consumers' expenditure (*see* Table II). However the pattern of growth has been uneven. In real terms spending has grown most rapidly on household durable goods, clothing and footwear and least rapidly on necessities—food, housing, fuel and light. This pattern of growth is typical of an economy whose citizens have already achieved a fairly high standard of living. (The exception to this pattern, a fall in spending on cars and motor cycles, is partly the result of the steep rise in the price of petrol.)

TABLE II. CONSUMERS' EXPENDITURE (1975 PRICES)

	1981 (£m)	Change 1971–81 (%)
Total	71,447	20
Food	12,398	2
Alcoholic drink and tobacco	7,620	17
Housing	10,001	15
Fuel and light	3,080	12
Clothing and footwear	6,447	37
Durable household goods	4,057	67
Cars, motor cycles	2,278	−3
Other goods	11,846	32
Other services	13,720	24

Source: *Economic Trends*

Investment expenditure

Investment expenditure has three marked characteristics. First, in recent years investment spending has risen less rapidly than total expenditure as a whole. Second, over time demand tends to fluctuate more for investment than for consumer goods. Third, the pattern of demand has varied considerably as between one sector of the investment goods industry and another.

The first point was demonstrated in our earlier discussion of final expenditure. The other two points are illustrated in Fig. 1. (This refers to the volume of new orders. Output fluctuates less because of changes in the length of order books.)

The volume of new orders has fallen dramatically in mechanical

1. THE ECONOMIC ENVIRONMENT

engineering orders received in 1981 being less than two-thirds of those for 1973. The product of this sector accrued throughout the early and the full order does reflect the overall decline in manufacturing, but technical change has also been important. New field devices being substituted for mechanical devices, a wide range of industries. It can be seen that the decline in orders for electrical equipment is much more modest, indeed orders received in 1981 were higher than in 1970, the base year, in electrical though not in instrument engineering.

Several declines in orders were experienced in 1974 (all sectors), 1975 (all sectors) and 1980 (mechanical engineering) balanced up in by increases in some sectors in 1974, and more notably from 1977 in the electrical sectors, 1978 (instrument and electrical engineering) and 1981 (mechanical engineering).

Government consumption. Government consumption comprises the operating, non-capital expenditure on goods and services by central government and the local authorities. Spending under this heading is sometimes affected by changes of government. But even it has recently this been for government consumption to account for a smaller share of total expenditure, as shown below.

Table I shows the relative importance in three years of the major items of expenditure. The full fall the relative importance of defence spending reflects the reduction in main UK overseas military commitments. The increase in 1981 reflects the more important financial and defence, the latter under new Government.

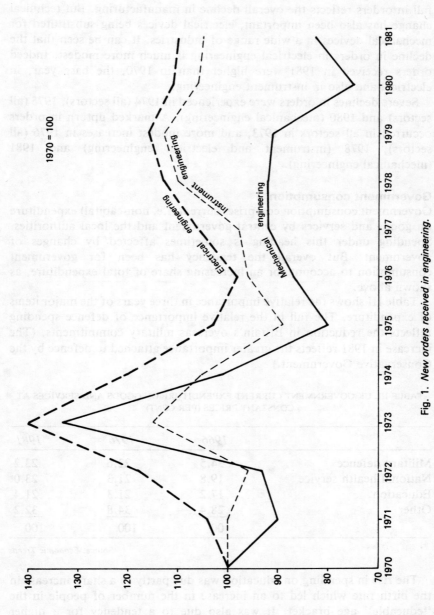

Fig. 1. *New orders received in engineering.*

The fall in the birth rate also was in part by a later increase in the birth rate which led to an increase in the number of people in the "teenage" age bracket. It was also due to a tendency for a higher proportion of these people to continue education beyond the minimum school leaving age. An expansion in the education service commonly occurs as incomes rise.

engineering, orders received in 1981 being less than two-thirds of those in 1973. The products of this sector are used throughout industry, and the fall in orders reflects the overall decline in manufacturing. But technical change has also been important, electrical devices being substituted for mechanical devices in a wide range of industries. It can be seen that the decline in orders in electrical engineering is much more modest. Indeed orders received in 1981 were higher than in 1970, the base year, in electrical and also in instrument engineering.

Severe declines in orders were experienced in 1974 (all sectors), 1975 (all sectors) and 1980 (mechanical engineering). A marked upturn in orders occurred in all sectors in 1973, and more modest increases in 1976 (all sectors), 1978 (instrument and electrical engineering) and 1981 (mechanical engineering).

Government consumption

Government consumption comprises current (i.e. non-capital) expenditure on goods and services by central government and the local authorities. Spending under this heading is sometimes affected by changes of government. But overall the tendency has been for government consumption to account for an increasing share of total expenditure, as shown above.

Table III shows the relative importance in three years of the major items of expenditure. The fall in the relative importance of defence spending reflects the reduction in Britain's overseas military commitments. (The increase in 1981 reflects the greater importance attached to defence by the Conservative Government.)

TABLE III. UK GOVERNMENT CURRENT EXPENDITURE ON GOODS AND SERVICES AT CONSTANT PRICES (PER CENT)

	1966	1976	1981
Military defence	34.5	22.6	23.2
National health service	19.8	21.3	23.0
Education	17.2	21.3	21.4
Other	28.4	34.8	32.2
	100	100	100

Source: *Economic Trends*

The rise in spending on education was due partly to a sharp increase in the birth rate which led to an increase in the number of people in the "educable" age bracket. It was also due to a tendency for a higher proportion of these people to continue education beyond the minimum school leaving age; an expansion in the education service commonly occurs as incomes rise.

A rise in the birth rate also required an increase in spending on health in the earlier part of the period. More recently an increase in the number of elderly people has emerged as a more important stimulus to spending. Another factor leading to higher spending has been the discovery and development of new, powerful, but often expensive, drugs.

Exports

Table IV shows that exports have accounted for an increasing share of the sales of every manufacturing industry. Exports are especially important in engineering, vehicles (including component manufacturing) and chemicals, although big increases in the sales ratio also occurred in other industries such as textiles, clothing and footwear.

TABLE IV. EXPORT AND IMPORT RATIOS

	Ratio of exports to manufacturers' sales 1974	1980	Ratio of imports to home demand 1974	1980
Food and drink	5	6	21	14
Coal and petroleum products	14	16	16	14
Chemicals and allied industries	34	39	27	29
Metal manufacture	17	29	24	36
Mechanical engineering	40	46	28	32
Instrument engineering	52	63	50	61
Electrical engineering	29	38	29	37
Shipbuilding and marine engineering	25	32	57	26
Vehicles	39	42	23	39
Metal goods n.e.s.	14	18	10	15
Textiles	25	34	24	35
Leather and leather goods	28	33	27	41
Clothing and footwear	11	19	20	30
Bricks, pottery, cement, glass etc.	13	14	9	9
Timber, furniture etc.	5	7	32	27
Paper, printing and publishing	9	11	23	20
Other manufacturing industries	18	21	16	20
Total manufacturing	21.4	26.1	23.3	25.4

Source: *Economic Trends*

It can be seen that the ratio of imports to home demand also increased during this period. These increases in UK exports and imports reflect a general expansion of international trade, which was itself due to several factors. First, the world economy expanded. Second, there was an increase in intra-industry trade, e.g. British consumers purchasing more electrical goods from Germany while German consumers purchase more British electrical goods. This increase was due partly to a reduction in barriers to trade, and partly to the tendency of consumers to use their higher incomes to widen their choice of suppliers (including the suppliers of imported goods).

THE IMPLICATIONS OF CHANGES IN EXPENDITURE

The changes in expenditure we have considered have arisen partly as a result of the activities of producers. To take an obvious example, spending on consumer durables has been stimulated by the introduction of a stream of new and improved products: colour television sets, automatic washing machines, fridge-freezers, video recorders, etc. However, as we have noted in passing, the changes in expenditure are also—and in many instances mainly—due to factors outside the control of the individual firm: reductions in barriers to trade, government policy, changes in the size and structure of population, changes in the level of national income etc.

It is important that firms should be aware of, and indeed should try to anticipate, such changes in the economic environment and to plan their activities accordingly. When a firm runs down some of its existing activities and concentrates its efforts on new products for markets which appear to have better growth prospects, it has to take decisions involving a wide range of issues: the purchase of new types of machinery and raw materials, the recruitment of workers with new skills, or the retraining of existing workers, the establishment of a new or enlarged distribution system, additional research and development work, the modification or enlargement of premises, perhaps the building of a new factory. The lead time, i.e. the time that elapses between a decision to produce a new product and its introduction, may be considerable, a fact which again emphasises the need to monitor and react quickly to changes in the economic environment.

THE DETERMINATION OF NATIONAL INCOME

Of the various factors influencing the firm's economic environment, the one of most general importance is the level of national income. Consequently we conclude this chapter by presenting a simple model of income determination.

FINAL EXPENDITURE, GROSS NATIONAL PRODUCT AND NATIONAL INCOME

Earlier in the chapter we considered the various components of final expenditure in the UK. Much of this expenditure flows to UK producers (and is subsequently paid out as wages, salaries, rent and dividends). However not all of the expenditure flows to UK producers. Some flows to overseas producers (imports), some to the UK government (expenditure

1. THE ECONOMIC ENVIRONMENT

taxes). When we subtract these two items from final expenditure we arrive at *gross domestic product* (GDP):

$$\text{Final expenditure} - \text{imports} - \text{expenditure taxes} = \text{GDP}$$

Finally in order to arrive at the *gross national product* (GNP) of the UK, we have to take account of net property income from abroad. This comprises interest, dividends and profits arising from investments made overseas in previous periods, minus similar payments made to overseas holders of investments in the UK:

$$\text{GDP} + \text{net property income from abroad} = \text{GNP}$$

GNP provides a measure of the UK's income in the current period, and this is the measure we use below in our model of income determination. We follow the convention, long established in the economics literature, of using the terms GNP and national income as interchangeable. However we must point out that in the national accounts a further adjustment is made to GNP in arriving at *national income*. This adjustment takes into account the fact that in the act of production (and hence of earning income), the country's capital stock is run down or partly "consumed":

$$\text{GNP} - \text{capital consumption} = \text{national income}$$

The interrelationships among the various measures we have discussed in this section are shown in Table V. (The individual items are rounded and do not sum to the totals given.)

TABLE V. UK NATIONAL INCOME, 1981

	£ billion
Final expenditure on goods and services	309
minus Imports	−61
minus (net) Expenditure taxes	−38
Gross domestic product at factor cost	211
plus (net) Property income from abroad	1
Gross national product	212
minus Capital consumption	−31
National Income	181

Source: *National Income and Expenditure*

A SIMPLE MODEL OF INCOME DETERMINATION

As noted earlier, firms are especially concerned with *changes* in the level of income. But in order to show why changes in income occur it is helpful to consider first the conditions under which income would *not* change, i.e. would be in equilibrium.

Equilibrium national income

Equilibrium exists when planned expenditure in one period $(t+1)$ equals national income in the previous period (t). In Fig. 2 income (Y) in period t is £100 billion. Expenditure (E) planned—by consumers, producers and the government—in the following period $(t+1)$ is £100 billion. Provided that producers are able to supply the goods and services demanded, actual expenditure (and therefore income) in period $t+1$ will be £100 billion. From this income, expenditure of £100 billion is planned for period $t+2$, and so the process continues; national income is constant at this level.

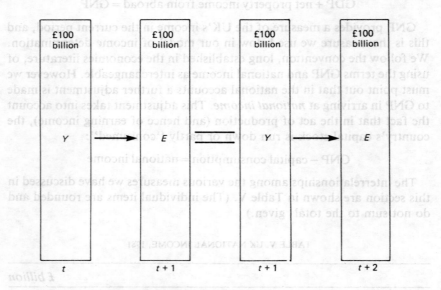

Fig. 2. *Constant national income.*

A changing level of national income

It follows from the analysis in the previous section that national income will change whenever planned expenditure in one period is *not* the same as national income in the previous period. We consider first the situation where planned expenditure is less than national income, giving rise to a declining income.

Declining national income

Figure 3 is based on the assumption that the expenditure plans of consumers, firms and the government are such that 80 per cent of the income in any period is spent in the next period. It can be seen that income declines from one period to the next.

1. THE ECONOMIC ENVIRONMENT

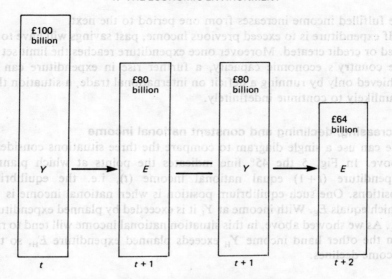

Fig. 3. *Declining national income.*

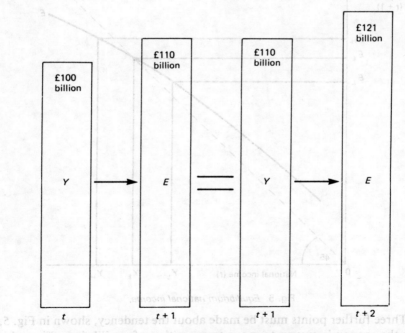

Fig. 4. *Increasing national income.*

Increasing national income
Figure 4 is based on the converse assumption, that planned expenditure exceeds income in the previous period. Provided these expenditure plans

are fulfilled income increases from one period to the next.

If expenditure is to exceed previous income, past savings will have to be used or credit created. Moreover once expenditure reaches the limit set by the country's economic capacity, a further rise in expenditure can be achieved only by running a deficit on international trade, a situation that is unlikely to continue indefinitely.

Increasing, declining and constant national income

We can use a single diagram to compare the three situations considered above. In Fig. 5 the 45° line indicates the points at which planned expenditure $(t+1)$ equal national income (t), i.e. the equilibrium positions. One such equilibrium position is when national income is Y_E, which equals E_E. With income at Y_L it is exceeded by planned expenditure, E_L. As we showed above, in this situation national income will tend to rise. On the other hand income Y_H exceeds planned expenditure E_H, so that income declines.

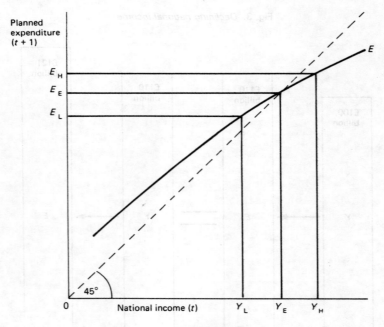

Fig. 5. *Equilibrium national income.*

Three further points must be made about the tendency, shown in Fig. 5, for the economic system to move to a position of equilibrium. First, this tendency depends upon the expenditure function E having the shape shown in the diagram. In other words it depends upon the assumption that as income increases there is a less than proportional increase in planned expenditure. There is a considerable amount of empirical evidence suggesting that this is often the case, but it does not follow that it must always be so. Second, the analysis is in real terms, i.e. it assumes that prices—of inputs and outputs—remain constant. This means that a change in expenditure corresponds to an equivalent change in output and (assuming no change in productivity) in employment. Finally there is nothing in the analysis to suggest that the economic system will reach equilibrium at full employment. These last two points are taken up in the next chapter when we examine government macro-economic policy.

QUESTIONS

1. What factors might explain the changes in consumers' expenditure shown in Table I?
2. On what products would you expect consumers to spend (*a*) an increasing, (*b*) a decreasing proportion of their income over the next decade?
3. Outline the implications for business policy of changes in the pattern of consumption.
4. Why does investment expenditure tend to fluctuate more over time than consumption?
5. What factors might explain the changes in the volume of orders for investment goods shown in Fig. 1?
6. What changes would you expect to occur during the next decade in the pattern of government current expenditure on goods and services?
7. What factors might explain the changes in export and import ratios shown in Table IV?
8. Explain briefly why firms should try to anticipate changes in the economic environment.
9. Explain the term equilibrium national income, and show how changes in expenditure affect national income.
10. Given the data below calculate (*a*) final expenditure, (*b*) gross domestic product at factor cost, (*c*) gross national product, (*d*) national income.

	£ billion
Consumers' expenditure	150
Government consumption	60
Investment	30
Exports	60
Imports	50
(net) Expenditure taxes	30
Property income from abroad	10
Capital consumption	30

CHAPTER TWO
Macro-economic Policy

OBJECTIVES

After studying this chapter the reader should be able to: explain why governments have attempted to influence the level of economic activity; list the main elements of fiscal and monetary policies; outline the possible consequences of fiscal and monetary policies; understand the relationships between changes in expenditure, employment and the price level; explain why attempts by governments to stimulate economic activity may not succeed.

INTRODUCTION

In the simple model of income determination presented in the previous chapter there was nothing to suggest that the economy would reach (or move towards) equilibrium at full employment. Indeed, J.M. Keynes demonstrated some half a century ago that under certain conditions substantial unemployment could persist for very long periods and perhaps indefinitely. Keynes suggested that higher government spending could help to ameliorate the situation.

Under the influence of Keynes's ideas, post-war governments have attempted to influence the flow of income and expenditure in order to modify the level of employment and the rate of inflation. (To simplify the analysis we assumed in our model of income determination that prices remained constant. In this chapter we relax this assumption). It is important that firms should monitor government policies designed to influence the flow of expenditure and income, and take account of changes in policy in planning their activities. In this chapter we outline the basic elements of macro-economic or demand-management policy, and indicate how this policy may influence the overall level of economic activity.[1]

AN INCREASE IN EXPENDITURE

As noted above, increased government intervention was initially justified on the grounds that the level of expenditure would otherwise result in too high a level of unemployment. Consequently we consider first the implications of policies designed to increase the level of expenditure and hence reduce unemployment.

In Fig. 6 Y_E indicates the equilibrium level of income in the absence of government intervention (expenditure E_1 includes government expenditure, but this is not designed specifically to increase the level of total expenditure). In order to increase national income to the full-

---

1. Policies designed to influence individual markets or industries are discussed in Chapter 3.

2. MACRO-ECONOMIC POLICY

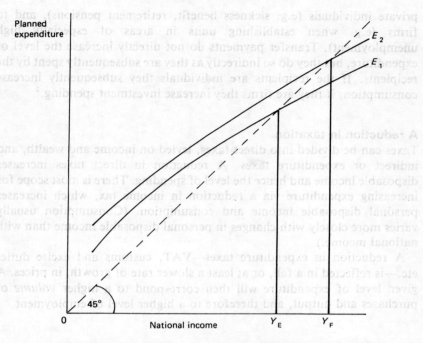

Fig. 6. *An increase in government expenditure and national income.*

employment level Y_F the expenditure function would have to increase from E_1 to E_2.

The government might adopt a range of policies in order to increase the level of expenditure. We briefly consider each of the major alternatives in turn.

An increase in government expenditure on goods and services

This measure is perhaps the most obvious, and it has certainly been used frequently, especially by Labour Governments. We saw in the last chapter that government consumption forms an important part of total expenditure, and increased spending under this heading might take the form of increased payments to public employees (civil servants, the police, teachers etc.), the buying of more books by libraries, the purchase of more medicines and drugs by the National Health Service, and so on.

Government expenditure also encompasses spending on investment or capital goods (included in total investment, as defined in the previous chapter). Increased spending under this heading might include the building of more roads, hospitals and schools.

An increase in transfer payments

Transfer payments comprise grants and subsidies made by government to private individuals (e.g. sickness benefit, retirement pensions), and to firms (e.g. when establishing units in areas of especially high unemployment). Transfer payments do not directly increase the level of expenditure, but they do so indirectly as they are subsequently spent by the recipients. If the recipients are individuals they subsequently increase consumption; if they are firms they increase investment spending.[2]

A reduction in taxation
Taxes can be divided into direct taxes, levied on income and wealth, and indirect or expenditure taxes. A reduction in direct taxes increases disposable income and hence the level of spending. There is most scope for increasing expenditure via a reduction in income tax, which increases personal disposable income and consumption. (Consumption usually varies more closely with changes in personal disposable income than with national income.)

A reduction in expenditure taxes—VAT, customs and excise duties etc.—is reflected in a fall, or at least a slower rate of growth, in prices. A given level of expenditure will then correspond to a higher *volume* of purchases and output, and therefore to a higher level of employment.

Easier monetary conditions
Governments have used a range of techniques designed to make monetary conditions easier. But these can be split basically into measures which facilitate and encourage an increase in the money supply and those which lead to a reduction in interest rates.[3] There is, in fact, a close interconnection between the two sets of measures. Given the demand for money, an increase in its supply leads to a reduction in its price, i.e. interest rates. Similarly, lower interest rates can normally be sustained only if the supply of money is increased.

Easier monetary conditions encourage higher spending in two ways. First, borrowers (firms and individuals) find it easier and cheaper to obtain the money with which to finance their expenditure. Second, some lenders, finding that the returns to lending have fallen, may spend the money they would otherwise have loaned. (The increase in the total amount of money made available to borrowers occurs mainly via the creation of credit by the banking system.)

Easier monetary conditions are felt to be especially beneficial to firms and hence to be a stimulus to investment spending. But personal borrowers, and therefore consumption, also benefit.

2. Purchases of new houses by individuals are also classified as investment.

3. The measures adopted in various periods are discussed in: R. Brown. *Monetary Control in Britain 1971–81*. Banking Information Service, 1981. For a fuller discussion of monetary policy *see* F. Livesey, *A Textbook of Economics*, Polytech, Stockport, 2nd edition, 1982, Ch. 12.

INTERRELATIONSHIPS BETWEEN EXPENDITURE FLOWS

In the previous sections we have seen how government might try to stimulate individual expenditure flows. There are two sets of interrelationships which may increase the impact of the initial stimulus to expenditure. These interrelationships can be expressed formally in terms of the multiplier and accelerator mechanisms.

The multiplier

The multiplier is defined as the ratio of the final change in national income, resulting from an autonomous change in expenditure, to that autonomous change in expenditure:

$$K = \frac{\Delta Y}{\Delta E}$$

where K is the multiplier, Y is national income, E is autonomous expenditure and Δ denotes a change in the variable.

If the value of the multiplier exceeds unity then national income will change by more than the initial change in expenditure, whether this be in spending by government, by firms or by consumers. This occurs because the initial increase in expenditure causes a rise in incomes which leads to further increases in expenditure. (The same point would apply in reverse to an initial fall in expenditure.)

The accelerator

The accelerator is the link between an initial change in consumption and a subsequent change in investment.

$$\Delta I = a(\Delta C)$$

where I is investment, C is consumers' expenditure, a is the accelerator coefficient and Δ denotes a change in the variable.

A more general formulation of the acceleration principle is

$$\Delta I = a(Y_{t1} - Y_{t0})$$

where $Y_{t1} - Y_{t0}$ is the change in output, sales or, more generally, national income, between one period and another. Investment is undertaken partly to maintain existing capacity—new plant and equipment being required to replace plant and equipment that wears out or becomes obsolete—and partly to expand capacity. Capacity is expanded in response to an increase in sales (experienced or anticipated). The accelerator coefficient is a measure of this response. (The incremental capital–output ratio is another term for the accelerator coefficient.)

Given the capital–output ratio, the effect of an increase in sales on investment will be most pronounced when (*a*) firms experiencing an increase in demand have little or no excess capacity and (*b*) firms in the capital goods sector are able to meet the additional demand for plant and equipment.

INCREASED EXPENDITURE AND THE PRICE LEVEL

Figure 6 encompassed the basic Keynesian analysis and the policy prescription derived from this analysis, namely that by increasing the level of expenditure, by one means or another, the government can increase the level of output and employment. In Fig. 7 we extend the analysis to take account of the impact of higher expenditure on prices.

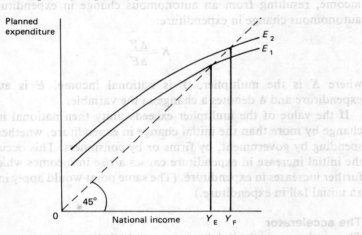

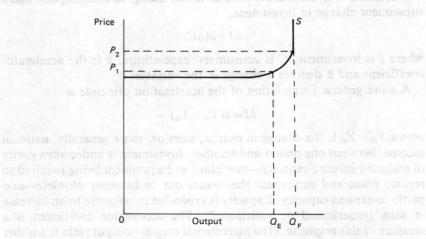

Fig. 7. *A change in expenditure, output and price.*

In the top diagram we reproduce Fig. 6, with the equilibrium output again being designated Y_E. This corresponds to the level of output Q_E in the bottom diagram. The aggregate supply curve S indicates the average price level relating to various output levels. It can be seen that output Q_E would be sold at price P_1. As the expenditure function shifts from E_1 to E_2, output, measured here in money terms, increases from Q_E to Q_F. But so too does average price, from P_1 to P_2. In other words, the increased national income Y_E Y_F represents partly an increase in the volume of output and partly an increase in price. Indeed if the expenditure function shifted upward yet again, any resultant increase in national income beyond Y_F would consist entirely of higher prices since, by definition, the volume of output cannot be increased beyond the full-employment level Q_F. (The multiplier and accelerator mechanisms, discussed above, make it very difficult to predict the extent to which the expenditure function may shift.)

Recognising the probable impact of higher expenditure on prices, Keynesian economists have suggested that it might be necessary to modify policy in one of two ways. First, governments should not attempt to achieve very low levels of unemployment, since this would lead to an unacceptably high rate of price increase, but should aim at an expenditure consistent with a margin of spare capacity (men and machines). Alternatively, if too high a margin of spare capacity, and especially too high a level of unemployment, was required to maintain an acceptable level of price increase then demand management policies should be supplemented by prices-and-incomes policies.

THE CONSEQUENCES OF INFLATION

The rate of price increase (inflation) may be deemed to be too high for several reasons. Purchasers, and especially housewives, may suffer psychological shocks as a result of rapidly rising prices. Moreover, some groups, such as pensioners, suffer because their incomes are "sticky", i.e. do not adjust, or adjust only with a lag, to the rate of inflation. (The more rapid the rise in prices the more difficult it is to devise adequate adjustment procedures, e.g. the uprating of pensions.)

In discussing the impact of inflation on business it is important to make a distinction between anticipated and unanticipated inflation. If the rate of inflation can be fully anticipated, i.e. if future price changes can be accurately predicted, then contracts can take such changes into account. The rate of interest on loans can be increased if prices are expected to rise. Employers may be able to offer (and employees will certainly expect to receive) higher wage increases if the prices of goods and services are expected to rise.

In principle it is possible to establish institutional arrangements that would fully offset these internal consequences of anticipated inflation. But even if such arrangements were established, the adverse external consequences of inflation would remain. If the inflation rate exceeds that of our main international competitors, the volume of exports is likely to fall and of imports to rise. This is likely in turn to lead to reductions in production, employment and profits, and a deterioration in the balance of payments.

If the rate of inflation cannot be fully anticipated—and this is, of course, the situation in practice—additional consequences follow. It becomes more difficult to agree the terms of a contract if the two parties have different expectations concerning future price changes. Moreover, even if they have the same expectations, one party will benefit and the other suffer if these expectations are not realised. If prices rise more rapidly than expected, debtors (borrowers) benefit at the expense of creditors (lenders). If product prices rise more rapidly than expected, employers tend to benefit at the expense of employees.

These are illustrations of the fact that unanticipated inflation causes a change in the distribution of income. It is impossible to say whether business as a whole will benefit or suffer as a result of these distributional effects. But there is no doubt that the inability to predict future price changes does have undesirable consequences for business. The additional uncertainty that is created makes firms more reluctant to enter into long-term commitments, especially when these involve investment in fixed assets: factories, machinery etc. (The consequences of this are discussed in Chapter 10.)

THE CHALLENGE TO KEYNESIANISM

There was a wide measure of agreement for much of the post-war period that policies based on the analysis presented above could be used to prevent the re-emergence of mass unemployment. However in the late 1970s and early 1980s governments in a number of countries, including the UK and USA, adopted a different mix of policies from those adopted by their predecessors.

Several factors help to explain this change in policy. In many countries both the rate of inflation and the level of unemployment rose, suggesting that Keynesian policies were less effective than previously thought. In addition, several specific deficiencies in the implementation of policy had been identified in the UK. First, as noted above, governments had frequently been obliged to modify expansionary policies in the face of an unsatisfactory international trading position. Second, it became evident that prices-and-incomes policies did little to moderate the rate of inflation except in the short term. Finally, increased government spending, the measure most frequently advocated by Keynesian economists, appeared to give rise to countervailing tendencies which reduced its effectiveness.

If the increased spending was financed by higher taxation this would lead to a fall in consumption and/or investment which could counteract the increased government spending. If, alterntively, the government financed its spending by higher borrowing, interest rates would rise and this again might cause other forms of spending to decline. (If the money supply increased in order to prevent the rise in interest rates this could have other undesirable consequences as shown below.) It was also claimed by some economists that as increased government spending led to an increase in the size of the public sector fewer resources (men and machines) would be available for employment in the private sector. This might mean that this sector was unable to meet the demand for goods and services.

In addition to these criticisms relating to the implementation of policy, the theoretical basis of the underlying analysis was attacked by a number of eminent economists, most notably Milton Friedman. As noted above, the implication of Fig. 7 is that the government could achieve a lower level of unemployment, albeit at the cost of higher inflation. Critics claimed that, except in the short term, this was not so. If the government induced a higher level of expenditure or demand the only long-term effect would be a higher level of prices; the rate of unemployment would be the same as if the government had not intervened. "There is an underlying rate of unemployment (and of output growth) which is the best that can be sustained for any period of time. . . . Any attempt to spend ourselves into levels of employment above this sustainable rate will lead to . . . accelerating inflation and, eventually, to a very nasty stabilisation crisis in which unemployment will shoot up to rates far higher than if the expansionary attempt had never been made."[4] This minimum sustainable rate of inflation was labelled the "natural rate" by Milton Friedman in 1967 and other terms used are the "non-accelerating or constant inflation rate of unemployment".

THE TWO APPROACHES COMPARED

These opposing viewpoints are illustrated in Fig. 8. Line PC_1, the so-called Phillips curve, reflects the belief that there is a trade-off between the rate of inflation and the rate of change of wages (and hence eventually of product prices). We assume that the initial rate of unemployment is N. Keynesian analysis would suggest that by boosting expenditure the government could reduce unemployment to M, but only at the expense of causing the rate of inflation to rise to P. (Further reductions in unemployment would require even sharper rises in the inflation rate. Compare Fig. 7 above.)

Point N represents the initial equilibrium in the sense that the number of jobs equals the number of people seeking work *at a given level of real wages*. If more workers are to be induced to enter employment, in order to supply the additional goods and services demanded, then an increase in

4. S. Brittan, *How to End the Monetary Controversy*. Insitute of Economic Affairs, 1982, p. 54.

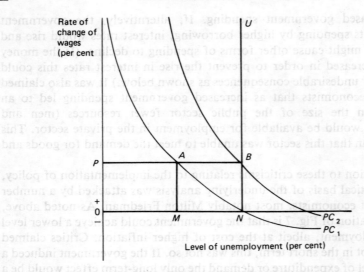

Fig. 8. *The natural rate of unemployment.*

real wages is required. Employers offer higher money wages because they believe that the more favourable demand conditions will allow them to set higher product prices. More employees (*MN*) are induced to take jobs by the increase in money wages. The new (temporary) point of equilibrium is *A*. But eventually employees realise that real wages have *not* risen, as product prices rise in line with money wages. The number of workers seeking work falls back to its previous level, i.e. unemployment returns to *N*. Now, however, the rate of price increase is higher than it was previously; the new equilibrium point is *B*. Moreover, further attempts by the government to boost demand would lead to even higher rates of inflation while leaving unemployment unchanged. In other words attempts to move up the new Phillips curve PC_2 would be frustrated; equilibrium would be re-established at a higher point on the line *NU*.

THE "MONETARIST" EXPERIMENT

The analysis presented in the previous section helps to explain the policies adopted by the Conservative Government that came into power in 1979. (The government's thinking was, of course, also influenced by many other factors, including an ideological preference for less government intervention in economic affairs.) The label "monetarist" has been attached to these policies, in recognition of the emphasis placed on monetary policy, and in particular on the need to reduce the rate of growth of the money supply.

However it should be stressed that there is nothing specifically monetarist about the underlying theoretical analysis. The boost to demand given by the government in an attempt to move up the Phillips curve to a lower level of unemployment (Fig. 8) could have been accomplished by fiscal policy (higher government spending or lower taxation) and/or by monetary policy (easier credit, lower interest rates). The central point made by the proponents of the theory is that this attempt to reduce unemployment will be frustrated, that in the longer term the movement will be from N to B, not A.

Similarly, if the government wished to move the system from B to N it could reduce expenditure by fiscal and/or monetary policy. (It is true, however, that economists such as Friedman favour monetary policy, with an emphasis on the desirability of a modest and steady increase in the money supply.)

The implications for firms of the monetarist experiment

In planning their activities firms pay more attention to policy decisions than to the theory that might underly those decisions. If for instance a firm is considering whether or not to build a new factory in order to increase its production capacity then it will try to assess the impact of changes in tax and interest rates on the demand for its products. However, some appreciation of the theory will aid understanding. For example Friedman and economists of a similar persuasion have argued that the sequence of events following the adoption of a restrictive monetary policy will be as follows. There will first be a rise in unemployment, then a fall in the rate of inflation, and finally a fall in unemployment.

It follows that a government whose policy is based on this analysis will maintain a restrictive policy in the face of an increase in unemployment, in the belief that this is a prerequisite to a fall in the inflation rate. Any firm which understood this point should not have been surprised when the Thatcher Government refused to reverse its policy (to make a "U-turn") despite pressure from the mass media, the trades unions, the CBI and some of its own MPs). Such a firm would benefit in that it would, for example, be less likely to expand capacity prematurely.

We have pointed out that the adoption of a different mix of policies by the Thatcher Government was partly a reaction to the fall in effectiveness of Keynesian policies. Furthermore, one of the aims of that government was to avoid excessive boosts to demand associated with some of its predecessors. (Incidentally, the most notorious of these was the "Barber Boom" of the early 1970s, under a previous Conservative Government.)

But the policy of the new government was not confined to trying to avoid the mistakes of its predecessors. We have already mentioned the attempt (only partly successful) to achieve a modest and steady rate of growth of the money supply. The government also attempted by various means to reduce the natural or minimum sustainable rate of unemployment, in particular by reducing imperfections in the labour market. The measures included additional support for training, reducing the immunities of trades unions, and taxing unemployment benefit. In addition, this and all other governments have adopted policies that have affected particular industries, markets or firms. These policies are outlined in the following chapter.

QUESTIONS

1. Outline the effects on the overall level of economic activity of each of the following policy changes: (*a*) an increase in government expenditure on goods and services, (*b*) a reduction in transfer payments, (*c*) an increase in direct taxes, (*d*) a reduction in expenditure taxes, (*e*) an increase in the money supply, (*f*) an increase in interest rates.

2. The government increases income tax in order to finance an expanded programme of school building. Explain how this might affect producers.

3. In what circumstances might an increase in government expenditure leave the overall level of economic activity unchanged?

4. Discuss the measures taken by recent governments to control inflation, and the consequences of these measures.

5. Role-play a television discussion between a government minister seeking to justify a decision to reduce government expenditure, a representative of the CBI and a representative of the TUC.

6. Explain why firms should try to anticipate major changes in macro-economic policy.

CHAPTER THREE

Micro-economic Policy

OBJECTIVES

After studying this chapter the reader should be able to: give the main reasons for government intervention in the operation of markets; outline current competition policy, policy regarding the nationalised industries, industrial policy, manpower policy and the economic policy of the EEC; understand how these policies can benefit companies, but also curtail their freedom of action.

INTRODUCTION

In the previous chapter we discussed government policies designed to influence broad (macro-) economic variables: the flow of expenditure, the rate of inflation, the level of unemployment and so forth. Although the implementation of these policies affects firms and markets, the focus of policy is not usually on the operations of an individual firm or the working of an individual market. (There are exceptions to this rule, e.g. when the government changes expenditure tax rates on certain products as part of an attempt to reduce the volume of expenditure. The distinction between the two sets of policies is therefore not absolutely clear cut.)

By contrast, the focus of the policies considered in this chapter is the operation of particular firms or markets. Policy is usually directed towards firms with certain characteristics or which meet certain conditions. For example, subsidies have been made available to firms investing in particular geographical areas or in certain types of machinery; competition policy is often applied to firms with a given market share.

There are many forms of micro-economic policy and we can examine only the main features of each. We do not attempt to evaluate the effectiveness of policy. Rather we seek to show how policy affects the operations of the firm. But we begin by considering the objectives of policy, the reasons why governments have felt it necessary to modify firms' activities and the operation of markets.

REASONS FOR GOVERNMENT INTERVENTION

Government intervention in the operation of markets clearly implies a belief that in the absence of intervention the market would not perform satisfactorily. Performance might be considered to be unsatisfactory in a number of respects.

Too high or inflexible prices

The prices of products may be too high because suppliers earn too high profits or because their costs are higher than necessary. Either outcome may arise because there is insufficient competition in the market. A failure of prices to change in line with changes in costs is believed to be another manifestation of a lack of competition.

An inadequate supply of goods and services
The government may decide that certain types of goods are extremely beneficial—examples of such "merit" goods are health care and education—and that their supply would be inadequate under free-market conditions. In other instances, e.g. energy, it may believe that adequate supplies would not be forthcoming at the time required to yield maximum benefit to society as a whole.

Too great a supply of goods and services
This is the reverse of the above situation; the government believes that the production of certain goods has undesirable consequences and so seeks to limit or control their production. In some instances production and sale is forbidden or strictly controlled, e.g. heroin. In other instances production may be discouraged, e.g. by the imposition of high taxes or by controls on advertising (e.g. of cigarettes).

An unsatisfactory rate of innovation
Innovation benefits consumers in two ways. New processes (process innovation) can make existing products cheaper or more reliable. New or improved products (product innovation) can widen consumers' choice. In the absence of keen competition there may be less incentive to innovate. (On the other hand, some economists believe that in certain types of market, competition leads to *too high* a rate of innovation, in the form of very minor product variations.)

A reduction of consumers' welfare
All the aspects of market performance considered above could lead to a reduction of consumers' welfare. But under this heading we also include factors that can lead to clear detriments to individual consumers, e.g. inadequate safety standards and the provision of misleading or inadequate information.

Other reasons for intervention
Governments have intervened in the operation of markets for various other reasons. These include a desire to improve the UK's international competitiveness, to reduce regional inequalities, and to improve the skills and efficiency of the workforce.

THE POLICIES
Having shown why governments might intervene to modify the working of

markets we now examine the major policy measures. We begin with competition policy since this relates to several of the aspects of performance listed above.

COMPETITION POLICY

Neo-classical economic theory suggests that economic performance will be optimised under perfect competition, i.e. when each market is supplied by a large number of producers, when the products supplied to each market are homogeneous or undifferentiated, and when the entry and exit of producers is not impeded. The other policy conclusion derived from neo-classical theory is that monopoly—the control of a market by a single producer—is undesirable. Output will be lower and profits higher than under perfect competition.

It was subsequently recognised that the model of perfect competition was at best an imperfect guide to policy for several reasons. First, the existence of a large number of producers may mean that economies of scale, leading to lower costs of production and distribution, cannot be achieved. Second, perfect competition is not consistent with rapid innovation. Third, if some markets are not perfectly competitive then overall performance will not necessarily be improved by making, or keeping, other markets perfectly competitive.

It was also recognised that the monopoly model is of limited applicability, since very few markets are supplied by a single producer. Moreover, studies of business behaviour revealed that monopolists (and others) do not necessarily attempt to obtain the highest possible profit. Finally, if above-average profits are achieved then these may be used to finance innovation.

However, although the neo-classical models do not constitute an adequate basis for policy, they do provide some useful insights. If a small number of suppliers account for a high proportion of sales in a given market they may be able to adopt policies, e.g. agreeing to set high prices, which yield above-average profit margins. Alternatively, in the absence of keen competition, they may become inefficient, high-cost producers, even if they are able to take advantage of economies of scale. These twin dangers, high profit margins and high costs, are obviously greatest where (*a*) producers are satisfied with their existing market shares, and in particular where they are reluctant to engage in price competition to try to enlarge their share of the market; and (*b*) barriers exist which prevent the entry of potential new suppliers (new entrants would make competition more intense).

We now consider how these considerations influence competition policy in the UK, and how the implementation of policy has affected particular firms. We begin with competition relating to mergers (including takeovers) and monopolies.

Policy relating to mergers and monopolies

Mergers may allow costs to be reduced in a number of ways. First, economies of scale may arise. Second, and connected with the previous point, duplication of plant and equipment may be eliminated. Third, a reduction in the number of competitors may reduce uncertainty and make forward planning easier. Fourth, a merger (and especially, perhaps, a takeover) may enable a more efficient management team to exercise control of the firm's assets. Mergers may also expand consumer choice if successful research and development (R&D) work can be undertaken only by large firms.

On the other hand, as we have seen, a reduction in the number of competitors may result in a weakening of the incentive to reduce costs,[1] and to the setting of prices which yield above-average profits.

In the light of these two opposing sets of forces a pragmatic policy has been adopted whereby each proposed merger is considered on its merits. Under the Monopolies and Mergers Act 1965, and the Fair Trading Act 1973, a proposed merger can be referred by the Secretary of State to the Monopolies and Mergers Commission if (*a*) it would result in at least one-quarter of the market being in the hands of a single supplier or (*b*) the assets acquired would exceed £15 million.

A large number of mergers come within the scope of the legislation—around two thousand between 1965 and 1980. Because of the size and composition of the Commission—most members serve in a part-time capacity—it cannot be expected to handle more than a small fraction of proposed mergers, and in practice about 97 per cent of proposed mergers have been allowed to proceed without reference to the Commission.

Only about 30 per cent of those referred have come to fruition. Moreover, even if the Commission recommends that the merger be allowed to proceed, the investigation involves the firm in considerable effort and expense. Consequently, if a firm is contemplating a merger, or launching a takeover bid, it will wish to know whether it is likely to be referred to the Commission. The Office of Fair Trading, which administers the policy, has indicated that markets or product sectors would be considered most worthy of investigation if they achieved "high marks" in terms of four conduct and four performance indicators.

The four conduct indicators are: complaints, from both trade and consumer sources; evidence or accusation of either price leadership or parallel pricing; the ratio of advertising expenditure to sales; and the degree of merger activity in the field concerned. The four performance indicators are: the ratio of capital employed to turnover (a high ratio possibly indicating inefficiency); changes in profit margins; return on

---

1. Two studies that suggest that many of the potential advantages of mergers are not realised are: G. D. Newbould. *Management and Merger Activity.* Guthstead, 1970; and: G. Meeks. *Disappointing Marriage: A Study of the Gains from Merger.* University of Cambridge Department of Applied Economics, 1977.

capital employed; and the movement of prices relative to the general rate of inflation.

When a merger is referred to the Commission, it has to decide whether the merger would be likely to be in, or against, the public interest. (The final decision on the merger is taken by the Minister in the light of the Commission's recommendations.) In making its recommendations the Commission takes account of criteria laid down in the Fair Trading Act. These include: maintaining and promoting effective competition in the supply of goods and services; promoting the interests of consumers, purchasers and users of goods and services; promoting the reduction of costs and the development and use of new techniques and products; the entry of new competitors; and maintaining and promoting a balanced distribution of industry and employment. It has been said that these criteria are so wide ranging that in practice they give little guidance to firms as to what behaviour is acceptable. Nevertheless, a proposed merger is more likely to be approved if a good case can be made out in terms of a number of these criteria.

In seeking to justify a merger with Birfield, GKN (Guest, Keen and Nettlefolds) claimed that the merged company would exploit technical developments more effectively. The Commission commented: "We are inclined to think that there may be some substance in this argument because we are not convinced that Birfield has an assured future on its own." The Commission described Birfield as "a company of high technological competence . . . but (which) appeared to lack some of the resources needed to exploit its advantages. . . . As a motor component producer it did not quite keep pace, in weight and size, with developments in this expanding industry." The Commission concluded that the merger would not be against the public interest.

One of the arguments put forward by Boots to justify a takeover of Glaxo was that the merged firm would be able to enjoy economies of scale in R&D. But the Commission pointed out that there are also grounds for believing that, provided the firms have attained a certain minimum size, the total R&D effort and the rate of innovation will be greater the bigger the number of independent R&D units. The Commission, presumably impressed by the past performance of Boots and Glaxo as separate firms, declared against the merger.

Existing monopolies, including export and local (geographical) monopolies, can also be investigated by the Monopolies and Mergers Commission. (Monopoly references to the Commission can be made either by the relevant Minister—at present the Secretary of State for Trade and Industry—or by the Director General of Fair Trading.)

The criteria taken into account are similar to those relating to mergers, and recommendations made by the Commission have included: the easing of restrictions on the type of outlet in which infant milks could be sold; the monitoring by the government of the prices of cornflakes; reductions in the prices of drugs (Librium and Valium) sold to the National Health Service; ending the practice of charging a price for colour film which included the cost of processing; and ending the agreements made by Turner and Newall, the dominant manufacturer of asbestos products, which restricted the right of customers to buy asbestos textiles, packing and jointing products from rival manufacturers.

In a mainly favourable report, *Building Bricks*, the Commission noted that the profits of London Brick Company, the dominant producer, had not been excessive, and that its prices had been reasonable. Indeed, one of the main reasons for the company's monopoly position was that its lower prices had driven other, less efficient, producers out of the market.

Policy relating to collective restrictive practices
The Restrictive Trade Practices Act 1956 required all restrictive agreements to be registered with the Registrar of Restrictive Trading Agreements (and subsequently, under the Fair Trading Act, with the Office of the Director General of Fair Trading). A restrictive agreement is defined as any agreement between two or more persons carrying on business in the production or supply of goods (and, since 1973, commercial services) under which restrictions are accepted by the parties in respect of the prices to be charged, the terms or conditions of sale, quantities or types to be produced, the process of manufacture, the persons or areas to be supplied, or the persons or areas from which the goods (or services) are to be acquired.

Economic theory implies that collective restrictive practices are more likely than mergers or monopolies to result in a loss of efficiency. The reason for this is that collective agreements can give rise to the dangers associated with monopoly, such as high prices yielding super-normal profits, but give less scope for the potential benefits of monopoly, such as cost reduction via economies of scale, less duplication of plant and equipment etc.

Consequently, whereas monopoly policy is pragmatic and neutral, there is a presumption in the legislation that collective restrictive practices are against the public interest. When an agreement is considered by the Restrictive Practices Court, the parties to the agreement have to satisfy the Court that the agreement yields benefits, and that these benefits outweigh the detriments inherent in a restrictive agreement.

The grounds on which the parties can attempt to justify the agreement (the "gateways") are:

(*a*) that the restriction is reasonably necessary to protect the public against injury;

(*b*) that the removal of the restriction would deny to the public, as purchasers, consumers or users of any goods, specific and substantial benefits;

(c) that the restriction is reasonably necessary to counteract measures taken by a person, not party to the agreement, with a view to restricting competition;

(d) that the restriction is reasonably necessary to enable fair terms to be negotiated with a large supplier or purchaser;

(e) that the removal of the restriction would be likely to have a serious and persistent adverse effect on unemployment in areas in which the industry is concentrated;

(f) that the removal of the restriction would be likely to cause a substantial reduction in export business;

(g) that the restriction is reasonably required for the purpose of supporting other restrictions in the agreement which are in the public interest;

(h) that the restriction does not directly or indirectly restrict or discourage competition to any material degree in any relevant trade or industry and is not likely to do so.

The three gateways that have received most prominence in the cases heard by the Court are (b), by far the most important, (e) and (f), all of which refer to aspects of an industry's performance. The improvements in performance which the Court has considered to be sufficiently important to outweigh the detriments inherent in a restrictive agreement, and thus to justify the agreement, include the three following:

First, the agreement results in lower prices, one of the benefits included under clause (b). The Cement Makers Federation argued that restricting price competition reduced member firms' risks and led them to accept lower prices than they would in more competitive conditions. The Distant Water Vessels Development Association claimed that although without the agreement prices would fall in the short run, this would lead to a reduction in investment and therefore in capacity, which in turn would result in higher prices in the long run. Similarly it was argued that if the Net Book Agreement were abandoned, price competition would lead to a reduction in the number of stockholding booksellers, a rise in the price of books and a fall in the number of published titles.

Second, co-operation on research and the dissemination of research results leads to product improvement and/or a reduction in costs—also benefits under clause (b). The Black Bolt and Nut Association argued that the exchange among their members of technical information and joint research depended upon the existence of a price agreement.

Third, the maintenance of export orders is enhanced by co-operation in overseas markets (clause (f)). The members of the Water Tube Boilers Association, whose products were used in power stations, had joint representation in overseas markets, a practice buttressed by a market sharing agreement for domestic orders.

As noted above, the Fair Trading Act 1973 extended the provisions of the 1956 Act to cover firms supplying commercial services, such as hairdressers, estate agents, and travel agents. Registration with the Office of Fair Trading is required for agreements relating to:

(*a*) the charges made, quoted, or paid for services;
(*b*) the terms or conditions on which services are supplied or obtained;
(*c*) the extent or scale on which services are supplied or obtained;
(*d*) the form or manner in which services are supplied or obtained;
(*e*) the persons, areas or places to, in or from which services are supplied or obtained.

The impact of the Act can be illustrated by the fact that when the first batch of agreements were registered it was found that the Association of British Travel Agents had dropped its recommendation to members to charge a standard 10 per cent commission on holidays sold, and that it had withdrawn its advice on minimum charges to be made for other services such as the sale of traveller's cheques.

Other policies relating to anti-competitive behaviour
Two other pieces of legislation have been introduced in order to counteract anti-competitive behaviour. The Resale Prices Act 1964 laid down that a manufacturer was allowed to enforce or maintain resale prices only if he could convince the Restrictive Practices Court that this would be in the public interest. The background to this Act was a rapid increase in the market share of multiple retailers, largely due to their policy of reducing prices in order to achieve a higher volume of turnover. The ability of manufacturers to prevent distributors from reducing prices inhibited the growth of such firms. The 1964 Act was, therefore, seen as a way of trying to improve market performance and economic efficiency in retailing.

Specific grounds for the justification of an agreement were again laid down, namely that in the absence of resale price maintenance (r.p.m.) the public would suffer in one of the following ways:

(*a*) the quality and variety of goods available for sale would be substantially reduced;
(*b*) the number of retail establishments in which the goods were sold would be substantially reduced;
(*c*) the retail prices of goods would increase;
(*d*) goods would be sold under conditions likely to cause danger to health in consequence of their misuse by the public;
(*e*) any necessary services provided in connection with the sale of the goods would cease to be provided, or would be substantially reduced.

Even if a manufacturer succeeds in justifying r.p.m. on one of these grounds, he has then to show that this advantage of r.p.m. outweighs the disadvantage of restricting the freedom of distributors. Only the manufacturers of books, maps, and certain medicaments have satisfied the Court in this respect.

More recently, the Competition Act 1980 extended the powers of the government in three areas. First, it gave the power to investigate price issues of major public concern. No power to control prices is attached to this provision—indeed the government had previously abolished the Price Commission—but if an investigation reveals that competition is limited, with undesirable implications for prices, then action can be taken through other provisions of this or other Acts.

Second, the Act provided for the investigation of nationalised industries and other enterprises operating in markets where competition is limited by statute or other special circumstances. The Secretary of State may direct the Monopolies and Mergers Commission to examine questions of efficiency and costs, standards of service, and possible abuses of monopoly power. There does not seem to be any reason for excluding public monopolists from scrutiny simply because they have been granted their monopoly by statute, and many economists have advocated "efficiency audits" of public enterprises, similar to that provided for by this Act.

Early references to the Commission related to British Rail commuter services, the postal services, the activities of the Severn–Trent Water Authority and the Central Electricity Generating Board. These references resulted in reports containing a total of 180 detailed recommendations, most of which were accepted by the industry concerned. These were considered to be among the most valuable of the Commission's reports, and in 1981 the government announced that the Commission would be asked to undertake six investigations a year, thus covering all the nationalised industries within a four-year period.

Finally, despite the large body of legislation aimed at preventing anti-competitive practices, it was felt that some practices existed which fell outside the scope of this legislation, or which could be investigated only in a very cumbersome manner. Consequently the Competition Act made it possible for specific practices by named individual firms to be investigated by the Commission without there being a full investigation of all the major suppliers in that market. Should the Commission find a practice to be against the public interest then the Minister may act to control it. Examples of practices which might be investigated, according to the Director General of Fair Trading, include: arrangements under which a distributor agrees to sell the products of a specified manufacturer only; the refusal to supply one product unless the distributor buys other products from the same manufacturer; selling below cost in order to force competitors out of business.

The first investigation made under this provision of the Act was into the distribution policy of TI Raleigh, the bicycle manufacturer. Certain cut-price retailers, e.g. Argos, had complained to the Office of Fair Trading that Raleigh had refused to supply them. Raleigh's policy favoured small specialised retail outlets, which it believed offered a better service to consumers as well as ensuring higher safety standards. The Commission arrived at a compromise verdict: the company manufactures bicycles under various brand names, and the Commission recommended that it should supply all except the Raleigh brand to any retailer who wished to be supplied.

Patents

We noted above that perfect competition is not conducive to innovation. The reason for this is that the condition of free entry would mean that any new product introduced by one firm could be immediately copied by competitors. In these circumstances the incentive to introduce new products would be weak or absent.

The need to provide protection to the originators of new products and processes is recognised in the establishment of a patents system. The holder of a patent is given the exclusive right to exploit an invention for commercial gain. Anyone else wishing to make the patented article must either buy the patent from the proprietor or use it under licence and pay a royalty to him.

Under the Patents Act 1977 a UK firm can apply to the Patent Office for a patent relating to the UK, or to the European Patent Office for a patent applying throughout the EEC. Once granted, a patent continues in force for twenty years, with the possibility of renewal.

Policy relating to consumer protection

In one sense all aspects of competition policy are designed to protect the consumer, by ensuring that he or she has an adequate choice of supplier, that "fair" profits are earned, and so forth. But the Fair Trading Act contained a number of provisions designed to directly protect consumers' interests. It gave the Director General a duty to keep under review commercial activities relating to the supply of goods and services that might adversely affect the economic interests of UK consumers. If he identifies a practice which he considers to be against the public interest, he may propose that an order of Parliament be made to regulate or prohibit the practice.

The Director General may also propose changes in the law if he considers that a "consumer trade practice":

(a) misleads customers as to their rights and obligations;
(b) is otherwise misleading or confusing to customers;
(c) subjects customers to undue pressure; or
(d) contains "inequitable" terms or conditions.

In practice, rather than invoke the force of law, the Director General has preferred to obtain a voluntary undertaking that a practice he considers to be unsatisfactory will be changed. Voluntary codes of conduct have been agreed which cover a wide variety of industries, including electrical servicing, laundries and dry cleaning, motor traders and travel agents. A common feature of these codes is that the industry should set minimm standards of conduct and establish an independent arbitration service for complaints.

NATIONALISATION

Political factors help to account for programmes of nationalisation (and de-nationalisation). But an economic case has also been advanced for nationalisation, some of the arguments overlapping with those presented in the section on competition policy. It is claimed first that nationalisation ensures an adequate supply of goods and services, and second that these goods and services will be sold at reasonable prices. In many of the industries, such as the telephone service and electricity generation, there is substantial scope for economies of scale, a situation conducive to monopoly. It is argued that nationalisation ensures that these benefits will be passed on to consumers in lower prices, rather than accruing to private monopolists as higher profits.

It is difficult to evaluate the first of these arguments (adequate supply) when there is only a single supplier. When the market has been opened to other, private-sector, suppliers, output has been expanded, e.g. in air travel, and, more recently, in telecommunications equipment. This suggests that supply, either in total or of certain types, was previously inadequate. Supply was also rendered inadequate when the unions called a national strike, as in coal-mining and the Post Office. (Of course many strikes occur in the private sector, but it may be more difficult for a union to bring about the closure of an entire industry in which there are a larger number of suppliers.)

The claim that nationalised industries are less likely to earn supernormal profits is certainly borne out in practice. In fact there are strong grounds for saying that on the whole the profits of these industries have been inadequate. Private-sector producers, after paying dividends to their shareholders, are normally able to finance about two-thirds of their capital expenditure from retained earnings. The nationalised industries have been able to attain a comparable figure only because several of them have received substantial government grants. (The government has also written off large amounts of capital debt, resulting in substantial savings in interest payments.)

Many factors have contributed to the relatively low profitability of the nationalised industries. The fact that the industries are sheltered from the full force of competition, including competition in the market for finance, has allowed inefficiencies to persist. There must also be less incentive to reduce inefficiency when it is known that losses will be met by the government.

Other aspects of government policy have also resulted in lower profits. For example the Central Electricity Generating Board has been persuaded to buy domestically produced coal in preference to cheaper imported coal. More generally it has been assumed that the nationalised industries would fulfil social obligations which private sector producers would be reluctant to shoulder. For example the National Coal Board has kept open unprofitable pits and British Airways has maintained unprofitable routes to sparsely populated areas. (In some instances specific grants are received from the government to cover the costs of unprofitable operations.)

Government has frequently curtailed the opportunities of the nationalised industries to diversify their activities, when diversification might have increased profits. Indeed in recent years the tendency has been to force the industries to concentrate on "core" activities. Pressure has been brought to bear on the British Gas Corporation to sell its retail outlets and its interests in the Wytch Farm natural gas deposits.

Profits have been lower despite the fact that the prices of the nationalised industries have on the whole risen more than those in the private sector. Labour costs have also risen more rapidly, partly because of a higher rate of wage increases and partly because of a lower rate of increase in productivity.[2]

INDUSTRIAL POLICY

Industrial policy comprises several elements, the most important being the provision of financial assistance to firms meeting certain conditions or undertaking certain activities. Assistance has been given to various firms on an *ad hoc* basis, e.g. grants towards R&D expenditure in the computer and shipbuilding industries. Under the Industry Act 1972 assistance has been provided to encourage investment in sectors of the economy in which it was felt the supply of goods might otherwise be inadequate. (If "bottlenecks" occur in industries supplying machines or components to other industries, this will affect the efficiency of those other industries.) Since 1975 sixteen schemes have been introduced, the latest relating to the microelectronics industry. Also under this Act, a Market Entry Guarantee Scheme has been established to help towards the cost of entering new export markets.

The Industry Act 1975 established the National Enterprise Board, with access to funds of £1 billion, subsequently increased to £4½ billion. The NEB took over assets that the government had acquired under previous Acts, including British Leyland (BL) and Rolls Royce. However these companies were subsequently returned to the government, and more

---

2. The performance of the nationalised industries is discussed at length in: R. Pryke. *The Nationalised Industries: Policies and Performance Since 1968.* Martin Robertson, 1981.

recently the NEB has invested in smaller companies, with an emphasis on advanced technology, e.g. microchips and computer software. In 1981 the NEB merged with the National Research Development Corporation, which has financed a large number of (mostly small) projects, to form the British Technology Group.

Assistance for small firms

Government assistance to small firms has been a regular feature of post-war government policy. Most of the measures were taken on an *ad hoc* basis. But the Conservative Government elected in 1979 adopted a more systematic policy than its predecessors. In its first two years of office it announced a series of measures designed to aid small firms:

(*a*) Schemes to augment the flow of capital to the small-firms sector. The most important of these schemes were:
 (i) The Business Start Up Scheme, introduced in 1981, and designed to overcome the problems of raising equity in the initial stage of a firm's existence. In order to counteract the risks of investing in new businesses, the scheme allows tax relief for "outside" investors in "qualifying" new businesses.
 (ii) The Loan Guarantee Scheme, also introduced in 1981. Some worthwhile projects may fail to find adequate finance because of the potential borrower's lack of "track record" or his unwillingness to provide personal guarantees. The government guarantees up to 80 per cent of the cost of the loan, the total money available being £150 million for each of the first two years.

(*b*) Modifying the tax regime so as to increase the rewards going to small businesses, e.g. raising the lower limit below which the special "small companies" rate of corporation tax applies.

(*c*) Reducing the amount of government administrative interference in the small-firms sector, e.g. the Employment Act 1980 provides for the exemption of certain small firms from requirements relating to unfair dismissal procedures, maternity reinstatement, etc.

Rationalisation

An element of industrial policy that has been far more important in some periods than others (such as the present) is the rationalisation of production facilities. This has taken two forms. First, in some industries, e.g. cotton textiles, shipbuilding, incentives have been provided to firms which have scrapped and/or modernised plant and equipment. Second, mergers have been sponsored with the intention of creating larger and stronger units. ICL, the dominant UK computer manufacturer, is the end-result of a series of mergers, the final stages of which were promoted by the government-financed Industrial Reorganisation Corporation.

Licensing

In some instances the government does not wish production to be confined to the public sector, but wishes to retain some control over the activities of private sector products. This can be achieved via a system of licensing. This solution is frequently adopted in the exploitation of natural resources, and one of the most extensive licensing operations undertaken in recent years related to the right to exploit oil resources off Britain's coastline.

Under the Continental Shelf Act 1964 licences have generally been issued by "administrative discretion". The government lays down guidelines for licence issue, and civil servants decide which areas shall be allocated to which companies. The payment made by licence holders is relatively modest, and the government's main source of revenue is taxation of various kinds relating to the sale of oil.

This system of licensing helps to ensure that the government can control the rate at which oil resources are developed. The government also has the power, under the Energy Act 1976, to control the rate of production from individual oil fields.

An unusual feature of policy relating to the North Sea was the establishment of a state oil company, British National Oil Corporation, with two sets of functions. First, the company was given access to substantial quantities of crude oil by various means, including participation agreements with private-sector licencees under which BNOC could buy up to 51 per cent of the oil at market prices. Second, BNOC acted as the government's advisor on North Sea policy. This dual role was criticised since it meant that BNOC advised the government on matters relating to companies with which BNOC, as an oil producer, was in competition. In 1982 BNOC's production and exploration assets were transferred to a new company, Britoil, a majority of whose shares were offered to the public.

The manufacture of medicinal drugs is subject to an elaborate system of licensing and regulation. Since this system is designed primarily to protect the safety of consumers it is considered in the following section.

Policy relating to health and safety

There is a vast body of legislation designed to protect the health and safety of consumers, workers and the man in the street. For example the Food and Drugs Act 1955 provided the basis for regulations concerning the description, composition and nutritional quality of food. The objectives of the Medicines Act 1968 were to protect consumers by improving the safety, quality and efficacy of drugs. The Act laid down that drugs can be manufactured only after a licence has been granted by the Department of Health and Social Security.

The licensing system regulates clinical trials, marketing, importation, manufacture and distribution of medicinal products. Among the costs of protecting the customer through this elaborate mechanism are an increase in spending by firms on quality control, and a lengthening of the average period for the testing of new drugs. (Critics of regulation point out that these factors may give rise to disbenefits to consumers—higher prices and a slower rate of innovation—which may counterbalance and even outweigh the benefits of protection.)

REGIONAL POLICY

The main aim of regional policy is to equalise (or at least make less unequal) employment opportunities in different parts of the country. This aim is pursued (*a*) by offering financial incentives to firms locating or expanding in areas of heavy unemployment (these Assisted Areas comprise Special Development Areas and Development Areas), (*b*) by restricting development in areas of lower unemployment.

The present pattern of assistance was established by the Industry Act 1972, although this built on earlier legislation introduced over a period of almost forty years. The two main policy instruments are Regional Development Grants and various forms of Regional Selective Assistance.

Regional Development Grants

RDGs are automatic grants of a specified percentage of cost—22 in Special Development Areas and 15 in Development Areas—payable on plant, machinery, buildings and works. RDGs are the main channel for government funds in support of regional policy.

Regional Selective Assistance

RSA is available throughout Assisted Areas (AAs) for projects which provide new jobs or safeguard existing ones. Applications for assistance are assessed against three main criteria. First, the project must be viable, have a clear employment benefit, and be financed mainly by the applicant or from other private sources. Second, the assistance must be necessary for the project to proceed as planned. Third, the project should seem likely to lead to a significant improvement in performance and strengthen the regional and national economy.

The four main categories of RSA are as follows:

(*a*) Grants to the mining, manufacturing and construction industries. The grants are normally related to the capital costs of the project and the number of jobs created.

(*b*) The Office and Service Industries Scheme. Grants linked to the number of jobs created are available to company offices, R&D units and service industry activities setting up and expanding in the AAs. Assistance is restricted to those activities with a real choice of location between AAs and elsewhere, and the grant offered is the minimum necessary to secure the project.

(c) The In-Plant Training Scheme. Introduced in 1980, this scheme applies to job creation and modernisation projects in Assisted Areas where training is an essential part of the project and accounts for a significant proportion of total costs. The grant covers 40 per cent of training costs and attracts a matching contribution from the European Social Fund.

(d) Exchange Risk Guarantee Scheme. This covers private-sector manufacturing firms in the AAs against the exchange risk on foreign-currency loans from the European Coal and Steel Community. The value of the scheme lies in the risk-free access it provides to European funds.

Factory building
The provision of factories of various sizes, including nursery units for small firms, is undertaken by the English Industrial Estates Corporation and the Scottish and Welsh Development Agencies. The factories are available on favourable terms, to either rent or purchase.

Controls on development
Despite the extensive coverage of the AAs, governments have felt unable to rely entirely on incentives; consequently these have been supplemented by controls on developments in other areas. The basic means of control is the Industrial Development Certificate, which is required for developments in the non-assisted areas of more than 50,000 square feet. Before 1979 the minimum figure was much lower, and the change represented a considerable softening of policy. Furthermore, the policy has been applied less rigorously: for example in 1974–5 about 9 per cent of applications for IDCs in the South East and West Midlands were refused; in the period 1976–8 the refusal rate was little more than 1 per cent.

MANPOWER POLICY

In the early 1980s increasing importance was given to manpower policy. Many of the new measures were designed to alleviate the consequences of steeply rising unemployment and were of more significance for unemployed workers than for employers.

Employers are more directly affected by policies relating to training. In seven industries there are Industrial Training Boards, designed to increase the level and improve the quality of training. Under the Employment and Training Act 1981 the financing of these boards became the responsibility of the firms in the industry.

Firms in a wide range of industries benefit from government-sponsored training under the Training Opportunities Scheme. TOPs courses are offered in different types of institutions, including Skillcentres (Government Training Centres) and Colleges of Further Education, and on employers' premises. In the year 1981–2 over sixty thousand adults completed TOPS training, and more than half a million school leavers entered the Youth Opportunities Programme.

Gross spending on special employment measures rose from £8 million in 1975–6 to £1,572 million in 1982–3, of which almost half was accounted for by the Youth Opportunities Programme.[3] Dissatisfaction with the extent and quality of training given under the YOP led to a decision to replace it as from September 1983 by the Youth Training Scheme.

The scheme aims to "equip unemployed young people to adapt successfully to the demands of employment; to have a further appreciation of the world of industry, business and technology in which they will be working; and to develop basic and recognised skills which employers will require in the future." To achieve these objectives the scheme combines work experience with a minimum of three months off-the-job training or further education. Sponsoring organisations receive £1,850 a year per trainee, out of which they pay a training allowance of £1,300.

The need for increased vocational training for young people was discussed in *A New Training Initiative*, a consultation document published by the Manpower Services Commission in 1981. This document showed that the proportion of young people undertaking post-school full-time vocational training was 40 per cent in France, 18 per cent in West Germany and only 10 per cent in Great Britain. The proportion undertaking apprenticeships was 14 per cent in France and Great Britain and 50 per cent in West Germany.

THE UNITED KINGDOM AND THE EUROPEAN ECONOMIC COMMUNITY

UK membership of the EEC has implications for both macro- and micro-economic policy. At the macro level the UK is a net contributor to the European Community budget which might imply that taxes are higher than they would otherwise be. On the other hand employers and employees are entitled to a range of benefits from the budget, as follows.

Employment and training grants

Grants for employment and training, retraining, resettlement and job-creation schemes are available from the European Social Fund. These schemes are available from within one of the Fund's "areas of intervention" which include Assisted Areas (see the discussion of regional policy above), textile and clothing workers, unemployed young people, disabled people, and women aged twenty-five or over. In 1981 the UK received about one-quarter of the total expenditure of the Fund.

---

3. D. Metcalf. "Special Employment Measures: an Analysis of Wage Subsidies, Youth Schemes and Worksharing". *Midland Bank Review*, 1982.

Finance for agriculture
Projects in the UK receiving finance from the European Agricultural Guidance and Guarantee Fund include the construction and improvement of fishing vessels, and the modernising of a milk-bottling plant.

Regional grants
Grant aid from the European Regional Development Fund takes two forms. First, the bulk of the aid is provided as a fixed amount or "quota" to each member state. About two-thirds of the quota is used to help finance infrastructure projects run by public authorities, and the remainder to finance industrial, tourist and service-sector projects. The UK's quota is almost one-quarter of the total. Second, the quota-free section is used for projects in any country, as dictated by the Community's regional problems, e.g. aid for small and medium-sized enterprises in steel closure areas such as Corby and Cleveland.

Loans for economic development
Loans for economic development are available from the European Investment Bank at advantageous interest rates. One-third of the lending in the UK has been to improve energy supplies, e.g. the building of a pumped-storage hydroelectric station in North Wales.

Other forms of assistance
These include aid to coal and steel regions from the European Coal and Steel Community, support for research and development work and support for energy-saving projects.

The other important implication of membership of the EEC is, of course, that the pattern of trade is affected. The absence of barriers to trade among member states means that UK producers have easier access to markets in Germany, France etc., but also that German and French producers have easier access to UK markets. The share of UK exports going to the European Community increased from 30 per cent in 1970 to 43 per cent in 1980, the corresponding increase in imports being from 27 per cent to 41 per cent.

QUESTIONS

1. Discuss the proposition that "what is good for ICI is good for Britain."

2. Explain why governments might seek to influence the operations of firms and markets.

3. You have been engaged as an economic consultant by a prominent biscuit manufacturer. This manufcturer wishes to merge with a rival, but this would give the enlarged firm 40 per cent of the market, and the proposed merger has been referred to the Monopolies and Merger

Commission. Prepare a short brief (*a*) indicating what objections to the proposed merger might be raised, (*b*) suggesting how your client might attempt to persuade the Commission that the merger be allowed.

4. Explain how and why legislation relating to collective restrictive agreements curtails firms' freedom of action.

5. Present and evaluate the arguments for allowing manufacturers to enforce the prices at which their products are sold to distributors.

6. Explain how competition policy can affect the welfare of consumers.

7. Evaluate the economic case for nationalisation.

8. "Since businessmen know more about their business than civil servants, government should not seek to influence firms' location decisions." Discuss.

9. Discuss the implications for firms of government manpower policy.

10. Assess the implications for manufacturing firms of UK membership of the EEC.

PART TWO

Measurement in Economics

CHAPTER FOUR

The Assessment of Demand

OBJECTIVES

After studying this chapter the reader should be able to: understand the principles underlying extrapolation, time-series analysis and regression analysis; give examples of leading, coincident and lagging indicators; describe the strengths and weaknesses of surveys; discuss the conditions required for successful test marketing; outline the advantages of market evaluation and scenario analysis; discuss the relative merits of alternative methods of assessing demand.

INTRODUCTION

As noted in Chapter 1, firms acquire resources only because they believe that there is a demand for the goods and services into which these resources can be transformed. It is therefore appropriate to begin our discussion of measurement by examining the various methods and techniques that might be used in assessing or predicting demand. In some instances these methods are applied directly to the demand for the products of an individual firm. In other instances the firm begins by forecasting total market size, and then calculates its own sales by estimating its share of that market, taking into account the strength of competition.

We consider first how the demand for existing products might be assessed.

EXTRAPOLATION

Extrapolation or trend projection is based on the assumption that the behaviour of sales in past periods is a useful guide to their behaviour in the future. (The volume of sales is a reasonable approximation to the level of demand, except in periods when supply cannot match demand.) This method does not attempt to identify the factors which determine sales. Consequently it is most useful when little or no change is taking place in these determinants. This requirement is especially important if naive models are to perform satisfactorily.

Naive models

A number of naive models might be used. Although they are of varying complexity, as a group they constitute the simplest form of extrapolation. The most basic model predicts that sales in the current period (year) will equal sales in the previous year:

$$Q_t = Q_{t-1}$$

A slightly more complex model predicts that the proportionate change in sales in the current year will be the same as in the previous year.

$$\frac{Q_t - Q_{t-1}}{Q_{t-1}} = \frac{Q_{t-1} - Q_{t-2}}{Q_{t-2}}$$

Time-series analysis

This method assumes that sales can be analysed in terms of one or more of four components: the secular trend (T), cyclical movements (C), seasonal variations (S) and a residual or random element (R).

The secular trend reflects long-term changes, e.g. in population or technology. Cyclical movements reflect more or less regular fluctuations in sales, usually occurring over a period of several years. These movements are often part of a movement affecting a sector of the economy or even the economy as a whole. "Seasonal" variations may occur on an annual basis, e.g. sales of holidays, or they may be of a much shorter duration, e.g. the demand for many forms of entertainment varies from one day to another. The random element may relate to identified unique events, e.g. wars, strikes, or to unidentified events.

Which of these components can be identified with respect to any particular product will, of course, depend upon the availability of sales data. Some products have been on the market far longer than others. Moreover, a firm which has been supplying a product often has access to more detailed data than a firm which is considering entering the market. Whereas the potential supplier may have to rely on published annual data, the existing supplier, drawing on its own experience, may have data on a monthly, weekly or even daily basis.

Furthermore, the usefulness of the information on the various components depends upon the decision to be made. Information on seasonal variations may be used in deciding manning levels, whereas information on the secular trend is required for decisions on the building of a new factory.

As a hypothetical example of time-series analysis let us consider the market for domestic telephones. The strong upward trend in sales shown in Fig. 9 is due to an increase in the number of households and in disposable income, and to a fall in the price of telephone calls relative to that of letters. (In order to simplify the analysis we have not considered sales trends on a month-by-month basis. But it would be very important to take account of such trends for some products, e.g. ice cream, rainwear, gas for heating.)

Cyclical variations around the trend reflect fluctuations in income. Although income grew during the period the pattern of growth was uneven, mainly because of changes in government policy, which was sometimes expansionary and sometimes restrictive. A seasonal pattern of orders, with sales highest in autumn and winter, reflects climatic influences and the fact that more time is spent in the home at this time of

4. THE ASSESSMENT OF DEMAND

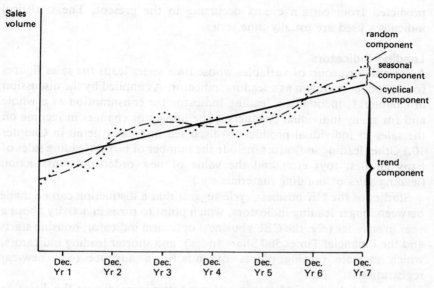

Fig. 9. *The demand for telephones.*

year than in spring and summer. Finally "shocks", such as the impact of the partial privatisation of telecommunications, are felt as part of the otherwise unexplained variations in the short-term regular patterns.

One time-series model sees the various components as acting additively, i.e.

$$Q = T + C + S + R$$

More commonly used is the multiplicative model, in which the effects of C, S and R are proportional to the trend level of sales, with C, S and R being expressed as percentages of T.

$$Q = T \times C \times S \times R$$

Once the model has been set up, time-series analysis is cheap and simple to undertake. But since it does not identify causal relationships its predictions are always vulnerable to changes in these relationships. When such a change occurs it may not be clear for some time whether the resultant change in sales constitutes a cyclical or seasonal change or a change in the secular trend. Furthermore, if causal relationships have not been identified it is more difficult to anticipate future changes in the factors which influence sales. These problems can be at least partly overcome by the use of barometric techniques.

BAROMETRIC TECHNIQUES

These techniques are based on the assumption that the future can be predicted from certain events occurring in the present. The statistical indicators used are usually time series.

Leading indicators

A variable or group of variables whose time series leads the sales figures for a product is known as a leading indicator. As implied by the discussion in Chapter 1, income is a leading indicator for consumption as a whole and for many individual products. (The impact of changes in income on the sales of individual products is discussed in greater detail in Chapter 10.) Other leading indicators include the number of births (leading sales of baby clothes, toys etc.) and the value of new orders in construction (leading sales of building materials etc.).

Studies of the UK business cycle suggest that a distinction can be made between longer leading indicators, which point to turns in activity about a year in advance (e.g. the CBI's business optimism indicator, housing starts and the Financial Times 500 Share Index), and shorter leading indicators, which indicate turning points six months in advance (e.g. new-car registrations).

In general, leading indicators perform better in predicting the direction of movement in sales than the magnitude or timing of the change. Moreover, although they have the advantage, compared with extrapolation, of identifying causal relationships, it must always be remembered that these relationships can themselves undergo substantial and sudden changes. For example during the recession of the early 1980s firms attempted to reduce their stocks. Consequently when distributors received orders for finished goods their orders for replacement goods, and hence the orders for components and raw materials, were considerably less than would have been expected on the basis of past experience.

Coincident and lagging indicators

These indicators coincide with or lag behind market trends. Their main value is in confirming or refuting the validity of a leading indicator. A full list of the economic statistics included in the Central Statistical Office's cyclical indicators is given in Table VI.

ECONOMETRIC MODELS

Econometric models are quantified relationships between one or more variables and another. The relationships may be deduced from economic theory or suggested by past experience. The models most frequently used in demand forecasting incorporate regression analysis.

Regression analysis

A simple regression model relates the forecast, or dependent, variable to a single independent variable. Pindyck and Rubinfeld developed a model to

4. THE ASSESSMENT OF DEMAND

TABLE VI. CYCLICAL INDICATORS

Indicators	Timing relative to reference cycle dates* (−) leads, (+) lags months		
	Average (mean)	Earliest	Latest
Longer leading			
Composite longer leading index	−13	−21	−7
Component series:			
Rate of interest, 3 months prime bank bills	−18	−26	−11
Financial surplus/deficit, industrial and commercial companies	−14	−21	−8
Total dwellings started, Great Britain	−11	−25	+6
Financial Times–Actuaries 500-Share Index	−9	−20	−4
CBI Quarterly Survey: change in optimism	−8	−18	−1
Shorter leading			
Composite shorter leading index	−5	−12	0
Component series:			
Credit extended by finance houses, retailer and other credit grantors	−6	−15	0
New-car registrations	−8	−26	0
CBI Quarterly Survey: change in new orders	−7	−28	+4
CBI Quarterly Survey: expected change in stocks of materials	−5	−15	+2
Gross trading profits of companies, excluding stock appreciation and mineral oil and natural gas extraction	−8	−26	+1
Roughly coincident			
Composite coincident index	+1	−1	+6
Component series:			
Gross domestic product (expenditure)	+1	−9	+10
Gross domestic product (output)	−1	−4	+2
Gross domestic product (income)	+2	−3	+7
Index of volume of retail sales	−4	−15	0
Index of production, manufacturing industry	0	−3	+2
CBI Quarterly Survey: capacity utilisation index	+2	−3	+7
CBI Quarterly Survey: change in stocks of materials	0	−6	+3
Lagging			
Composite lagging index	+10	+6	+17
Component series:			
Unemployment, excluding school-leavers and adult students, Great Britain	+7	−1	+16
Vacancies notified to employment offices and remaining unfilled	+4	−2	+16
Investment in plant and machinery, manufacturing industry	+11	−6	+18
Engineering industries, volume index for orders on hand	+10	+5	+15
Level of manufacturers' stocks and work in progress	+12	+3	+20

*Assessed on performance up to last identified peak, May 1979

Source: *Economic Progress Report*, September 1982

explain the relationship between car sales in the USA (the dependent variable) and wages (the independent variable).[1] The regression function (equation) was

$$V = 1767.1 + 7.48W$$

where V is monthly sales ($ billion) and W is wages paid by private employers ($ billion).

When the equation was applied to monthly sales for the period 1963 to 1970 the correlation coefficient (R^2) was 0.8, implying that 80 per cent of changes in sales were due to changes in wage payments.

Multiple regression

It is unusual to find a single variable with a very high explanatory power. Moreover, even if one factor has a very strong impact on sales, the degree of explanation can usually be improved by including additional independent variables in the regression equation. A high correlation coefficient ($R^2 = 0.983$) was obtained by the multiple-regression model for sales of radio and television receivers in the USA developed by Houthakker and Taylor.[2]

$$Q_t = 0.6599 Q_{t-1} + 0.0167 \Delta x_t + 0.0060 x_{t-1} - 0.0946 \Delta P_t - 0.0340 P_{t-1}$$

where

Q_t = quarterly expenditure per head on radio and television receivers ($)
Q_{t-1} = expenditure per head in previous quarter ($)
Δx_t = change in total personal quarterly consumption expenditure ($)
x_{t-1} = total personal consumption in previous quarter
ΔP_t = price relative in present quarter (with 1954 as base year)
P_{t-1} = price relative in previous quarter

This equation shows that expenditure on television and radio receivers was affected by factors operating in both the current and the previous quarter. Lagged relationships are often found to be important and some models have included lags extending over several periods. The signs in the equation have the expected values. A change in total consumption (itself probably reflecting a change in income) was positively related to expenditure in this market; a change in relative price was negatively related to expenditure.

Regression models can be used to predict sales on the assumption that the values currently included in the models are maintained. They also enable the firm to explore the impact of changes in these values. This is

---

1. R. S. Pindyck and D. L. Rubinfeld. *Econometric Models and Econometric Forecasting*. McGraw-Hill, New York, 1976, p. 39.

2. H. Houthakker and L. Taylor. *Consumer Demand in the United States 1920–1970*. Harvard UP, Cambridge, Mass., 1966.

especially useful if the firm has developed a model including variables within its own control, e.g. price, advertising expenditure. By simulating changes in these variables and observing the consequences, the firm can use the model in formulating its marketing policy.

However, econometric models should be seen as complementing, not replacing, judgment and experience of the market. As with the other forecasting methods considered so far, they are based on past experience and behaviour. This can be captured only imperfectly. Moreover, there are many reasons why consumers may behave differently in the future than in the past. This leads to a consideration of methods that do not rely on past data.

SURVEYS

Surveys can take different forms. But all surveys involve asking people what they believe will happen, or what they intend to do, in the future. Although the respondents' answers may reflect their own past experience, there is no attempt to link the future with the past, as there is with the models considered above. (However, the evidence from surveys is often considered together with the predictions of such models.)

Surveys relating to aggregated items

A number of surveys relating to aggregated items are published on a regular basis. For example, four times a year the CBI surveys companies' expectations with respect to exports, capital expenditure, new orders, output, stocks etc. (As noted above, this survey is seen as an important leading indicator.) Such surveys can help to give a feel of likely broad movements in economic activity. But most firms will require more detailed information relating to their own products.

Surveys of purchasers' intentions

Pioneering work into the attitudes and intentions of purchasers was carried out by the Survey Research Centre at the University of Michigan, beginning in 1953. More recently, similar work has been undertaken at the London Business School and the University of Sussex. These surveys have proved to be more accurate at the level of groups of products, e.g. consumer durables as a whole, than individual products. The reason for this is probably "switching" within the total durables market, with money which it was stated was to be spent on one product actually being spent on another.

To survey an adequate number of final purchasers would be extremely expensive for a single manufacturer. It is much less expensive to survey the attitudes and intentions of the distributors buying from that manufacturer. However, the manufacturer should be aware of the possibility of bias being introduced into the responses. Distributors may paint an over-optimistic picture of future sales in order to avoid the danger that manufacturers might not produce sufficient to meet their requirements. On the other hand, distributors may be tempted to paint a gloomy picture if they feel that manufacturers would thereby be encouraged to offer a better deal, e.g. a lower price or a bigger promotional allowance.

Surveys of the sales force
Many firms obtain information about market prospects on a routine basis from their sales force. There is again the possibility of bias: salesmen are by nature optimistic! But if information is found to be systematically biased then the firm can correct for this.

Surveys of expert opinion
In order to reduce the possibility of bias, the opinions of a range of expert observers might be canvassed. The Delphi technique attempts to increase the accuracy of these opinions by providing feedback. The first round of questioning attempts to establish median (average) values of a variable and this is passed back to the group together with extreme values. Those who made extreme values give the reasons for their decisions, and this information is also passed to the other members of the group. The questions are then repeated and the process continues until a consensus is reached. In 1972 and 1973 an extensive Delphi exercise was run with grocery manufacturers and major retailers. Their estimates included the following changes between 1970 and 1990 in the percentage of households owning various products: washing machines 64 per cent to over 80 per cent; refrigerators 63 per cent to 85 per cent; food and drink mixers 24 per cent to almost 50 per cent.[3]

Sales-growth models
It has been found that the sales of products that are entirely new in conception often follow the time pattern shown in Fig. 10. (The curve shown there is a Gompertz curve.) The vertical axis shows the proportion of households (or firms for industrial goods) that have "adopted" the product. If it is possible to estimate the final adoption rate, e.g. 80 per cent of households for video recorders, it is then possible to estimate the number of adopters each year.

It would, of course, be sensible to use this information in conjunction with data obtained in other ways, and to adjust the estimates to take account of changes in incomes, competitive activity etc. Moreover, account should be taken of replacement sales, which become more important over time. Finally, as noted in chapter 14, the firm should not assume that it is unable to prevent the transition from the growth and saturation stages to the decline stage of the product life-cycle. Provided

3. D. Walters. *Distribution and Retailing in the Eighties*. Cranfield School of Management, 1974.

4. THE ASSESSMENT OF DEMAND

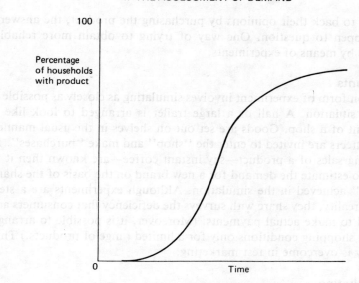

Fig. 10. *The adoption of a new product.*

these qualifications are borne in mind, the product life-cycle concept can provide useful guidance in assessing the future demand for existing products.

ASSESSING THE DEMAND FOR NEW OR MODIFIED PRODUCTS

Models using past data—extrapolation, barometric techniques and econometric models—can obviously not be used for new or substantially modified products. We consider below alternative techniques that might be used. But first we consider the use of surveys with regard to new and modified products.

Surveys and new products

Potential purchasers—distributors or final users—may be asked whether or not they would be likely to buy a new (or modified) product. To help them to reach a decision they could be shown a prototype, or mock-up, of the product, or given a verbal or visual description of it. (It is necessary to provide more information on a new than a modified product.)

The opportunity is usually taken during the survey to seek purchasers' reactions to different "offers". In some instances the variations may be confined to price. (The impact of price on sales is considered at length in later chapters). But if the formulation of the product has not been finally determined, product variations—in colour, size, styling and even function—may be introduced.

A large number of potential purchasers can be questioned at a relatively low cost. However, since they are not in a purchasing environment and are not asked to back their opinions by purchasing the product, the answers must be open to question. One way of trying to obtain more reliable answers is by means of experiments.

Experiments
A common form of experiment involves simulating as closely as possible a shopping situation. A hall or a large trailer is arranged to look like a department of a shop. Goods are set out on shelves in the usual manner and volunteers are invited to enter the "shop" and make "purchases". If the existing sales of a product—say instant coffee—are known then it is possible to estimate the demand for a new brand on the basis of the share of "sales" achieved in the simulation. Although experiments are a step nearer to reality, they share with surveys the deficiency that consumers are not asked to make actual payments. (Moreover, it is possible to arrange simulated shopping conditions only for a limited range of products.) This deficiency is overcome in test marketing.

Test marketing
In test marketing the product is marketed in one part of the country—perhaps a single town or an Independent Television region—and an assessment of demand is made on the basis of its performance in this area. Test marketing is usually considered to be the most reliable way of assessing the demand for a new product. However, great care must be taken in the choice of test area and in the analysis of the results.

The test area should have a socio-economic mix as near as possible to that of the whole area in which the product would be sold. Also the conditions in the test market should be typical. The first requirement is within the control of the company, the second is not. There may be more (or less) advertising of competitive products than normal. Supplies of competitive products may be temporarily in short supply e.g. because of a strike.

Even if the test conditions are satisfactory, the results of the test may be difficult to interpret. If the firm's information is derived from its own records, or those of distributors, it may not know the split of sales as between initial and repeat purchases. But this is a very important distinction since future demand will in many instances—and especially for low-value goods—mainly comprise repeat purchases. The firm may attempt to obtain more detailed information by asking a sample of consumers about their purchases. But this will increase the cost of an already expensive exercise.

MARKET EVALUATION

Market evaluation may be undertaken as a preliminary to the types of analysis discussed above, or as an alternative if it is thought that this analysis would not yield useful results, e.g. because economic conditions are very unsettled. In evaluating the opportunities offered and the ability of the firm to take advantage of these opportunities, it is sometimes useful to attach numerical scores to the various markets which might be entered. Table VII shows a typical, although simplified, example of this procedure. The external score indicates the firm's assessment of the conditions in each market. It can be seen that toys and greeting cards appear to be the most promising markets from this point of view. However when the internal factors, indicating the firm's orientation towards each market, are taken into account, fruit juice appears to be the most promising choice.

TABLE VII. A MARKET-EVALUATION SCHEDULE

Factors	Maximum score	Baby foods	Canned meat	Fruit juice	Greeting cards	Toys
Market size	15	4	14	7	15	15
Past growth	10	1	2	9	6	5
Profitability	20	8	2	13	18	19
Competition	20	6	8	15	16	16
Chance of originality	20	5	7	9	14	17
Seasonality	5	5	3	3	1	1
External total	90	29	36	56	70	73
Fit for:						
Company production	25	2	5	5	0	0
Sales force	20	8	14	14	7	7
R&D	10	7	7	7	2	2
Branding	15	2	8	9	1	2
Distribution	10	6	8	8	5	5
Internal total	80	29	42	43	15	16
Total score	170	58	78	99	85	89

Source: P. Krausher. "Developing a New Consumer Product". In: M. Rines (ed.). *Marketing Handbook*. Gower, 2nd edition, 1981, p. 135

SCENARIO ANALYSIS

Another response to unsettled economic conditions has been the willingness, especially by large firms, to "depart from reliance on analytically derived forecasts and to place more reliance on the results of speculative or conjectural approaches."[4] This may seem to be a retrograde

[4]. H. E. Klein and R. E. Linneman. "The Use of Scenarios in Corporate Planning—Eight Case Histories". *Long Range Planning* Vol. 14 (1981).

step in view of the development of an increased range of planning techniques. However "conventional environmental forecasting techniques, predicted on analysis of past data, have difficulty dealing with structural discontinuities or what might be called "historyless situations". Unfortunately this is the situation in which many corporations find themselves; hence the need to consider the non-analytic approaches to future forecasting."[5]

These "non-analytic", or less formalised, approaches take account of a wide range of variables, economic, demographic, social, political, technological and ecological. A firm which was considering whether to establish a petrochemical complex in an undeveloped country would try to assess the demand for the various products that could be produced. It would also examine other factors that might affect the profitability of the project: the possibility that political power might pass to a government pledged to the nationalisation of foreign-owned assets; the advent of a new and far more efficient technology; the social unrest which might follow from the introduction of a large plant paying higher wages than usual in that country; possible restrictions on the level of operation because of fears that the gases discharged from the plant could harm the crops grown by nearby farmers, and so on.

As an example of how an apparently promising project can founder, consider the experience of BP in the manufacture of industrial proteins. The company began protein research in 1959. This led to the building of several pilot plants in the 1960s and finally to an agreement to share the costs of building a £40 million commercial-scale plant with Anic, the chemicals arm of ENI, the Italian state hydrocarbons corporation. The plant was completed in 1976, but was never allowed to enter full production.

The decrees allowing the plant to operate were suspended in 1976, on the ground that the Italian authorities had found a residue of n-paraffins in the back fat of pigs fed on Toprina (the protein's brand name) at a level of 70 parts per million. (BP point out that rice on sale in Italy has traces of n-paraffins at 1,400 parts per million. Moreover, in the USA the Food and Drug Administration, one of the toughest regulatory authorities in the world, allows an n-paraffin level of 950 p.p.m.)

The plant was allowed to operate for the commissioning stage at the beginning of 1977, but was then closed on the further ground that dust emission was too high. (BP point out that the dust level was one-fortieth of that allowed for other plants in Italy such as cement works. The managing director of BP Nutrition commented: "It is an absolute scandal that it should be brought to nothing for reasons that do not have any scientific justification whatsoever.")

A study by Linneman and Klein found that 150 of the 1000 largest

---

5. Klein and Linneman. *Op. cit.*

corporations in the USA used multiple-scenario planning. This usually involved constructing three scenarios relating to optimistic, most likely and pessimistic cases, extending over five years or longer. All the alternative scenarios were taken into account when the companies constructed their final strategies.[6]

The corollary of scenario analysis is that business plans need to be flexible enough to handle the possibility of any of the alternative scenarios developing. This has implications for investment policy, especially in industries where plant and equipment is expected to have a long life, say twenty years. In these industries such investment may be limited to that which is justified under all likely scenarios. The importance of flexibility in planning is considered again in Chapter 6.

QUESTIONS

1. Discuss the possible behaviour of the sales of the following products in terms of the secular trend, cyclical movements, seasonal variations and random elements: (a) television sets, (b) video recorders, (c) railway travel, (d) potatoes, (e) health foods, (f) shoes.

2. Prepare a list of the products for which each of the following items might be an important leading indicator: (a) number of dwellings started, (b) credit extended by finance houses, (c) new-car registrations, (d) number of births.

3. Explain why each of the following items is considered to be an important leading indicator: (a) rate of interest, (b) financial surplus/deficit of industrial and commercial companies, (c) CBI Quarterly Survey: change in new orders, (d) CBI Quarterly Survey: expected change in stocks of materials, (e) CBI Quarterly Survey: change in optimism.

4. Assess the usefulness of econometric models in demand forecasting.

5. Prepare a series of briefs for surveys to be undertaken in order to obtain information that will be used by manufacturers in forecasting the sales of the products listed below. The brief should indicate what information is required, what questions should be asked, and to whom the questions should be addressed: (a) car batteries, (b) a small yacht that can be produced more cheaply than existing models, (c) a new type of packaging for potato crisps and similar snack products, (d) a portable, battery-operated, mini-vacuum cleaner that could be used for such things as cleaning the interior of cars.

6. Explain the advantages and disadvantages for the purposes of test marketing of the town or city in which you live.

7. What factors might enter into scenario planning undertaken by a car manufacturer? Explain why it might be useful to this manufacturer to construct alternative scenarios.

6. R. E. Linneman and H. E. Klein. "The Use of Multiple Scenarios by U.S. Industrial Companies". *Long Range Planning* Vol. 12 (1979).

CHAPTER FIVE

Cost Analysis

OBJECTIVES

After studying this chapter the reader should be able to: define opportunity cost, fixed cost, variable cost, marginal cost, incremental cost, escapable cost and sunk cost; explain how average cost is likely to change as the level of output changes; list and give examples of the various economies of scale; explain why average cost may rise as a firm grows; explain the meaning and significance of the experience effect.

INTRODUCTION

In answer to the question "What was the cost of your holiday?" the man in the street would probably answer "£400" or whatever figure was appropriate. An economist, on the other hand, might answer "a television set" or "a washing machine". This answer would be explained by the fact that the economist sees the cost of any action (e.g. booking a holiday) as the maximum alternative benefit forgone as a result of that action. The technical term for this forgone benefit is opportunity cost.

The economist also views cost as being subjective; only the decision-taker can know what alternative benefit he would have expected to enjoy (the satisfaction expected to be obtained from a television set or a washing machine) had he not taken the holiday. This viewpoint has been concisely expressed by Professor Buchanan: "Cost is that which the decision-maker sacrifices or gives up when he selects one alternative rather than another. Cost consists therefore in his own evaluation of the enjoyment or utility that he anticipates having to forgo as a result of choice itself."[1]

We illustrate the significance of opportunity cost at various points in this and later chapters. But in this chapter we devote most of our attention to what might be called accounting cost. By this is meant cost which relates to the expenses incurred by the company. (Companies have a legal duty to prepare accounts based on expense-related costs.)

Since cost is related to expenses incurred it might be considered to be objective. However, the procedures for estimating and calculating costs require judgment to be exercised concerning, for example, the period of time over which fixed assets are depreciated and hence the annual depreciation charge, whether depreciation charges should be based on the historic (actual) or the replacement cost of the assets, whether raw materials should be valued at historic, current or replacement cost, and how joint costs are to be allocated among two or more products. The considerable scope that exists for exercising judgment means that accounting cost is less objective—and that the gap between the respective

1. J. M. Buchanan. *Cost and Choice*. Markham, Chicago, 1969, p. 14.

viewpoints of economist and accountant is less wide—than might be thought.

Many factors can influence a firm's level of costs, the most obvious being the price the firm pays for its inputs. But in the early part of the chapter we take the price of inputs as given and examine the effect on costs of a change in the volume of output. We consider first the situation when the scale of organisation is given.

THE BEHAVIOUR OF COSTS AS OUTPUT CHANGES WITH A GIVEN SCALE OF ORGANISATION

The scale of organisation refers to the capacity or effective potential output of the firm, i.e. the output that could be produced in a standard working week with an allowance for normal delays. The effective potential output is normally less than technical capacity, which assumes production on seven days a week, each day comprising twenty-four working hours, and ideal operating conditions.

The capacity of a manufacturing plant is determined by the number of machines installed, the capacity of each machine, the number of hours per week for which labour can be found to operate the machines, the ability and skill of this labour, etc. The capacity of a hairdressing salon is determined by the type and amount of equipment, the hours during which the salon is open (which may be due partly to the availability of labour and partly to licensing regulations), and by the number of customers an assistant can deal with in a given period of time. In retailing the capacity of a shop may be determined by such factors as the amount of selling space, the number of check-out points (in a self-service store), the amount of car-parking space (in out-of-town shops) and, once more, the availability of labour.

In choosing its scale of organisation, the firm takes into account both the conditions of demand and its objectives. For example demand may be rising and the firm may wish to increase its market share. Having chosen the scale of organisation, the firm has to acquire the appropriate resources or inputs.

Although, as noted above, the firm's planned capacity is related to the output that it expects to supply in the forthcoming (or planning) period, many firms choose a scale greater than the expected *average* output in that period. There are several reasons why such a policy may be adopted.

First, there may be substantial fluctuations in orders during the planning period. As we saw in Chapter 4, sales may have a seasonal component, being higher in, say, winter than summer. If the firm is to meet the peak demand it will have spare capacity at other times of the year. Furthermore, the average demand may turn out to be higher than expected. (As we also saw in Chapter 4 it is often difficult to accurately predict demand.) If, in either of these situations, the firm was unable to meet its orders, some customers might transfer their trade, perhaps on a permanent basis, to rival suppliers able to fulfil their immediate requirements.

Second, and this is the opposite side of the coin, a firm which has the capacity to cope with peak or unexpectedly high demands may expect to gain customers from rival suppliers whose capacity proves inadequate at such times. In markets where there are no important physical differences between the products of rival suppliers, the ability to give a quicker service may be the most effective way of increasing market share. Even when products are differentiated early delivery can be an important competitive weapon, as shown in Chapter 15.

Finally, it is not normally possible to increase the scale of organisation by infinitely small amounts. Even if the firm wished to install capacity in line with the expected average demand, it might have to choose between capacities above and below this level. If the firm is not interested in growth it may choose the lower capacity. If, like most firms, it is interested in growth, it is likely to choose the higher level for the reasons already mentioned. In making decisions about what quantities of the various inputs are required, most attention is usually given to the amount of plant and equipment to be installed. Although some flexibility in the utilisation of plant and equipment may exist by way of overtime or extra shift working, the firm may not be able to rely on it. (As we showed above, capacity is based on a standard or normal working week.) Consequently the capacity of plant and equipment becomes the factor determining the output limit.

Moreover, there is often a considerable time-lag between a decision to expand the amount of plant and equipment and the ability to obtain and install additional units. This lag may be due partly to the inability of suppliers to meet orders immediately—a delay of several months is common for many types of equipment—and partly to the need to create space for the new equipment, perhaps by buying land and building a new factory.

This suggests that buildings, plant and equipment are the inputs whose quantities are most likely to be fixed given the scale of organisation. Costs attaching to fixed inputs are known as fixed costs.

Fixed costs

As output increases, and the cost of fixed inputs is spread over a greater number of units of output, the cost per unit of output, or average fixed cost, falls (Fig. 11). Average fixed cost continues to fall beyond output E, the expected level of output, to L, the maximum output that could be produced, given the scale of organisation. (Any further increase in output would require the scale of organisation to be increased by means of an increase in the quantity of the fixed or limiting input. This increase in scale

5. COST ANALYSIS

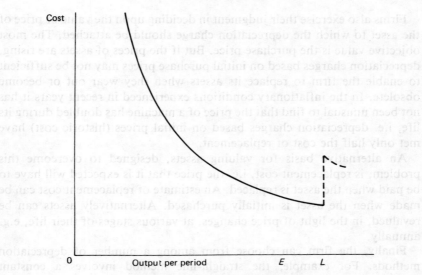

Fig. 11. *Average cost: buildings, plant and equipment.*

would lead to an increase in average fixed cost as shown by the dotted line.)

If buildings are rented and plant and equipment are leased, the costs incurred correspond to the cash payments made by the firm during the current period. But in many instances these assets are purchased by the firm. The full purchase price is paid in the first year of ownership and nothing (apart from operating costs) in subsequent years. If the costs were taken into the accounts as they were incurred, this could produce undesirable fluctuations in reported profits. To prevent this, the cost of these assets is spread more evenly; it is depreciated over the life of the assets.

As noted above, judgment has to be exercised concerning the period over which an asset is depreciated or written off. The measurement of cost is therefore partly subjective, and in this sense cost becomes more akin to the economist's definition.

In order to explain this more clearly let us consider a firm which could use its resources in several alternative, highly profitable ways. By buying machines to increase the output of one product the firm is prevented from exploiting another profitable opportunity. The firm could take this forgone opportunity into account by creating a high annual depreciation charge, i.e. by writing off the machines over a short period. An early write-off, a high depreciation charge, might also be chosen if, in another situation, considerable risk attached to the purchase of machines, e.g. because the demand for the product was highly uncertain or because technological change could soon render the machines obsolete. (The degree of aversion to risk is again subjective.)

Firms also exercise their judgment in deciding upon the value or price of the asset to which the depreciation charge should be attached. The most objective value is the purchase price. But if the prices of assets are rising, depreciation charges based on initial purchase prices may not be sufficient to enable the firm to replace its assets when they wear out or become obsolete. In the inflationary conditions experienced in recent years it has not been unusual to find that the price of a machine has doubled during its life, i.e. depreciation charges based on initial prices (historic cost) have met only half the cost of replacement.

An alternative basis for valuing assets, designed to overcome this problem, is replacement cost, i.e. the price that it is expected will have to be paid when the asset is replaced. An estimate of replacement cost can be made when the asset is initially purchased. Alternatively assets can be revalued, in the light of price changes, at various stages of their life, e.g. annually.

Finally, the firm can choose from among a number of depreciation methods. For example, the straight-line method involves a constant depreciation-charge in each year, whereas the declining balance method involves higher depreciation-charges in earlier than in later years. Although this may be mainly a technical choice, it gives a further opportunity for the firm to take account of some of the factors discussed above.

Other fixed costs

There are other inputs whose costs are considered as fixed for a given scale of organisation. Local authority rates and insurance premiums on buildings, plant and equipment are treated as a fixed cost in some, but not all, situations.

Indirect labour can be defined as those employees who do not work directly on the product itself, but whose services are related to the process of production, e.g. maintenance staff, fork-lift-truck drivers, foremen. The term could also be widened to include staff further removed from the production process, such as planning, marketing and personnel staff. (In some organisations the costs of such staff are included in "general overhead" costs.)

There are two justifications for treating the costs of indirect labour as fixed. First, if the staff are obliged to work longer hours as output increases then they may do so without receiving additional remuneration. (In fact this is more likely to apply to, say, the marketing manager than a maintenance fitter.) Second, if output falls, the costs of these staff are less likely to fall than the costs of direct labour. Indirect workers are often on a fixed salary, as noted above, and also are less liable to be made redundant following a reduction in output. However if the fall in output is prolonged then the firm may reduce its indirect labour costs while retaining all its plant and equipment, i.e. leaving the scale of organisation unchanged. In other words, some fixed inputs are more fixed than others!

The likely behaviour of indirect labour costs is shown in Fig. 12. As output falls below L the total of these costs remains unchanged and so average cost rises. But once output falls to N then the firm reacts by reducing the amount of indirect labour employed, i.e. fixed costs fall. Given this lower amount of labour, if output falls below N then average cost will again rise until point M is reached, when a further reduction in the quantity of labour is effected. (The reverse process would apply if output increased from a low initial level.)

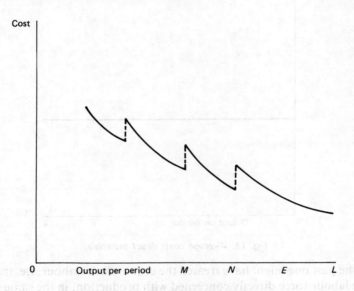

Fig. 12. *Average cost: indirect labour.*

We referred above to general overheads, a cost category found in many firms. This category includes many costs which vary as shown in Fig. 12. For example the costs of the R&D department include the costs of materials, fuel etc. as well as (indirect) labour. The level of activity of this department is unlikely to be affected directly by a change in output, but if output, and hence profit, suffers a prolonged fall then the firm may be obliged to cut back on expenditure in this area. (However an alternative response to a fall in output may be to increase spending on R&D, if the money is available.)

Variable costs

The firm varies the quantities of some inputs in accordance with the level of output. The costs attaching to these variable inputs are known as variable costs. Figure 13 shows the behaviour of average variable cost when the amount of the input used varies in direct proportion to output. This will apply to direct materials, where the quantity used per unit of output is determined by technical specifications. (At very high output levels the increased pace at which both men and machines work sometimes causes a slight increase in material usage per unit of output, i.e. a slight rise in average variable cost. On the other hand, larger purchases of materials may enable the firm to buy at slightly better prices.)

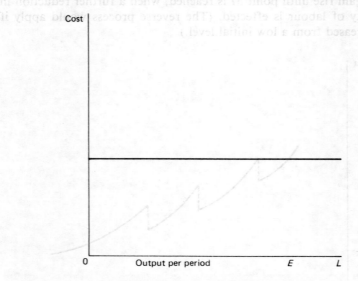

Fig. 13. *Average cost: direct materials.*

In the past one might have treated the cost of direct labour, i.e. that part of the labour force directly concerned with production, in the same way as direct materials. However, it has become increasingly difficult for a firm to change the quantity of labour in line with changes in output. Such a policy would meet with opposition from the unions, moreover its cost to the firm has been increased by legislation, including that relating to redundancy payments. Consequently there is often a lag between a change in output and a change in the amount of direct labour employed. In other words, average variable cost has a stepped function, as shown in Fig. 14. This is similar to the function for indirect labour, although the number of steps is greater for direct labour.

It will be noticed in Fig. 14 that average cost rises as output increases beyond the expected level. This is likely to happen for either of two reasons. First, unless the firm is convinced that the rise in demand is permanent, it will be reluctant to engage more workers who may subsequently have to be dismissed. Instead it will prefer to ask the existing workers to work overtime. Since overtime working by direct labour usually involves premium payments, average labour cost rises.

Alternatively, if the firm does engage more workers in the belief that the increase in demand is permanent then these new workers may initially have

5. COST ANALYSIS

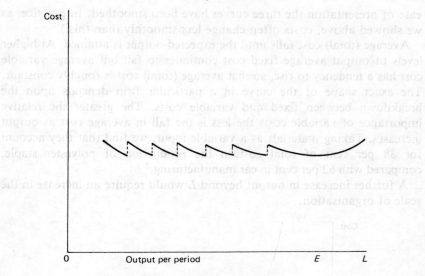

Fig. 14. *Average cost: direct labour.*

a lower productivity than existing workers who are familiar with the firm's operations and who may also have a higher level of skill. If new workers are paid at the same rate as existing workers then the cost per unit of output will rise.

There is less scope for subjective judgment in the allocation of variable than fixed costs. However, the allocation is not always entirely objective. Some variable inputs are employed in the production of more than one product, and it is often necessary to make an arbitrary allocation of costs among products.

Semi-variable costs

We have made a distinction between two groups of inputs, and thus two types of cost, fixed and variable. However we have shown that within each group differences in the behaviour of costs are to be expected. We noted that some fixed costs are more fixed than others, and we can add that some variable costs are more variable than others. In addition, some inputs do not fall easily into either group, since their costs are semi-variable, e.g. power and fuel, some indirect materials, and plant maintenance. We assume that semi-variable costs can be divided into two elements, fixed and variable; thus we can retain a two-fold classification. In practice firms often use a more complex classification.

THE BEHAVIOUR OF COSTS WITH A GIVEN SCALE OF ORGANISATION: SUMMARY

The behaviour of costs as output changes is summarised in Fig. 15. (For ease of presentation the three curves have been smoothed. In practice, as we showed above, costs often change less smoothly than this.)

Average (total) cost falls until the expected output is attained. At higher levels of output average fixed cost continues to fall but average variable cost has a tendency to rise, so that average (total) cost is roughly constant. The exact shape of the curve in a particular firm depends upon the breakdown between fixed and variable costs. The greater the relative importance of variable costs the less is the fall in average cost as output increases. Taking materials as a variable input, we find that they account for 38 per cent of total cost in the production of polyester staple, compared with 62 per cent in car manufacturing.[2]

A further increase in output beyond L would require an increase in the scale of organisation.

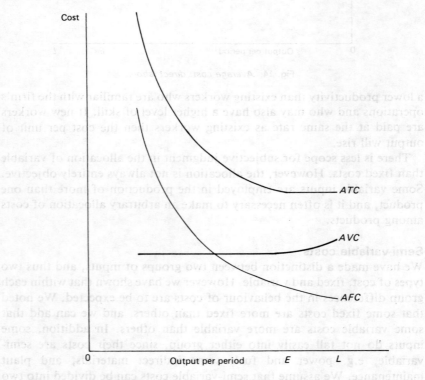

Fig. 15. *Average fixed, variable and total cost.*

THE BEHAVIOUR OF COSTS WITH A CHANGING SCALE OF ORGANISATION

As we show in Chapter 10, growth is an important objective for many firms. Consequently in this section we concentrate on increases in the scale

2. P. S. Johnson (ed.). *The Structure of British Industry.* Granada, 1980, Ch. 8 and 9.

of organisation. However we also refer briefly to the implications of a decrease in scale.

Economies of scale

When the scale of organisation is increased, the firm is able to take advantage of certain economies that are not available, or are of much less importance, at a lower scale. The classification of economies of scale presented here is one of several alternative classifications.

Technical economies

The first type of technical economy arises from the physical properties of plant and equipment, and in particular from area–volume relationships. The volume of three-dimensional objects increases faster than the surface area. Consequently when output depends on volume and cost upon area, as in the construction of oil and gas pipelines, cost per unit of output falls as scale increases.

Technical economies also arise when it is possible to obtain an increase in output by increasing only some parts or components of equipment while leaving other parts unchanged. For example, one size of motor may be sufficient to drive machinery of different sizes and capacities. The capacity of stone-cutting machinery can be increased to a certain extent by adding extra cutting blades without making significant modifications to the rest of the machine.

However some of the most outstanding economies of scale have been obtained not by installing bigger machines of the same basic type, but by using a different technology that can be efficiently utilised only when the level of output is increased substantially. A simple example is the automatic weaving loom where the recharging of the shuttle, previously performed by hand, is now performed by machine. A bigger advance in technology was represented by the introduction of the continuous strip-mill in steel and plate-glass manufacture.

The output required to take full advantage of modern methods of production can be very high indeed. It has been estimated that in car manufacturing the minimum efficient scale is 1 million units a year in the casting of engine blocks and 1 to 2 million units in the pressing of various panels.[3] (The significance of minimum efficient scale is discussed further below.)

All the economies listed above could be obtained by firms which continued to undertake the same processes as previously (although perhaps using different methods), i.e. where the firm grew horizontally. Other economies can result from vertical expansion, where growth entails a move into an additional stage of production, enabling separate processes to be linked.

---

3. P. S. Johnson. *Op. cit.*, Ch. 8.

It has been estimated that to locate a cotton spinning mill and a weaving shed on the same site would result in a saving in transport costs, in relation to the existing pattern of location, which would represent up to 2½ per cent of the selling price of the cloth. Transferring molten pig-iron direct to steel furnaces, rather than allowing it to cool and then subsequently reheating it, could reduce fuel costs by an estimated 22 per cent.

The "law of large numbers" lies behind a further group of technical economies of scale which arise when firms, being unable to foresee the future pattern of events, need to guard against possible adverse circumstances. Firms often keep spare machinery to be used when other machines break down. Stocks of raw materials and components are maintained in case the firm suddenly needs to increase output or because of the fear that the supply of materials or components might be interrupted, e.g. by a strike at a component manufacturer's factory. In all these instances the required level of "reserves" increases less than proportionately to output or capacity.

Marketing economies
It is often possible to achieve an increase in turnover with a less than proportionate increase in the cost of such resources as warehousing and the sales fleet. (This is analogous to technical economies considered above, and could have been included under that heading.)

Economies in advertising may arise from two sources. First, there may be a threshold below which certain types of advertising cannot be undertaken, e.g. many small firms are unable to finance advertising on television and may be obliged to adopt a less cost-effective form of advertising. Second, there is some evidence to suggest that a firm that has achieved a large scale of operations can maintain a given level of advertising effectiveness at a lower cost than a smaller, less well-known firm.

Purchasing economies
As noted above the firm may be able to purchase inputs at a lower cost as it expands output at a given scale of organisation. But greater purchasing economies are clearly available as the scale of organisation increases. Many suppliers offer quantity discounts, but large purchasers can often obtain better terms than those contained in the published discount schedules.

Purchasing economies are especially important in retailing since the cost of goods sold is by far the most important cost. The discounts granted by individual manufacturers are a well-kept secret. But in its report *Discounts to Retailers,* published in 1981, the Monopolies and Mergers Commission showed that the additional discounts (i.e. outside the normal rebates) obtained by the three largest multiple grocery chains from 15 major manufacturers averaged almost 8 per cent.

Purchasing economies can also be obtained in services. For example the unit price of advertisements sometimes falls with an increase in the number of advertisements such as television spots and newspaper insertions. The charges made for professional services, e.g. legal services, and by agents of various kinds, are often on a sliding scale.

Financial economies

Firms can obtain finance from a number of sources, as shown in Chapter 6, but whichever source is used large firms are often able to obtain finance more easily and cheaply than smaller firms. If money is borrowed from a bank the rate of interest charged may be 1 or 2 per cent lower. If permanent loan capital is raised from the public a similar differential might apply. If money is raised by means of an issue of shares then the smaller firm may need to offer a slightly higher prospective dividend. (Moreover, when money is raised via the stock exchange, whether by the issue of shares or by debentures, the costs of the issue—underwriting etc.—rise less than proportionately to the amount of money raised.)

The main reason why institutions and individuals are often willing to provide finance at a slightly lower rate to large than to small firms is the belief that the investment will be more secure. There is evidence to suggest that the profitability of large firms tends to fluctuate less than that of small firms. Indeed the reduction in risk conveyed by size can be considered as a separate economy of scale.

Risk reduction

Large firms can reduce their risks in two ways. First they may achieve such a dominant position in their existing markets that competitors find it difficult to challenge that position. As we show below, a firm's average cost is influenced by its cumulative output of a given product, and the dominant firm may therefore have much lower costs than competitors.

Alternatively, large firms may attempt to reduce their risks by diversification, as shown in Chapter 10. Diversification is most likely to be undertaken when the long-term prospects in the firm's existing markets are poor, e.g. in tobacco, or when the existing markets generate a cyclical pattern of profits which can be counterbalanced via diversification. When a merger was announced between J. & P. Coats and Paton & Baldwin it was pointed out that the profits from the two companies' main products—sewing thread and knitting wool respectively—were both subject to cyclical fluctuations, but that the two cycles were usually out of phase with each other. The move by W.H. Smith, whose base is in newspaper and periodical distribution, into the travel agency business, which peaks in January and February, was influenced by the fact that cash inflow from its other retailing activities peaked sharply in the three months before Christmas.

Managerial economies
This covers a miscellaneous group of economies relating to the administration of the firm. It includes the ability to offer the high rewards needed to attract highly talented staff, and to make full use of administrative procedures, including computerisation, which might be too costly for the smaller firm. It is difficult to overestimate the impact on a firm's fortunes of highly talented individuals. Note the success of GEC under Sir Arnòld Weinstock, of BTR under Sir David Nicholson, of Sainsburys under the Sainsbury family. However, many small firms prosper without employing such outstanding talent and without elaborate administrative procedures. Indeed it is sometimes claimed that such procedures are required to prevent the emergence of managerial or administrative diseconomies of scale.

Diseconomies of scale

The limitations imposed by the current state of technology sometimes mean that increasing the size of plant would cause costs per unit of output to rise, i.e. technical diseconomies of scale would arise. For example in the late 1970s the largest ethylene cracker in production had an annual capacity of 500,000 tons of ethylene. Up to that size substantial economies were achieved; it was estimated that the cost per unit of output of this cracker, when working at full capacity, was only 30 per cent of the cost of the smallest cracker. However, the construction of plants with a greater capacity would have resulted in diseconomies, for several reasons: on-site fabrication of towers and vessels would be required; more capital would be tied up, making delays in commissioning very expensive; the technical limit to compressor size had been reached.

Since engineering data of this kind is often available, firms should be aware of potential technical diseconomies and hence be able to avoid them. (They may, of course, accept a technical diseconomy if this is balanced by an economy of scale elsewhere.) The empirical evidence shows that firms seldom operate with technical diseconomies, and it is believed that insofar as diseconomies of scale exist they are most likely to be managerial or administrative in nature.

Higher costs may arise for several reasons. First, large firms, and especially firms operating large plants, may become very impersonal and bureaucratic, leading to a loss of job satisfaction. This can manifest itself in high absence and turnover rates, poor timekeeping and a high incidence of strikes. Figures published by the Department of Employment in 1978 showed that 99.3 per cent of small establishments (11 to 99 employees) were strike-free each year, as compared to only 51 per cent of very large establishments (1000+ employees).

Second, large firms with potentially lower costs than their smaller competitors may provide extra perquisites of one kind or another to senior staff, and thus dissipate their potential advantage. (This form of managerial behaviour is built into Williamson's theory of the firm, as noted in Chapter 8.)

Finally, costs may be allowed to rise in various ways (including spending on management perquisites) because managers wish to enjoy a quiet life, or simply because they are inefficient. This concept of "X-inefficiency" has been developed at length by Leibenstein[4] (*see* Chapter 8).

It is difficult to find comprehensive data relating to managerial diseconomies, and to a large extent the evidence is circumstantial; despite the existence of economies of scale, large firms do not on the whole earn above-average profits and this suggests that compensating diseconomies must operate. Whatever the status of the evidence, many large firms have in recent years modified their organisational structures in order to avoid or overcome diseconomies. There has been a tendency to move from a unitary form (U-form) enterprise to a multidivisional enterprise (M-form).

The U-form enterprise has a chief executive with functional divisions—marketing, production etc.—responsible to him for their functions as applied to all company products. The M-form enterprise usually has a general office with advisory staff, a series of operating divisions (e.g. one for each product) responsible to the general office, and functional departments responsible to the divisional heads. Each division operates like a quasi-firm—its managers being responsible to the main board for that division's performance—while the board concentrates on the formulation of strategy for the company or group as a whole.

THE BEHAVIOUR OF COSTS WITH A CHANGING SCALE OF ORGANISATION: SUMMARY

The behaviour of costs with a changing scale of organisation is summarised in Fig. 16. The three average-cost curves relate to three alternative scales of organisation. At levels of output up to Q_1 the lowest costs are attained by operating at the smallest scale (AC_1). Beyond that output and up to Q_2 lower costs are attained at the larger scale (AC_2). Finally, beyond Q_2 the lowest costs are attained with the largest scale (AC_3). The unbroken line running from AC_1 to AC_3 shows the average cost of the firm as, over a long period of time, it expands its output and scale of organisation.

Three additional points need to be made about Fig. 16. First, some of the economies discussed above depend upon the firm making more than one product (perhaps via diversification or vertical integration). If the cost curves in Fig. 16 are interpreted as applying to a single product, as is usual, the diagram fails to encompass these economies.

Second, Fig. 16 shows output per period. We noted above that some economies are related to the firm's cumulative output of a product, and hence are not fully encompassed by this diagram.

---
4. H. Leibenstein. "Allocative Efficiency *v.*X-Efficiency". *American Economic Review* Vol. 56 (1966).

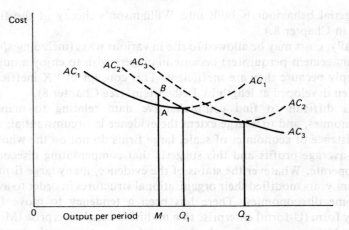

Fig. 16. *Average cost with a changing scale of organisation.*

Third, the curve AC_1AC_3 is unlikely to be reversible. We can see that if output M were produced with scale 1 the average cost would be MA. We suggested above that if output increased beyond Q_1 the firm should move to scale 2. But it is quite possible that output would not remain at the higher level. If it fell back to M the average cost, with scale 2, would be MB.

It might appear that the firm should now revert to scale 1, but this might not be feasible. The move to scale 2 would almost certainly have involved the purchase and installation of additional plant and equipment. As we showed above it is usual to spread the cost of plant and equipment over a number of years. This means that selling these assets would not leave the firm in the same financial situation as before they were bought (unless it received an extremely favourable second-hand price). Moreover, other factors might prevent the firm from returning to its initial position: redundancy payments might have to be made to additional workers recruited and then dismissed, or penalties might be incurred if contracts for the supply of materials had to be broken.

MEASUAREMENT OF ECONOMIES OF SCALE

A firm considering increasing its scale of organisation will wish to know what benefits (and disbenefits) are likely to arise. Four methods of measuring economies of scale can be identified, although in practice it might be very difficult for an individual firm to obtain the data required for some of these methods:

(*a*) Cross-section studies, involving a comparison of the costs (per unit of output) of firms of different sizes.

5. COST ANALYSIS

(b) Time-series studies, involving a comparison of the costs of firms as their size changes over time.

(c) Engineering studies, in which an estimate is made of the costs that would be incurred at different scales.

(d) The survivor technique. Firms are grouped into size classes and a comparison is made of the share of output accounted for by each group at two or more points in time. It is assumed that the size category that shows an increased share has the lowest average cost.

Table VIII illustrates the results obtained from the third method. The data was originally published in the *Journal of Political Economy,* 1967, by Haldi and Whitcomb. Using figures collected mainly by industrial cost estimators (the underlying observations being derived from catalogues of industrial equipment), Haldi and Whitcomb found that the relationship applying in many basic industrial processes could be best represented by the equation

$$C = aX^b$$

where C represents cost, X represents output capacity, a is a constant, and the exponent b may be called the "scale coefficient".

TABLE VIII. ESTIMATES OF TECHNICAL ECONOMIES OF SCALE

Value of the scale coefficient b	*Basic industrial equipment*	*Plant investment costs*	*Total operating costs*	*Labour costs*
Less than 0.40	10.7	4.1	12.5	71.2
0.40 – 0.49	14.9	5.4	3.1	9.6
0.50 – 0.59	20.8	10.0	15.6	15.4
0.60 – 0.69	21.4	20.4	9.4	1.9
0.70 – 0.79	13.4	27.6	31.3	1.9
0.80 – 0.89	8.7	16.7	28.1	—
0.90 – 0.99	4.4	9.0	—	—
1.00 – 1.09	2.9	2.7	—	—
1.10 +	2.8	4.1	—	—
Total	100	100	100	100

Distribution of values of b (%) in relation to:

A value of $b<1.00$ would indicate the existence of economies of scale, or increasing returns. But given the quality of the data, Haldi and Whitcomb defined increasing returns to be where $b<0.90$, to exclude those values of b which did not differ significantly from one.

II. MEASUREMENT IN ECONOMICS

It can be seen that technical economies of scale were widespread. Of 687 types of basic equipment, 618 (90 per cent) showed increasing returns. Of 221 estimates of costs for complete plants, 186 (84 per cent) showed increasing returns. Finally, increasing returns were found to apply to total operating costs in all instances.

These estimates allow the firm to assess the potential savings available. But these savings will be achieved only if the plant and equipment are fully utilised. The firm must therefore assess its chances of selling the required output, and an important factor here is the share of the market that it would need to capture in order to do so. The first column of Table IX shows that the minimum efficient scale—i.e. the level of output at which costs become constant, scale economies being exhausted—may constitute a very small part of the domestic market (bread, shoes) or a very large part (turbo-generators, aircraft).

TABLE IX. SCALE COEFFICIENTS AND MINIMUM ECONOMIC SCALE

Industry etc.	MES as % of UK market	% increase in cost at 50% MES	Scale coefficients
Oil refining	10	5	0.66
Ethylene	25	9	0.62
Sulphuric acid	30	1	0.75
Dyes	>100	22	0.47
Polymer manufacture	35	5	0.70
Filament yarn	16	7	0.85
Beer	3	9	0.37
Bread	1	15	0.62
Detergent powder	20	2.5	0.74
Cement	10	9	0.77
Bricks	0.5	25	0.62
Steel production	33	5–10	0.80
Rolled steel products	80	8	0.82
Iron castings: cylinder blocks	1	10	0.80
Cars: range of models	50	6	0.82
Aircraft: one type	>100	20	0.68
Machine tools: models	>100	5	0.86
Diesel engines: models	10	4	0.86
Turbo-generators	100	approx. 5	0.86
Electric motors	60	15	0.74
Footwear factory	0.2	2	0.93
Newspapers	30	20	0.51

Sources: Columns 1 and 2: C.F. Pratten, *Economies of Scale in Manufacturing Industry*, University of Cambridge, Department of Applied Economics, Occasional Papers No. 28, Cambridge University Press, 1971. Column 3: Z.A. Silberston. "Economies of Scale in Theory and Practice". *Economic Journal* vol. 82, 1972.

If it appears that in total the firm will fail to achieve the minimum efficient scale then it will have to consider the implications of this failure. If a competitor is operating at this scale the firm will incur higher costs. The second column of Table IX shows that the cost penalty incurred by a firm producing at half MES ranged from 1 per cent (sulphuric acid) to 25 per cent (bricks).

ECONOMIES OF SCALE, SPECIALISATION AND JOINT VENTURES

If it appears that a single firm is unlikely to attain the scale of organisation required to obtain certain economies of scale it may have to choose between abandoning the activity in question and purchasing the required inputs from a specialist supplier, or undertaking the activity in conjunction with another firm or firms.

A very large number of specialist organisations exist to provide marketing services, such as advertising, market research, package and product design and merchandising. These specialists enjoy economies of scale, especially in being able to employ experienced and talented personnel. Hence they are able to offer their services at a cost less than the purchaser—manufacturer, retailer etc.—would incur if it provided these services itself. (One of the most important reasons for this is that the specialist firms undertake these activities on a continuous basis and hence can spread their costs over a much bigger output than purchasers who may require the services only from time to time.)

Purchasers should, of course, constantly review the relative merits of purchase versus production "in-house". ("Make or buy" decisions also occur frequently with respect to manufacturing activities.) Large purchasers may be able to undertake trials which help in this process of review. For example in the early 1980s Lever Brothers employed their own staff to demonstrate products in a limited number of stores. Sales through these stores increased so markedly that the scale of the operation was substantially expanded.

Joint ventures are undertaken in various areas, e.g. joint sales-forces have been established to handle the products of two or more companies, and co-operative advertising has been undertaken for many products including insurance and banking services. But in recent years the most notable instances of joint ventures intended to capture economies of scale have occurred in research and development.

An article in the *Financial Times* (2nd September 1980), entitled "Increase in joint research ventures", began: "The 1980s will be the decade of joint ventures within the motor industry. The burdens are so heavy on the car and truck makers that, as they attempt to bring the new breed of fuel-efficient vehicles quickly to the market place, they are having to join together—or with outside component manufacturers—because there simply is not enough in the way of human resources or finance to accomplish the job any other way."

Numerous joint ventures were detailed in the article. Some involve research only, for example an agreement signed by six major companies—BL, Fiat, Peugeot, Renault, Volkswagen and Volvo—to work together on long-term, high-technology research. They agreed to pool resources in such areas as combustion technology, corrosion surface treatment, computerised engineering methods and the properties of new materials. Other agreements go beyond the research stage. Fiat, Alfa-Romeo and Renault each have one-third of an engine production facility. BL and Honda are collaborating in the development of new cars.

In computers, where the costs of development are often very high, there have been a number of joint ventures. ICL agreed to market the very large data-processing centres manufactured by Fujitsu, the Japanese company. In exchange ICL gained access to Fujitsu's technology in very-large-scale integrated-circuit chips. ICL also entered into a technical exchange agreement with the US manufacturer CDC.

The experience effect

The experience or learning effect can be illustrated by reference to Fig. 17 in which AC_1 indicates the average cost of producing various quantities of a product within a given period. Average cost is lower with an output of OM than ON per period because of the scale factor. (The scale factor is an amalgam of the two factors considered separately above. Cost may be lower at OM because of economies of scale and/or a higher rate of capacity utilisation.)

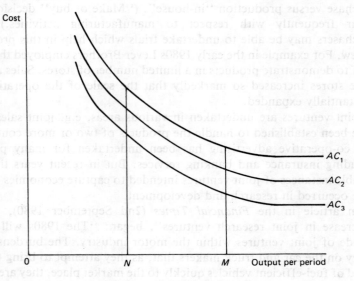

Fig. 17. *The experience effect.*

If we were to measure cost in a subsequent period, we would expect to find that real cost (i.e. after allowing for changes in input prices) had fallen. The extent of the fall would be influenced by the amount produced within the previous period. Output ON would give rise to cost AC_2, output OM to cost AC_3. The difference between AC_2 and AC_3 is a measure of the experience or learning effect.

The first systematic observations of the experience effect were made in the production of aircraft in the USA in the 1930s. In the Second World War the production of the famous Liberty ships showed similar effects, the first taking many months to build, and the last being completed within three days. The Boston Consulting Group found that the decline in unit cost "is consistently 20 to 30 per cent each time accumulated production is doubled. The decline goes on in time without limit (in constant prices) regardless of the rate of growth of experience. The rate of decline is surprisingly consistent, even from industry to industry."[5] This consistency is illustrated in Fig. 18.[6] (Note that a logarithmic scale is used on the horizontal axis. The underlying relationship between cumulative output and unit cost is a curve and not, as might be thought at first sight, linear.)

The experience curves shown in Fig. 18 represent the aggregate effect of several cost trends associated with the cumulative volume of output:

(*a*) the learning curve for labour and management;
(*b*) technological improvements in product design;
(*c*) improved manufacturing technology;
(*d*) movement towards maximum scale economies;
(*e*) development of plants to operate at economic capacity.

ADDITIONAL COST CONCEPTS

In the foregoing sections we have presented a broad picture of the way in which costs may change as output changes. We now fill in some of the detail in that picture. We introduce a number of additional cost concepts and indicate how these concepts might be used in decision making. (We examine these decisions in greater detail in later chapters and especially in Chapter 14.)

Marginal cost
Marginal cost is the cost incurred when output is increased by one unit (or, more generally, when output changes by one unit). If the product is manufactured in large quantities then a change in output of one unit will have very little effect on cost, e.g. the cost of producing an additional can of soup on an automated line will probably be the cost of materials. If, on

---

5. Boston Consulting Group. *Perspectives on Experience*. Boston, 1970, p. 12.
6. These exhibits were prepared by the Boston Consulting Group for the Department of Trade and published in: *A Review of Monopolies and Mergers Policy*. HMSO, 1978.

II. MEASUREMENT IN ECONOMICS

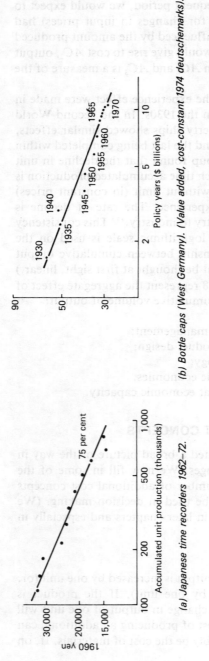

(a) *Japanese tape recorders 1962–72.*

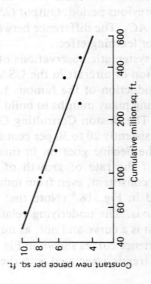

(b) *Bottle caps (West Germany). (Value added, cost-constant 1974 deutschemarks).*

(d) *Pilkington Brothers float glass (1962–7): total cost per square foot.*
Source: The Monopolies Commission.

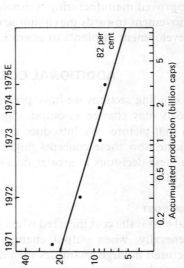

(c) *Life insurance industry (US): operating expense per policy-year.*
Source: Institute of Life Insurance.

Fig. 18. *Experience curves.*

the other hand, production is on a one-off basis, e.g. the construction of a power station, marginal cost will be much higher. In traditional economic theory marginal cost is applied to the first of these situations. But in practice very few decisions relate to such infinitesimal changes in output, and therefore marginal cost is of limited use in the analysis of business decisions.

Incremental cost

Incremental cost is the cost incurred by a given increase in output. The value of incremental cost is largely dependent upon the size of the output increase. We noted earlier that firms often operate with spare capacity. The bigger the increase in output the more of this spare capacity is taken up, the more additional inputs are required and thus the greater is the additional cost incurred. A small increase in output may require an increase only in material costs; a larger increase may require more labour to be employed; an even larger increase may require additional machinery to be installed and perhaps even a new factory to be built. In all cases, however, the firm should take account of the incremental cost and should compare it with the incremental revenue, i.e. the additional revenue resulting from the increase in output.

Escapable cost

When a firm is considering whether to contract its output, and even whether to cease supplying certain products, it should attempt to estimate the costs that it would save thereby, i.e. its escapable cost. In one sense escapable cost is the reverse of incremental cost, but it is important to recognise that there is not an exact correspondence, in terms of either the accounting or the economist's view of cost.

In discussing economies of scale we pointed out that a cost curve may not be reversible (*see* Fig. 16). A major reason for this non-reversibility is the accounting convention that the cost of a machine is spread over its life so that it continues to incur costs even when it produces a lower, or indeed a zero, level of output. But if the firm took account only of escapable costs, the costs of machinery already installed would not, of course, be included. Finally, for the economist the cost of reducing output is the consequent loss of revenue.

The concept of escapable cost is also very important when joint costs exist, an extremely common situation. Reducing the output of a product will cause little change in cost (i.e. escapable cost is low) if the resources—men or machines—used in making that product have to be retained in order to continue making other products.

Sunk cost

A sunk cost is a cost that has been incurred and so, it can be argued, ought not to be taken into account in decisions relating to, say, the future level of output. A good example would be the cost of machines, as noted above. If sunk costs are ignored then average cost will be less than suggested by the diagrams appearing earlier in the chapter (e.g. Fig. 15). For increases in output, cost will approximate to variable cost. (For an increase of a given size incremental cost will be the appropriate measure.)

Opportunity cost and linear programming

At the beginning of the chapter we said that economists define the opportunity cost of any course of action as the benefit forgone, and that this benefit is subjective. Opportunity cost is treated slightly differently when applied to linear programming. It is defined as the benefit forgone, but the benefit is objectively measured. It commonly happens that the capacity of a machine, or group of machines, used in the manufacture of two (or more) products is insufficient to meet the demand generated by both products taken together. It is then possible to increase the output of one product A only be reducing the output of the other product B. The opportunity cost of the additional output of A is the loss of revenue from B.

Consider an engineering factory in which two components, A and B, are produced on two types of machine, drills and lathes. The capacity of the drills is 1,000 hours per month, and of the lathes 800 hours per month. The production of component A requires 1 drilling hour and 2 cutting hours per unit; the production of component B requires 2 drilling hours and 1 cutting hour. Given that the profit per unit of the two components is equal, what combination of the two products should be manufactured?

The constraints in the system, i.e. the capacity of machines and the input per unit of output required, can be shown graphically, as in Fig. 19. Line *DE* indicates the limits to the various combinations of products A and B that could be produced, given the amount of drilling capacity available (1,000 hours) and assuming that there was no limit on the cutting capacity. It would be possible to produce 1,000 units of A and no B, 500 units of B and no A, or any other combination on *DE*. Similarly, line *FG* indicates the limits to the various product combinations that could be produced, given the amount of cutting capacity available (800 hours). It would, for example, be possible to produce 400 A and no B, or 800 B and no A. In fact there are limits to capacity in both drilling and cutting. Consequently the limits to output are indicated by the line *FHE*; in other words the feasible combinations of output are bounded by the area *FHE*0.

One can demonstrate easily that the optimum output will lie on the line *FHE*, rather than to the left of it, at a point such as *J*. *J* cannot be the optimum output since it is possible at some other point, say *K*, to produce more of both *A* and *B*. What is not so immediately obvious is which of the points on the line *FHE* is the optimum. To solve this problem we utilise the concept of opportunity cost.

We know that the profit per unit of product A equals the profit per unit

5. COST ANALYSIS

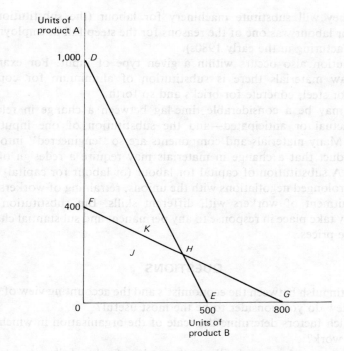

Fig. 19. *Opportunity cost and linear programming.*

of product B. Consequently the optimum output is that which maximises the total number of units of A and B aggregated together. It would be possible to find this point by trial and error, calculating total production at all the various points on the line. However a little thought will lead us to the answer much more quickly.

Let us take a point at one end of the line, say *F*, representing an output of 400 A and no B. As we move away from *F* the increase in the quantity of B exceeds the fall in the quantity of A, i.e. the revenue forgone by remaining at *F* exceeds the revenue at *F*. This continues until the gradient of the line changes, at *H*. Similarly if we start from *E*, the increase in A exceeds the fall in B as we move towards *H*. *H* indicates the maximum combined output that could be produced, the output that would maximise profit.

CHANGES IN INPUT PRICES

In the discussion above we assumed that input prices were unchanged except when the firm was able to purchase in larger quantities. But the relative prices of inputs change constantly and firms have to take these changes into account when deciding what "mix" of inputs to employ. If they believe that the price of labour will rise relative to the price of capital goods, they will substitute machinery for labour (the substitution of capital for labour was one of the reasons for the steep fall in employment in manufacturing in the early 1980s).

Substitution also occurs within a given type of input. For example within raw materials there is substitution of aluminium for copper, plastics for steel, concrete for bricks and so forth.

There may be a considerable time-lag between a change in relative prices—actual or anticipated—and the substitution of one input for another. Many materials and components are so "engineered" into this final product that a change in materials may require a redesign of the product. A substitution of capital for labour (or labour for capital) may require prolonged negotiations with the unions, retraining of workers and the recruitment of workers with different skills. But substitution will eventually take place in response to any permanent and substantial change in relative prices.

QUESTIONS

1. Distinguish between the economist's and the accounting view of cost. Which view do you consider to be the most useful?

2. Which factors determine the scale of the organisation in which you study or work?

3. Briefly explain and illustrate each of the following terms: opportunity cost, depreciation, technical economies of scale, the experience effect, sunk cost, marginal cost.

4. Why is it said that it is impossible to obtain a completely objective measure of cost?

5. What advantage would you expect to accrue in each of the following situations?
   (a) Two biscuit manufacturers merge.
   (b) A firm making ice cream takes over a firm specialising in the production of Christmas cakes and puddings.
   (c) A merger occurs between two firms of solicitors located in the same city.

6. With reference to Tables VIII and IX write an essay on the incidence of economies of scale.

7. Explain, with relevant illustrations, the statement that different cost concepts are required for different decisions.

8. Which cost concept(s) would be relevant in the following situations?
   (a) A firm increases output beyond the expected level.
   (b) A firm ceases operations.
   (c) A decision has to be made as to which of two machines to buy.

9. Wessex Engineering manufactures a range of machine tools, most of which are produced in limited quantities to the order of individual customers. Many of the components are common to more than one type

5. COST ANALYSIS

of tool and although Wessex could in principle make most of these components itself, it has traditionally bought its components from outside suppliers as and when required. Following a reorganisation of senior management it was decided that this policy should be reviewed. To aid this review data was obtained on the cost at which Wessex might produce a sample of components at present bought outside, and the outside suppliers' prices.

Wessex classified its costs as follows:
 Variable cost: direct materials and labour
 Variable overhead cost: indirect labour, maintenance, fuel and power
 Fixed overhead cost: depreciation, selling and administrative expenses

Although it was recognised that this classification might not be fully accurate, e.g. direct labour might not always be a variable cost, it was felt to be adequate for the purpose of this exercise.

Both fixed and variable overhead costs were allocated to particular products in the form of a given cost per direct-labour hour expended on that product. The ratios were obtained by calculating, twice a year, the total fixed overhead cost, total variable overhead cost, and total direct-labour hours for the previous six months, and by dividing each of the first two figures by the third. The ratios in use at the time of the review were:

 Variable overhead cost (per direct-labour hour)   £3.00
 Fixed overhead cost (per direct-labour hour)   £1.60

The current cost of direct labour was £2.40, giving a total "basic manufacturing cost" of £7.00 per direct-labour hour. The cost per unit for a product was obtained by adding to the basic manufacturing cost the cost of direct materials.

The company had in the past compared unit cost, derived in this way, with the outside purchase price, and had invariably found the purchase price to be lower. However some of the new members of the management team felt that the existing method of calculation was not appropriate when substantial spare capacity existed, as it had done for some years, and as appeared likely in the foreseeable future. They believed that in these circumstances fixed overhead costs should be excluded.

The annual requirements of three components, and the inputs required, were estimated as follows:

	Toughened steel bushes	Bronze bushes	Steel springs
Annual requirement (units)	38,000	3,600	20,000
Material cost (£)	2,584	1,584	1,520
Direct labour hours	342	219	963

The best prices that could be obtained from outside suppliers were:

	Pence per unit
Toughened steel bushes	10
Bronze bushes	80
Steel springs	32

Which, if any, of the components should be purchased outside?
Would you have made the same decision if Wessex did not have spare capacity?

CHAPTER SIX

The Cost of Finance and Investment Appraisal

OBJECTIVES

After studying this chapter the reader should be able to: list the sources and uses of funds of a typical large company; explain why a company may choose one source of funds in preference to another; list the measures taken to meet the special financial needs of smaller companies; explain how a company can calculate its cost of finance; understand how a change in the cost of finance may affect the level of investment; compare and contrast the discounted cash flow and net present value methods of investment appraisal; evaluate alternative methods of investment appraisal; list areas of application of investment appraisal; discuss the implementation of investment appraisal in the public sector.

INTRODUCTION

In this chapter we discuss the ways in which firms might mesure the cost of capital and how they might try to assess the returns to be obtained from investment projects. But first we examine the various sources of funds available to firms, and the uses to which these funds are put.

SOURCES AND USES OF FUNDS: AN OVERVIEW

Figure 20 gives a summary view of the flow of funds of a typical public company.[1] On average, 90 per cent of sales revenue is used to meet the current costs of production: labour, materials etc. The remainder—gross trading profit (assumed to be £27.1 million here)—is allocated in three ways. First, provision is made for the depreciation of fixed assets. (We noted in Chapter 5 that in the estimation of cost, depreciation is treated as a non-cash expense.) Second, payments are made to external bodies in the form of interest, dividends and taxation. Finally the remainder is retained within the business.

Depreciation provisions and retained earnings together constitute the internal cash flow. This is the most important source of long-term funds. But from time to time additional funds may be raised in the form of long-term debt finance, e.g. debentures, and the proceeds of new equity issues. The long-term funds are used—roughly in the ratio one third to two thirds—to build up the firm's current assets and to finance investment expenditure.

---

1. This figure is adapted from D. A. Hay and D. J. Morris. *Industrial Economics, Theory and Evidence*. Oxford UP, 1979, p. 324. The values are based on average figures for manufacturing companies as they appear in the national accounts. There are, of course, variations from company to company and from year to year.

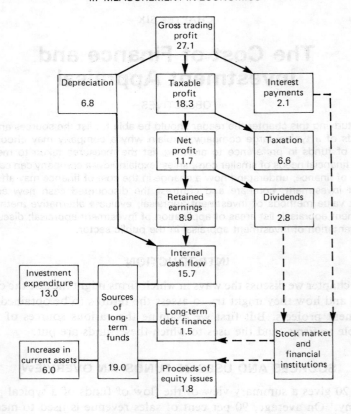

Fig. 20. *The flow of funds of a public company.*

Current assets
Current assets mainly comprise stocks and work in progress, financial assets, short-term loans to debtors and cash balances. As output expands one would expect to see an expansion in current assets, and especially in stocks and work in progress. But current assets may also expand in other circumstances. If sales are below expectations then stocks and work in progress may rise. The firm may acquire financial assets which it is felt will yield a better return than long-term investments. Short-term financial assets may be acquired pending long-term investment. If competition becomes more acute then the firm may grant extended credit. Finally, since current assets are measured net of current liabilities, they may increase because of a fall in liabilities, e.g. because the firm makes payments to creditors or repays bank loans.

Investment expenditure
The second use of long-term funds comprises investment in physical facilities—factories, offices, machinery etc.—in research and

development, and in market promotion activities, e.g. advertising. All three forms of expenditure compete for investment funds, although an individual project may involve all three. For example the introduction of a new product may require expenditure on research and development, the building and equipping of a new factory and an increase in advertising. We discussed investment in physical facilities in Chapter 5; research and development expenditure is discussed in Chapter 12, and market promotion activities in Chapter 15.[2]

Having given a brief overview of the sources and uses of funds we now discuss the sources in more detail.

INTERNAL SOURCES OF FINANCE

During the period 1963–81 internal funds (depreciation provisions and retained earnings) accounted for 62 per cent of the increased funds of industrial and commercial companies. Moreover there is no evidence of a decline in importance; indeed since 1977 they have accounted for over two-thirds of the total.

EXTERNAL SOURCES OF FINANCE

The sources of finance that are available depend to some extent upon the legal form of the enterprise. We briefly examine each of the main forms in turn.

Unincorporated businesses: sole traders and partnerships

There are about 1¼ million unincorporated businesses in the UK, making this the most important form numerically. However they are mainly very small, and together account for only about one-tenth of the capital expenditure of all businesses.

External finance for sole traders, who are particularly common in retailing, farming and the building trades, is largely short-term, comprising bank loans, trade credit, hire-purchase finance, leasing etc. Longer-term credit may sometimes be obtained by means of a mortgage on land or buildings. (Specialist sources of finance for small firms are examined below.)

External sources of finance for partnerships, which are very common in the professions—law, accountancy, medicine etc.—are similar to those for the sole trader.

Joint stock companies

There are almost 700,000 companies registered in Great Britain. Over 97 per cent are private companies, but these are exceeded in aggregate size by

---

2. Expenditure on research and development and market promotion activities may be treated as current costs in accounting records, but conceptually it is similar to other forms of investment expenditure.

the much smaller number of public companies. In addition to having access to all the sources of finance available to unincorporated businesses, joint stock companies are able to raise permanent capital by the issue of shares. The maximum number of shareholders in a private company is fifty, which can limit the amount of permanent finance that such firms can raise. No such limitation is imposed on the public company. Moreover the securities issued by public companies, unlike those issued by private companies, can be freely traded. This provides an additional incentive to investors to make funds available to public companies.

The new-issue market
New issues of securities may take several forms. When a *public issue by prospectus* is made the company offers, directly to the general public, a fixed number of shares or debentures at a stated price. The Stock Exchange requires that a prospectus be issued, setting out the nature of the company's business and giving details of its past turnover, profits etc. An *offer for sale* is similar to a public issue, but the company sells the securities to an issuing house (usually a merchant bank) which in turn offers them to the general public. With a *private placing* the shares are again acquired by an issuing house, which in this instance places them with its clients and with jobbers. In order to ensure that an adequate market is created, the Stock Exchange stipulates that a minimum number of securities be placed with jobbers, who conduct the trading on the floor of the Stock Exchange.

An *offer for sale by tender* is the only method in which the amount of money to be raised by a new issue is not known in advance. A minimum price is stipulated at which a tender will be accepted. If investors believe that the securities are worth more than this minimum then they will put in a higher offer in order to try to secure an allocation. Offers for sale by tender are used most when it is difficult to decide what an appropriate offer price would be. This can happen because at the time of the issue the market as a whole is volatile, or because there are no similar quoted companies whose price can be used as a guide in setting a price for the newcomer. In 1982 the government made a public issue of shares in Amersham International, a producer of radioactive materials. The offer price was far too low and the issue was heavily oversubscribed. Dealing opened at a premium of more than a quarter above the subscription price, suggesting that an offer for sale by tender would have raised a substantially larger amount.

Rights issues are confined to existing shareholders, who are offered additional shares in proportion to their holdings. The new shares are issued at a price below the current market price, and this can be seen as a reward to shareholders. Even though the shares are initially available only to existing shareholders, rights issues can raise substantial sums. In 1981 existing shareholders in BP subscribed some £500 million. (Rights issues should not be confused with scrip or bonus issues, which do not raise additional finance for the company, the additional shares being *given* to shareholders.)

When planning a new issue the company should take account of market conditions. The return that has to be offered—the rate of interest on debentures and preference shares and the prospective yield on equity (ordinary shares)—is strongly influenced by the yield available on existing securities. Stock market prices—and hence yields—fluctuate over time, and companies try to offer their shares for sale when existing prices are high. (A company may not be able to choose the *best* time because the Stock Exchange regulates the flow of new issues. Also, the company's capital requirements may induce it to raise money at a time that would otherwise not be propitious.)

The method chosen may be influenced both by market conditions and by the company's characteristics. Whereas a well-known company may choose an issue by prospectus, a less well-known one may choose an offer for sale or private placing. There is also evidence of considerable variations in the costs of different methods. Looking first at the accounting costs—advertising, legal fees etc.—it was estimated in 1978 that for an issue of £2 million, costs as a percentage of proceeds would be 7.6 per cent for an issue by prospectus or offer for sale, 4 per cent for a rights issue and only 2.6 per cent for a placing.[3] (Tender issues were then out of favour and, unfortunately, no estimate of their cost was given.) However, it seems that these cost differentials may be outweighed by bigger differentials in opportunity cost, in revenue forgone. In a study of new issues in the period 1965 to 1971 it was found that the average discount—the difference between the issue price and the average price during the first five days of trading—was 19 per cent (of the issue price) for placings as compared with 9 per cent for offers for sale and 7 per cent for tenders.[7] (The disparity was most marked in rising markets.)

The Unlisted Securities Market

The costs involved in securing a Stock Exchange listing, and the requirement that a minimum of 25 per cent of the company shares be made available to the general public, were felt to be partly responsible for the sharp reduction in the number of companies seeking a listing in the 1970s. To overcome these obstacles the Stock Exchange introduced the Unlisted Securities Market (USM) in 1980. (The Wilson Committee had previously made recommendations along these lines.)

A minimum of only 10 per cent of shares must be made available to the public. Moreover the costs of issue are much lower: by

---

3. *Report of the Committee to Review the Functioning of Financial Institutions; Evidence on the Financing of Industry and Trade.* HMSO, 1978, Vol. 3.

4. E. W. Davis and K. A. Yeomans. *Company Finance and the Capital Market.* University of Cambridge, Department of Applied Economics, 1976.

introduction—under £10,000; by placing—around £40,000; by offer for sale—around £65,000. In its first year the USM attracted more than seventy companies, many in micro-electronics, computer services and other high-technology industries.

External sources of finance for smaller companies
The USM has been of benefit to smaller companies wishing to go public. A number of other measures have been taken to improve the sources of finance available to smaller companies, public or private. These measures include the establishment of institutions catering for the needs of smaller firms.

The first group of institutions, including Charterhouse Industrial Development and Credit for Industry, were established following the report of the Macmillan Committee on Finance and Industry, published in 1931. The resources of these early institutions were very modest and met only part of the needs of the smaller firms. Since it was anticipated that the end of the war would lead to an increase in these needs, in 1945 the clearing banks, with the support of the Bank of England, established the Industrial and Commercial Finance Corporation. ICFC had initial resources of £45 million, with a remit to provide long-term loans and subscribe equity capital within the range £5,000 to £200,000. In 1959 the Radcliffe Committee identified a need for additional finance to facilitate the commercial exploitation of technical innovations. To meet this need ICFC established a subsidiary, Technical Development Capital Ltd.

These and other institutions have continued to expand the scale of their operations, and in 1975 ICFC along with the Finance Corporation for Industry, which supplies finance to large companies, became a subsidiary of Finance for Industry. FFI, whose shareholders are the clearing banks (85 per cent of shares) and the Bank of England (15 per cent), has access to funds of £1,000 million, intended mainly for medium-term lending.

The activities of FFI are complemented by two other institutions established more recently. Equity Capital for Industry (ECI) was established in 1976 with a capital of £50 million, provided by various institutional investors. As suggested by the name of the institution, these funds are intended as a source of permanent capital, and ECI acquired its first shares, at a cost of £1.75 million, early in 1977.

The National Enterprise Board (NEB) was originally established to enable the state to acquire holdings in large companies, such as British Leyland and Rolls Royce. However more recently the NEB has provided finance for an increasing number of small businesses.

The Conservative Government that took office in 1979, as already mentioned in Chapter 3, introduced several measures to augment the flow of capital to small businesses. The most important of these measures were:[5]

5. These and other measures are discussed in: M. Jarrett and M. Wright. "New Initiatives in the Financing of Small Firms". *National Westminster Bank Quarterly Review*, 1982.

(a) The Business Start Up Scheme, introduced in 1981 for three years. This is designed to overcome the problems of raising equity at the start-up stage of a business. In order to counteract the risks of investing in new businesses, the scheme allows tax relief for "outside" investors at the individual's top marginal rate on investments up to £20,000 a year in "qualifying" new businesses.

Individuals can make investments in single companies or in institutions which in turn invest in a range of companies. One such institution is Electra Risk Capital, which started operations in 1981 with £8.6 million of capital subscribed by more than 1,800 investors, the average individual holding being £4,700.

(b) The Loan Guarantee Scheme, also introduced in 1981 for three years. Some worthwhile projects may fail to find adequate finance because of the potential borrower's lack of a "track record" or his unwillingness to provide personal guarantees. In such instances the government will guarantee up to 80 per cent of the cost of the loan. The scheme began in June 1981 with an initial allocation of £50 million a year, or £150 million in total. This proved inadequate; the ceiling was raised and by August more than £200 million had been loaned to over six thousand companies.

(c) The Venture Capital Scheme, introduced in 1980. This enables losses on equity shares in certain unquoted companies to be offset, for tax purposes, against income instead of against only capital gains.

These schemes reflected the proposals of the Wilson Committee which found the provision of finance to small firms to be a "main area of difficulty".

The relative importance of the various sources of finance

Table X shows the relative importance of the various forms of external finance discussed above. It can be seen that bank borrowing was by far the most important of these external sources.

TABLE X. SOURCES OF EXTERNAL FUNDS OF INDUSTRIAL AND COMMERCIAL COMPANIES 1963–81

	£ billion	%
Bank borrowing	44.8	61
Other loans and mortgages	6.6	9
UK capital issues*	12.0	16
Overseas†	11.7	16
Import and other credit received (net)	−1.5	−2
	73.6	100

*Issues of ordinary shares, preference shares and debentures.
†Overseas capital issues, overseas direct investment in securities, and intra-company investment by overseas companies.

Source: *Bank of England Quarterly Bulletin*, June 1982

Bank borrowing has tended to increase in importance, as shown in Table XI. This increase is the result of a combination of three factors. First, the unfavourable economic conditions made equity investment less attractive in the 1970s. Second, high rates of interest made companies more reluctant to issue debentures and preference shares at the prices required to attract investors. (The rate of interest charged by banks also increased, but borrowers are not locked into the higher rates as they are when they issue long-term debt.) Finally, banks have widened their range of lending instruments, particularly with respect to longer-term lending.

TABLE XI. BANK BORROWING BY INDUSTRIAL AND COMMERCIAL COMPANIES

Annual Average	£ million
1963–6	500
1967–71	580
1972–6	3,240
1977–81	4,960

Source: *Bank of England Quarterly Bulletin*, June 1982

UK capital issues are a relatively minor source of finance. Of the total of £12 billion, shown in Table X, about two-thirds comprised issues of ordinary shares, and one-third issues of fixed-interest securities. The market in fixed-interest securities virtually collapsed in the 1970s, due to high nominal rates of interest allied to uncertainty about future rates. The equity market also declined in the early 1970s, but it subsequently revived and in 1981 it provided about one-sixth of external funds.

For all companies together, net credit appears to be insignificant (and indeed was negative in the period in question). But for individual companies—and especially companies trying to grow rapidly and those facing difficult trading conditions—credit can be a valuable source of finance.

THE FINANCING OF PUBLIC-SECTOR PRODUCERS

Public-sector producers of goods and services that are sold at zero or very low prices are financed mainly by taxation of one form or another. The pattern of financing of the nationalised industries is more akin to that of private-sector producers in that both generate income from the sale of goods and services. However the financing of the two groups differs in two respects.

First, on the whole the nationalised industries do not generate sufficient revenue from the sale of products to finance as high a proportion of their capital expenditure as do private-sector producers. In the absence of

6. THE COST OF FINANCE AND INVESTMENT APPRAISAL

government grants, internal funds, as a proportion of capital requirements, would have been less than 50 per cent for most of the 1970s.

Second, the nationalised industries do not normally seek external funds through the usual financial markets. They usually derive all their long-term external finance from the government. Even though they obtain this money on favourable terms, the interest payments can constitute a burden, when business is poor, which would be less acute in an organisation with a mix of equity and debt financing. One way of trying to overcome this problem has been to provide public dividend capital to some of the industries, the dividends being payable only when profits are satisfactory. More recently shares in certain industries, Britoil and British Aerospace, have been sold to the public.

The maximum amount of external finance that can be raised is specified by the government, account being taken of each industry's economic circumstances. Moreover the government expects industries which are in danger of exceeding the limit to reduce their costs by increased efficiency, rather than by raising their prices to obtain more revenue. For 1983–4 the government set positive external financing limits for twelve industries (including £1.1 billion for the National Coal Board and £973 million for British Rail), a zero limit for two industries, and a negative limit—implying a net repayment—for the electricity industry and the Post Office (Table XII).

TABLE XII. EXTERNAL FINANCING LIMITS FOR THE NATIONALISED INDUSTRIES (1983–4)

	£ million
National Coal Board	1,130
Electricity (England and Wales)	– 300
North of Scotland Hydro-Electric Board	7
South of Scotland Electricity Board	284
British Gas Corporation	0
British Steel Corporation	200
British Telecom	120
Post Office	– 20
National Girobank	0
British Airways Board	8
British Airports Authority	33½
British Railways Board	973
British Waterways Board	42
National Bus Company	69
Scottish Transport Group	19½
British Shipbuilders	150
Total	2,716

Source: *Economic Progress Report*, November 1982

THE COST OF FUNDS

We have made several references in preceding sections to the cost of funds obtained from various sources. In this section we present a more comprehensive, theoretical explanation of the relative costs involved, and of the overall cost of finance when the firm obtains funds from several sources.

The relative costs of equity and debt finance

Equity finance is more expensive than funds raised via the issue of loan stock. This is due partly to the fact that there is a higher element of risk in equity investment, for which potential investors require compensation in the form of a higher prospective return. The risk arises partly because payments to equity holders—in the form of dividends (and repayment of capital if the company is wound up)—are made after all other liabilities, including payments to holders of loan stock, have been discharged (*see* below). Another explanation of the differential costs of the two forms of finance is that the company's tax liability is reduced by the amount of interest paid on loan stock. (The same applies to interest payments on other forms of loans.) For a company borrowing money at a rate of, say, 12 per cent, and subject to corporation tax at a rate of, say, 50 per cent, the cost of borrowing would be 6 per cent. (Dividends, on the other hand, are deducted from profits *after* the payment of corporation tax.)

Capital gearing and the cost of finance

The capital gearing ratio indicates the relative proportions of a company's fixed-interest and variable-interest capital. The higher the ratio, the more highly geared the company is said to be. The "book" gearing ratio is given by the expression:

$$\frac{\text{Debentures} + \text{preference shares}}{\text{Equity share capital} + \text{reserves}}$$

Reserves are included in the denominator because they represent further investment in the company by shareholders.

An alternative ratio is the market gearing ratio, given by the expression:

$$\frac{\text{Market value of debentures and preference shares} + \text{Short-term borrowing}}{\text{Market value of equity shares}}$$

The impact of gearing can be illustrated by reference to Table XIII.

Firm A has raised £500,000 by the issue of debentures and the same amount by the issue of shares, whereas firm B has raised £800,000 by the issue of debentures and only £200,000 by the issue of shares. In year 1, of the £100,000 profits, interest payments account for 50 per cent in firm A and 80 per cent in firm B. The amount available for dividends is

6. THE COST OF FINANCE AND INVESTMENT APPRAISAL

TABLE XIII. THE IMPACT OF GEARING

Firm A			Issued (£000)	Firm B			Issued (£000)
£1 Ordinary shares			500	£1 Ordinary shares			200
10% Debentures			500	10% Debentures			800
			1,000				1,000

	Year 1 (£000)	Year 2 (£000)		Year 1 (£000)	Year 2 (£000)
Profits	100	80		100	80
Interest	50	50		80	80
Dividend	50	30		20	—
Dividend yield	10%	6%		10%	—

correspondingly less in B than in A. (To simplify the discussion we ignore tax payments and retained earnings and assume that the bank and market values of equity are identical.) In year 2 profits fall to £800,000. Interest payments are maintained but dividends are cut, and indeed fall to zero in firm B.

This illustrates the greater risk experienced by equity holders, referred to above. It also explains why a higher potential reward has to be offered to equity holders as the level of gearing increases. (When profits increase, the rewards to shareholders increase inversely to the level of gearing; this can be seen by examining what would happen if in year 3 profits returned to their level in year 1. Shareholders in firm B would benefit more than shareholders in firm A. It might be thought that this prospect would compensate for the undesirable effect of high gearing when profits fall, leaving shareholders indifferent as between different levels of gearing. However this is so only if shareholders are risk-neutral. It is assumed than in general shareholders are risk-averse, i.e. that they would prefer the certainty of receiving £100 to equal probabilities of receiving nothing or £200.)

Table XIII also shows that the holders of debentures face a higher degree of risk in firm B than in firm A, since there is a smaller "cushion" in the form of payments to shareholders. Indeed in year 2 this cushion has disappeared. Any further reduction in profit would leave the company unable to fulfil its obligations to debenture holders (unless, of course, it could draw on profits retained in earlier years). We see, then, that an increase in gearing increases the risk faced by stock holders. To compensate for this higher risk a company would have to offer a higher rate of interest.

These considerations lead to the conclusion that high gearing increases the cost of finance. But very low gearing can have the same effect. As we have seen, loan stock is a cheaper form of capital than equity finance, and low gearing means that the firm utilises only a small proportion of this low-cost finance. We can conclude therefore that the cost of external finance (and therefore the overall cost of finance) is minimised when the level of gearing is moderate, neither very high nor very low.

The cost of retained earnings

As we showed above, retained earnings have accounted for a high proportion of the increase in company assets. The cost which the company should impute to retained earnings is the cost of equity, adjusted to take account of tax considerations. If shareholders provide £1 million through subscribing to a new share issue the cost to them is £1 million. On the other hand if they provide the £1 million through retained earnings, and dividends are taxed at the rate of, say, 33⅓ per cent, then the cost to shareholders would be only £⅔ million. (However, this differential will be reduced if the retention of earnings causes the share price to rise, making shareholders liable to capital gains tax.) The use of retained earnings rather than new equity capital is therefore likely to reduce the overall cost of finance.

The effect of gearing: an alternative view

The conclusion arrived at above—that the overall cost of finance is minimised at a moderate level of gearing—has been challenged by a number of economists, notably Modigliani and Miller.[6] They argue that under certain conditions the cost of capital is not affected by the level of gearing. However the conditions required are extremely restrictive; their model assumes perfect capital markets and no growth in retained earnings, and does not take taxation into account.[7]

The cost of finance and investment

The overall cost of finance to an individual company is affected by all the factors considered above and also by factors pertaining to that company, and in particular its past and prospective profitability and its policy with regard to dividends. Differences in these respects can mean a considerable difference in the cost of finance to companies employing an identical mix of retained earnings, equity and loans.

It is sometimes argued that in estimating the cost of financing a given investment programme, the firm should consider only the cost of those forms of finance utilised for that programme. So if, for example, a new

---

6. F. Modigliani and M. H. Miller. "The Cost of Capital, Corporation Finance and the Theory of Investment". *American Economic Review* Vol. 48 (1958).

7. The limitations of the Modigliani–Miller approach are discussed in detail in: Hay and Morris, *op. cit.*, Ch. 10.

factory was financed entirely by retained earnings and the issue of new capital, the cost of loan stock would not be taken into account. However this ignores the effect that raising this finance might have on the future cost of finance. Reducing the gearing ratio from a high level may facilitate the future issue of (low-cost) debentures. Considering each increment of capital in turn would seem to be justified only for short-term, self-liquidating investments whose financing does not impinge upon subsequent investments, e.g. the financing of temporarily increased stocks by a bank loan. In other instances it is probably preferable to apply the company's overall cost of finance to each investment project.

INVESTMENT APPRAISAL

Having examined the factors influencing the cost of capital, we now consider how the firm might decide whether or not to undertake particular investments. These decisions often require the expected costs and revenues of each proposed investment to be quantified, and the impression could well be gained from the discussion below that investment appraisal is a precise art. It is therefore appropriate to preface the examination of investment appraisal techniques with a reminder that in practice firms operate in a world of uncertainty.

UNCERTAINTY AND INVESTMENT APPRAISAL

In a recent article Mr M. Barnato wrote as follows: "It would be difficult to tell from most textbooks on appraisal of capital investment that the uncertainties surrounding the projections of cash flows are the critical factor. Instead they frequently give the impression that correct investment decision making depends solely on applying the appropriate cash flow technique to forecasts of costs and revenues. In the real world this is of course necessary. It is however not sufficient unless the forecasts of cash inflows and outflows are certain to be correct and are not subject to error. This is obviously never likely to be the case. In fact there are likely to be increased uncertainties over the coming decade which will manifest themselves in financial terms (such as highly variable interest rates, tax rates and structure etc.), in economic terms (the collapse of most of the historical macro-economic relationships), in marketing terms and via the vicissitudes of government policy. These factors are unlikely to become any easier to forecast accurately."[8]

Barnato goes on to explore the implications of uncertainty for investment appraisal. He suggests two ways in which forecasting procedures might be changed in order to make them more useful in investment appraisal. First, where future values of environmental factors

---

8. M. Barnato, "Wrong Macro Economic Forecasts and the Implications for Business Strategy". *Business Economist,* Vol. 13 (1982).

are vital, point forecasts should be supplemented by ranges and probabilities. It would not be sufficient to allow for uncertainty by adjusting the target rate of return upwards, as sometimes suggested.

Second, the decision-maker needs to consider what value of the environmental variable could change the investment decision (the principle of the reverse question). "For example, at what exchange rate would an import substitution project be rendered non-viable?" Having found the critical number or crossover point between two alternative projects, the decision-maker asks the forecaster to give a view on the likelihood of that value coming about.

Another implication of uncertainty noted by Barnato is that preservation of flexibility should be an important aspect of investment policy: "It is worth considering what will happen if the forecast proves to be incorrect—will the project still be viable or would an alternative project be able to cope with the situation? The optimal solution may be the more brittle. It may, for example, be most profitable on any given set of forecasts of demand to make the product on a new line within an existing factory. But if there is uncertainty on future demand—clearly the likely situation—then an initial period of sub-contracting production might be worthwhile".

Barnato's experience in industry leads him to conclude that: "The recognition of uncertainty has frequently not fully permeated organisations. Top management frequently receive for review what amounts to a single option (e.g. one acquisition candidate, one new product) and are then asked to make a 'yes or no' decision rather than to choose from a set of alternatives."

Where several alternatives are presented for consideration then uncertainty can be allowed for in various ways. Probabilities may be attached to future cash flows, with the earlier flows carrying a higher probability than later ones. Alternatively, projects involving a great deal of uncertainty may be accepted only if the prospective gain is substantially above the target or norm. Sensitivity analysis can be used, whereby a number of alternative returns are calculated using different assumptions about future costs and revenues. (This can be done when competing projects have to be compared or when a yes–no decision on a single project is required.)

Having considered how the information yielded by investment appraisal should be presented and interpreted, we examine the main appraisal methods that might be used. We begin with discounting methods.

DISCOUNTING METHODS OF INVESTMENT APPRAISAL

The major advantage of discounting methods is that they take account of the pattern of cash flows over time and of the fact that money received today is worth more than money received in the future. The two discounting methods, considered in turn, are the discounted cash flow (DCF) method (also known as the internal rate of return, compound interest rate of return, investor's return and actuarial method) and net present value (NPV) analysis.

The discounted cash flow method

The two basic pieces of information required in calculating the return on any investment, whatever the method used, are:

(a) The outflow of cash which that investment involves. This often comprises a single transaction as when a machine is purchased. But large investment projects, such as the construction of an electricity generating station or the building and equipping of a large factory, may involve a series of payments made over a number of years.

(b) The subsequent net inflows of cash resulting from the investment. Whereas the cash outflow frequently comprises a single transaction, the inflows usually extend over a considerable period of time. Revenue may be received from a new product for five or ten years. A new, more efficient machine may reduce production costs (and thus increase net revenue) over a similar period.

Having obtained this information—and we should remember that "information" means the firm's best estimate, especially of future cash inflows—the firm is able to derive the DCF or internal rate of return. The rate of return is the discount factor that brings the sum of the cash inflows into equality with the initial cash outflow. The relevant formula is:

$$CO = \sum \frac{NCI}{(1+r)^n}$$

where CO is the initial cash outflow, NCI is the cash inflow in a given year, n is the number of the year in question and r is the DCF or internal rate of return.

To illustrate the operation of the method we can apply the formula to a simple example, the purchase by a farmer of a herd of young bullocks for fattening and subsequent resale. The initial purchase price is £100,000 and the farmer expects to receive, net of all expenses (labour, feed etc.), £60,000 in each of the next two years from the sale of the bullocks:

$$£100,000 = \frac{£60,000}{(1+r)^1} + \frac{£60,000}{(1+r)^2}$$

By consulting tables or by using a computer program we can find the discount rate that makes the present value of the cash inflows equal to the cash outflow. It can be seen from Table XIV that the relevant discount factor, the DCF or internal rate of return, is just over 13 per cent.

TABLE XIV. THE PRESENT VALUE OF £x RECEIVED FOR 2 YEARS

£	*Discount factor*				
	10%	*11%*	*12%*	*13%*	*14%*
1	1.73554	1.71252	1.69005	1.66810	1.64666
60,000	104,132	102,751	101,403	100,086	98,800

The farmer would be able to borrow money at (just over) 13 per cent, invest it in this project and out of the proceeds repay both the principal and the interest.

If the cash flows vary from year to year more calculation is involved. But the underlying principle is unchanged. By comparing the internal rate of return (IRR) with its cost of capital, the firm is able to see whether or not a particular project would be profitable. Any project is profitable, in accounting terms, if the IRR exceeds the firm's cost of capital.

However, this method does not tell the firm by how much profits would be increased. This is, of course, an important question whenever a choice has to be made between alternative investment projects, two or more of which have estimated returns in excess of the cost of capital. In these circumstances net present value analysis can be used.

Net present value analysis

The net present value (NPV) of a project is the present value of the project's net cash inflows discounted at the firm's cost of capital to the time of the initial capital outlay (cash outflow), minus that capital outlay.

$$\text{NPV} = \sum \frac{\text{NCI}}{(1-i)^n} - \text{CO}$$

where i is the cost of capital and the other terms have the same meaning as before.

Taking our previous example, and assuming that the farmer's cost of capital is 10 per cent, we have:

$$\text{NPV} = \frac{£60,000}{(1.1)^1} + \frac{£60,000}{(1.1)^2} - £100,000$$
$$= £54,545 + 49,587 - 100,000$$
$$= £4,132$$

The farmer would be better off by £4,132, in present value terms, than if he did not undertake the project. However, whether he should undertake the project depends upon the alternative projects that are available. The farmer may well have to choose between alternatives, since he is unlikely to have unlimited access to funds. Moreover, all investment decisions should take account of uncertainty, as noted above.

6. THE COST OF FINANCE AND INVESTMENT APPRAISAL

Multi-period capital outlays
We have assumed so far that the entire capital outlay is incurred at the beginning of the project's life (conventionally designated as year nought). But, as noted earlier, with large projects the outlay may extend over several years, i.e. the cash flow can be negative for more than year nought. The net present value method can be applied to such projects in the normal way. Consider a firm whose cost of capital is 8 per cent, and which has the opportunity of investing in a project with the following cash flows:

Year	0	1	2	3	4	5
Cash flow (£)	−10,000	−5,000	3,000	5,000	10,000	5,000
Discounted at 8%	−	−4,630	2,572	3,969	7,350	3,403

NPV = £12,664 − 10,000
    = £2,664

Discounting methods compared

Both methods give the same answer to the question: Would this project lead to an increase in the firm's profits? This is illustrated in Fig. 21, which shows how the net present value of a project varies with the cost of capital, the discount factor. As the cost of capital (CC) increases, NPV declines. NPV is zero at point *A*, where the cost of capital equals the internal rate of return. At a capital cost less than *A*, the project would lead to increased profits (NPV positive, IRR>CC). At a capital cost greater than *A*, the project would lead to reduced profits (NPV negative, IRR<CC).

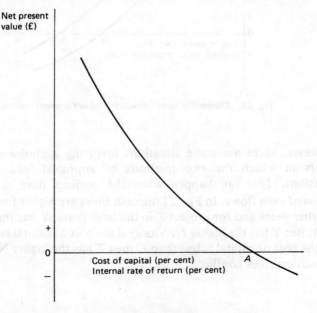

Fig. 21. *The cost of capital and net present value.*

Furthermore, when a decision has to be made as to which of two (or more) projects should be undertaken, the two methods will frequently produce the same result. The project with the higher internal rate of return will often have the higher net present value.

This is illustrated in Fig. 22, which shows the NPVs, at various costs of capital, for two projects Y and Z. The IRR is higher for Z (B per cent) than for Y (A per cent). Similarly at any cost of capital NPV is higher for Z than for Y. Both methods lead to the conclusion that Z is to be preferred to Y.

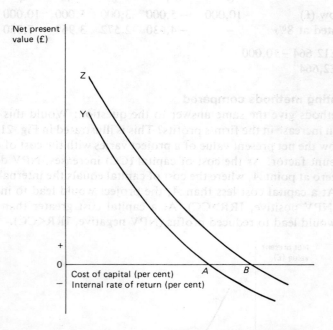

Fig. 22. *Alternative rates of return and net present values.*

However, there are some situations involving a choice between two projects in which the two methods of appraisal lead to different conclusions. This can happen when the projects have different time patterns of cash flows. In Fig. 23 the cash flows are higher for project Y in the earlier years and for project Z in the later years. Y has the higher IRR ($A>B$). But Y has the higher NPV only if the cost of capital is greater than C. If the cost of capital is less than C then Z has the higher NPV, and the two decision rules conflict.

6. THE COST OF FINANCE AND INVESTMENT APPRAISAL

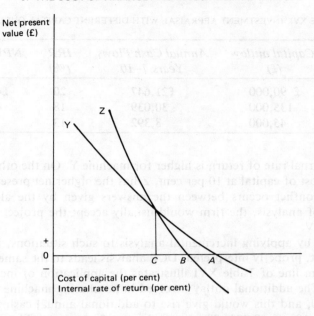

Fig. 23. *The time pattern of cash flows and investment appraisal.*

TABLE XV. A COMPARISON OF DISCOUNTING METHODS

Project	\multicolumn{6}{c}{Cash flows (£000) by year}	IRR (%)	NPV at 5%
	0	1	2	3	4	5		
Y	−100	40	40	30	9	—	9	£7,695
Z	−100	25	25	25	25	25	8	£8,237

The two projects shown in Table XV might be alternative versions of a new product that the firm is about to launch. The capital outlay would be £100,000 for each version. Version Y has a higher fashion content and is expected to produce higher cash inflows in its earlier years than Z. However Z, with a greater emphasis on performance, is expected to have a longer market life. Y has the higher IRR, but Z, with a cost of capital of 5 per cent, has the higher NPV.

Incremental analysis
It frequently happens that alternative projects involve different initial capital outlays. For example firms frequently have to choose between two machines having different costs and capacities. In Table XVI the more expensive machine, Z, has a substantially greater capacity than machine Y, and so is expected to earn substantially more revenue.

TABLE XVI. INVESTMENT APPRAISAL WITH DIFFERENT CAPITAL OUTLAYS

	Capital outlay (£)	Annual Cash Flows Years 1–10	IRR (%)	NPV at 10% (£)
Y	£ 90,000	£21,647	20	£43,012
Z	135,000	30,039	18	49,577
Z – Y	45,000	8,392	13	6,565

The internal rate of return is higher for machine Y. On the other hand, with the cost of capital at 10 per cent, Z has the higher net present value. When a conflict occurs between the answers given by the alternative methods of analysis, the firm would usually accept the project with the higher NPV.

In fact, by applying incremental analysis to such situations, it can be shown that, properly interpreted, DCF analysis leads to the same answer. The bottom line of Table XVI illustrates the application of incremental analysis. The additional outlay involved in purchasing machine Z would be £45,000, and this would give rise to additional annual cash flows, in years 1 to 10, of £8,392. The internal rate of return on this additional investment is 13 per cent. Since this exceeds the cost of capital, 10 per cent, the additional investment should be undertaken. This is confirmed by the fact that the NPV at 10 per cent would be positive (£6,565).

Dual rates of return

In certain instances the DCF method gives two internal rates of return. This can happen when there are reversals of sign in the net cash flow during the project's life, e.g. where the cash inflow is negative at the beginning of the project, subsequently becomes positive, but becomes negative again towards the end of the project's life. When this happens it is possible to have two IRRs, one less than and the other greater than the cost of capital. Fortunately instances of meaningless results yielded by DCF analysis are rare.

An operational comparison of NPV and DCF

We have shown that NPV analysis and DCF analysis usually yield the same answer—and always do so when the decision relates to the profitability of a single project—but that there are some situations in which NPV analysis is technically preferable. This might suggest that firms using discounting methods would always choose NPV analysis. However, it has been argued that on operational grounds DCF is the superior method. "This superiority is particularly marked in the context of assessing the return offered for risk bearing because the DCF measures profitability as a return per unit of capital per unit of time it is invested (that is exposed to risk). It is therefore measuring profitability in the same dimensions of quantity and time as risk, since risk generally depends on the amount of capital exposed to risk over time. NPV, which takes the form of an absolute quantity of money, lacks this important advantage".[9]

Merrett and Sykes believe that this is the primary reason why the DCF method is more readily accepted by senior managers. They also see economy of presentation as a second major operational advantage of DCF. "Given the very considerable opportunity cost of senior management time, this advantage is extremely valuable." The provision of a single DCF return "enables senior management to perceive immediately whether or not the DCF is sufficiently above the various desired rates of discount considered appropriate for a particular category of investment".[10] (On the other hand, economy of presentation can have dangers, as noted in the earlier quotation from Barnato.)

OTHER METHODS OF INVESTMENT APPRAISAL

We have shown that discounting methods of investment appraisal have the very important advantage that they take account of the time pattern of cash flows and the cost of finance. Despite these advantages discounting methods are not always used. In some instances firms may believe that they have to undertake particular investments if they are to survive—*see* the discussion of this point in Chapter 10—rendering all forms of investment appraisal superfluous. (In fact even in such situations formal methods of investment appraisal can often play a useful role.) In other instances firms may prefer to use one of the other methods of investment appraisal discussed in the following sections.

The payback method

The payback period is that in which the net cash inflows become equal to the initial capital outlay or cash outflow. (In other words it is the period over which *undiscounted* NPV becomes zero.) The payback method can be illustrated by reference to Table XVII, which shows the estimated cash inflows expected to result from the introduction of two new products. Each product requires an initial investment of £500,000, and the firm has to choose between the two.

The total income generated (and also the IRR) is greater for product B than for product A. But A would be chosen if the decision rule for mutually exclusive projects was that the one with the shorter payback period should be chosen. (The payback period is 5 years for A and 6 years for B.) Product A would also be chosen if the decision rule was to accept only those projects with a payback period of 5 years or less. (A study by the National Economic Development Council found that the payback

---

9. A. J. Merrett and A. Sykes. *Capital Budgeting and Company Finance.* Longmans, 1966, p. 118.
10. Merrett and Sykes. *Op. cit.,* p. 119.

TABLE XVII. THE PAYBACK METHOD OF
INVESTMENT APPRAISAL

Year	Estimated Net Cash Inflows (£) Product A	Product B
1	100,000	80,000
2	100,000	90,000
3	100,000	90,000
4	100,000	90,000
5	100,000	80,000
6	—	70,000
7	—	70,000
8	—	70,000

period stipulated by firms ranged from 3 to 7 years, with 5 the most common.[11])

The obvious disadvantage of the payback method is that it does not take account of cash inflows outside the payback period, or of the cost of capital. (The NEDC study suggested that the use of the payback method led to rejection of some projects that might have been accepted had other methods of appraisal been used.) The advantage of payback is its ease of calculation and presentation.

Payback can be best justified on technical grounds when the firm's liquidity position is unsatisfactory or when there is a great deal of uncertainty about the returns to the project in later years, for example because of rapid changes in technology or fashion. In such situations firms seek to invest in projects likely to yield high returns in earlier years. (In order to "steer" decisions towards such projects, discounting methods would incorporate a high cost of capital, a high discount-factor. In the first situation, when the firm's liquidity position is unsatisfactory, its cost of capital is likely to be high since investors would be reluctant to supply funds. In the second situation, the uncertainty arising from rapid technological or market change would be taken into account by adjusting the cost of capital by an appropriate risk factor.)

The book rate of return method
This method—sometimes known simply as the rate of return method—is especially popular with small firms lacking sophisticated financial expertise. The strengths and weaknesses of the method can be illustrated by means of a simple hypothetical example. Table XVIII shows the expected profit (after depreciation) from two alternative projects, each of which has an initial cost of £500,000 and a life of five years.

11. NEDC. *Investment Appraisal.* HMSO, 1969.

6. THE COST OF FINANCE AND INVESTMENT APPRAISAL

TABLE XVIII. THE BOOK RATE OF RETURN METHOD

Year	Profit (after depreciation) (£) Project A	Project B
1	250,000	50,000
2	100,000	50,000
3	50,000	100,000
4	50,000	200,000
5	50,000	100,000
Total	500,000	500,000

For each project the average annual return is £500,000 ÷ 5 = £100,000. The rate of return, defined as the average return divided by the initial cost, is £100,000 ÷ £500,000 × 100 = 20 per cent. In order to decide whether a particular project should be undertaken, the estimated return is compared with the firm's target rate of return, which is influenced by the firm's cost of capital.

It can be seen that the rate of return is easy to calculate. However the method suffers because it does not take account of the time pattern of cash flows. This is shown clearly in the example above. Both projects have the same rate of return. But the cash flows are such that project A would be ranked above B if either discounting or the payback method were used.

AREAS OF APPLICATION OF INVESTMENT APPRAISAL

The decisions referred to in this chapter have mainly been of two types. The first is whether a particular project, e.g. the purchase of a new machine or the introduction of a new product, should be undertaken. The second is which of two alternative projects should be undertaken.

There are several other important types of decision to which the various methods of investment appraisal can be applied. As machines approach the end of their useful life, decisions have to be made concerning the timing of their replacement. The purchase of a new machine involves a cash outflow against which have to be set lower costs of maintenance (higher net cash inflows) subsequently. Manufacturers have frequently to choose between making a component and buying it from other manufacturers. Make-or-buy decisions again require the initial cash outlay (required for internal manufacture) to be balanced against the subsequently higher cash inflows. A similar balancing exercise is involved in the choice between purchasing and leasing machines. Furthermore, if the company decides to lease then it may be able to choose between alternative schemes with different terms, one requiring higher payments in earlier years and the other higher payments in later years.

Location decisions have to be made by many firms, especially when they are expanding. Retailers, building societies, banks etc. have to balance the additional costs involved in acquiring city-centre premises against the higher revenue likely to be generated by such premises. Firms deciding where to build a new factory frequently have to balance the lower capital outlay required in Development Areas (because of government subsidies) against the possible additional costs of operating in such areas (due to remoteness from markets, shortages of skilled labour etc.). Multinational companies have to take account of an even wider range of factors, as shown in Chapter 10.

In principle a takeover can be looked at in the same way, since the bidder expects the purchase to give rise to higher profits in future years. However, takeovers are usually determined by strategic considerations, as shown in Chapter 11, rather than by a precise evaluation of costs and benefits.

CAPITAL RATIONING AND INVESTMENT DECISIONS

We have discussed above the various factors that might affect the availability of funds and a firm's cost of capital or finance. In this section we take the cost of capital as given and examine the relationship between the availability of funds, the cost of capital and investment decisions.

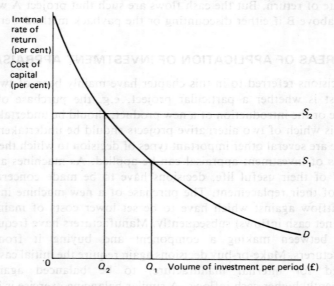

Fig. 24. *The cost of capital and the volume of investment.*

In Fig. 24 the line D indicates the volume of investment expected to yield given (internal) rates of return. The line S_1 indicates the cost at which capital is available. If the firm wishes to maximise its profits it will invest

6. THE COST OF FINANCE AND INVESTMENT APPRAISAL 111

up to the point where the rate of return and the cost of capital are equal, that is point Q_1. (This is also the point at which NPV becomes zero.) An increase in the cost of capital, shown by the shift from S_1 to S_2, leads to a fall in the profit-maximising volume of investment to Q_2. Conversely, a fall in the cost of capital would lead to an increase in investment.

As noted earlier, firms may seek to take account of uncertainty by adding a risk premium to the cost of capital. This can also be illustrated by reference to Fig. 24. Where S_1 is the cost of capital, S_2 would be the adjusted cost, the minimum acceptable rate of return.

The shape of the supply curve in Fig. 24 implies that the cost of capital is constant however much finance is raised. In practice, as a firm seeks to raise more finance in a given period it likely to find that the cost rises, as shown in Fig. 25. The firm is able to identify the profit-maximising volume of investment (Q) by comparing the rate of return and the cost of capital, as before. But a variable cost of capital makes net present value analysis more complicated, since a set of NPVs has to be estimated for each cost of capital within the possible range.

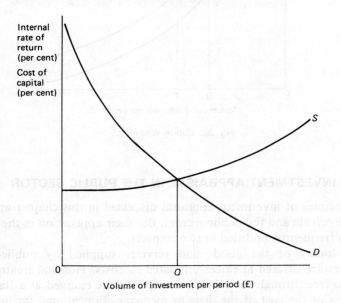

Fig. 25. *An increasing cost of capital.*

Firms sometimes decide to undertake only such capital expenditure as can be financed out of retained earnings. Such a policy might be adopted if the firm was afraid that control would be diluted, increasing the chance of a takeover bid, if more shares were issued. This situation is illustrated in Fig. 26, where SQ refers to the supply of internally generated funds. If the prospective profitability of investment is as indicated by D_1, the volume of funds available would be sufficient to finance all projects ($0Q$) yielding a return greater than or equal to the cost of capital, I. But if the prospective profitability is as indicated by D_2, insufficient funds would be available to finance all potentially profitable projects. The volume of investment would be $0Q$ and QT potentially profitable projects would be rejected. For these projects the internal rate of return exceeds the cost of capital, and the net present value is positive.

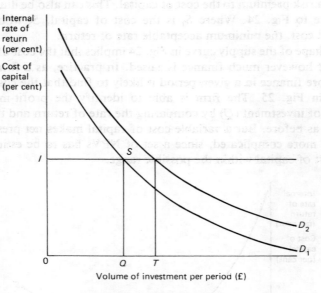

Fig. 26. *Capital rationing.*

INVESTMENT APPRAISAL IN THE PUBLIC SECTOR

The principles of investment appraisal discussed in this chapter apply to both the private and the public sectors. But their application in the public sector is frequently modified in two respects.

First, many of the goods and services supplied by public-sector producers are offered at prices unrelated to costs. Hospital treatment is available free through the NHS; prescriptions are charged at a flat rate, regardless of the cost of the drug or medicine. Educational facilities are provided for children at a zero price; the fees charged for further and higher education are usually well below the costs involved.

In such instances it becomes inappropriate or even impossible to balance cash outflows and inflows in the ways outlined above. Another measure of benefit has to be substituted for revenue. Output is perhaps the most promising alternative, although it is easier to measure quantity than quality. For example we know the exact number of school children, but can only imperfectly assess educational standards.

6. THE COST OF FINANCE AND INVESTMENT APPRAISAL

Consequently, investment appraisal tends to be used most in helping to answer the question: how can a given level of output (however defined) be most efficiently supplied? In answering this question account can be taken of the relative costs that would result from locating activity in different areas, from purchasing and leasing equipment, from the use of different types of equipment etc.

The second factor that requires the modification of investment appraisal methods in the public sector is the difficulty of identifying the cost of capital. This is particularly true when the capital is obtained via taxation.

Investment appraisal in the nationalised industries

The nationalised industries are less subject than other public-sector producers to the limitations on investment appraisal outlined above. These industries attempt to sell their products at prices that cover their costs. Moreover, they are required to take account of the cost of capital. However, this cost is determined by the government, not by the financial markets.

The test discount rate

A White Paper issued in 1967 advocated that a proposed investment by a public corporation should be undertaken only if it promised to yield more than the test discount rate (TDR). The TDR was set initially at 8 per cent in real terms, in line with the existing average rate of return on low-risk projects in the private sector. The TDR could therefore be seen as the opportunity cost of capital expenditure in the nationalised industries. Ensuring that investment in these industries produced a return in line with this opportunity cost would contribute to an optimum allocation of resources in the economy as a whole.

Although this approach has considerable merit in principle, in practice it has limited application. The uncertainty surrounding the return to investment that we considered with reference to private-sector producers applies also to the public sector. (Public-sector producers usually have fewer direct competitors and from this point of view are subject to less uncertainty. On the other hand they face more uncertainty from possible changes in government policy.)

Furthermore, as large organisations the nationalised industries invest relatively little in projects whose merits can be considered in isolation. As noted in an NEDC report, "the major part of the investment programme in the Post Office and British Gas is determined by prior strategic decisions to maintain a certain standard for telecommunications services or to purchase the output of North Sea gas fields. Investment cannot in these cases be disaggregated for appraisal purposes because it relates to a total system—the telephone network or gas distribution grid—and consequently most of the investment programme becomes classified as inescapable or essential."[12] NEDC found that of four industries studied, only in steel were discounted rates of return calculated. In gas, telecommunications and rail, investment projects were adopted that had the lowest discounted costs.

The required rate of return

To try to allow for the interdependence of projects, a White Paper issued in 1978 specified a Required Rate of Return that should apply to an industry's investment programme as a whole rather than to individual projects. The RRR was specified as 5 per cent in real terms and before tax. The change from the 1967 figure presumably reflected the decline in private-sector profitability. Incidentally, a common RRR does not imply a common financial target for the whole of the industries' operations. The government sets different targets for different industries, reflecting their varying economic circumstances. British Gas was set a target of 6½ per cent profit on turnover for 1979–80, whereas the target for British Shipbuilders was a maximum trading loss of £100 million in 1979–80 and £90 million in 1980–81.

It would be logical if funds were made available to the nationalised industries at the RRR. But in fact they are able to borrow more cheaply from the National Loans Fund. (As noted above, the cost of capital is not a market-determined cost.)

Cost benefit analysis

Appraisal techniques may also be applied in a modified manner to public-sector investment in order to take account of external costs and benefits. These are costs and benefits which result from trading transactions, i.e. the production and sale of goods and services, but which accrue to firms or individuals not party to these transactions. For example, if some people pay to be immunised and as a result do not contract a disease, the people to whom they would have transmitted the disease benefit. People who suffer noise and fumes because an airport or motorway is built near their house incur a cost.

Cost benefit analysis has been undertaken in connection with a number of public-sector investment projects—actual or proposed—including the building of the underground Victoria line in London, the building of the M1 motorway, the siting of the third London airport, the Channel Tunnel and the Morecambe Bay barrage.

Investment in transport schemes can yield benefits of three main kinds: savings in time and operating costs to existing travellers over the route, benefits to those who transfer from other routes and other modes of travel to the new facility, and other benefits to people and firms when the new facility brings about significant changes in the overall pattern of travel. Estimates of all three types of benefit are usually made. Costs might

12. NEDC. *The Nationalised Industries*. HMSO, 1976.

include loss of amenity, e.g. green spaces, noise and pollution. A different set of benefits and costs arise from other types of investment.

QUESTIONS

1. What sources of funds are likely to be used to finance (*a*) an increase in stocks, (*b*) the building and equipping of a large factory, (*c*) a series of takeovers?

2. Discuss the advantages and disadvantages of alternative methods of raising new capital.

3. Explain why small firms may find it difficult to attract new capital, and describe the measures that have been taken to overcome the difficulties.

4. What factors might explain the changes in bank borrowing shown in Table XI?

5. Evaluate the case for allowing public sector producers to raise finance from the capital markets.

6. Explain the term gearing and discuss the implications of gearing for (*a*) firms, (*b*) investors.

7. "A firm should finance as high a proportion of its activities as possible from retained earnings, since no cost is involved." Discuss.

8. The information below refers to three pairs of hypothetical companies. Say, in each case, for which company you would expect the cost of finance to be higher, and briefly explain your answers.

(*a*) Company A has assets of £100 million and manufacturers a wide range of leisure products. Company B has assets of £3 million and manufactures mechanical components for vehicles.

(*b*) The profits of the two companies, which have equal assets and are in the same line of business, have been as follows (£ million):

Year	Company A	Company B
1	5	5
2	7	5
3	3	5
4	5	5
5	7	5

(*c*) Company A plans a modest programme of expansion which it intends to finance entirely from retained earnings. Company B has a much more ambitious growth target, despite being highly geared.

9. Outline the advantages and disadvantages of each of the following methods of investment appraisal: (*a*) DCF method, (*b*) net present value analysis, (*c*) payback method, (*d*) book rate of return method.

10. "Investment projects should only be undertaken by nationalised

industries if they pass the same tests as projects undertaken by private sector producers." Discuss.

11. List the factors that might be taken into account in a cost-benefit analysis of the following projects: (*a*) building a barrage across the river Avon to generate electricity, (*b*) the siting of a third London airport, (*c*) building a ring-road around the south of London, (*d*) building reservoirs in a national park.

12. A company is considering whether it should replace an existing machine by an improved model that has just appeared on the market. The improved model costs £50,000 and is expected to reduce the cost of production by £7,000 for each of the 10 years of its estimated life. (*a*) Using present value tables calculate the net present value of the investment when the company's cost of capital is (*i*) 6 per cent, (*ii*) 8 per cent. (*b*) Explain how the net present value would be affected by each of the following: (*i*) the prices of the items produced on the machine increase more rapidly than expected; (*ii*) the wages of the workers manning the machine rise more rapidly than expected; (*iii*) the machine has a lower scrap value than expected; (*iv*) the machine has a longer life than expected.

13. Chemico plc is faced with the choice between repairing some laboratory equipment and purchasing new equipment. The cost of the new equipment is £100,000, and its useful life is estimated at ten years, after which it is expected it would be superseded by a new generation of equipment with a much improved performance. To repair the existing equipment would cost £20,000, and this would allow the purchase of new equipment—of the present vintage—to be deferred for five years. Given a cost of capital of 10 per cent, which of the two alternatives would you recommend?

14. John Shaw is about to set up business as a hairdresser. He has identified the premises that he would like to occupy, but has to decide whether to take out a lease for (*a*) 10 years at an annual rent of £5,000 with no review, or (*b*) 10 years at an annual rent of £4,000 with a review at the mid-point. In recent years rents have risen at an average rate of 10 per cent a year. Which alternative would you advise?

15 A firm of bullion dealers buys gold for £1 million which it resells for £1.2 million two years later. Calculate the DCF (internal) rate of return.

16. The owner of a block of flats is considering installing insulation in order to reduce heating costs. The average heat loss for an uninsulated building of that type is estimated at 90 pence per year per square foot of exterior wall. Insulation is available in sheets one half-inch thick at a price of 50 pence per square foot installed. The heat loss for successive thicknesses of insulation is as follows:

6. THE COST OF FINANCE AND INVESTMENT APPRAISAL

Thickness of insulation (inches)	Heat loss per sq. ft. (pence)
½	64
1	46
1½	34
2	23
2½	16
3	13
3½	12

What thickness(es) of insulation would enable the owner to:

(*a*) recover his investment within four years;
(*b*) maximise the (book) rate of return on his investment;
(*c*) maximise the net present value of the investment, assuming a life of 20 years and a cost of finance of 8 per cent?

PART THREE

Models

CHAPTER SEVEN
Models of Markets

OBJECTIVES

After studying this chapter the reader should be able to: describe the various market forms; explain how price is determined in perfect competition, monopoly and monopolistic competition; derive a supply curve; construct simple models of oligopolistic markets.

INTRODUCTION

The focus of this book is on the behaviour and performance of firms rather than markets. But in traditional, neo-classical economic theory a firm's behaviour and performance is seen as being strongly conditioned by the form of market that it supplies. Therefore in this chapter we briefly examine some basic models of markets. Reference is made to firms only insofar as this is required in order to explain the determination of price and output in different forms of market. The firms are not intended to bear any resemblance to actual organisations.

A CLASSIFICATION OF MARKETS

It is conventional to classify markets in accordance with two characteristics: the number of sellers or suppliers, and the degree of product differentiation. Table XIX shows that five forms of market can be distinguished, each having a different combination of these two characteristics.

TABLE XIX. MARKET FORMS

Number of sellers	Product Homogeneous	Differentiated
Many	perfect competition	monopolistic competition
Few	oligopoly	oligopoly
One		monopoly

It should be emphasised that this classification is designed to facilitate the construction of models of markets. In practice it is often difficult to decide what product(s), and therefore which suppliers, constitute the market. For example is it sensible to talk about the market for fresh cod fillets, or should our definition be extended to include fresh cod steaks, other types of fresh fish, frozen fish, processed fish, fish products, other foods? The answer to this question will determine which market form we model.

The two extreme or polar markets are perfect competition and monopoly. In perfectly competitive markets a large number of suppliers sell a homogeneous product. The number of sellers is large because there are no barriers to entry into the market and because economies of scale are unimportant.

The fact that the product is homogeneous or undifferentiated means that consumers have no preference for the products of one supplier over those of other suppliers. This situation requires that the methods of production can create undifferentiated products and that producers do not wish to differentiate their products. Many agricultural products satisfy the first condition, but fewer satisfy the second. For example, most vegetables are undifferentiated—branded fresh carrots or brussels sprouts are uncommon—whereas differentiation is more common in fruit, e.g. bananas, grapefruit and oranges.

In a monopoly one firm accounts for the total supply. (This is a more restrictive definition than that adopted in connection with competition policy—*see* Chapter 3.) Since there is a single supplier, product differentiation within that market is not a meaningful concept. But the product is, of course, differentiated from products sold in other markets.

The term monopolistic competition indicates that this market has characteristics in common with both perfect competition and monopoly. There are many suppliers but the product of each is differentiated—in one way or another—from those of rival suppliers.[1]

The primary characteristic of oligopoly is that a high proportion (perhaps 100 per cent) of the market is supplied by a few sellers. Oligopoly, which may be either homogeneous (undifferentiated) or differentiated, if often stated to be the dominant market form, a point to which we return below.

Having presented a classification of markets, we now consider how firms might behave in each type of market, beginning with perfect competition.

PERFECT COMPETITION

Since purchasers are indifferent between the products of the many suppliers, any supplier which set a price above that set by other suppliers would sell nothing. Each supplier therefore accepts the market price, which results from the interaction of market demand and supply. A supplier would not benefit from reducing price below this level since it can sell all it wishes at that price. We summarise this by saying that each firm's demand or average-revenue curve is horizontal at the market price. This

---

1. The theory of monopolistic competition was developed by E. H. Chamberlin in the USA in the 1930s. At roughly the same time in England Joan Robinson developed a model in which she used the term imperfect competition to describe the same market form. But imperfect competition is now sometimes applied to any market that is not perfectly competitive.

7. MODELS OF MARKETS

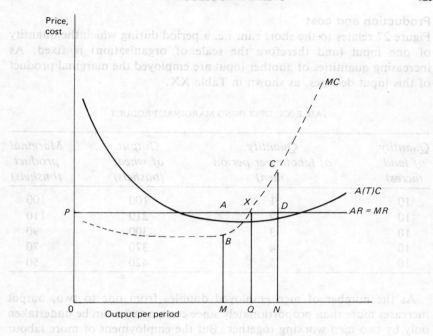

Fig. 27. *Profit maximisation in a perfectly competitive market.*

means that average revenue equals marginal revenue, the revenue from an additional unit (Fig. 27).

Firms in perfectly competitive markets are assumed to maximise short-run profits. This requires that the firm shall produce to the point at which marginal cost equals marginal revenue, i.e. at Q in Fig. 27. To see why this is the profit-maximising position consider alternative outputs, remembering that marginal revenue and marginal cost denote the change in revenue and cost that result from a change in output of one unit. If output were reduced from Q to M, revenue would fall by $QMAX$ whereas cost would fall by only $QMBX$. Conversely if output were increased to N then revenue would increase by $QNDX$ whereas cost would increase by $QNCX$.

It is conventional in these models to assume that cost includes normal profit, defined as the profit required if the firm is to remain in this market. (Normal profit is a similar concept to opportunity cost.) It can be seen that at the profit-maximising output Q, average revenue exceeds average cost, indicating that the firm is achieving supernormal profits, i.e. it is earning more than is required to remain in the market. The implications of this situation are explored below, but first we show why the cost curves are said to have the shape shown in Fig. 27. (The shape of the average cost curve is somewhat different from those presented in Chapter 5.)

Production and cost

Figure 27 relates to the short run, i.e. a period during which the quantity of one input (and therefore the scale of organisation) is fixed. As increasing quantities of another input are employed the marginal product of this input declines, as shown in Table XX.

TABLE XX. DECLINING MARGINAL PRODUCT

Quantity of land (acres)	*Quantity of labour per period (men)*	*Output of wheat (bushels)*	*Marginal product (bushels)*
10	1	100	100
10	2	210	110
10	3	300	90
10	4	370	70
10	5	420	50

As the number of men employed doubles from one to two, output increases more than proportionately since certain tasks can be undertaken only by two men working together. But the employment of more labour results in a less than proportionate increase in output, as each man works with less land.

If each man is paid the same wage, the average and marginal cost of labour falls until two men are employed, but rises thereafter. Generalising from this example we can say that as the quantity of the variable factors of production, and hence output, increases, average variable cost and marginal cost fall at first but subsequently rise. The rise in averge variable cost is at first balanced by the fall in average fixed cost, as fixed cost is spread over a greater output. But eventually the rise in average variable cost outweighs the fall in average fixed cost, and average (total) cost begins to rise, as shown in Fig. 28. (In Chapter 5 we showed that in practice average cost is roughly constant over a wide range of output and begins to rise only as the limit to output is approached.)

Equal-product curves

An alternative method of deriving the shape of cost curves is by means of equal-product curves or isoquants. Figure 29 shows a series of equal-product curves, each of which indicates the combinations of land and labour required to produce a given level of output. For example, 50 units of output can be produced by $0L$ land plus $0M$ labour. (To simplify the analysis it is assumed that only two inputs are required.) It can be seen that if the quantity of land is held constant, say at K, then the productivity of labour at first rises but subsequently declines as more labour is employed.

Given a constant wage-rate this again implies cost curves with the shape shown in Fig. 28.

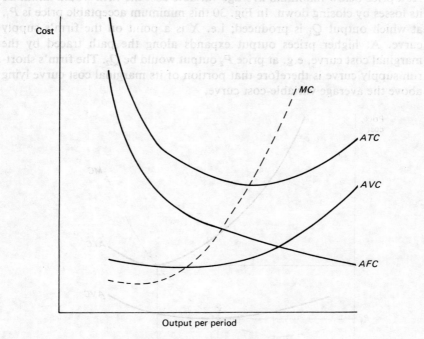

Fig. 28. *Average and marginal cost.*

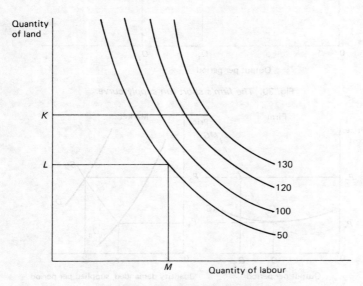

Fig. 29. *Diminishing returns to labour.*

The short-run supply curve

The firm will supply a market only if revenue covers average variable cost. At a price below minimum average variable cost the firm would minimise its losses by closing down. In Fig. 30 this minimum acceptable price is P_1, at which output Q_1 is produced; i.e. X is a point on the firm's supply curve. At higher prices output expands along the path traced by the marginal cost curve, e.g. at price P_2 output would be Q_2. The firm's short-run supply curve is therefore that portion of its marginal cost curve lying above the average variable-cost curve.

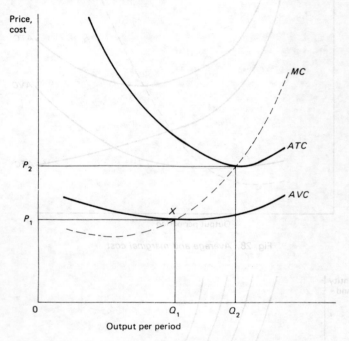

Fig. 30. *The firm's short-run supply curve.*

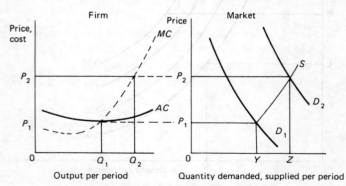

Fig. 31. *The short-run market supply curve.*

The market supply curve is obtained by aggregating the individual firms' supply curves. Figure 31 assumes that there are n suppliers, each with identical cost conditions. When market demand is D_1 market supply is Y, giving an equilibrium price P_1. The output of each firm is Q_1, where $n(Q_1) = Y$. With demand D_2 market supply is Z and price is P_2. The output of each firm is Q_2, where $n(Q_2) = Z$.

The long-run supply curve

In the long run all costs are variable. Consequently we have to consider the relationship between price and average total cost. In Fig. 32 the initial equilibrium price is P_1, at which the output of the firm is Q_1 and the market supply is Y, where $Y = n(Q_1)$ as before. An increase in demand to D_2 leads to an increase in the equilibrium price to P_2 and in equilibrium output to Q_2 (firm) and Z (market).

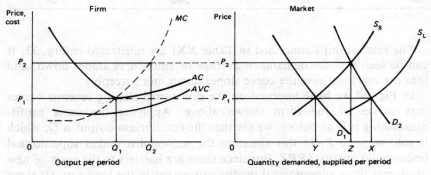

Fig. 32. *The long-run market supply curve.*

But P_2 is the equilibrium price only in the short run. At this price the existing suppliers earn supernormal profits and so in the long run new firms are attracted into the market. (It will be remembered that an absence of barriers to entry is a primary characteristic of perfect competition.) The additional output supplied by these new entrants causes the price to fall. This is shown in Fig. 32 by the shift of the supply curve from S_S to S_L. The entry of new firms, the expansion of capacity and supply, continues until the supernormal profits have been competed away. If we assume that the increased demand leaves input (factor) prices unchanged, and if the cost conditions of entrants are the same as existing suppliers, then the long-run equilibrium price will be the same as the initial price, equal to minimum average cost (P_1 in Fig. 32). Output is OX, equal to $m(OQ_1)$, where there are m firms.

Conversely a fall in demand leads to a fall in price in the short run. But in the long run, supply falls as some firms leave the market, and price returns to its original level, equal to minimum average cost.

MONOPOLY

Since there is only one supplier, market demand and the firm's demand are identical. In most markets demand varies inversely to the price, as shown in Table XXI.

TABLE XXI. DEMAND IN A MONOPOLY MARKET

Price (£)	Quantity demanded (Units)	Total revenue (£)	Marginal revenue (£)
50	10	500	–
60	9	540	40
70	8	560	20
80	7	560	0
90	6	540	– 20

The relationships contained in Table XXI are illustrated in Fig. 33. It can be seen that the demand or average revenue curve slopes down, and that the marginal revenue curve slopes down more steeply.

In Fig. 34 we have imposed on the downward sloping revenue curves cost curves of the form shown above. Applying the same profit-maximising rule as before, we see that the equilibrium output is Q, which is sold at price P. In this situation the monopolist makes supernormal (monopoly) profits $TRPZ$. But since there are barriers to the entry of new producers these supernormal profits can persist in the long run. (If there are no barriers to entry the monopoly is likely to be temporary.)

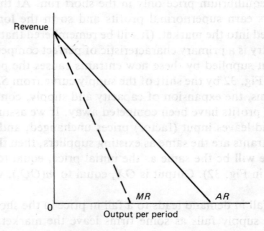

Fig. 33. *Average and marginal revenue curves.*

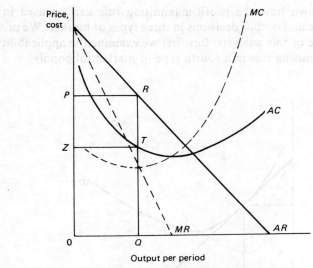

Fig. 34. *Profit maximisation in monopoly.*

MONOPOLISTIC COMPETITION

In monopolistic competition each firm supplies a product that—in the eyes of the consumer—is differentiated from similar products supplied by competitors. The basis of product differentiation may be the quality of the product, its styling, a brand name, etc. Whatever the basis, since the competing products are not seen as identical, one producer can raise its price above those of competitors without losing all its sales, as it would in perfect competition. In other words the firm's demand curve is downward sloping, not horizontal.

The firm's short-run equilibrium is similar to that of the monopolist. We can illustrate this by reference to Fig. 34, although the existence of (imperfect) substitutes, of alternative brands, means that the demand curve of the firm is likely to be more elastic in monopolistic competition than in monopoly.

We showed above that the monopolist continues to earn supernormal profits in the long run, i.e. Fig. 34 applies to both short and long run. In monopolistic competition, on the other hand, the existence of supernormal profits induces new firms to enter the market and existing firms to modify their product offerings. Some customers transfer from the firm with supernormal profits to other firms, causing the first firm's demand curve to shift to the left. This process continues until the supernormal profits have been competed away.[2] The long-run equilibrium position, with price P_E and output Q_E, is shown in Fig. 35.

2. Chamberlin recognised the possibility that some firms might continue to earn supernormal profits in the long run.

We have shown how the profit-maximising rule can be used in the analysis of price and output decisions in three types of market. We present below a critique of this analysis. But first we examine the applicability of the profit-maximising rule in a fourth type of market, oligopoly.

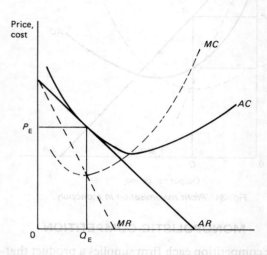

Fig. 35. *Long-run equilibrium in monopolistic competition.*

OLIGOPOLY

As noted above, the primary characteristic of oligopoly is that a large (perhaps a 100 per cent) share of the market is accounted for by a few large suppliers. This is said to result in a degree of interdependence among suppliers different from that in other types of market. In perfect and monopolistic competition interdependence exists as part of the generalised market relationships, but producers do not take into account the possible reactions of particular competitors. Each producer attempts to maximise short-run profits. In monopoly, since there is a single producer, interdependence is ruled out by definition.

By contrast, in oligopolistic markets each producer has so large a share of the market that it cannot ignore the reactions of competitors to its actions. (This is especially important when the products are homogeneous.) These reactions are subject to considerable uncertainty, and the introduction of uncertainty into the analysis is another feature that distinguishes the oligopoly model from the others.

The assumption underlying the basic oligopoly model is that each producer believes that competitors would not match an upward price-change but would match a downward change. It follows that each producer sees its demand curve as being highly elastic for upward price-changes and inelastic (mirroring the market demand curve) for downward price-changes. This is shown in Fig. 36, where the demand curve has a kink at the existing price P.

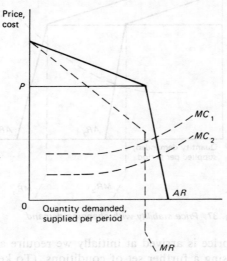

Fig. 36. *The kinked demand curve.*

An important feature of the kinked demand curve is the discontinuity in the marginal-revenue curve. This discontinuity means that a given price is consistent with a range of cost conditions. For example, P would be the profit-maximising price if marginal cost was MC_1 or MC_2. This fact is used to support the hypothesis that prices tend to be more "sticky", less responsive to changes in costs, in oligopolistic than in other markets.[3]

In Fig. 37 a fall in demand is shown by the shift to the left of the average and marginal revenue curves. The marginal cost curve continues to cut the marginal revenue curve in the region of the discontinuity, suggesting that prices will be sticky in the face of changes in demand.

The conclusion drawn from this is that oligopolists usually engage not in price competition, but in various forms of non-price competition: advertising, product development etc. (This can apply, of course, only to differentiated oligopolies.)

In the basic oligopoly model presented above, the decision rule for maximising profits—set output at the point where marginal cost equals marginal revenue—explains why prices tend to be sticky. In order to

---

3. The empirical support for this hypothesis is not strong. Stigler has shown that prices tend to be less sticky in oligopoly than in monopoly (G. J. Stigler. "The Kinky Oligopoly Demand Curve and Rigid Prices". *Journal of Political Economy* Vol 55 (1947)). Moreover, Stigler and Kindahl showed that transactions prices are much less sticky than the list prices which have been used in many other studies (G. J. Stigler and J. K. Kindahl. *The Behaviour of Industrial Prices.* Columbia UP, New York, 1970). For a further discussion of empirical evidence and theory see: G. C. Reid. *The Kinked Demand Curve Analysis of Oligopoly.* Edinburgh UP, 1981.

III. MODELS

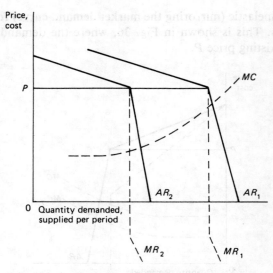

Fig. 37. *Price stability with changing demand.*

explain how the price is arrived at initially we require a more elaborate model, encompassing a further set of conditions. (To keep the model as simple as possible we assume that there are only two producers.)

Figure 38 refers to a market in which the two producers supply an undifferentiated product. The producers have identical cost structures and perfect knowledge of cost and demand conditions. Given these conditions

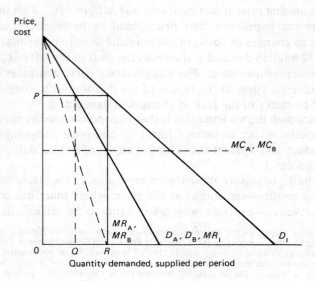

Fig. 38. *Profit maximisation in oligopoly.*

and the assumption that both producers are rational profit maximisers, it can be shown that price and output will be the same as under monopoly.

D_I is the industry demand curve. Since the product is undifferentiated it is reasonable to assume that the two individual demand curves, D_A and D_B, are identical. (These demand curves also coincide with the industry marginal revenue curve MR_I.) Each supplier produces Q, where its marginal cost equals marginal revenue. At the combined output R, industry marginal cost and revenue are equal. A monopolist would produce R for sale at price P.

The importance in this model of perfect knowledge is clear. Each producer is able to identify the joint-profit-maximising position. Moreover he knows that his competitor is also able to do so. Consequently each producer chooses the price–output combination that maximises joint profits, believing that the other will also do so.

The dependence of the solution on the other assumptions can be shown by relaxing these assumptions. For example Fig. 39 illustrates an industry in which the producers have different cost structures. (To simplify the analysis we retain the assumption of undifferentiated products and, consequently, of market shares that are intitially equal.) D_A and D_B—and also the industry marginal revenue curve MR_I—coincide. In this situation B would prefer a higher price and a lower output than A.

There is nothing in the model that allows us to predict what will happen in this situation. One possibility is that the firms might agree to set a price which would maximise joint profits. But it seems more likely, especially when price agreements are illegal or difficult to sustain, as in the UK, that A would set the price that would maximise its own profits.

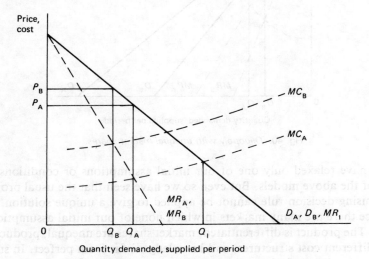

Fig. 39. *Oligopoly with different cost structures.*

Further analysis must be conjectural and is complex. The demand curves D_A and D_B are drawn on the assumption of identical prices. So if prices P_A and P_B were set, the demand curves would shift, the limiting case being where all customers of B transfer to A. A's marginal-revenue curve would become MR_1 and it would produce Q_1. However there is no reason to think that B would allow this process to occur. It is more likely that it would follow A's lead, set price P_A and produce Q_A. In other words it would not adopt the decision rule adopted in all the models considered previously.

Finally let us consider a situation in which equal prices result in unequal market shares (Fig. 40). This could be due to product differentiation (relaxing another of the previous assumptions), but it could also be due to differences in capacity, arising from the respective histories of the firms. Given the shape of the marginal cost curve, B would prefer a lower price than A. On the other hand if the marginal cost curve sloped down, A would prefer a lower price than B. In either instance further analysis again becomes conjectural. Only if marginal cost is constant would the profit-maximising prices be identical.

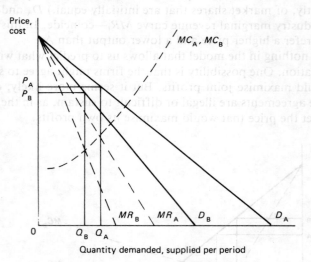

Fig. 40. *Oligopoly with unequal market shares.*

We have relaxed only one of our initial assumptions or conditions in each of the above models. But even so we have seen that the usual profit-maximising decision rule cannot be applied to give a unique solution. In practice there are many markets in which none of our initial assumptions holds. The product is differentiated, market shares are unequal, producers have different cost structures, and knowledge is far from perfect. In such situations unique solutions are even less easy to find.

The same point applies to other models such as the limit-pricing model and models incorporating game theory. It is possible to arrive at a determinate solution by assuming a certain pattern of actions and reactions on the part of the various "actors". But there is no guarantee that the actors would not follow a path different from that specified.

MARKET MODELS AND THE FIRM

We said in the introduction to this chapter that the behaviour and performance of a firm is conditioned by the type of market that it supplies. The most obvious point to emerge under the performance heading is the earning of higher profits (rate of return) in monopoly than in perfect competition, with monopolistic competition as the intermediate case. If monopolisation had no effect on cost conditions we could deduce that price would be higher, and output (and hence resource utilisation) lower, than in perfect competition. However we cannot make such a deduction since economies of scale are likely to mean that costs are lower in monopoly than in perfect competition.

Some economists would claim that product differentiation, especially when due to advertising, is undesirable, implying that perfectly competitive firms have the better performance. (Product differentiation is sometimes deemed to be a performance and sometimes a behaviour variable.) On the other hand there is a strong argument to the effect that product differentiation widens consumer choice. Consumer choice is also widened by the technical progress which is inhibited by the conditions pertaining in perfect competition, and especially by perfect knowledge and an absence of barriers to entry.[4]

Turning to behaviour, the profit-maximising rule, that output should be set at the point where marginal cost equals marginal revenue, is incorporated in all the models. However it "explains" behaviour far less well in oligopoly than in other models. Indeed it is often claimed that there is no satisfactory theory of oligopoly, a serious matter in view of the widespread existence of oligopolistic markets.

In view of the number of references in this chapter to individual firms, it might be thought that these models of markets would provide a great deal of insight into the behaviour of firms in practice. However it has been said that " 'the firm' as understood in the real world plays virtually no role in the theory, which is in reality a theory of supply. Supply is produced by firms, and the theory is consequently designated as the theory of the firm and is immediately thrown into conflict with reality."[5] Commenting on the development of theories of imperfect competition, Professor O'Brien

---

4. *See*, for example: G. B. Richardson. *Information and Investment*. Oxford UP, 1960.

5. R. Jones. *Supply in a Market Economy*. George Allen and Unwin, 1976, p. 73.

has said: "Marshall held that there is no substitute for a good knowledge of firms; the Cambridge economists of the 1930s almost seem to have adopted the view that it was *irrelevant*."[6]

But the fact that the models we have considered in this chapter are not meant to be applied to the operations of firms "in the real world" does not mean that they provide *no* insight concerning the operations of such firms. Indeed in the next two chapters, in which we present a series of models that are closer to reality, we demonstrate the significance of product differentiation, barriers to entry, the number of suppliers, and marginal or incremental analysis, all of which appear in one or other of the models presented above.

QUESTIONS

1. Say whether each of the following statements is true or false:

   (*a*) There are a large number of producers in both perfect competition and monopolistic competition.

   (*b*) Average revenue equals marginal revenue in both perfect competition and monopolistic competition.

   (*c*) Monopoly can be either homogeneous or differentiated.

   (*d*) Short-run profits are maximised when marginal cost equals marginal revenue only in perfect competition.

   (*e*) If price falls below minimum average total cost the firm would minimise its short-run losses by closing down.

   (*f*) In the short run suppliers can earn supernormal profits in both perfect competition and monopoly.

   (*g*) In perfect competition a firm's short-run supply curve is the portion of its marginal-cost curve that lies above its marginal-revenue curve.

   (*h*) Market demand and the firm's demand are identical in oligopoly.

   (*i*) Monopolistic competition refers to a situation in which a few suppliers account for a large share of the market.

   (*j*) The assumption underlying the basic oligopoly model is that each producer believes that competitors would match an upward but not a downward price change.

2. Explain the relationship between declining marginal product and the shape of short-run cost curves.

3. Explain, using diagrams and carefully stating your assumptions, how (*a*) short-run, (*b*) long-run market supply curves are derived.

4. Why does a change in demand have a bigger impact on price in the short run than in the long run?

---

6. D. P. O'Brien. "The Evolution of the Theory of the Firm". Unpublished: presented at an SSRC conference in Economics and Work Organisation, York University, 1982.

5. Explain the significance of the statement that in the long run all costs are variable.

6. Discuss the relationship between barriers to entry and profits.

7. Explain why the demand curve for an oligopolist might have a kink at the existing price, and discuss the implications.

8. Under what conditions will price and output be the same in oligopoly as in monopoly?

9. Discuss the importance of perfect knowledge in models of the firm.

10. How satisfactory do you consider the theory of the firm to be, given that "the firm as understood in the real world plays virtually no role in the theory"?

CHAPTER EIGHT

Models of the Firm

OBJECTIVES

After studying this chapter the reader should be able to: show how assumptions regarding firms' objectives influence models of firms' behaviour; explain the significance of the divorce between ownership and control; distinguish between models incorporating maximising and satisficing behaviour.

INTRODUCTION

The models presented in the previous chapter incorporated the assumption that firms always act so as to maximise their short-run profits. This assumption has been criticised on two main grounds.

First, it is pointed out that firms operate in a world of uncertainty and so are unable to identify the price–output combination that would maximise profits.[1] If we wish to maintain the assumption of profit maximisation, it must be in terms of subjective estimates of cost and revenue. In other words the firm takes decisions in the light of *its perceptions* of the likely behaviour of cost and revenue.

Modifying our assumption in this way means that the conclusions derived from the models also have to be modified, since different firms may have different perceptions of a given situation. For example the earning of supernormal profits will not necessarily lead to new entry into an industry since other firms may not perceive these profits.

Second, it is argued that even if firms were able to identify the price–output combination that would maximise short-run profits, they would be unlikely to choose that combination, since short-run profit maximisation is not a common objective. In order to assess the validity of this criticism we review in the following sections the alternative objectives that have been proposed. We first consider two contrasting views of the firm, and then examine a number of models incorporating one or other of these views.

FIRMS' OBJECTIVES

We can discuss firms' objectives from two quite different standpoints. First, we can take as our starting point the assumption that the firm is an entity with, as it were, a collective mind and will. This enables us to see the firm as having a single objective. For example we have seen that the objective posited by traditional neo-classical theory is the maximisation of profits during the current period or short run. More advanced theory recognises that firms may attempt to maximise their long-run profits or,

---

1. We saw that oligopoly models become indeterminate under uncertainty.

more precisely, the present value of the future stream of profits, suitably discounted. This view of the firm as an entity with a collective mind makes most sense when the firm is small and run by its owners.

The alternative starting point is the recognition that in many instances the firm is composed of people with differing objectives. An important aspect of this situation is the divorce between ownership and control. A number of writers have shown that the typical large company is run by people who hold only a small proportion of the shares. Florence found that in a sample of 102 large firms in the UK the proportion of voting shares in the hands of the directors was only 3 per cent in 1936 and that this had fallen to only 1½ per cent by 1951.[2] Prais found that in 1972 in only 11 of the largest 100 UK manufacturing firms did directors own more than 10 per cent of the shares while in 73 they owned less than 2 per cent.[3]

Despite this (partial) divorce between ownership and control, directors (and senior managers) continue to give close attention to the impact of their decisions on the firm's profitability. Even holding a small percentage of the total shares in a large company may mean that dividend payments (linked to the company's profitability) constitute an appreciable proportion of the directors' and managers' income. Moreover, even though the shareholders may not be in a position to evaluate the firm's performance precisely (if only because they are not aware of the opportunities missed by the firm), directors and managers of a firm which earns poor profits are in danger of losing their jobs. (This may happen because of action taken by the shareholders or because lower profits lead to a fall in the share price and hence leave the firm vulnerable to a takeover bid.) Finally the directors' non-monetary or "psychic" income will increase with the firm's profitability. Although profit is a dirty word to some members of the community, there is in general more prestige to be gained by presiding over a profitable than an unprofitable company.

However, although attention is still given to profitability, the divorce between ownership and control does mean that directors can take some decisions which are of benefit primarily to themselves rather than to the shareholders. If they gain prestige or satisfaction from running a large organisation they may pursue growth for its own sake. In order to avoid conflict with trades unions they may concede high wage claims. If they put a high value on leisure activities they may take an extended lunch hour or spend considerable time on the golf course. (Such activities may also be undertaken by owner-managers.)

There is a second feature of large firms that can lead to a diversity of objectives, namely the division of the firm into a number of functional departments, each with a high degree of responsibility and autonomy. Consider for example the situation that might arise in a pharmaceutical

---

2. P. S. Florence. *Ownership, Control and Success of Large Companies.* Sweet and Maxwell, 1961.
3. S. J. Prais. *The Evolution of Giant Firms in Britain. NIESR, 1976.*

company following the discovery by the research and development department of a new drug. The R&D department would wish to see the product introduced on to the market because it would provide evidence of their usefulness to the company and would enhance their standing in the eyes of the scientific community. The marketing department would also welcome its introduction if it believed that the drug would give it an edge over competitors; otherwise it might resent the additional effort involved in introducing the drug. The production department might also prefer not to have to rearrange production schedules to accommodate the new product.

One could take the view that personnel in all departments should willingly accept any additional effort or inconvenience if it is for the good of the firm as a whole, and very often they do so. But one must recognise that people are often motivated by self-interest and frequently act in a way that may not be best for the firm as a whole. (One should bear in mind the widespread existence of uncertainty as noted earlier. Since no one can be sure that the introduction of the new drug would benefit the firm, negative reactions can be more easily understood.)

Two major alternative lines of analysis have followed from the recognition of the diversity of objectives and motives. Mainstream economists have generally continued to work with models which incorporate the maximisation of one variable or another. Many models assume long-run profit maximisation. Baumol's sales maximisation model assumes that the firm attempts to maximise sales revenue provided that profits are above a certain minimum level.[4] Williamson has constructed a model based on the maximisation of managerial utility, which is said to depend upon monetary income, the number and quality of staff controlled, control over investment funds, and perquisites such as company cars and lavish offices.[5] Marris's model is based on the assumption that firms attempt to maximise growth.[6]

Although these models take account of a wider range of factors than profit-maximising models, they still assume that the firm as a single entity, or the directors and senior managers acting as a coherent group, consistently follow a given objective. Quite a different model is adopted in the behavioural theory of the firm.[7] At the centre of this theory is the proposition that over time the firm has to satisfy five main objectives or goals. In certain circumstances the firm may not be able to achieve all its objectives at any given point in time. It will then seek to cope with the resulting conflict by paying particular attention first to one goal and then to another. This may be the only way in which the firm can continue to

4. W. J. Baumol. *Business Behaviour, Value and Growth*. Harcourt Brace Jovanovich, New York, 1967.

5. O. E. Williamson. *The Economics of Discretionary Behaviour*. Prentice-Hall, Englewood Cliffs, 1964.

6. R. Marris. *The Economic Theory of Managerial Capitalism*. Macmillan, London, 1966.

7. R M. Cyert and J. G. March. *A Behavioural Theory of the Firm*. Prentice-Hall, Englewood Cliff, 1963.

operate, given the conflicting desires of its members (managers, workers, shareholders, etc.).

Having indicated the range of possible objectives, and having outlined the models which incorporate alternative objectives, we now examine these models in detail.

LONG-RUN PROFIT MAXIMISATION[8]

The time horizon of most firms extends beyond the current period, and most firms consider the effect of future policies on future profitability. A firm may set a price lower than required to maximise current profits if it believes that this lower price will deter potential new entrants and so enable it to earn higher profits in the future. A firm may invest—in new machinery, in the development of a new product, in an advertising campaign etc.—in the expectation that this expenditure will depress current profits but will yield higher profits in the future.

In balancing the short-term and long-term consequences of its policies the firm must take account of the fact that today's profit is worth more than an identical sum earned tomorrow. In fact the firm is assumed to maximise the present value of the future stream of profits, suitably discounted. While this reformulation makes the model more realistic than the short-run profit-maximising model, it also raises additional questions.

First, how can the firm predict the effect of its current actions on future opportunities? (We outlined in earlier chapters some of the methods adopted by firms in practice, but these serve to reduce, not eliminate, uncertainty.) Second, how can the firm identify the discount factor to be applied to future profits? The cost of capital to the firm may be taken as the basis for the discount factor, but this cost may change substantially over time.

Another criticism of the basic model follows from the argument that accounting cost (used in the model) is a less appropriate measure than opportunity cost. This means that the true profit-maximising position may not be that derived from accounting data. This argument has very wide-ranging implications, since part of the opportunity cost of a given action (say, increasing output) may be forgone leisure, defined to include both time spent away from work and work done with less than 100 per cent effort. The directors of a firm may substitute leisure for profit, thus taking the firm away from the (accounting) profit-maximising position.

Costs and competition

These ideas have been incorporated in the concepts of organisational slack and X-inefficiency. Organisational slack, an important element in the behavioural theory of the firm (*see* below), is defined as the difference

---

8. Long-run profit maximisation is discussed only briefly here, since it is an important aspect of the models considered in Chapter 9.

between the resources available (used) and those necessary to meet the current demands of members of the firm; in other words the difference between acceptable and maximum or optimum performance. X-inefficiency, a concept first developed by Leibenstein, is the difference between actual cost and minimum attainable cost.[9]

There are many reasons why actual cost may deviate from the minimum attainable. Leibenstein emphasises the fact that effort is discretionary, i.e. the employees can decide—within limits—how hard he will work. The employee will take this decision in pursuit of his own objectives, which may not coincide with those of his employer. Moreover, effort is required in order to change the allocation of resources; inertia may prevent or inhibit a move to an optimum allocation.

Both organisational slack and X-inefficiency imply that the (accounting) cost curve lies above the minimum-attainable-cost curve. Firms are able to survive, despite the divergence between minimum and actual cost, because of the weak state of competition in the market.

MODELS INCORPORATING THE MAXIMISATION OF OTHER VARIABLES

It is not only a desire for increased leisure that might take the firm away from the profit-maximising position. Other important motivating factors are salary, status, power and security, factors which it has been argued lead to a desire for large size. There is strong evidence to suggest that a firm's growth will yield the directors increased salary, status, power and security,[10] and we consider in the following sections models which take account of these factors. However it is by no means clear that directors and senior managers achieve these benefits from growth which is achieved at the expense of profits.

A sales-revenue-maximisation model

This model,[11] first proposed by Baumol, can be illustrated with reference to Fig. 41. Output is measured on the horizontal axis, and revenue, cost and profit at each level of output on the vertical axis. The difference between total revenue, R, and total cost, C, is profit, PR. The profit-maximising output is Q, where total revenue exceeds total cost by the greatest amount. (This is also, of course, the point at which marginal cost equals marginal revenue; this is shown by the fact that the gradients of curves R and C are equal at that point.)

---

9. H. Leibenstein. "Allocative Efficiency *v*. X-Efficiency". *American Economic Review* Vol. 56 (1966); "Microeconomics and X-Efficiency Theory" in: D. Bell and I. Kristol (eds). *The Crisis in Economic Theory*. Basic Books, New York, 1981, p. 100.

10. The evidence is reviewed in: Hay and Morris, *Op. cit.*, p. 259 ff.

11. The predictions of the sales-revenue-maximising model are summarised in: K. Heidensohn and N. Robinson. *Business Behaviour*. P. Allan, Dedington, 1974, p. 78 ff.

8. MODELS OF THE FIRM

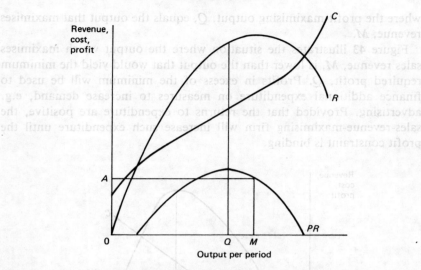

Fig. 41. *Sales revenue maximisation subject to a profit constraint.*

The sales maximiser will increase output beyond the profit-maximising level, Q, until he runs up against the minimum-profit constraint A. (The level of minimum acceptable profit depends upon the rewards required to satisfy shareholders.) He will therefore choose output M.

Shepherd has pointed out that if there is a kink in the demand curve, as assumed in the basic oligopoly model, the sales-revenue-maximising and profit-maximising outputs may coincide.[12] This is illustrated in Fig. 42,

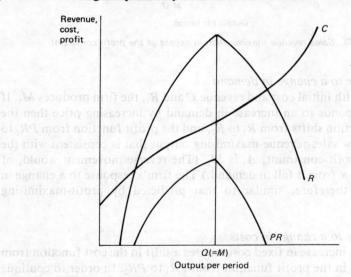

Fig. 42. *Profit and Sales revenue maximisation.*

12. W. G. Shepherd, "On Sales Maximizing and Oligopoly Behaviour". *Economica* Vol. 9 (1962).

where the profit-maximising output, Q, equals the output that maximises revenue, M.

Figure 43 illustrates the situation where the output which maximises sales revenue, M, is lower than the output that would yield the minimum required profit, Q. Profits in excess of the minimum will be used to finance additional expenditure on measures to increase demand, e.g. advertising. Provided that the returns to expenditure are positive, the sales-revenue-maximising firm will increase such expenditure until the profit constraint is binding.

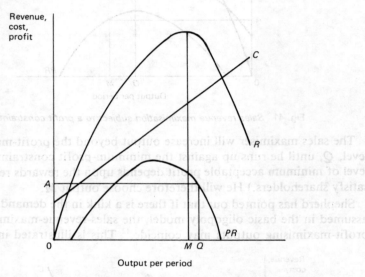

Fig. 43. *Sales revenue maximisation in excess of the profit constraint.*

The response to a change in demand

In Fig. 44, with initial cost and revenue C and R_1, the firm produces M_1. If the firm responds to an increase in demand by increasing price then the revenue function shifts from R_1 to R_2, and the profit function from PR_1 to PR_2. The new sales-revenue-maximising output that is consistent with the minimum profit constraint, A, is M_2. (The reverse movement would, of course, follow from a fall in demand.) The firm's response to a change in demand is, therefore, similar to that predicted by profit-maximising models.

The response to a change in costs

In Fig. 45 an increase in fixed costs causes a shift in the cost function from C_1 to C_2 and in the profit function from PR_1 to PR_2. In order to continue to earn the minimum profit required, A, output must be reduced from M_1 to M_2. With a downward sloping demand curve, this implies an increase in

8. MODELS OF THE FIRM

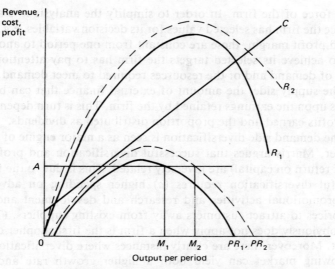

Fig. 44. *Sales revenue maximisation with a change in demand.*

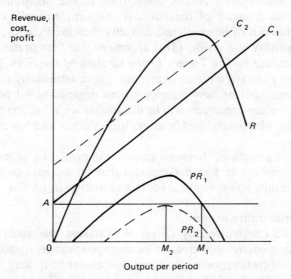

Fig. 45. *Sales revenue maximisation with a change in fixed cost.*

price. This response is *not* the same as those profit-maximising models which assume that output changes only in response to a change in variable, and hence marginal, cost. (Both types of model yield similar predictions following a change in variable cost.)

A growth model
In the model first proposed by Robin Marris growth is seen as the prime

driving force of the firm. In order to simplify the analysis it is assumed that once the firm has selected values for its decision variables, e.g. growth rate and profit margin, these are constant from one period to another. In order to achieve its selected targets the firm has to pay attention to the growth of demand and of the resources required to meet demand.

On the supply side, the amount of external finance that can be raised depends upon the earnings retained by the firm. This is turn depends upon total profits earned and the proportion distributed as dividends.

On the demand side diversification is seen as a major engine of growth. However, Marris argues that successful diversification and profitability (rate of return on capital) are inversely related. This is due to the fact that successful diversification requires (*a*) higher spending on advertising, other promotional activities and research and development and/or (*b*) lower prices to attract customers away from existing suppliers. (This last factor obviously does not apply when a firm is the first supplier of a new product. Moreover there are clearly instances where diversification into a fast-growing market can yield both a higher growth rate and higher profitability, at least for some time.)

There is also a limit at any given time to the decision-making and organisational capacity of the firm. If the firm embarks on a rate of diversification out of line with this capacity then inefficiency, higher costs and lower profits will result. (This argument was first presented in detail by Edith Penrose in *The Theory of the Growth of the Firm*, published in 1959.) If the firm attempts to overcome this constraint by increasing the rate of recruitment of new managers then organisational problems will arise, since the new managers will be unfamiliar with the firm's procedures and routines. Managerial inefficiency, higher costs and lower profits will again result.

The idea of a trade-off between growth and profits is, of course, similar to the presumption in Baumol's model that an increase in sales volume beyond a certain point would involve a reduction in profits.

A managerial utility model
In the model constructed by Oliver Williamson, the goals of the firm reflect the immediate objectives of its managers: monetary compensation, the number of staff reporting to a manager and their quality, control over investment of the firm's funds, and perquisites, such as lavish offices, in excess of those necessary for the firm's operations. Williamson's model concentrates on these individual objectives rather than on the goals of the firm as a whole, but it is likely that the growth of the firm would help these objectives to be met.

A behavioural theory of the firm
In the models discussed above the maximand (the variable maximised) differs from one model to another. Moreover, maximisation of one

variable is sometimes subject to a constraint relating to another variable. Nevertheless the principle of maximisation prevails. These models can therefore be contrasted with the behavioural theory of the firm, which is based on the assumption that firms "satisfice", i.e. their targets specify an acceptable, rather than an optimum (e.g. maximising), level of performance.

One reason for satisficing is managerial conflict. The various managers within a firm will have different views and objectives, and these objectives will often be incompatible. This conflict is resolved by a process of continuous bargaining, the outcome being that the firm does not attempt to maximise any variable. Rather, it seeks an acceptable level of performance in terms of several goals. These are:

(a) a production goal: production should not fluctuate too much, nor fall below an acceptable level;

(b) an inventory goal: the level of inventory (stocks) should not fall below a certain minimum figure;

(c) a sales goal: sales should be maintained or expanded;

(d) a market-share goal (may be an alternative to the sales goal);

(e) a profit goal: sufficient profit should be earned to provide satisfactory dividends for shareholders and sufficient resources for the expansion of the firm.

It is clear that these various goals may not always be compatible. For example an increase in price, required if the profit goal is to be achieved, may lead to a failure to achieve the target volume of sales or market share.

The fact that objectives may be incompatible is also incorporated in some of the models considered earlier. Baumol's model recognises that the firm will seek to maximise sales revenue only up to a certain point (minimum acceptable profit). In Williamson's model the managerial utility function (the variable maximised) comprises several elements (none of which may individually be maximised). But there is an important difference in that the behavioural theory sees the individual managers, as well as the firm as a whole, as indulging in satisficing behaviour, i.e. objectives are set in terms of an acceptable rather than an optimum level of performance. Actual performance may exceed this acceptable level with respect to some goals. Consequently, if action has to be taken to get back on target in terms of one goal, it does not follow that this will cause the firm to fail to meet other goals. To return to the previous example, if the volume of sales is well ahead of target, a price increase designed to raise profits may still leave sales at an acceptable level.

Moreover, firms often operate with a certain degree of organisational slack (defined as the difference between the resources available (used) and those necessary to meet the organisation's goals). When performance is unsatisfactory with respect to one goal some of the slack will be taken up in order to get back on target. So as an alternative to raising prices in order to increase profits it may be possible to lower costs by reducing manning levels, cutting back on expenses etc.

Two other aspects of the behavioural theory should be mentioned. First, it acknowledges the widespread existence of uncertainty, which the other models tend to ignore. Second, it emphasises learning. If a firm succeeds in comfortably achieving a target, it will probably raise its aspiration level, i.e. set a higher target in the succeeding year. Learning can also work in the opposite direction; a failure to achieve a target in one year may lead to a lowering of the aspiration level. Learning also helps to increase the firm's efficiency and hence reduce its costs. When a decision has to be made for the first time it will involve a considerable amount of time. Subsequently, as experience is gained with this type of decision, the decision process will be reduced to a routine, less costly, operation.

EQUILIBRIUM

One of the major factors distinguishing some of the models discussed above from others is the significance attached to equilibrium. The term equilibrium denotes a situation of stability, an absence of any tendency towards change. In traditional, neo-classical economic theory a firm is said to be in equilibrium when it is maximising its profits. When it has reached this position it will, if possible, continue to produce the same output in succeeding periods and to sell that output at the same price.

There are a number of reasons why this traditional concept of equilibrium is not very helpful in an analysis of business decisions. It implies that the firm has a much greater degree of knowledge—both of its own cost and revenue conditions and of the activities of its rivals—than is the case. In other words it assumes that firms can accurately predict the consequences of their actions, whereas in practice firms operate in a highly uncertain environment.

Moreover, the traditional theory ignores the fact that firms learn from their experience. Learning means that a firm would not necessarily take the same decision as previously when faced by the same situation. For example if a price increase led to a much bigger loss of sales than was expected, the firm would probably not increase its price if a similar situation arose. (As noted above neo-classical theory need not concern itself with learning, since it assumes perfect knowledge in every situation.)

Furthermore, even if things turn out as expected, learning often causes firms to adopt different policies from those adopted previously. Note the following example from the toothpaste market. In the mid-1970s several producers were considering whether to introduce a fluoride toothpaste. The majority decided not to do so, no doubt being influenced by the fact that the fluoride toothpastes introduced in the 1960s had not been well received by consumers and had been withdrawn. However, Procter and Gamble was the exception. It introduced Crest, backed with heavy promotional expenditure. Consumer attitudes towards fluoride proved to have changed over the previous decade, and Crest sold well. (It is now the fourth-largest-selling brand in the UK.) Other producers, realising that they should have introduced a fluoride toothpaste and devoted fewer resources to some non-fluoride brands, subsequently followed the lead set by Procter and Gamble.

Moreover, placing emphasis on the attainment of equilibrium gives a misleading impression of the quantity of resources that can be devoted to taking decisions. Decisions are, of course, taken at various levels of the firm. But major decisions, e.g. whether to introduce a new product or to try to break into a new market, are taken by a relatively few, highly paid senior executives.

The fact that only limited resources are available means that it is impossible to ensure that the best possible decision is always taken, that the best solution to every problem is found. Consequently it is sensible for senior executives to allocate their time so as to ensure, as far as possible, that they find a good solution to every problem.[13]

This point is so important that it is worth quoting a chief executive at some length: "I submit that most top policymakers, in dealing with the issues they must decide, do not pretend or necessarily desire to examine their decision until they conclusively find the best answer. [They] are much more inclined to generate numerous options, consider the pros and cons, eliminate poor alternatives, narrow the list to two or three acceptable answers and then allow intuition, judgement, experience, savvy, executive feel or any other words you wish to use, to make the final selection." And again: "We are content to know that we have found a good solution, and we rely on implementation to make it work. This is preferable to being continuously in pursuit of the one best solution, and hence incurring the opportunity costs of not being able to give our attention to other needy projects."[14]

In the same article Dr Beesley emphasises the importance of flexibility (this importance deriving, of course, from the existence of uncertainty): "I cannot stress strongly enough to you how important it is to management to preserve flexibility for the future. It is not enough to say that, if other things are equal, a manager would choose the flexible option. It is not even close. For example I would prefer an option with a 15 per cent return and with flexibility to an option with a 20 per cent return without flexibility—and maybe to an even higher return."

As an illustration of this precept consider a firm which has to decide how much additional capacity (machinery etc.) to install in order to meet an

---

13. It is sometimes argued that a firm should increase the resources devoted to decision taking until the marginal cost equals the marginal return. But by definition the marginal return cannot be known in advance.

14. W. H. Beesley (President and Chief Executive Officer, Velsicol Chemical Corp, USA). "Can Managerial Economics Aid the Chief Executive Officer?" *Managerial and Decision Economics* Vol. 2 (1981).

increased demand for one of its products. It estimates that if its competitors' policies remain unchanged it will be able to sell 100,000 units a year. Installing just enough machinery to supply this demand would yield a return of 20 per cent. If more machinery than this was installed and 100,000 units were sold the return would be only 15 per cent. However, installing additional machinery would enable the firm to meet demand should it turn out to be higher than expected. This might happen if, for example, competitors are unable to satisfy the demand from their usual customers who then seek alternative suppliers.

In this situation greater flexibility might also be obtained by installing general-purpose machinery rather than less-expensive specialised machinery dedicated to the production of only a single product. If demand turns out as expected the return will be higher on the specialised machinery. But if demand is lower than expected the general-purpose machinery can be used in the production of other products.

QUESTIONS

1. Discuss the implications for company policy of the divorce between ownership and control.

2. Explain why firms may attempt to maximise long-run profits, and discuss the problems that can arise in trying to operationalise this objective.

3. Compare the predictions yielded by the profit-maximising and sales-revenue-maximising models.

4. "The more realistic the model of the firm the fewer useful predictions it yields." Discuss.

5. "Any theory of the firm that fails to take account of learning is inadequate." Discuss.

6. Explain the statement that the traditional concept of equilibrium is not very helpful in an analysis of business decisions.

7. In the light of the following statements, made by representatives of various companies, discuss the objectives of firms.

"The goal of the organisation must be this—to make a better and better product to be sold at a lower and lower price. Profit cannot be the goal. Profit must be a by-product. This is a state of mind and a philosophy. Actually an organisation doing this job as it can be done will make large profits that must be properly divided between user, worker, and stockholder." (Lincoln Electric Co.)

"If we were to isolate the one factor, above all others, that transformed the tiny company of 1902 into the industrial giant of 1952, while hundreds of competitors failed and are forgotten, I should say that it has been Texaco's settled policy of thinking first of quality of product and service to the customer, and only second of the size of its profit. . . . In a highly competitive industry such as ours, the highest rewards are reserved for those who render the greatest service." (The Texas Co.)

"To make and sell quality products competitively and to perform those functions at the lowest attainable cost consistent with sound management policies, so as to return an adequate profit after taxes for services rendered." (US Steel Corp.)

"Everyone in the factory knows the customer by name and the word goes round, 'Sam needs those cuff-links tonight.' There's a feeling of personal involvement that you don't get with a larger firm." (Small jewellery manufacturer.)

8. A company is considering whether to increase the number of varieties of its main product. Simulate a board meeting attended by the chairman, marketing director, production director and finance director.

9. Items (*a*) to (*n*) each contain five options (*i*) to (*v*). Indicate which of the options is correct.

(*a*) Which of the following *cannot* be true? In the short-run, as output falls a fall occurs in:
   (*i*)   average total cost;
   (*ii*) average variable cost;
   (*iii*) average fixed cost;
   (*iv*) marginal cost;
   (*v*)   opportunity cost.

(*b*) If, as output increases, the short-run average variable cost rises, it must be true that:
   (*i*)   average total cost rises;
   (*ii*) average fixed cost rises;
   (*iii*) marginal cost is greater than average fixed cost;
   (*iv*) marginal cost is greater than average variable cost;
   (*v*)   average variable cost is greater than average fixed cost.

(*c*) The supply curve of a firm in a perfectly competitive industry is:
   (*i*)   its average cost curve;
   (*ii*) its average variable cost curve;
   (*iii*) that portion of its average variable cost curve lying above its marginal cost curve;
   (*iv*) its marginal cost curve;
   (*v*)   that portion of its marginal cost curve lying above its average-variable-cost curve.

(*d*) The best explanation of the fact that the short-run supply curve of a perfectly competitive firm slopes upward is that in the short run:
   (*i*)   as the firm increases output it must pay more for its factors of production;
   (*ii*) an increase in output can be obtained only by using additional capital equipment;
   (*iii*) one factor of production is fixed, and returns to the variable factors diminish as more of these factors are employed;

(iv) the perfectly competitive firm is in equilibrium where average cost is at a minimum;
(v) since marginal revenue is constant, equilibrium can be achieved only where marginal cost is rising.

(e) A firm that wishes to maximise its short-run profits will cease production if there is no output at which:
(i) total revenue exceeds total variable plus fixed cost;
(ii) marginal revenue exceeds average cost;
(iii) average revenue exceeds average total cost;
(iv) average revenue exceeds average fixed cost;
(v) average revenue exceeds average variable cost.

(f) Which of the following applies to the short-run equilibrium in both perfect competition and monopoly?
(i) Average cost equals average revenue.
(ii) Average revenue equals marginal revenue.
(iii) Average revenue exceeds marginal revenue.
(iv) Marginal cost equals average revenue.
(v) Marginal cost equals marginal revenue.

(g) A firm is in long-run equilibrium, and the conditions in the market are as follows: average revenue exceeds average cost, average revenue exceeds marginal revenue, average cost exceeds marginal cost. The market is one of:
(i) perfect competition;
(ii) monopolistic competition;
(iii) monopoly;
(iv) homogeneous oligopoly;
(v) differentiated oligopoly.

(h) The hypothesis that the marginal productivity of labour eventually declines is based on the assumption that:
(i) the average productivity of labour eventually declines;
(ii) as the cost of labour increases, firms substitute capital for labour;
(iii) the quantity of at least one factor of production, other than labour, is fixed;
(iv) a firm will employ the most efficient workers first;
(v) the efficiency of workers declines as they become tired.

(i) Current assets include all of the following *except*
(i) factories;
(ii) work in progress;
(iii) short-term loans to debtors;
(iv) stocks;
(v) cash balances.

(j) A company can obtain additional finance by all of the following *except*:
(i) a public issue by prospectus;

 (*ii*) an offer for sale;
 (*iii*) a private placing;
 (*iv*) a scrip issue;
 (*v*) a rights issue.
 (*k*) A company's capital gearing ratio is:
 (*i*) debentures ÷ equity share capital;
 (*ii*) debentures ÷ (equity share capital + reserves);
 (*iii*) equity share capital ÷ reserves;
 (*iv*) (debentures + preference shares) ÷ equity share capital;
 (*v*) (debentures + preference shares) ÷ (equity share capital + reserves).

(*l*) Which method of demand forecasting is based on the assumption that the behaviour of the sales of a product in past periods is a useful guide to sales of that product in the future?
 (*i*) Extrapolation.
 (*ii*) Coincident indicators.
 (*iii*) Lagging indicators.
 (*iv*) Surveys of purchasers' intentions.
 (*v*) Test marketing.

(*m*) In which method of demand forecasting is feedback given to the participants?
 (*i*) Extrapolation.
 (*ii*) Test marketing.
 (*iii*) Multiple regression.
 (*iv*) Barometric techniques.
 (*v*) Delphi technique.

(*n*) "These non-analytic or less formalised approaches take account of a wide range of variables, economic, demographic, social, political, technological, and ecological." This statement can be best applied to:
 (*i*) simple regression analysis;
 (*ii*) multiple regression analysis;
 (*iii*) barometric techniques;
 (*iv*) scenario analysis;
 (*v*) extrapolation.

Items (*o*) to (*t*) each have three options, 1, 2 and 3. Answer
A if 1, 2 and 3 are correct
B if 1 and 2 only are correct
C if 2 and 3 only are correct
D if 1 only is correct
E if 3 only is correct

(*o*) If a monopolist, previously in equilibrium, were to reduce his price, this must lead to a fall in
1 marginal revenue
2 total revenue
3 total profit

(p) When costs rise as output increases in the short run, which of the following curves is/are intersected from below at its/their minimum point by the marginal cost curve? The average
1 fixed cost curve
2 variable cost curve
3 total cost curve

(q) Which of the following methods of investment appraisal take(s) account of the fact that money received today is worth more than money received next year?
1 DCF
2 Net present value
3 Book rate of return

(r) Time-series analysis assumes that sales can be analysed in terms of
1 the secular trend
2 cyclical movements
3 seasonal variations

(s) With an unchanged scale of organisation an increase in output must lead to a fall in
1 average fixed cost
2 average variable cost
3 average total cost

(t) A firm's internal cash-flow comprises
1 the proceeds of new equity issues
2 depreciation provisions
3 retained earnings

CHAPTER NINE
Price Takers and Price Makers

OBJECTIVES
After studying this chapter the reader should be able to: understand the relationship between the structure of a market and the pricing behaviour of the firms in that market; distinguish between price takers and price makers; explain the relationship between cost and price; show how a firm is likely to respond when demand is higher, or lower, than expected; list the factors which facilitate the co-ordination of price and output decisions; list the means by which producers may attempt to co-ordinate their price and output decisions.

INTRODUCTION

In Chapters 7 and 8 we examined numerous models of markets and firms. We now draw upon the analysis of both chapters in presenting a final set of models. The title of the chapter indicates that attention is focussed on firms' behaviour, especially with respect to the determination of price and output. But the structural features of markets also play an important role in the analysis.

PRICE TAKING IN OPEN MARKETS

An open market has the same structural features as a perfectly competitive market, namely a large number of suppliers of a homogeneous (undifferentiated) product, with insignificant barriers to the entry of new suppliers. Models of the two markets are also similar in that both assume that suppliers are price takers, i.e. they accept the going market price. However the models differ in their treatment of decisions on output.

As we showed in Chapter 7, the perfect-competition model assumes that the firm sets its output at the point at which marginal cost equals marginal revenue. (This gives rise to an upward sloping short-run supply curve.) But when we consider the markets that have the structural characteristics of perfect competition, such as foodstuffs, natural fibres and other agricultural products, we find that output decisions are typically made *before* market price is known. The initial decisions affecting output—the purchase of land, animals etc.—are made months or years before the date of supply. The final decisions on how much to supply may be made on a daily or weekly basis.

In many markets each producer decides to supply a given quantity and to sell that quantity at the best price obtainable. Given the supply S on a certain day, the price depends upon the demand. In Fig. 46 with demand D_1 producers obtain a price P_1. With demand D_2 price is P_2. The two curves might represent the demand for lettuces on two different days, the first warm and dry, the second cold and wet.

The reason why the producer accepts the best price, however unsatisfactory it may be, is that the alternative is often to throw away the product and thus obtain no revenue. (If an individual producer withdrew part of his supply from the market this would have a negligible influence on the price since each producer's supply represents a very small proportion of the total.)

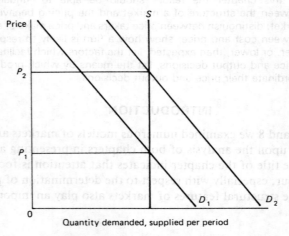

Fig. 46. *Price determination in an open market.*

Figure 46 is the basic model of price determination in an open market. Some open markets have particular features that require the basic model to be modified and extended in order to represent the behaviour of producers.

A floor price

Producers supplying goods to one market may make arrangements whereby these goods can be diverted to other markets if price in the primary market is unsatisfactory. Suppliers of meat or fish for human consumption may, as an alternative, sell it for conversion into pet food. Suppliers of fresh fruit to households may sell slightly less fresh fruit for jam manufacture.

In Fig. 47 P_F is the floor price, i.e. the guaranteed price in the alternative, secondary market. With demand D_1 the entire supply is sold in the primary market at price P_1. With demand D_2 price is P_F, $0Q$ being sold in the primary market and QM in the secondary market. Since the supplier is guaranteed an outlet in the secondary market the price will be lower than the expected average price in the primary market.

A floor price may also exist if producers are able to divert or reallocate supplies over time. If the product is not perishable, it may be withdrawn from the market and re-presented at a later date. At auction sales a reserve price is frequently attached to houses, furniture, paintings etc. (Such products are not, of course, homogeneous as assumed in the basic model.)

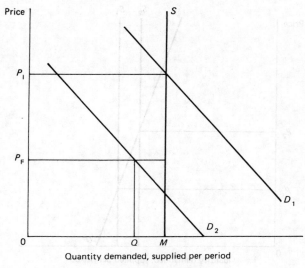

Fig. 47. *A floor price.*

The reserve price is determined by the price that the buyer expects to obtain and by the costs incurred in exit from and re-entry to the market.

The influence of cost on price in open markets

In the models discussed above no reference was made to the cost of production, in contrast to the role of cost in models of perfect competition. Cost is an important influence on price in open markets, but the influence is indirect.

In Fig. 48 S_1 and D represent the initial supply and demand conditions on day 1. Producers take account of the price, P_1, in deciding whether to enter the market on the following day. If they believe that the same price will rule, and if that price is less than variable cost, they will not enter the market. In the market for foodstuffs the variable cost may comprise the cost of picking or harvesting the crop, packing and transportation. (It should be remembered that time determines which costs are variable. Labour cost is unlikely to be variable on a day-to-day basis unless casual labour is used. Moreover, producers should take account of the opportunity costs of the inputs used. Workers employed in driving tractors etc. might otherwise have been used to repair machinery or buildings.)

Producers may temporarily withdraw from the market if the price on one day is less than they expect it to be at a later date. Whether producers are able to control the timing of their entry into the market is dependent, of course, upon the nature of the product and the techniques of production. Strawberry growers have less flexibility than the owners of sheep or beef cattle.

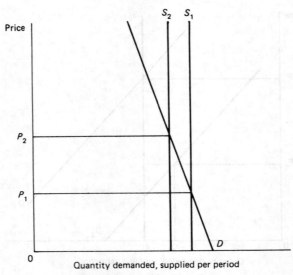

Fig. 48. *A fall in supply and an increase in price.*

If, as a result of the low price ruling on day 1, some suppliers leave the market on day 2, supply falls; the supply curve shifts from S_1 to S_2 (Fig. 48). As a result of the change in the balance between supply and demand, the suppliers who remain in the market obtain a higher price, P_2.

A changing scale of organisation

The analysis in Fig. 48 refers, of course, to the short run. In the longer run, when the producers are able to change their scale of organisation (*see* Chapter 5), they have to consider the relationship between average total cost and price (and also the opportunity cost of *all* the firm's resources). If the relationship is unsatisfactory, i.e. if the firm's profit is below target, or if revenue is exceeded by opportunity cost, the firm is likely to withdraw some or all of its resources from the market.

The techniques of production are again an important influence on this decision. A farmer who has grown peas one year can switch to the production of beans far more quickly than a grower of apples can switch to growing pears. For the owner of a fishing vessel the decision may be whether or not to sell the ship and re-invest the proceeds in entirely new productive assets.

These longer-term decisions are illustrated in Fig. 49, which relates to the market for carrots. The vertical supply curves indicate that the capacity of the industry is given and that this capacity yields a given output. We have seen that the quantity supplied may vary from one day to another, and the vertical supply curves (and also the demand curve) in Fig. 49 are to be seen as typical or representative for the year in question.

9. PRICE TAKERS AND PRICE MAKERS

In year 1, with supply S_1, price is P_1, which we assume yields a higher rate of return than was obtained from the growing of other crops such as lettuces. Consequently in year 2 some land is taken out of lettuce production and used for growing carrots. This results in an increase in supply (S_2). With an unchanged demand, price falls to P_2 at which the returns are less than those obtained from other crops. Consequently in year 3 supply decreases (S_3) with the result that price rises (P_3). In year 4, with supply S_4, price is P_2.

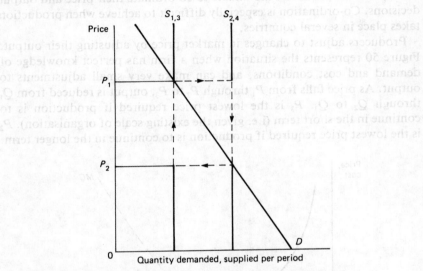

Fig. 49. *The cobweb: price fluctuations in an open market.*

The path traced by price, via the changing supply curves, is shown by the dotted line in Fig. 49. Because of the configuration of this path this process has been called the cobweb. There is no reason why price fluctuations should not continue indefinitely, since the actions of suppliers are unco-ordinated. Each supplier who considers entering the market may recognise that if sufficient suppliers enter, the price may fall to an unacceptable level. But he cannot tell, until after his own decision is made, what other suppliers have decided to do.

Figure 49 shows that price fluctuates between two points. This follows, of course, from the assumption that supply fluctuates between two levels. But in practice supply, and therefore price, may behave in other ways. If fluctuations in supply increased over time, i.e. if S_3 lay to the left of S_1 and S_4 to the right of S_2, price fluctuations would become greater. (This is known as a divergent cobweb.) Conversely if fluctuation in supply decreased (if S_3 lay to the right of S_1 and S_4 to the left of S_2) price fluctuations would decrease and eventually disappear (a convergent cobweb).

PRICE TAKING IN OTHER MARKETS

There are some markets which differ structurally from open markets, but in which firms usually act as price takers, i.e. they accept the going market price. For example in mineral production there are often barriers to the entry of new firms; moreover in some instances a few large firms account for a substantial proportion of output. Price taking occurs in these markets because no single producer is accepted as a price leader (*see* below) and the producers are unable to co-ordinate their price and output decisions. Co-ordination is especially difficult to achieve when production takes place in several countries.

Producers adjust to changes in market price by adjusting their output. Figure 50 represents the situation when a firm has perfect knowledge of demand and cost conditions, and can make very small adjustments to output. As price falls from P_1 through P_2 to P_3, output is reduced from Q_1 through Q_2 to Q_3. P_3 is the lowest price required if production is to continue in the short term (i.e. given the existing scale of organisation). P_2 is the lowest price required if production is to continue in the longer term.

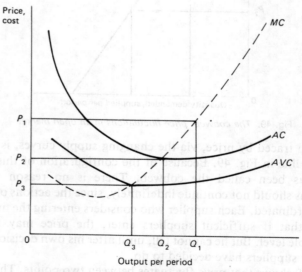

Fig. 50. *A fall in price and a reduction in output.*

In practice producers are unlikely to be able to adjust output as smoothly as indicated in Fig. 50. For example in mining a reduction in output may require the closure of a complete mine or pit. High-cost mines are closed and output is concentrated in the low-cost mines. In Fig. 51 the average variable cost curves refer to three mines. At price P_1 all three operate. When price falls below P_1 mine C is closed. A further fall in price below P_2, say to P_3, leads to the closure of mine B. (In the long run price would, of course, have to cover average total cost.)

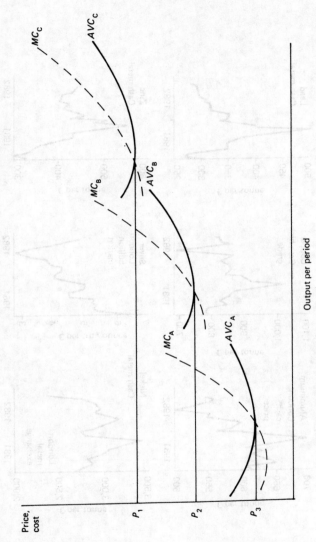

Fig. 51. A fall in price and a closure of production units.

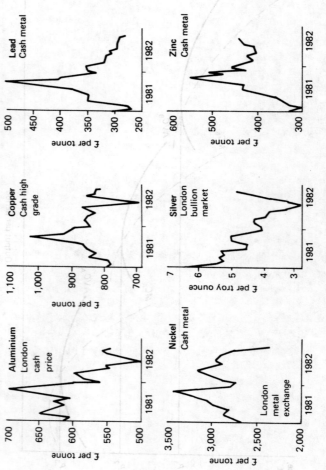

Fig. 52. Price changes in metal markets.

Source: Financial Times, 12th October 1982.

The behaviour of prices in a number of metal markets is shown in Fig. 52. The decline in price that occurred in virtually all markets in 1982 was due to a fall in demand as the world-wide recession intensified. Despite some drastic reductions in output, prices fell to very low levels. Reductions in output were easiest to effect where a few producers accounted for a large share of the market. For example large American producers of copper made enormous production cuts. But developing countries, dependent on copper exports for the bulk of their foreign exchange earnings, were much more reluctant to cut output.

Large producers also attempted to lead prices back up again, but with only limited success. In the USA Kennecott announced that it was returning to a producer price system and no longer basing its prices on the New York copper market quotations. It sought to establish a minimum price level, but that proved virtually impossible in the weak market conditions. American producers of zinc were able to increase domestic prices following production cutbacks. They also increased the price of zinc outside North America from $800 to $850 a tonne. But European producers refused to follow the increase, which they claimed was not justified by market conditions in Europe.

PRICE MAKERS

In constructing a basic model it is helpful to think in terms of a pricing season. In planning their activities producers decide what price to set for a forthcoming period or season. The length of the pricing season depends upon the product, the rate at which costs are changing, the pace of technological advance and so forth. But in many markets the season covers several months and it is not unusual to find an annual pricing cycle.

Cost estimation
The first step in setting price is to estimate the average cost during the pricing season. Since the season is usually defined in months rather than years, the producer is able to treat the scale of organisation as given. We showed in Chapter 5 that the average cost curve is likely to take the shape shown in Fig. 53. (The longer the pricing season the more likely it is that input prices will change; cost may be above AC at times and below AC at other times during the season.)

Target price
The next step is to derive the target price, i.e. the price that would enable the firm to achieve its profit target and any other objectives. In Fig. 53 the firm expects to produce E, at which output its average cost is estimated as EF. To this it adds a profit margin FG, yielding price $EG(=P_T)$.

This procedure contains an element of circular reasoning. The producer estimates average cost at the expected output, but this output is influenced by the price set. In many instances this circularity is not a serious matter, for two reasons. First, as shown in Fig. 53 and as explained in detail in Chapter 5, average cost is virtually constant over a wide range of output. Consequently, output can vary over this range without significantly affecting the cost and hence the profit margin achieved. Second, when a firm has been supplying a product for some time (several seasons) it has a fairly good idea as to which price–output combinations are feasible and which are not.

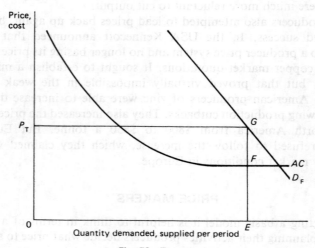

Fig. 53. *Target price.*

Target profit

Surveys have revealed that firms differ in terms of both the magnitude of the target profit and the form in which it is expressed. (The magnitude depends upon many factors, including profits earned in the past, profits earned by other firms, especially in the same industry, and the firm's opportunity cost of capital.) Profit is often expressed as a percentage of capital employed. Assume that the firm represented in Fig. 53 has a capital employed of £1 million and a target profit of 20 per cent or £200,000. If it expects to sell 100,000 units in a season its target profit per unit will be £2.

Having considered the various alternative price–output combinations, the firm might conclude that, given its present policies, there was no feasible combination that would allow it to attain its objectives. (Although a failure to sell the expected quantity might not affect the profit margin, it might cause the rate of return to fall below the target level.) It would then consider whether changes in policy might enable it to attain its objectives. It might seek to reduce costs through higher efficiency, keener purchasing etc. or to increase demand via a change in advertising strategy or by modifying the product's characteristics. (The longer the pricing season, the more opportunities for policy change are likely to be available.)

We return to some of these points below, but for the moment let us assume that policy changes are not required, and that the firm expects to achieve its objectives given existing cost and demand conditions, i.e. it sets price P_T at which it expects to sell E units. If demand is at D_E (Fig. 53) these expectations are fulfilled. However, given the various uncertainties faced by producers, it is unlikely that demand will turn out precisely as expected. Consequently we must consider how producers are likely to react when demand is not as expected.

Pricing when demand is higher than expected

In Fig. 54 demand D_H is higher than expected. This situation could arise because the firm's offer to consumers proved more attractive than expected, *vis-à-vis* the offers of competitors, giving the firm a higher than expected market share. Alternatively it could arise because market demand was higher than expected, to the benefit of all firms. The demand curve D_H is drawn on the assumption that relative prices within the market are unchanged, i.e. a change in price by one firm would be matched by other firms.

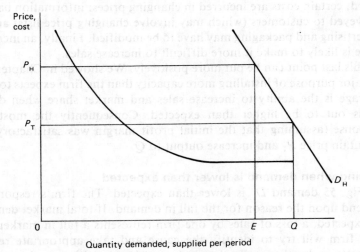

Fig. 54. *Pricing when demand higher than expected.*

The firm could take advantage of the higher demand in several ways. It could maintain output E and increase price to P_H. It could maintain price P_T and increase output and sales to Q. It could adopt an intermediate position, setting price between P_T and P_H and selling an output between E and Q. (It could even reduce its price, since the lower profit margin might be balanced by the higher volume of sales, leaving the rate of return unchanged. But this is more likely to happen in the longer term as greater opportunities for economies of scale become available.)

Several factors will influence the firm's choice from these alternatives.

If the initial profit margin was considered unsatisfactory the firm may take the opportunity to restore its margins to a more satisfactory level. This is especially likely if the profit margins of all suppliers have been depressed and an increase in demand has been experienced by all suppliers, since other suppliers would then be likely to match an upward price change. (It will be remembered that the demand curve is drawn on the assumption that relative prices are unchanged.)

In Fig. 54 we assumed that the initial profit margin was satisfactory. Even here the firm might decide to increase its price. But several factors would militate against a price increase. First, higher profit margins are likely to attract increased competition via new entry into the market. Thus higher profits may be achieved during the current season only at the expense of lower profits in the future. Second, the firm will be less sure about the extent of the increase in demand than is implied by Fig. 54. The higher demand will be experienced by the firm in the form of a higher level of orders than expected at the existing price, and the firm will be able only to guess what could be sold at higher prices. Moreover it cannot be sure that competitors would match a price change, as assumed in the diagram. Third, certain costs are incurred in changing prices: information has to be conveyed to customers (which may involve changing price lists) and also advertising and packaging may have to be modified. Finally, an increase in price is likely to make it more difficult to increase sales.

This last point can be put more positively. We showed in Chapter 5 that a major purpose of installing more capacity than the firm expects to use on average is the ability to increase sales and market share when demand turns out to be higher than expected. Consequently the most likely response (assuming that the initial profit margin was satisfactory) is to maintain price P_T and increase output to Q.

Pricing when demand is lower than expected

In Fig. 55 demand D_L is lower than expected. The firm's response will depend upon the reason for the fall in demand. If total market demand is as expected, a loss of sales by one firm represents a fall in market share. The firm will try to identify the cause and take appropriate remedial action, e.g. by changes in the product or in advertising, and possibly by reducing its price.

If all firms in the industry are facing a fall in demand, the response will depend mainly on the extent to which they are able to co-ordinate their activities. (Methods of co-ordination are discussed in detail below.) If there is a high degree of co-ordination the response is likely to be to maintain price P_T and accept a reduction in sales to Q. (This assumes that the market demand is not so elastic that a reduction in price would lead to an increase in profits.) Indeed there have been some recorded instances of prices being increased in response to a fall in demand, e.g. in the American steel industry, in which a high proportion of sales is accounted for by a few large producers. Higher prices would, of course, restore profit margins, but it is difficult to enforce price increases in the absence of increases in input prices, when demand is depressed.

Co-ordination of price and output decisions is most likely to occur when a few producers have a high share of sales, as in the example above, and when there is little opportunity for making "secret" price reductions (e.g. when the terms of a large order are negotiated with an individual purchaser rather than business being undertaken in accordance with a published price list). Given the cost and demand conditions in Fig. 55, a price reduction would clearly result in a fall in profit. Nevertheless, the firm might reduce its price in the expectation, or at least the hope, of *increasing* its profits. Sometimes this happens out of ignorance; a supplier believes that market demand is more elastic than it is. But in other instances a supplier may hope to be able to reduce price without competitors matching the reduction. (This would, of course, render demand far more elastic than indicated in Fig. 55.)

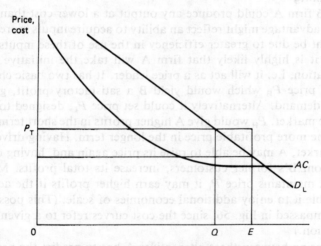

Fig. 55. *Pricing when demand lower than expected.*

If there are a large number of suppliers, some unmatched price reductions may be feasible. But if there are only a small number of suppliers it is extremely difficult for any one supplier to increase sales in this way without causing retaliation. As noted above, the best chance of doing so is to institute secret price reductions. (Effective price reductions can be made in various ways, including offering discounts for smaller quantities than usual, supplying a higher quality of product than normal for the price, and offering improved credit terms.)

Even secret price reductions, if successful, are likely eventually to cause retaliation. Once a price war breaks out it is very difficult to predict where it will stop. However there are two points at which the barriers to further price reductions are likely to be high. The first is average cost; a price below average cost implies that the firm makes an accounting loss. The second point is average variable cost; a price below average variable cost implies a negative cash flow, and firms will accept this outcome only in the most unusual circumstances, such as the need to obtain orders in order to avoid disbanding a skilled and experienced work force.

PRICING WITH DIFFERENT COST STRUCTURES

So far we have assumed that all the suppliers to a given market have identical cost structures. But in many markets some firms have lower costs than others, and we now explore the implications of this for price determination. (To simplify the analysis we consider two firms, one representative of low-cost producers, and the other representative of high-cost producers.)

Price making

In Fig. 56 firm A could produce any output at a lower cost than firm B. This cost advantage might reflect an ability to acquire inputs more cheaply or it might be due to greater efficiency in the use of these inputs. In this situation it is highly likely that firm A will take the initiative in price determination, i.e. it will act as a price leader. It has two basic choices. It could set price P_H which would yield B a satisfactory profit, given the expected demand. Alternatively it could set price P_L, designed to drive B out of the market. P_H would give A higher profits in the short term. But P_L may be the more profitable price in the longer term. Having driven B out of the market, A may be able to raise its price again and, having obtained orders from B's former customers, increase its total profits. Moreover even if A maintains price P_L it may earn higher profits if the additional sales enable it to enjoy additional economies of scale. (This possibility is not encompassed in Fig. 56, since the cost curves refer to a given scale of organisation.)

In choosing between these alternatives A has to predict the probability that a low price would drive B out of the market, and assess the likely demand and cost conditions after B's exit. It also has to compare the present value of profits earned in the immediate future with profits earned in the more distant future. As shown in Chapter 6, the higher the rate at which future profits are discounted, the greater the relative attractiveness of a course of action yielding early profits.

Figure 56 can also be used to illustrate the situation in which existing suppliers are faced by potential competition from firms which would enter the market if the price was right. If existing producers (represented by A) set price P_H, new entry (by firm B) would occur. Price P_L would deter new entry. If the new entrant's output represents a significant addition to total supply, the analysis is more complex. The entrant has now to consider

9. PRICE TAKERS AND PRICE MAKERS

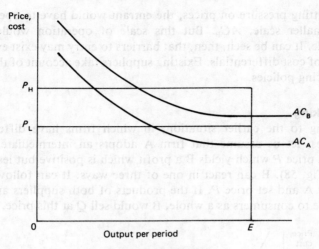

Fig. 56. *A price maker.*

what the price would be after entry. It is likely that price will have to fall if the higher output is to be sold. Consequently new entry might not occur even at price P_H.

The analysis is further extended in Fig. 57. Existing producers, operating with average cost AC_A, each supply $0Q$ at price P. A potential entrant has no inherent cost disadvantage and could also operate at AC_A.

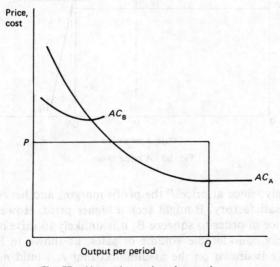

Fig. 57. *Alternative scales of operation.*

However, in order to accommodate the additional output price would fall, perhaps to a level at which no producer earned satisfactory profits. To avoid putting pressure on prices, the entrant would have to operate on a much smaller scale, AC_B. But this scale of operation would not be profitable. It can be seen, then, that barriers to entry may exist even in the absence of cost differentials. Existing suppliers take account of this fact in their pricing policies.

Price taking

Returning to the earlier situation, in which firms have different cost structures, let us assume that firm A adopts an intermediate strategy, setting a price P which yields B a profit which is positive but less than its target (Fig. 58). B can react in one of three ways. It can follow the lead given by A and set price P. If the products of both suppliers are equally attractive to consumers as a whole, B would sell Q at this price.

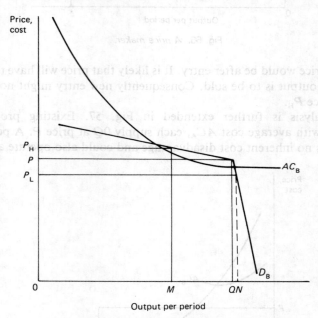

Fig. 58. *A price taker.*

Alternatively, since at price P the profit margin, and hence the rate of return, is unsatisfactory, B might seek a higher price. However, since A has set its price in order to squeeze B, it is unlikely to raise its price. B is likely to lose a considerable volume of sales, as shown in Fig. 58. (B's demand curve is drawn on the assumption that A would *not* match an upward price change.) At price P_H, sales would fall from Q to M. It is unlikely that a price above P would increase B's profits, unless its products are highly differentiated from those of A. In this latter case B's demand curve might be less elastic than indicated in Fig. 58.

The final alternative available to B is to set a price below P. This alternative would be profitable only if demand was highly elastic. But if the lower price causes customers to move from A to B, as is likely unless the products are highly differentiated, then A will probably match the price reduction. (Indeed, as the lower-cost firm, A may reduce its price below that of B as a disciplinary measure.) With prices equal, B will achieve higher sales only insofar as the market demand is elastic. In Fig. 58 sales at price P_L are N, and B incurs a loss. (The kinked demand curve is similar to those in the oligopoly models considered in Chapter 7.)

This suggests that B's optimum short-term strategy is to act as a price taker, i.e. to follow the pricing lead set by A. In the longer term B could attempt to ameliorate the situation in one of two ways. First, it could increase the degree of product differentiation by advertising, product modification etc. Product differentiation would make demand less elastic to price increases than indicated in Fig. 58.

Price-minus costing

The reverse strategy would be to try to reduce costs to such an extent that price P yielded satisfactory profits. There is frequently considerable scope for cost reduction. (See the discussion of X-inefficiency and organisational slack in Chapter 8.) For example in the 1970s many companies reduced their energy consumption by methods that had previously been available but were exploited only when the rise in the price of oil threatened profits. General Motors' consumption of energy in the USA and Canada was 3 per cent less in 1978 than in 1972 despite an increase in production of one-and-a-half million vehicles, yielding a saving of $180 million on an energy bill in 1978 of $925 million. The energy-saving measures included the installation of a refuse-recycling system burning wood, cardboard and paper, extended use of computers to control the operation of energy-using devices, and the introduction of lasers to treat metals that require hardening; the lasers replaced a heat furnace that used seven times as much energy. These measures were introduced primarily to counteract an increase in costs. But measures of the same sort can help to restore margins squeezed by low prices. When a firm accepts the going price and tailors its costs to match this price it can be said to follow a policy of price-minus costing.

THE CO-ORDINATION OF ACTIVITIES

We have seen that pricing behaviour may be influenced by the ability of producers to co-ordinate their activities. We now consider the various forms co-ordination might take, beginning with the most formalised.

Overt and covert agreements

In an oft-quoted remark Adam Smith said that "People of the same trade seldom meet together, even for merriment and diversion, but the conversation ends in a conspiracy against the public or in some contrivance to raise prices." Almost two centuries later R.A. Smith, an executive found to be involved in a conspiracy to fix the price of electrical goods in the USA in the 1950s, was quoted in *Fortune* magazine in 1961 as saying that for many American businessmen price-fixing was "a way of life".

Legislation has been introduced in many countries, including the UK and the USA, in order to prevent or control collusive pricing agreements. (The UK legislation was outlined in Chapter 3.) But there is little doubt that such agreements can exist, unbeknown to the authorities for many years. In recent years the Office of Fair Trading has discovered a series of agreements in industries as disparate as blacktop, telephone cables, concrete pipes, copying equipment, gas boilers and bread manufacture.

Agreements on prices are frequently buttressed by clauses relating to conditions of sale, product specifications, charges for extras, authorised outlets etc. An alternative means of attaining the same end as a price agreement is a market-sharing agreement which limits supply, e.g. by establishing quotas and imposing financial penalties on firms exceeding the quota.

Information agreements

There are different types of information agreement, but all involve agreement by some or all the firms in an industry to exchange information about certain of their activities, including prices, sales and costs. Price fixing is obviously most likely to be facilitated by the exchange of information on prices, and especially by agreements to notify competitors before changing prices (pre-notification agreements). Common costing-systems, if used as the basis for cost-based pricing, may give common prices. The exchange of information on future plans for output may also introduce a greater measure of stability into prices.

Information agreements can clearly be used to attain the same ends as agreements to fix prices. Consequently they have been brought within the scope of competition policy in a number of countries, including the UK.

Price leadership

Price leadership denotes a situation in which one firm sets a price which is followed by competitors. (This does not necessarily imply identical prices; rather a well-defined structure of prices which tends to persist over time.) The competing firms may reach an agreement or understanding about which firm is to act as price leader, although such an agreement, if discovered, might well run foul of competition policy. Alternatively the largest or lowest-cost firm may spontaneously emerge as the price leader. In some instances one firm may act as price leader at one time and another firm at another time.

9. PRICE TAKERS AND PRICE MAKERS

Professor Scherer has given numerous examples of price leadership in the USA, including the pre-war cigarette industry: "a classic example of price leadership used to establish a price structure that (barring miscalculations) tended to yield maximum collusive profits."[1] Over two-thirds of the output of cigarettes was accounted for by the three major producers: Reynolds, American Brands and Liggett and Myers. Between 1923 and 1941 there were eight standard-brand list-price changes, five up and three down. Reynolds led on six occasions and American on the other two; on each occasion the other majors followed quickly, normally within twenty four hours. Throughout the period the rate of return of the major producers averaged double the rate earned by manufacturing industry as a whole.

But even experienced price leaders can misjudge the situation. In 1931 Reynolds raised prices as the consumption of tobacco was beginning to fall and as leaf tobacco prices reached their lowest level since 1905. The other majors followed and this allowed the producers of cheaper cigarettes to expand their market share from 1 per cent in early 1931 to 23 per cent in late 1932.

The consequences of a lack of co-ordination are also illustrated by Scherer with reference to the US tin can industry. In September 1958 American Can announced a 6 per cent across-the-board price increase. American had been accepted as price leader, but on this occasion Continental Can responded by raising its prices by only 3 per cent. American retaliated with price reductions ranging from 2 to 5 per cent. These reductions were matched by Continental in order to maintain the initial differential. Further reductions followed and by mid-1959 prices were 10 per cent *lower* than a year earlier.[2]

Rule-of-thumb pricing
This term refers to the use of well-established procedures in setting prices, e.g. a conventional markup might be added to (estimated) average cost. This is most likely to contribute to price stability when a common costing system is used, and especially when (*a*) the cost base is common, e.g. published by a trade association or a price leader, and (*b*) producers reach an understanding concerning the markup to be applied.

In May 1963, two years after it was convicted for illegal price fixing, General Electric announced a new policy for pricing turbine generators. It published a more simplified pricing book that enabled its rival Westinghouse to compute the "book" price of any generator. A standard multiplier was to be applied to the book price on each bid, and changes in the multiplier would be publicly announced by General Electric.[3]

---

1. F. M. Scherer. *Industrial Market Structure and Economic Performance.* Rand McNally, Chicago, 2nd Edition, 1980, p. 177.
2. F. M. Scherer. *Industrial Pricing.* Rand McNally, Chicago, 1973, p. 40.
3. F. M. Scherer. *Industrial Market Structure and Economic Performance,* p. 182.

The extent to which suppliers can co-ordinate their activities depends upon the form of co-ordination adopted. Formal, overt agreements give rise to much tighter, more disciplined co-ordination than rule-of-thumb pricing (which is why overt agreements often run foul of competition policy). The analysis in the earlier part of this chapter suggested that co-ordination facilitates stability of prices and profits. It can also enable firms to attain higher profits, as shown by the experience of the US cigarette industry, quoted above.

QUESTIONS

1. Compare and contrast models of perfect competition with models of open markets.
2. How is a change in cost likely to affect price in an open market?
3. Specify the market conditions under which a price cobweb is most likely to arise. Draw diagrams to illustrate (*a*) a divergent cobweb, (*b*) a convergent cobweb.
4. Analyse the probable response of price to a fall in demand when producers are (*a*) able, and (*b*) unable, to co-ordinate their price and output decisions.
5. What factors would influence decisions on price and output taken by a firm when demand turns out to be higher than expected?
6. What conditions facilitate the co-ordination of price and output decisions?
7. In what circumstances is price-minus costing most likely to be adopted?
8. Discuss, with reference to the theory of the firm, the concept of equilibrium.
9. Enumerate (*a*) the advantages, (*b*) the disadvantages, of models incorporating the assumption that firms attempt to maximise profits.
10. Further evidence that the whole future of raw material supplies and prices is entering a new era of control by producers, which could be similar to OPEC in oil, has been provided recently in both the copper and tin markets. Rio Tinto-Zinc, the British-based international mining group, has been acting on behalf of a number of leading copper-producing countries to deal with the problem of surplus supplies, especially in Japan, which are depressing copper prices to a level that is below the cost of production for many mines.

The basic idea is to organise a financial consortium to take over, and effectively remove from sale at current prices, the huge surplus of copper supplies in Japan—estimated at some 250,000 tonnes—and also to obtain world-wide agreement to cut back production to levels more suited to the present low demand.

It was the export of surplus copper by Japanese smelters, who refine ore concentrates into copper, when domestic demand plummeted after the oil crisis, that was the major influence in the collapse of world copper prices last year from a peak of £1,400 to £500 a tonne in the space of a few months.

The Japanese Government, bowing to requests from developing countries dependent on copper for the bulk of their export earnings, banned further exports in November. Since then, however, it has been faced with surplus stocks piling up and threatening to bankrupt the smelters.

The above passage was extracted from an article in the *Financial Times* of 21st April 1975.

(*a*) How would you explain the fact that copper prices had fallen to a level "below the cost of production for many mines"?

(*b*) Can selling copper at this price ever be a sensible policy?

(*c*) Assuming that a consortium could be formed which would buy up the surplus supplies of copper, what factors would influence the extent to which such a policy would be commerically successful?

(*d*) Indicate in two or three sentences the basis on which a reasonable target-price might be determined.

PART FOUR

Strategy Formulation

CHAPTER TEN

Corporate Strategy

OBJECTIVES

After studying this chapter the reader should be able to: understand the role of corporate strategy; list the stages of the strategic planning process; understand the factors causing changes in demand for individual products; understand how planning can help a firm to exploit opportunities and counteract threats; explain how a firm might evaluate its strengths and weaknesses; understand the process of product portfolio selection; explain the principles underlying product protfolio analysis, a product–resource matrix and a resource portfolio matrix; understand the factors influencing strategy formulation in multinational enterprises.

INTRODUCTION

Having discussed the objectives that might be set by firms, we now examine how they might formulate a strategy by means of which these objectives can be achieved. Examples of the strategy adopted by particular firms are given later in the chapter. But first we consider in more general terms the role of corporate strategy.

THE ROLE OF CORPORATE STRATEGY

Strategy is concerned with developing long-term advantage. Competitive advantage can come from superiority in product, in marketing (including service) and/or advantage in price. Cash funds competitive advantage in the sense that cash is required for investment in low-cost production facilities to sustain low prices, in research and development and in marketing activities. In a given market segment at a given price, the lowest cost producer will have the most cash to invest in building competitive advantage.

In striving to become the lowest-cost producer the firm must make an assessment of its costs against the estimated costs of competitors. Each element of product cost is incurred through the use of a resource, e.g. a machine centre, a salesforce, a warehouse. Consequently if the economics of each resource are understood, it is possible to reduce unit product cost elements over a number of products using the same resources. (The links between the firm's product and resource portfolios are discussed at greater length later in the chapter.)

THE STRATEGIC PLANNING PROCESS

In this section we examine the strategic planning process, assuming that the firm's objectives have been agreed. (In practice, there is an interaction between current objectives and past strategy. We are entering at a particular point what is in effect a continuously evolving situation.)

The strategic planning process can be divided into four stages:

(*a*) Examination of the current and expected future state of the environment in which the firm operates, in order to identify the opportunities and threats that may arise.

(*b*) Evaluation of the firm's relative strengths and weaknesses in responding to these opportunities and threats. (These strengths and weaknesses are also taken into account in setting objectives.)

(*c*) Identification of the directions in which the firm should try to move in order to achieve its objectives, given its resources and environment.

(*d*) Selection of the firm's portfolio of products and markets, and determination of the priority to be allocated to each.

This strategic planning process usually gives rise to a series of detailed plans for each department or division of the firm. However we will not follow the process through to that point. Instead we examine in detail each of the four stages listed above.

EXAMINING THE FIRM'S ENVIRONMENT

The trend of demand

The most important aspect of the firm's environment is usually the trend of demand. We examined broad changes in the pattern of demand in Chapter 1. In this chapter we narrow the focus by considering changes in the demand for individual products, and the factors causing these changes.

Income

The response of demand to a change in income is measured by the income elasticity of demand (IED). This is defined as follows:

$$\text{Income elasticity of demand} = \frac{\text{the proportional change in demand}}{\text{the proportional change in income}}$$

Using symbols, this can be expressed as

$$\text{IED} = \frac{\Delta Q}{Q} \div \frac{\Delta Y}{Y}$$

Estimates of IED are usually obtained by considering past changes in income and sales, an allowance being made for other influences on sales. Some examples are given in Table XXII.

It may be very difficult for a firm to make an accurate estimate of IED. But even a broad approximation can form a useful input to a firm's strategy. For

10. CORPORATE STRATEGY

TABLE XXII. INCOME ELASTICITIES OF DEMAND

Product	IED
Recreational goods	4.28
Wines and spirits	3.55
Meat and bacon	1.36
Bread and cereals	0.72
Rail travel	−2.52

Source: A. Deaton, *Models and Projections of Demand in Post-War Britain*. Chapman and Hall, 1975.

instance, IED for many foodstuffs is low; consequently a food manufacturer aiming at a rapid increase in sales will have to stimulate demand, e.g. by advertising or by introducing new products.

Population

Since a change in total population affects national income it is unlikely to be given much weight as a separate influence on the trend of demand. (Also, total population changes only very slowly.) But for some firms changes in the *structure* of population are a very important influence on demand. For example the post-war population "bulge" led to successive increases in demand for baby foods, toys for young children, teenage clothes, pop records and so forth. As the number of elderly people increases towards the end of this century, demand will increase for bungalows, false teeth and spectacles.

Government policy

We showed in Chapters 2 and 3 how government policies can affect the aggregate level of demand, and demand in particular sectors and industries. Monitoring of White Papers, government statements etc. can often allow changes in policy to be anticipated. But in some instances sudden policy decisions are taken which cause unexpected changes in demand. The decision by the Argentine government to invade the Falkland Islands, and the decision by the British government to defend the Islands, resulted in a sharp increase in demand for certain types of military equipment. On the other hand the decision by OPEC to substantially increase the price of oil led to a slow-down in the world economy, and to a fall in demand for oil-fired central heating systems, large cars etc.

Substitution

An important aspect of a market economy is the freedom of consumers to choose from among competing products. This freedom means that firms must constantly take into account the possibility of being able to wean customers away from the products of other suppliers and, conversely, the possibility that they may lose sales to these other suppliers.

In trying to assess the likelihood of substitution occurring the firm should be aware of the fact, emphasised by Lancaster, that it is not goods in themselves that yield utility, but their characteristics.[1] If television programmes are watched for their entertainment value, a substitution relationship will exist between television sets and other forms of entertainment such as cinemas and sporting events. If television programmes are watched for their information value, the substitution relationship will be with other sources of information such as newspapers and magazines.

Substitution may occur for several reasons. First, the relative prices of products may change. The fall in the price of gas relative to other fuels was accompanied by an increase in its share of the domestic fuels market from around 10 per cent in 1960 to over 50 per cent in 1980. The demand for butter is very sensitive to the price differential between butter and margarine.

Second, a new product, or a vastly improved version of an existing product, may be introduced on to the market. The decline of the traditional fish-and-chip shop has been hastened by the spread of alternative quick-food outlets selling hamburgers, baked potatoes, Chinese meals etc. The introduction of the pocket calculator heralded the virtual demise of the slide rule.

Third, advertising and other promotional activities may persuade consumers to transfer some of their spending to other products. (These promotional activities may be linked to other changes, such as the introduction of new products.)

Finally, consumers' tastes may change. The change may be stimulated by the factors discussed above, or by other factors such as overseas travel and extended education. Sometimes a change in tastes has a substantial effect on demand, as when the advent of the mini-skirt led to a fall in demand for cloth and an increase in demand for nylon. In other instances the change is much more gradual, e.g. the increase in wine drinking and in the consumption of such foreign foods as pasta, stemming in part from the increase in overseas travel.

Changes within the market

We have seen that the overall demand for a product may be affected by changes in other markets. The demand for one "brand" of a given product may also be affected by changes in other brands of that product. Substitution, leading to changes in market share, may result from a

---

1. K. J. Lancaster. *Consumer Demand: A New Approach*. Columbia UP, New York, 1971. *See also:* J. Mark, F. Brown and B. J. Pierson. "Consumer Demand Theory, Goods and Characteristics: Breathing Empirical Content into the Lancastrian Approach". *Managerial and Decision Economics* Vol. 2 (1981).

change in relative prices, improvements made to products, changes in promotional activity, etc.

It is extremely difficult to predict some changes in competitive activity and to assess the likely consequences, e.g. the nature and impact of the advertising that will be undertaken by competitors in two years' time.

In other instances prediction may be easier. For example if a mineral producer, A, knows that a competitor, B, has discovered and is about to exploit low-cost deposits, it is a reasonable assumption that this competitor will reduce his prices. This will cause either a fall in the quantity sold by A if the price reduction is not matched, or a fall in profit margins if it is. (The relationship between demand and profit is examined below.) If it is known that a competitor has taken out a patent on a vastly improved product then a change in market shares can again be predicted fairly confidently.

Even when there is a high probability that a change will occur, it is not easy to assess the precise effect of this change on demand. But as a general rule one can say that the effect of a given change depends upon the degree of product differentiation. (A product is said to be highly differentiated from that of a rival producer if the two are seen by consumers as having very different qualities or characteristics, e.g. a "high roast" and a "mild blend" instant coffee. Undifferentiated products are seen as identical by consumers, e.g. wheat of a given grade produced on different farms.)

If the change in the environment takes the form of a change in the price of another brand (or product) we can express the impact in terms of the cross elasticity of demand, defined as

$$\frac{\Delta Q_A}{Q_A} \div \frac{\Delta P_B}{P_B}$$

where A and B are two brands (or products), Q is quantity demanded, P is price and Δ represents a small change in the variable.

The cross elasticity of demand will be low where the two brands are highly differentiated (poor substitutes) and high when they are undifferentiated or mildly differentiated (good substitutes).

The balance of demand and supply
We saw in the previous chapter that growth is often an important objective, suggesting that firms will seek to enter markets with good growth prospects. Moreover in many instances production for fast-growing markets leads to higher profits. However this is not always so. The profits earned in any market reflect the balance of demand and supply, and the corporate strategy should take account of possible changes in this balance. This involves trying to assess the capacity of competitors, existing and potential.

The capacity of competitors
Capacity refers to the volume of output that can be produced, but in the present context account should also be taken of the quality of that output. It is obviously easiest to estimate the capacity of existing competitors. But it is important to try to identify potential competitors and to assess the probability of their entering the market. The extent of new entry will depend very largely upon the existence and height of entry barriers. Barriers to entry include control by existing producers of resources essential in the production process, the attainment by existing producers of low costs through experience, and strong loyalty to existing producers on the part of consumers.

Changes in the environment and the firm's conditions of supply

Changes in the environment that can affect the firm's conditions of supply, i.e. its capacity and costs, include: loss of access to vital raw materials (note the widespread changes in British Petroleum's business caused by the nationalisation of Middle Eastern oil); a substantial change in costs (equal-pay legislation posed particular threats to firms employing a high proportion of women); legislation relating to product quality and characteristics (the cost of producing cars for some export markets was increased by the need to meet safety and anti-pollution regulations); a restriction of supplies following the takeover of a supplier by a rival (some small car assemblers were unable to obtain car bodies when suppliers were taken over by the major assemblers).

These changes might raise the firm's costs and/or reduce its capacity and hence its output. In either instance profits would suffer. To counteract these threats it may be necessary to effect a substantial change in the firm's activities. For example a threatened restriction of supply may lead a manufacturer to integrate backwards, i.e. to take over a supplier or begin production of the component or raw material.

Opportunities and threats: summary

The above analysis will have suggested the types of opportunities and threats that a firm might discover in an examination of its environment. The opportunities comprise an increase in sales and/or profits, from either existing or new markets. The threats comprise a loss of sales and/or profits. The next stage of the corporate planning process is to consider whether the firm is able to take advantage of the opportunities and counteract the threats. This requires an evaluation of the firm's strengths and weaknesses.

EVALUATING THE FIRM'S STRENGTHS AND WEAKNESSES

There are a large number of factors that might be included in a profile of a firm's strengths and weaknesses, and Fig. 59 should therefore be seen only

10. CORPORATE STRATEGY

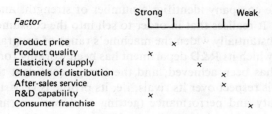

Fig. 59. *A profile of strengths and weaknesses.*

as illustrative of such a profile. Furthermore the five-point scale used in this figure is only one of several possible measures. The values are comparative; they indicate the position of the firm relative to that of competitors.

Applications of the strengths–weaknesses profile

In order to show how a strengths–weaknesses profile can aid the development of strategy, let us consider two situations. In the first, to which Fig. 59 refers, the firm is presented with an opportunity. In the second the firm faces a threat. (In practice many firms face opportunities in some markets and threats in others, as illustrated by the discussion of British Petroleum's diversification programme in the following chapter.)

An opportunity

The first situation concerns a (hypothetical) firm whose main business is the manufacture of a range of cleansing devices supplied to industrial and commercial customers. Its products include air purification plant, equipment used in the recycling of waste products, and industrial laundering equipment. The firm has for some time manufactured a machine that cleans clothes by sonic means. The machine uses no water or detergents and hence its running costs are very low. On the other hand it is much less flexible than a conventional washing machine, having fewer cleaning programmes; it is most commonly used for cleaning large quantities of identical products such as dirty overalls or roller towels.

The firm has for some time contemplated entering the consumer market, but has always considered its competitive profile to be too weak. However it believes that a number of factors have given rise to an opportunity that it may be able to exploit. A proposal by the government to insert water meters in all houses and to charge for the volume of water used will increase the running costs of conventional washing machines. Running costs are also likely to increase as the relative price of electricity continues to rise. Furthermore there seems little scope for the manufacturers of conventional machines to offer consumers increasing value for money, since all current machines make full use of microtechnology, and no other new technology is on the horizon.

In considering how well placed it is to take advantage of this opportunity the company identifies a number of strengths and a number of weaknesses. It realises that in order to sell into the consumer market it will have to substantially widen the machine's range of programmes. This is a project on which its R&D department has been working for some time. Some success has been achieved, and the firm is confident that it has a clear lead in this respect over its rivals, i.e. its profile is very strong at this point. Reliability and performance (getting clothes clean) are the most important aspects of product quality in this market, and in the light of its previous experience the firm believes that it is strong here also. Furthermore the company has always tried to incorporate the latest technology in its manufacturing processes, and its costs of production and hence its prices have tended to be below average.

On the other hand the firm has a number of obvious weaknesses with respect to the new market. It has virtually no experience of consumer markets; hence it has no consumer franchise. It has always sold direct to its industrial and commercial customers and has no contact with the distributors (wholesalers and retailers) of consumer durables. Finally, its after-sales network is very limited by comparison with those of the major manufacturers of domestic machines.

Elasticity of supply refers in this context to the ability of the firm to increase production. This is determined partly by the availability of physical production capacity, partly by access to an increased volume of other inputs (especially raw materials and components), and partly by experience of the relevant manufacturing processes. Although the firm has extensive experience in the manufacturing processes it would be at a disadvantage on the other two points, since manufacturers of conventional machines would be able to switch part of their existing plant to the production of the new machine.

If the firm decided that its overall competitive profile was not strong but it still wished to pursue the opportunity, it might seek to co-operate with a firm with a complementary profile, i.e. a manufacturer of conventional washing machines, strong in terms of consumer franchise, channels of distribution, after-sales service and elasticity of supply, but weak on R&D capability, product quality and price. Co-operation might enable an opportunity to be exploited, which neither firm could exploit independently. If the project was very large in relation to the firms' assets and existing business then a merger might be effected. A more limited form of co-operation would be the formation of a jointly owned subsidiary to manufacture and market the new machine. (These alternatives are considered in greater detail below.)

A threat

We can describe the second situation more briefly, since it is very familiar. Many British firms have found their markets undermined by competition from foreign products of better quality or at lower prices. These advantages enable the foreign producers to overcome the disadvantages of an initially weak consumer franchise, lack of experience with distribution channels and a limited service network.

An example of this situation is the penetration by Japanese producers of the market for motor cycles, television sets, radios etc. These producers have taken steps to correct any competitive weaknesses as soon as possible, and they have posed an extremely formidable threat. In some instances the sensible response to such a threat is to try to diversify into other products.

Another possibility is to make a partial withdrawal from the market, and to concentrate a limited volume of resources on a specific market segment in which the firm has advantages. However even this strategy sometimes fails, as illustrated by the experience of the UK motor cycle industry. British manufacturers had always devoted most attention to the production of medium and large bikes. Consequently when Japanese manufacturers attacked the small bike segment of the market, British manufacturers withdrew from this segment without putting up much resistance. However the Japanese were subsequently able to use their dealer and service network to market larger bikes. The British manufacturers then found that with a more limited production range their average costs were higher than those of their competitors, and eventually they had to withdraw from the remaining segments of the market.

The emergence of spare capacity

Spare capacity sometimes emerges as a by-product of planned growth, "partly because the process of growth and diversification generates new skills and hence capacity for further growth, and partly because each growth project will temporarily absorb management or other capacity which is then freed for further use once the project has been completed."[2]

A common example is when a producer develops a product for internal use and subsequently sells the product in external markets, e.g. computer service bureaux established by a number of firms (see Chapter 11). When external sales are substantial it is often convenient to set up a subsidiary company with responsibility for the product, e.g. Scicon, the management consultancy owned by BP, and Lintas, the advertising agency founded by Unilever.

In this section we have illustrated how a firm's competitive profile, together with an examination of the environment, can suggest the direction in which the firm may have to move, the ways in which it may have to modify its pattern of activities in order to achieve its objectives. We develop this theme further in the following section, which deals with the third stage of the strategic planning process.

2. C. J. Sutton. *Economics and Corporate Strategy*. Cambridge UP, 1980, p. 53.

IDENTIFYING THE DIRECTION OF CHANGE

In some instances the examination of the environment suggests that if the firm maintains its existing pattern of activities, i.e. if it continues to supply the same products to the same markets, it is likely to achieve its objectives. If growth is an objective then this will be achieved by horizontal expansion.

In other instances firms find that a gap exists between objectives and the likely outcome if the present pattern of activities is maintained. In order to fill this "planning gap", in order to achieve its objectives, the firm has to change its policies, to develop its strategy.

In developing its strategy it will look first to the opportunities that have already been identified. This might involve entering new markets with existing products; the opportunity to do this might arise, for instance, because of a reduction in tariff barriers in overseas markets. Or the change might involve diversification, the development of new products for either new or existing markets, perhaps taking advantage of an opportunity arising from a change in consumers' tastes or in government regulations, e.g. new safety regulations resulting in an increased demand for flameproof nightwear. Finally the firm might need to integrate vertically, either backward to secure access to supplies, as noted above, or forward, undertaking activities that bring it closer to the consumer.

If it appears that these developments would not be sufficient to close the planning gap, a more intensive "strategic search" will be undertaken. This search is likely to begin with a reappraisal of existing products. It may be possible to increase sales and profits by various means, e.g. finding cheaper sources of raw materials, improved working practices or a new advertising campaign.

Further consideration may also need to be given to the introduction of new products and entry into new markets. (There is no guarantee that the initial examination of the firm's environment will have revealed all the available opportunities.)

At this stage of strategy formulation the broad parameters are set for the final stage, the selection of the firm's portfolio of products and markets. tools last twenty five years."[3]

SELECTION OF THE FIRM'S PORTFOLIO

In the previous section we showed that the firm may have to search the environment on more than one occasion before identifying the opportunities that will enable it to achieve its objectives. In one sense there is an almost unlimited number of opportunities open to a firm, an almost unlimited number of ways in which it can allocate its resources. But the potential profit offered by many of these opportunities may be unacceptable, or the firm may not have the resources required to exploit them. Consequently in the final stage of strategy formulation the firm has to select its portfolio, i.e. it decides which of the opportunities it wishes and would be able to exploit, and how its resources are to be allocated among products and markets.

Product portfolio analysis

The Boston Consulting Group has suggested that the products in a firm's portfolio often fall into four groups. "Wild cats" are products which have not been on the market long enough to gain consumer acceptance and are currently absorbing cash. It is hoped that this cash will turn wild cats into "stars". These products are currently profitable and are likely to remain so for a considerable period. The third group comprises "cash cows", more mature than stars and unlikely to achieve further growth. These mature products require less support, e.g. in terms of expenditure on R&D and advertising, and less management time. Consequently they generate even more profit currently than the stars. Finally there are the "dogs", reaching the end of their life-cycle, and yielding very poor and perhaps even negative profits.

The implication of this approach for portfolio selection is that cash cows should be milked and dogs liquidated to provide the cash required by the wild cats and stars. However this approach must be treated with caution, especially when it is combined with the often expressed view that products follow a similar life cycle, in accordance with a fairly predictable time scale.

This can lead to a rigid approach to portfolio selection which has a number of dangers. First, support can be withdrawn from mature products too early, thus hastening the transition from star (via cash cow) to dog. Insufficient attention is given to the possibility of extending the profitable part of the life cycle by means of developing or reformulating the product, entering new market segments (e.g. selling by mail order), or by selling into new geographical markets.

The importance of model development has been emphasised by Ernst Fuhrmann, managing director of Porsche, the West German sports car manufacturer: "There are two possibilities for handling model development. One is to invest a big amount in a model and produce it for four or six years with a very limited further investment; this is the way most big companies do it. The other way is to develop a car to a reasonable limit. Then you can build it for fifteen years, having a further stab at development every two years or so. This is the way we do it. . . . There is no point in our changing tooling every five years—at the rate we build, tools last twenty five years."[3]

In 1978, when Fuhrmann made this statement the 911 model had been in production for thirteen years, using the same body shell and therefore the same basic tools. But it had frequently been uprated in terms of

3. Quoted in *Financial Times*, 3rd January 1978.

performance and equipment, including the introduction of a turbo-charged version.

A second danger is that managers may overemphasise the brightness of some of the stars. Two members of a firm of international management consultants write: "Kearney has found many firms using the wrong market definitions in calculating their shares and thus seriously over-estimating their position. A common error is to define the market so narrowly that the firm is bound to appear as market leader. Brand managers are adept at this self-delusion: 'We have leadership of the sugar-coated breakfast cereal market', they may say—all they have done is to define the market in terms of their product, ignoring the fact that other products satisfy exactly the same market.

"Other firms fail to recognise the true internationalism of their business. For example, a manufacturer of controls for refrigeration and air-conditioning equipment drew up a portfolio matrix which showed relative market shares in Europe only. In commercial reality, the business was world-wide—and quite different strategic conclusions were indicated when the portfolio was drawn up on an international basis. To become the lowest-cost producer the company required to move on a world scale, specifically to gain volume from major markets outside Europe."[4]

Third, many wild cats become dogs without ever being stars or cash cows. The firm is sometimes better advised to spend money on improving its existing products than on introducing new ones, especially when the new products require new expertise in production or marketing. For example among the tobacco companies Philip Morris, which has diversified least, has consistently improved its tobacco performance. Competitors which have invested heavily in other businesses have found that these businesses frequently yield lower returns (and sometimes losses). Major UK manufacturers, Imperial Tobacco and British American Tobacco, attempted to buy expertise by taking over established companies in food manufacturing, retailing etc. but with somewhat unsatisfactory results. (Diversification is discussed at greater length in Chapter 11.)

Finally, care must be taken in liquidating dogs which share resources with profitable products. If the output of these other products cannot be increased in order to absorb the capacity released, their average cost of production will rise—since they are now carrying the share of the resource cost previously carried by the dogs—and their profitability will therefore decline.

A product–resource matrix

Clarke and Scanlon suggest that there is a need to exploit the virtues of product portfolio analysis, but to add a means of analysing the company's skills and key resources, and to relate the latter to markets and potential

---

4. C. J. Clarke and B. Scanlon. "The Quality Volume Mix". *Management Today* June 1982.

markets. The first step in the analysis is the preparation of a product–resource matrix. This shows the major resources and products, and indicates the percentage of each product cost which is incurred in each resource area, and the percentage of each resource cost which goes into each product (Fig. 60).

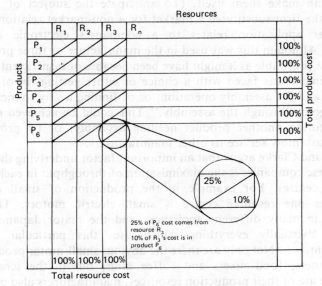

Fig. 60. *A product–resource matrix.*

In a recent study carried out by A.T. Kearney, and reported by Clarke and Scanlon, the business of an engineering company was found to comprise forty-six product classes and more than eighty major resources. The product–resource matrix revealed that one dog product, which management felt to be closely related to other products and was therefore reluctant to drop, was almost entirely separate in the resources it used.

A resource portfolio matrix
A further step in the strategy proposed by Clarke and Scanlon is the development of a resource portfolio matrix. We have discussed above the application of experience curves to products. Clarke and Scanlon argue that "experience curves can be developed for particular resources, for example, sales forces, machine centres, purchasing sections and warehousing. In each case, the cost per unit handled by the resource centre falls as cumulative volume increases. It follows that the firm using the largest share of that type of resource has the lowest costs."[5]
An application of this concept quoted by Clarke and Scanlon relates to

---
5. Clarke and Scanlon *op. cit.*

a manufacturer of electrical–mechanical components who was making little use of some of his equipment, e.g. single-spindle automatic lathes. The company made contact with a German manufacturer whose cumulative experience with this type of equipment was twelve times as great. The company decided to buy components from the German manufacturer rather than make them itself. (To anticipate the subject of the next chapter, the firm substituted a market for a non-market relationship.)

Another application relates to a company's electronic assembly resource. Although this was used in the manufacture of three products it was not as profitable as it might have been because of insufficient volume. "Management was faced with a choice of either getting rid of the dog products and the assembly operation, or of finding a way to increase the volume going through the assembly." This could be achieved either by manufacturing another product needing assembly, or by providing a contract assembly service to other manufacturers.

Banks and Clarke argue that an important factor underlying the success of Japanese companies is the maximisation of throughput in each of their resource centres. For example in the production of small domestic appliances one resource centre is small electric motors. These are included in many different appliances and the major Japanese firms produce "virtually everything which uses this particular type of component. . . . Not only are there the obvious small-motor products like floor-cleaners, food-mixers and coffee mills, but in the scramble to maximise use of their production resources, manufacturers also produce a plethora of more exotic devices. An electric letter-opener incorporating a motor, and an electric foot-warmer incorporating a heating element (another resource centre) are just two examples."[6]

STRATEGY FORMULATION IN MULTINATIONAL ENTERPRISES

A multinational enterprise (MNE) is an organisation that owns income-generating assets in more than one country. Most MNEs operate in several countries and together MNEs are estimated to account for over one-fifth of the world's output (excluding the centrally planned economies).

The USA has given birth to more MNEs than any other country. A study of 400 US MNEs undertaken at the Harvard Business School found that in 1970 they operated nearly ten thousand wholly or partly owned foreign manufacturing subsidiaries. The largest, such as General Motors (one of whose British subsidiaries is Vauxhall Motors) and Exxon (parent of the Esso oil company), had annual sales which exceeded the national income of many countries, including Denmark and Norway. Prominent European MNEs include the Anglo-Dutch Unilever, with operations in Europe, Africa, America etc., Shell (another Anglo-Dutch company) and

---

6. P. Banks and C. Clarke. "How to Tackle Japan". *Management Today* February 1983.

BP in oil, Fiat, Renault, Volkswagen and other major vehicle manufacturers (vehicle production is considered at greater length below). The 1980s have seen an extension of the overseas operations of Japanese companies, e.g. Sony and Hitachi manufacture televisions in the UK for sale in European markets.

All the principles discussed above apply to purely domestic producers and to MNEs. But MNEs have to take additional decisions, particularly relating to the establishment of production facilities in overseas countries. Product facilities may be established overseas for various reasons, and we examine the most important of these in the following sections, beginning with the factors incorporated in the product cycle model.

The product cycle model

The concept of the product life cycle is discussed in Chapter 14. We show there that firms might attempt by various means to prolong the growth stage of the cycle in the domestic market. An expansion of sales can also be achieved by introducing the product into overseas markets. Firms usually do this initially by exporting and subsequently by establishing manufacturing units overseas. (It is, of course, this latter step that characterises the MNE.)

Vernon has argued that the operations of MNEs typically pass through four stages.[7] In the first stage the balance of advantage is clearly in favour of domestic production and sale. The firm's target growth can be achieved in the domestic market. Moreover the firm does not seek potentially low-cost overseas production locations because cost minimisation is not the primary consideration at this point. More importance is attached to the central control of production so that changes in the mix of inputs or sources of supply, required by changing customer needs or changes in technology, can be effected quickly.

During the second stage the product becomes more mature and a certain degree of standardisation is attained. This allows technical economies of scale, and hence lower unit costs, to be achieved. Furthermore, more regular procedures relating to the supply of inputs have been established. More attention has now to be paid to costs because competition has become stronger. (This assumes that the growth in sales has resulted from an innovation to which competitors have now reacted.)

The firm begins to export, to sell into less competitive overseas markets. The additional sales allow full advantage to be taken of economies of scale in production. Many of these economies depend upon the centralisation or linking of production processes (*see* Chapter 5), and this provides an incentive to expand the domestic production facilities and to export to overseas markets.

---

7. R. Vernon. *Sovereignty at Bay: the Multinational Spread of US Enterprises.* Basic Books, New York, 1971. R. Vernon. "The Location of Economic Activity", in J. H. Dunning (ed.). *Economic Analysis and the Multinational Enterprise.* George Allen and Unwin, 1974.

On the other hand there are incentives to establish production units overseas. The cost of some inputs, including land and labour, may be less. (However, firms locating overseas have found that cheaper wage rates are sometimes accompanied by lower labour efficiency—especially when workers are faced with entirely new production processes—leaving labour costs per unit of output at least as high as in domestic plants.) Foreign governments can also encourage overseas manufacture, either by providing financial incentives or by creating barriers to imports. In previous chapters we have noted the importance of flexibility in company strategy. As the more flexible alternative, exporting may continue until the superiority of direct foreign investment has been clearly demonstrated.

Once exports have reached a certain level (stage 3) several factors lead inevitably to direct foreign investment, according to Vernon. Production economies become exhausted, the requirements of overseas customers, including the supply of spare parts and the provision of service, can be fulfilled more quickly from local production units, and further controls are imposed on imports. If the firm does not respond to the changed circumstances by establishing plants overseas, competitors seeking to increase their sales are likely to do so. In other words direct foreign investment may be required to protect market share. Considered in isolation, the returns to such investment may be less than the firm's usual target. Nevertheless the investment may still be justified on broader, strategic grounds. By denying competitors a foothold in this market the firm reduces the possibility that the market can be used to launch a counter-offensive in international trade. This takes us to stage 4.

In this final stage foreign subsidiaries supply both the market in which they are located and, in certain circumstances, other markets, including the parent country. Shipment to the parent country is obviously most likely if production costs are lower overseas, or if the products of the foreign subsidiary do not compete directly with domestic products, e.g. subsidiaries of US car manufacturers have exported compact cars to the USA.

An extension of this final stage occurs when the responsibility for making a product is shared among various subsidiaries, perhaps in conjunction with plants in the parent company. This process has been most fully developed in the production of cars. In order to take the fullest possible advantage of economies of scale, production of various parts of the car—engine, gearbox, axles etc.—is concentrated in different plants, located in different countries. The output of one plant may go to any of several countries for use in the final assembly of the vehicle.

OTHER DETERMINANTS OF DIRECT FOREIGN INVESTMENT

The desire to increase sales, and so exploit to the full an innovation or technical advantage, is the basis of the product-cycle model. But our discussion of the model has shown that decisions on direct foreign investment can be influenced by numerous other factors, and we now explore some of these other factors in greater detail.

Lower costs of production and distribution

Firms often establish production units in overseas countries in order to take advantage of lower production costs, which may result from lower wage rates, cheaper sources of raw materials, nearness to markets etc. These advantages are also available to domestic producers but they may be less well placed to take advantage of them. This is because the multinationals are able to combine these advantages with others specific to themselves.

Specific advantages of MNEs

The MNE has certain advantages over the domestic producer whose activities are confined to the host country. Professor Caves has identified three types of advantage:[8]

(*a*) *Technological advantage in products or processes.* We emphasised the importance of this factor in our discussion of the product cycle model.

(*b*) *Entrepreneurial excess capacity.* This is a specific example of the point made in Chapter 11, that growth is often the preferred way of dealing with the emergence of excess managerial capacity. If the excess capacity comprises personnel with specific skills associated with the production and marketing of existing products, it makes sense to use these products and processes as the base for overseas expansion. (If the excess capacity is in management whose skills are not specific to products, e.g. in computer services, then it is likely to make more sense to aim for conglomerate expansion at home. In such instances the advantage conveyed by excess managerial capacity is likely to be outweighed by the disadvantages *via-à-vis* host country producers, e.g. lack of knowledge of the local market and of sources of inputs).

(*c*) *Multi-plant economies.* There may be certain economies of scale, e.g. in advertising and R&D, that can be enjoyed fully only by building additional plants, whose output is sold in overseas markets. (It would be possible to achieve these economies by building more plants at home and exporting the output, but this can give rise to additional costs.)

Capital abundance

Another advantage enjoyed by the MNE arises from the fact that most MNEs are based in developed countries. This means that they are often able to acquire capital more easily and/or cheaply than firms in underdeveloped countries.

---

8. R. E. Caves. "Causes of Direct Investment: Foreign Firms' Shares in Canadian and UK Manufacturing Industries". *Review of Economics and Statistics*, 1974.

Government policy

As noted above, the governments of foreign countries can encourage foreign investment in two ways. First, they can restrict imports by imposing tariffs and quotas or by requiring importers to adopt time-consuming and costly procedures. (A good example of the latter was the decision in 1982 that all video recorders imported into France had to pass through a small, under-staffed customs point in the remote town of Poitiers.)

The main purpose of these barriers to imports is usually to protect domestic producers or to achieve a more favourable trade balance. An increase in direct foreign investment would be a subsidiary effect. But governments also directly encourage foreign investment by offering a range of financial inducements: grants, subsidies, tax incentives, etc. As unemployment has risen, competition to attract foreign investment has become keener. In the early 1980s several European countries are believed to have offered substantial incentives to Nissan, the Japanese car manufacturer, which was considering establishing a plant in Europe. (In the UK assistance is available on both an automatic basis (Regional Development Grants) and a discretionary basis (Regional Selective Assistance). Discretionary assistance has often been used to attract overseas investment.)

Governments can also encourage foreign investment by providing a stable economic and political environment. This is probably especially important in underdeveloped countries. Foreign investment will be inhibited if firms fear that a government may nationalise foreign assets, block the repatriation of profits or in some other way interfere with their operations.

THE OWNERSHIP OF PRODUCTION FACILITIES

Once a firm has decided to establish production facilities overseas, it must then decide whether to retain complete ownership of these facilities or whether it should enter into alternative arrangements. An advantage of joint ownership is that the operation is less vulnerable to the political risks noted above. Furthermore, local partners can offer local expertise and better access to local markets and sources of supply. It may be possible to acquire expertise by employing local managers. But better access to suppliers and markets may require joint ownership, e.g. with a supplier or major customer. Some raw material producers in the aluminium, copper and oil industries have set up joint ventures to provide downstream marketing outlets for their materials.

The major disadvantage of joint ownership is that it makes future policy less flexible. As a result of changing market or technological conditions, the firm may wish to adjust the geographical allocation of its resources, transferring processes and products from one plant to another. This is likely to be much more difficult to achieve when the subsidiaries are jointly owned.

Another alternative is to license overseas manufacturers to use any patents required for efficient operation. We show in Chapter 12 that this can give the licensor firm a more rapid return on capital employed, and this is especially attractive if there is political instability in the host country. Reciprocal licensing agreements may be established, especially between manufacturers in two (or more) industrialised economies.

PATTERNS OF CONTROL

The main alternative patterns of control adopted by MNEs are shown in Fig. 61. As noted in Chapter 5, there has been a tendency in recent years

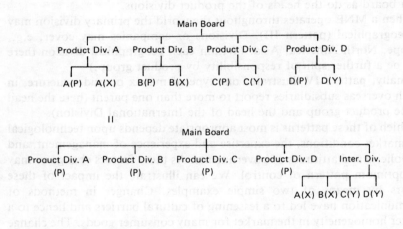

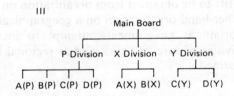

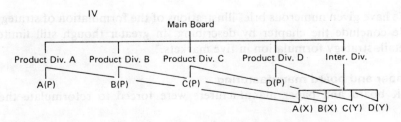

Fig. 61. *Alternative patterns of control.*

for large firms to move from a unitary (U-form) to a multidivisional (M-form) organisation, and this is reflected in the patterns of control shown in Fig. 61.

The hypothetical firm makes four groups of products A, B, C, and D in the parent country P, products A and B in host country X, and products C and D in host country Y. With pattern I authority—below main-board level—is vested in the four product divisions and the head of each division is responsible for its performance in both parent and host country. (The heads of the divisions may, of course, delegate some authority to the managers in the host countries. Indeed European MNEs have typically sought to achieve co-ordination via consensus.)

In pattern II the operations in the parent country are organised on a product-group basis, as before. But the operations in the host countries are combined in an "international division" whose head reports to the main board as do the heads of the product divisions.

When a MNE operates throughout the world the primary division may be geographical (pattern III). Divisions or companies may cover, e.g., Europe, North America, Asia. (Within each geographical division there may be a further split of responsibility by product group.)

Finally, pattern IV illustrates one type of matrix or grid structure, in which overseas subsidiaries report to more than one parent (here the head of the product group and the head of the International Division).

Which of these patterns is most appropriate depends upon technological and market conditions, the expertise and experience of management, and the policies and attitudes of governments. As these factors change so may the optimum pattern of control. We can illustrate the impact of these factors by means of two simple examples. Changes in methods of communication have led to a lessening of cultural barriers and hence to a greater homogeneity in the market for many consumer goods. The change has increased the benefits to be obtained from organisation on a product-group basis. On the other hand organisation on a geographical basis may become more appropriate as governments attempt to increase their influence over the activities of foreign firms, and as regional institutions such as the EEC are formed.

CASE STUDIES

We have given numerous brief illustrations of the formulation of strategy. We conclude the chapter by describing, in greater though still limited detail, strategy formulation in five markets.[9]

Paper and board manufacturing

UK board and paper manufacturers were forced to reformulate their

---

9. These case studies draw on articles appearing in the *Financial Times*.

strategy when tariffs with other members of the European Free Trade Area were ended in the 1960s. Almost overnight the UK changed from a highly protected market to one fully exposed to Scandinavian producers enjoying the advantages of cheap energy and much larger local supplies of wood. Especially vulnerable were the manufacturers of those grades of paper, such as newsprint and kraft liner, which are most economically produced in large, integrated pulp and paper mills. Firms which had to import pulp and convert it into paper in non-integrated mills could not compete in some of these mass production grades.

Import penetration, as a proportion of total UK consumption of board and paper products, increased from 30 per cent in the 1950s to over 50 per cent by 1980.

Firms which have been most successful in meeting competition from imports have adopted a strategy with two important elements. First, they concentrated on the manufacture of products using local raw materials (waste paper and local timber), products, such as tissues, which are difficult to transport, or products which need a mix of pulps and can profitably be made in non-integrated mills, e.g. glossy papers.

The second element of the strategy was investment in machinery to increase the quality of these products and the efficiency of the production process. Wiggins Teape spent £35 million over five years on its carbonless paper operation. Tullis Russell built a £12 million coating plant for the production of a new glossy magazine paper. Thomas Tait and Sons, a small company with trading profits of only around £1 million a year, mainly from the production of upmarket tinted and watermarked papers, spent £6½ million on capital projects in three years. This included a £1 million paper and wrapping line which trebled labour productivity.

One indication of the magnitude of the change in the mix of output is that while UK output of newsprint fell from 760,000 tonnes in 1964 to 114,000 tonnes in 1981, the output of tissues in the corresponding period rose from 186,000 tonnes to 440,000 tonnes.

Banking

As multinational companies have become responsible for an increasing share of production and trade, the major banks have sought to establish international links. Several large consortium banks, jointly owned by a number of European banks, were established. In addition, banks sought direct representation in overseas markets. In the last fifteen years several British banks have taken over banks in the USA. These takeovers gave the British banks access to a large and fast-growing market: many of the acquisitions were on the West Coast of the USA, considered to have very good growth prospects.

The banks also had a particular requirement which distinguished the takeovers from those made by manufacturing companies. This was the need to establish a dollar base. In 1980, when the Midland Bank announced an $820 million plan to acquire a controlling interest in Crocker National Corporation in California, one-third of its world-wide assets were denominated in dollars. But those assets were funded without access to the largest and most secure source of dollar deposits—the American saver.

UK banks obtain "wholesale" deposits from multinational companies and from other banks through the eurodollar markets. They also take substantial deposits from dollar-rich oil exporting companies. But there is always a chance that political upheaval could halt the flow of OPEC dollars to specific groups of banks or banking centres. Moreover, another advantage of retail banking is that in certain circumstances retail deposits are much cheaper than wholesale.

A second important aspect of the banks' strategy has been to widen their product range. Banks now provide finance in a variety of forms in addition to loans and overdrafts—leasing, factoring, hire purchase etc. They also offer, either directly or via subsidiaries, a range of other financial services: insurance broking, the sponsoring of new issues, registrar facilities etc.

Retailing

The merger in 1981 between Habitat and Mothercare brought together two of the most successful retail chains built up in the post-war period. In the early 1960s Selim Zilkha, Mothercare's founder, was the first person to see the opportunity presented by the increase in the number of births. He built up a chain of about four hundred stores (half in Britain, half overseas) specialising in clothes and equipment for babies and expectant mothers: nappies, prams, maternity clothes, medications etc. He exploited the advantages of chain-store buying—lower overheads, bulk ordering, centralised stock control. (Mothercare's stock control and sales reporting systems were generally acknowledged to be among the best to be found in retailing.)

Growth continued through the 1960s and 1970s but as competition increased—for example from the three hundred Baby Boots departments established within the larger Boots stores—Mothercare began to lose market share and its profit margins slipped. (In fact total profits in 1981 were one-seventh less than in 1980.) It appeared that a major cause of this reversal of fortunes was a lack of marketing expertise.

On the other hand Habitat's success in developing a chain of fifty stores selling furniture, furnishings etc. owed a great deal to its marketing skills. It designed a range of furniture with clean lines and a functional appearance, and fabrics with bright but not gaudy colours, with uncluttered patterns. These appealed strongly to young marrieds owning their first home and with a high disposable income. But they were also well received by other segments of the market.

Habitat saw in the merger the opportunity to apply their marketing and design skills to a combined business whose turnover was three-and-a-half times as big as that of Habitat itself. Skills were applied in a number of areas.

Market research was undertaken to discover the characteristics of Mothercare's customers. It was found that a wide range of customers bought necessities for babies (nappies etc.) seen as giving good value for money. But sales of maternity and children's wear were mainly confined to the C_2DE socio-economic groups: "working class" mothers. Mothercare's low-price, high-volume policy had established it as a down-market chain for maternity and children's clothes, and the challenge for the new management was to broaden its appeal.

The key to this was the introduction of more fashionable clothes and a wider product range, e.g. baby foods. Changes were also introduced in advertising, the responsibility for which was given to Habitat's own agency, and in shop design and fittings, drawing on the experience of Habitat's design consultancy unit.

Bus manufacturing

In many European countries the domestic market provides relatively few new opportunities for bus manufacturers. Demand is growing only slowly. Moreover the markets are characterised by substantial barriers to imports. Therefore there is relatively little intra-European trade. These barriers often result from local legislation. Sometimes the encouragement of local producers is overt, as when grants towards mass-transit services are available to local authorities only when local manufacturers supply the vehicles.

European manufacturers have therefore given increasing attention to overseas markets where demand is rising more rapidly. For example in 1980 Saudi Arabia announced their intention to buy 4,000 buses over the next five years, and asked for bids in lots of 400. The importance of this single market can be judged from the fact that the current output of the two major European manufacturers, Leyland and Daimler-Benz, was around six-and-a-half thousand vehicles each.

There are, however, dangers in committing too many resources to these overseas markets. The market in individual countries can be volatile, with high peaks and low troughs. In developing countries in particular, bus orders can arise or be cancelled for basically political reasons which have little to do with mass-transit needs. Moreover in the longer term it is likely that these countries will develop their own bus body-building capacity, possible in partnership with the Europeans. The technology involved is relatively low—much lower than in engine production—and manufacture is labour-intensive, an advantage when a government is seking to create employment. The costs of transportation also favour local assembly. In

1980 it was estimated that the cost of shipping a built-up double-decker from Europe to Hong Kong was £6,000, whereas a separate chassis could be shipped for £1,500 and a body for £200.

These doubts about the long-term viability of exporting assembled vehicles has led manufacturers into offering transport systems or packages. These systems and packages go much further than simply providing service support and training for mechanics. The bus makers can produce for a potential customer a model of a transit system which takes into account the likely number of passengers and vehicles, the nature of the infrastructure and planning regulations.

Using their experience in Europen markets they can demonstrate ways of increasing the efficiency of the mass-transit system (and thus improve the demand conditions for buses). This might involve separating the modes of transportation by providing bus lanes, bus streets, overpasses or tunnels. They can offer advice on bus-stop equipment which can increase reliability and safety, such as elevated boarding platforms. They can explain to local authorities how improvements at intersections can be gained by controlling traffic lights from the bus, providing special bays for buses, and so forth.

In order to provide these services, the bus manufacturers have had to devote resources to the development of expertise not traditionally associated with manufacturing.

Joint ventures in the car industry

The development of the car industry illustrates several aspects of the operations of MNEs: joint ownership of production facilities, reciprocal and non-reciprocal licensing agreements, and collaborative R&D programmes. (This last aspect was discussed in Chapter 5.) Some of the more important links involving European manufacturers are shown in Fig. 62. (Many of these links are operational, but some are still at the planning stage at the time of writing.)[10]

The links referred to in the diagram are as follows:

1. BL makes the Honda Ballade under licence in Britain and sells it, with some modifications, as the Triumph Acclaim.

2. Volkswagen makes body panels for BMW's Six-series cars.

3. Nissan produces a version of the VW Passat for sale in Japan.

4. Nissan and Alfa Romeo have agreed to jointly produce a small car in Italy for sale in Europe. Nissan will supply the bodies from Japan and Alfa the engines and mechanical equipment.

5. Alfa Romeo and Fiat are co-operating in the development of components, e.g. chasses and gearboxes.

6. Seat in Spain has produced cars under licence from Fiat for many years.

10. This diagram, and part of the accompanying commentary, appeared in an article in the *Financial Times*, 19th October 1982.

10. CORPORATE STRATEGY

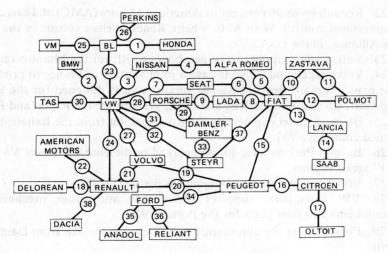

Fig. 62. *European car component links.*

7. After the Fiat–Seat arrangement expires in 1985, Seat will produce 100,000 Volkswagen cars a year.

8. Fiat provided the Soviet Union with the technology required for the production of Lada saloons, based on the old Fiat 124.

9. Porsche of West Germany is doing much of the development work required for a more modern Lada model.

10. The Zastava company in Yugoslavia makes the Fiat 128. The two companies swap components with an annual value of around $500 million.

11. Zastava exchanges components with Polmot of Poland.

12. Polmot makes a version of the Fiat 126 for sale through Fiat's Western European dealership network.

13. Fiat owns Lancia.

14. Lancia and Saab of Sweden are jointly developing a new car. Each company will produce its own distinctive car from a common components "pool".

15. Fiat and Peugeot have a joint project to build one million engines a year in two plants, one in Italy, the other in France.

16. Peugeot owns Citroen (and Talbot).

17. Citroen has a joint venture with the Romanian company Oltoit, which produces a small car, half of the output being for sale through Citroen's Western European dealership network.

18. Renault supplied engines to De Lorean before the collapse of the latter company.

19–20 Peugeot, Volvo and Renault jointly own the FSM company, based in France.

21. Renault owns 15 per cent of Volvo's car business. The two companies are co-operating on the development of new vehicles and components.

22. Renault owns 46 per cent of American Motors (AMC) and exercises management control. With AMC's help, Renault sells a version of the R9, the Alliance, in the USA.
23. Volkswagen supplies some gearboxes to BL for the Maestro range.
24. Volkswagen and Renault have a joint venture in France to produce two new automatic gearboxes. The smaller unit is designed for the Polo and Golf, R5 and R14 models, and the larger unit for the Passat and R18.
25. BL buys diesel engines for the Rover saloon from the Italian state-owned company, VM.
26. BL and Perkins have jointly worked to dieselise the Rover V8 and "O" series engines.
27. Volvo uses a VW diesel engine for the 160 GLE.
28. VW assembles, supplies the engine and other mechanical components and trim parts for the Porsche 924.
29. Porsche buys the automatic gearbox used in the 928 from Daimler-Benz.
30. Volkswagen owns 49 per cent of the TAS company in Yugoslavia, which makes Golfs and Jettas for the local market.
31. Volkswagen and Daimler-Benz own DAUG, a company which undertakes research and development work in electrical engineering and electrical storage systems.
32. Steyr-Daimler-Puch of Austria produces a version of the VW Minibus, using VW bodies and engines.
33. Daimler-Benz supplies components for Steyr's cross-country vehicle.
34. Ford buys Peugeot diesels for the Granada and Sierra.
35. Ford of Britain supplies engines to Anadol of Turkey.
36. Ford supplies the engine used in Reliant's Scimitar sports saloon.
37. Steyr supplies components for the Fiat Panda.
38. Dacia of Romania builds several Renault models under license.

The above list is not comprehensive. For example it excludes the long-term agreement on basic research concluded by the six major European manufacturers: BL, Fiat, the Peugeot group, Renault, Volkswagen-Audi and Volvo. Nevertheless it clearly illustrates the fact that the development of the MNEs may involve a great deal of collaborative activity.

QUESTIONS

1. Explain what is involved at each stage of the strategic planning process.
2. Discuss the role of corporate strategy with reference to (a) a manufacturer of television sets, (b) a producer of high-performance saloon cars, (c) British Airways.
3. Explain how estimates of (a) income elasticity of demand, (b) price elasticity of demand might be useful to manufacturers.

4. How would you expect the demand for the following products to change over the next ten years: (*a*) video recorders, (*b*) school textbooks, (*c*) wines and spirits?

5. Construct a strengths–weaknesses profile for the following retailers: (*a*) Sainsburys, (*b*) Marks and Spencers, (*c*) Harrods.

6. Suggest ways in which the following firms might attempt to fill a planning gap: (*a*) a firm owning a chain of hairdressing salons, (*b*) a publisher of textbooks sold in UK schools, (*c*) a construction company that has specialised in building bridges.

7. What threats and opportunities might face the following organisations over the next ten years: (*a*) a supplier of defence equipment, (*b*) British Rail, (*c*) a firm supplying a contract cleaning service to offices, shops and factories?

8. Discuss the benefits that a firm might expect to obtain from product portfolio analysis, and the dangers of a rigid approach to portfolio selection.

9. Explain the uses to which a resource portfolio matrix might be put.

10. What factors does a multinational enterprise have to take into account, when formulating its strategy, which do not apply to the firm whose activities are confined to a single country?

11. Discuss the relative merits of exporting from a domestic production unit and establishing production units overseas.

12. In what circumstances would each of the forms of control depicted in Fig. 61 be most appropriate?

13. With reference to Fig. 62 and the accompanying text, discuss the benefits of joint ventures under the following headings: (*a*) production and technical, (*b*) marketing, (*c*) financial. Discuss the possible disadvantages of joint ventures.

CHAPTER ELEVEN

Market and Non-market Relationships

OBJECTIVES

After studying this chapter the reader should be able to: explain how a firm can change its mix of activities via market and non-market relationships; describe and give examples of vertical and horizontal relationships; list the advantages of vertical integration, horizontal integration and diversification; give examples of quasi-market relationships.

INTRODUCTION

In the previous chapter we showed that corporate strategy often involves a change in the "shape" of the firm, in the mix of its activities. The firm increases its output of some products and reduces the output of others; it extends or contracts its product range; it withdraws from some of its existing geographical markets and enters others.

The firm can attempt to change its shape by either market or non-market activities. This distinction can be illustrated most simply with reference to a firm that wishes to enter a new product market. It could do this by beginning the production and marketing of the product from scratch (market activities). Alternatively it could merge with or take over a supplier of the product (non-market activities). In this chapter we examine the relative merits of these two approaches, with particular reference to an expansion of activity. We begin by considering vertical relationships. We then discuss horizontal expansion (very briefly) and diversified growth. We conclude by examining two types of quasi-market relationship.

VERTICAL RELATIONSHIPS

Buyer–seller relationships, e.g. between manufacturer and retailer, are established because both buyer and seller benefit. The terms of the relationship may, of course, favour one more than the other. For example an increase in the price of the product, other things remaining equal, favours the seller at the expense of the buyer. Nevertheless the buyer continues to benefit from the relationship. Otherwise he would buy the product from another seller or cease to buy it altogether. Alternatively he could replace market by non-market activities or transactions, i.e. he could begin to manufacture the product himself.

Market relationships
Firms (and individuals) usually plan their activities in the expectation that they will develop long-term relationships with their trading partners. In some instances these plans are very firm, e.g. vehicle manufacturers often

11. MARKET AND NON-MARKET RELATIONSHIPS

"engineer" into their cars components of a design, specification and quality that can be provided by only one or two suppliers, at least at short notice. (When plans are firm, the relationship may extend to co-operation on design and development work between supplier and purchaser. For example Marks and Spencers lay down detailed specifications for their suppliers and institute checks to ensure that these specifications are met.) In other instances the plan is more flexible, as when the housewife usually buys her groceries from a particular shop but also shops elsewhere, e.g. when a visit to the doctor takes her to another part of town.

Several benefits arise from long-term relationships. Costs are usually less when the firm (or the individual) conducts a series of transactions with a small number of trading partners than individual transactions with a much larger number of partners. We can again illustrate this with reference to the shopping habits of housewives. The bulk of purchases are made from the shops usually patronised; if the housewife started from scratch each time, going round all the shops to assess prices, the quality of the products, the level of service etc. she would incur substantial additional costs in time and/or money. Similarly the retailer can reduce his costs by dealing with representatives from only a limited number of manufacturers or wholesalers. The manufacturer's negotiating costs are lower when he sells to a multiple retailer than when he sells the same total quantity to a large number of small retailers. (On the other hand he will obtain a lower price from the multiple). All these are examples of lower transactions costs.

Another, and often more important, reason for developing long-term relationships is the greater continuity of supply inherent in such a relationship. Continuity of supply enables the purchaser to plan his activities more efficiently. The vehicle manufacturer plans his production schedule on the assumption that components of the required quality and in the required quantity will be delivered by the suppliers at specified times. The retailer undertakes local advertising on the assumption that manufacturers will supply him with the goods required to satisfy the consumer demand generated by the advertising. The housewife does not have to include milk on her grocery shopping list because she knows that the milkman will leave three pints on her doorstep at approximately eight o'clock.

Long-term relationships benefit sellers by reducing large and unpredictable fluctuations in sales. Stability of sales facilitates the planning of investment in that plant and equipment can be designed for output capacities in line with expected demand. Complete stability of demand cannot, of course, be guaranteed. Indeed, as pointed out in Chapter 5, firms often install capacity in excess of expected average demand. Nevertheless planning will be easier the greater the degree of certainty concerning the average demand.

Furthermore, the utilisation of plant, equipment and labour will be most effective with a steady pattern of orders. If orders fall below the expected level then average cost may rise, for the reasons explained in Chapter 5, and profits are reduced. If orders are greater than expected, costs are likely to be higher, and hence profits lower, than if the higher output had been anticipated; in order to meet an unexpectedly high demand it may be necessary to introduce overtime working at premium rates; it may be necessary to operate machines at greater than the rated speeds, leading to higher scrap rates.

The firm will still face uncertainty, even when long-term trading relationships have been developed. Purchasers can insure against the worst consequences of uncertainty by maintaining stocks. Suppliers can moderate the impact on output of fluctuations in sales by producing for stock and subsequently drawing on these stocks. This is most feasible when (*a*) the financial costs of carrying stocks are low, e.g. because the product is compact and easily stored, or because interest rates are low, (*b*) the product is standardised so that future demand does not depend upon the orders of a few customers, and (*c*) the product has a long (physical and technological) life.

An alternative way of coping with uncertainty is to produce only to order. This implies a lag between the receipt of the order and delivery, and is feasible only when this practice is accepted in the market in question, as in the markets for such industrial goods as machinery and large computers. Fluctuations in orders are then accommodated by changes in the length of the order book. (Even if production to order is accepted practice, the firm may still lose orders if its delivery dates are not competitive.)

Vertical integration

Having weighed up the costs and benefits of a market relationship, the firm may decide that it would prefer to substitute a non-market relationship, to internalise transactions previously undertaken through the market. This form of internalisation is known as vertical integration or expansion. The advantages of vertical integration can be discussed under several headings.[1]

Increased efficiency

The internalisation of transactions helps to ensure that production processes are linked in the most technically efficient way. Many of the processes in steel making are carried out at high temperatures. Common control of linked processes facilitates their being located in close proximity and hence leads to a saving in the cost of fuel for heating and reheating.

---

1. The classification adopted here follows that in C. J. Sutton, *op. cit.*, Ch. 3. Alternative classifications are used by Hay and Morris, *op. cit.*, pp. 57–62; and : S. Moss. *An Economic Theory of Business Strategy; an essay in dynamics without equilibrium*. Martin Robertson, 1981, pp. 149–54.

Savings in transport costs can also be achieved including the costs arising from damage caused to intermediate products.

Vertical integration may result in savings in administrative costs in two ways. First, if integration occurs by merger or takeover it may be possible to eliminate duplicate facilities such as office buildings and data-processing equipment. Alternatively, if integration is by internal expansion, it may be possible to make fuller use of existing buildings and equipment. Second, administrative costs may be reduced because certain activities inherent in market transactions are not required, or require fewer resources, when these transactions are internalised. (Transactions costs are reduced.)

In illustrating this point Sutton quotes the example of metal castings, which involves the processes of preparing the moulds and casting the metal in the moulds. Since the processes are physically linked, with each mould being built for a specific casting, if they were undertaken by different firms these firms would have to sell to, and buy from each other. But they would be willing to do so only if a firm contractual basis for their relationship could be agreed. They would want a contract "that would not only give reasonable guarantees of quantities and prices but would also specify how prices were to be fixed if patterns or other technical characteristics were to change, and would provide for arbitration in the case of dispute over (say) the quality of the moulds or the causes of any imperfections in the castings".[2] If both processes were undertaken by the one firm it might not be necessary to enter into such elaborate arrangements. Instead the relationship between divisions could be specified by central management.

A reduction in input prices

Even if vertical integration does not lead to an increase in efficiency it may enable inputs to be acquired at lower prices, i.e. at a cost below the purchase price. (Integration which involves a move into earlier processes in the chain of production and distribution is known as backward integration.) This could happen in the short term if the firm has spare capacity and so incurs only variable costs such as the cost of materials and direct labour (*see* Chapter 5).

However, in the longer term the firm would have to take account of all the costs involved in the production of the input, including the cost of replacing plant and equipment as it wears out. Moreover it would have to add to its costs a "profit" margin reflecting the opportunity cost of using its resources in this way (*see* Chapter 5). Only if cost calculated in this way is less than the purchase price can the firm be said to have achieved a reduction in input price(s).

If we continue to make the assumption that backward integration does

---

2. C. J. Sutton. *Op. cit.*, p. 28.

not lead to increased efficiency then a reduction in input prices implies one of two things. First, the expanding firm is willing to accept a lower profit margin than existing producers. Second, the prices charged by existing producers do not reflect the true cost of supplying this firm. For example Oi and Hurter argued that one reason why some American companies met their own transport needs was that the prices charged by specialist transportation organisations were based on average costs for a range of distances or time periods.[3]

Securing access to inputs or outlets
Vertical integration may be undertaken to secure access to inputs or to outlets. (This might be seen as an extreme example of ensuring continuity of supply or purchase.) In some instances firms beginning the production of a product may be obliged to manufacture components because of the absence of reliable or conveniently located suppliers. This situation faced British manufacturers of clocks and watches when they started up in business after the end of the Second World War. In other instances the purchasers of inputs may fear that suppliers will be taken over by rival purchasers who will deny them access to the inputs. In the post-war period the independent builders of car bodies were taken over one by one by the vehicle manufacturers and today no independent of any size survives. Jowett, once a prominent manufacturer, failing to acquire body-building capacity, went out of business.

An extension of this principle is that vertical integration may constitute a barrier against competition. The ownership by brewers of public houses (an example of forward integration) restricts the market opportunities of new brewers since it is difficult to obtain planning permission for new public houses. (However a number of producers of "real ale" have successfully expanded without acquiring more pubs.) Moreover the money required to take over an integrated brewer is very large. (But in practice this has not prevented takeovers in this sector.)

Although backward integration gives greater security of supply, if the firm begins production from scratch (as opposed to taking over an existing producer) it cannot guarantee that the goods will be of the required quality. Similarly, although forward integration gives access to outlets, it does not guarantee that these outlets will themselves achieve satisfactory sales. (The danger of unsatisfactory sales is especially acute when new outlets are opened.) Cyril Lord, a leading manufacturer of tufted carpets, incurred such heavy losses in retailing that the entire business collapsed.

Reduction of uncertainty
Gaining access to outlets and inputs itself reduces uncertainty. In addition forward integration can reduce uncertainty by giving the manufacturer

---

3. W. Y. Oi and A. P. Hurter. "Economics of Private Truck Transportation". In: B. S. Yamey (ed.). *The Economics of Industrial Structure.* Penguin, Harmondsworth, 1973.

better information about market trends, changes in fashion and consumers' tastes etc. Courtaulds, the textiles and clothing manufacturer, claimed that this was one of the biggest advantages accruing from their ownership of retail shops. Backward integration can provide information on technological change, the development of new materials, changes in costs etc.

Problems in vertical integration
The preceding discussion has shown that a firm deciding whether or not to integrate vertically has to take a large number of factors into account. The difficulty of balancing these factors is increased by the fact that it is much easier to predict some of the consequences of integration than others. For example we noted earlier that a potential advantage of integration is that it allows a central authority, such as the board of directors, to specify the relationships between the departments or divisions within the company. However, the board's decisions may be preceded by time-consuming consultations and negotiations, and may give rise to controversy. An example is the decision concerning the "price" to be charged when goods are transferred from one division to another. (Transfer pricing is discussed in Chapter 14.)

A potential disadvantage of vertical integration is that it removes a greater proportion of the firm's activities from the discipline exerted by the market. A supplier to captive outlets may have less incentive to reduce its costs or improve the quality of its products. This loss of efficiency is impossible to measure but it may easily outweigh such benefits as lower expenditure on advertising and distribution, and a reduction in other transactions costs.

Finally, vertical integration may give rise to administrative or mangerial diseconomies. In very large firms diseconomies of scale may arise and it appears that these are most likely to be administrative in nature (*see* Chapter 5). In addition, or alternatively, problems may arise because different management skills are required at the various stages of the vertical chain. Probably the most obvious example is integration of manufacturing and retailing. If integration occurs by merger the individual managements may retain their original authority, in order to ensure that their ability is deployed most appropriately. But this, of course, prevents the firm attaining some of the other potential advantages of integration.

HORIZONTAL EXPANSION

Horizontal expansion—whether by internal growth or merger—comprises an increase in the scale of the firm's existing activities. The car assembler increases the output of cars; the bank lends more money; the advertising agency acquires more clients. We say very little about horizontal expansion in this chapter. This is not because it is unimportant. Indeed it is probably the most important form of growth, at least externally; in most years horizontal mergers are the most numerous. But the two main benefits of horizontal expansion are discussed at length in other chapters, and so are mentioned only briefly here.

First, as shown in Chapter 5, there is a tendency for average cost to fall as the output of a given product increases. This is likely to lead to higher profit margins and a higher rate of return on capital employed. Second, as shown in Chapter 9, firms which achieve a high market share may have more discretion in pricing. This discretion may be used to obtain higher and/or more stable profits.

DIVERSIFICATION

Diversification occurs when a firm undertakes two or more activities which are not vertically related to each other, although they may use the same inputs or be sold through the same channels of distribution. (The introduction of products that are related neither to the existing production base nor to existing channels of distribution is known as conglomerate diversification.)

Figure 63 charts the diversification strategy of the top 200 UK companies. The proportion of single businesses (not less than 95 per cent of sales accounted for by one "basic business") fell from 35 per cent in 1950 to 9 per cent in 1980. The proportion of dominant businesses (less than 95 per cent but more than 70 per cent of sales from one "major business") also fell, from 41 to 26 per cent. On the other hand the proportion of related businesses (sales distributed among a series of "related businesses" such that no one business accounted for 70 per cent of sales) rose from 20 to 47 per cent. Finally, the proportion of

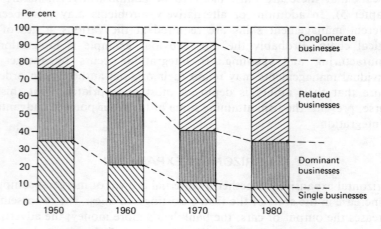

Fig. 63. *Diversification strategy of top 200 UK companies.*

conglomerate businesses (sales distributed among a series of "unrelated/conglomerate businesses" such that no one accounted for 70 per cent of sales) rose from 4 to 18 per cent, most of the increase occurring after 1970.[4]

Motives for diversification

The fundamental reason for diversification is the belief that it constitutes the best strategy for achieving the firm's objectives, whether expressed in terms of profitability or in terms of growth.

Diversification and profitability

As noted in Chapter 10, all firms face a range of threats and opportunities affecting (for ill or good) their profitability. By definition, the threats arise in the firm's existing markets, whereas at least some of the opportunities arise in other markets. Consequently diversification—the seizing of opportunities—can be seen as a means of protecting the firm's profitability.

Profitability may also be enhanced in situations in which the firm's capacity cannot be fully utilised in its existing activities. New products may utilise spare or excess capacity in production, in marketing or in both. The firm should not, of course, assume that spare capacity must be used in this way. An alternative that should always be considered is to dispose of the surplus capacity. But this may not be feasible because of indivisibilities. Machinery which is not fully utilised may still be required for the manufacture of other products. Moreover, potential buyers may undervalue the assets because they lack the information needed for a true appraisal. Only the seller has all the information, and he may not be believed.

Excess capacity may also exist in the management team. Indeed, as we saw above, Edith Penrose has argued that excess managerial capacity will constantly tend to appear as more and more tasks become routinised. Penrose saw the emergence of excess managerial capacity as one of the main forces leading to growth. The disposal of managerial capacity can obviously raise problems, since the senior managers have themselves to make the decisions. Moreover, managers are less likely to strive for increased efficiency if it puts their jobs at risk. Furthermore, there can be indivisibilities in management as in physical assets. Finally, firms are unable to sell managers and thus be recompensed for the skills that the managers have acquired through experience. Together these reasons constitute a strong incentive to seek growth as an alternative to dismissing managers.

A good example of diversification arising from the desire to utilise spare

---

4. D. Channon. "Distribution and Diversification of Large Companies". *Long Range Planning* Vol. 15 (1982).

capacity is given by Sutton.[5] Large-scale computer users frequently find that they have spare capacity in both computer time and in programming and data-preparation services. In order to utilise this spare capacity several large computer users established computer service bureaux alongside their existing businesses. By the end of the 1960s the service bureaux included offshoots from nationalised industries such as the Coal Board and the Post Office, and private firms such as Laing and Wates in civil engineering. Some of these bureaux were so successful in the outside market that their parent companies accounted for only minor parts of their business.

Diversification and growth
A somewhat different perspective underlies Marris's growth theory. As noted in Chapter 8, this theory assumes that diversification is undertaken to enable the firm to attain its target rate of growth. In some instances diversification is highly profitable. But Marris argues that successful diversification and the rate of return on capital employed may be inversely related. As noted in Chapter 8 this is due to the fact that successful diversification requires (*a*) additional expenditure on advertising, other promotional activities, and research and development; and/or (*b*) lower prices to attract customers away from existing suppliers. It is also worth repeating a point made during our discussion of vertical integration. If growth requires new skills—as is likely in diversification—and these are not readily available then a loss of managerial efficiency may result.

It seems possible, then, that diversification may not always be to the advantage of shareholders, who are more interested in profitability (return on capital employed) than growth for its own sake. The shareholders might benefit more from a lower or even zero rate of growth, and by having surplus cash paid out as higher dividends rather than being ploughed back into the business. (This principle could be applied to any form of growth. As we saw in Chapter 8, Baumol's model, which demonstrates the possibility of a trade-off between sales and profitability, does not apply specifically to diversification.)

EXTERNAL GROWTH

The discussion so far has mainly referred to internal growth. But diversification frequently occurs by external growth, i.e. merger or takeover. Of the proposed mergers covered by the Monopolies and Mergers Act 1965, diversified mergers accounted for 12 per cent during 1965–9, 31 per cent during 1970–3 and 27 per cent during 1974–8.[6]

In diversification by merger (or takeover) factors additional to those

---

5. C. J. Sutton. *Op. cit.*, p. 58.
6. *Trade and Industry*, 14th September 1979.

considered above may be important. If two firms have cyclical profits which are out of phase, i.e. the profits of one firm peak when the profits of the other are in a trough, a merger will increase the stability of the combined profits. (Stability of profits may also be achieved by internal expansion, but this is likely to take longer.) Second, the loss of managerial efficiency, referred to above, is less likely to occur if expansion involves an enlargement of the management resource. On the other hand, as noted during our discussion of vertical integration, if the two sets of managers continue to apply their skills to the same range of activities as before, one would not expect to see much of an increase in managerial efficiency.

Some mergers, and especially takeovers, are instituted on the understanding that one set of managers will infiltrate, or even oust, the other set. The belief is that one firm has a particular resource—management expertise—that could be best utilised not by internal expansion but by being applied to the assets of the other firm.

Trans-European mergers

The history of recent trans-European mergers has been disappointing. In 1971 tyre manufacturers Dunlop (UK) and Pirelli (Italy) took large minority stakes in each other's businesses. But the arrangement soon came under strain. Because of losses at Pirelli, Dunlop's investment of £41 million yielded no return until 1980, and in 1981 the arrangements were dissolved. In 1964 two major photographic firms Agfa (owned by Bayer, West Germany) and Gevaert (Belgium) came together on a 50–50 basis. When additional funds were required in 1980 these were provided by Bayer, which thus achieved a 60 per cent holding. The following year Bayer assumed complete control. In 1973 three companies, Siemens (West Germany), Phillips (Holland) and CII (France) merged their computer operations. The arrangement lasted only until 1975 when the French government decided that CII would fit better with Honeywell Bull.

A case study: diversification in British Petroleum[7]

It is not surprising to find that all the major oil producers have begun to diversify. Supplies of the basic raw material will eventually become exhausted, and although no one can predict when this will happen, and although the major producers are continuing to explore for new fields, the rate of depletion of existing proved reserves is such that all the major producers are considering alternative uses of their assets. Moreover, the substantial profits earned in recent years (although not currently) have been sufficient to finance a substantial programme of diversification. Finally, for many companies there is no pressure from shareholders to increase dividend payments rather than use the money to finance new activities.

7. This section draws on an article appearing in the *Sunday Times*, 21st June 1981.

On the whole the major producers have been content to proceed slowly, although Mobil already derives one-fifth of its revenue from outside oil and gas. Most of the companies have moved into energy- or geology-based industries, although some developments have involved unrelated businesses, e.g. Exxon's move into office equipment and information systems and Mobil's move into retailing via the purchase of Montgomery Ward.

In the 1970s BP brought on stream two very large and profitable oil fields, Forties in the North Sea and, through its US subsidiary Sohio, Prudhoe Bay in Alaska. Some of the profits from these fields were ploughed back into oil exploration work, and in 1981 exploration was being undertaken in twenty-six countries, ranging from onshore Britain to offshore China. But expenditure was constrained by a shortage of potentially viable prospects. Profits have therefore been increasingly used for diversification. The broad strategy has been to move into four main business areas which have at the same time widened the geographical basis of the company. These are:

(*a*) The energy sector. BP is moving into the long-distance transmission of natural gas, being active in Abu Dhabi, New Zealand, Nigeria, Northern Europe etc. It has interests in solar energy and uranium mining, but has committed little to synthetic fuels and nuclear energy. It believes that the economies of the business do not justify the former, and the experience of other oil companies does not encourage the latter.

(*b*) Natural-resources industries—basically coal and minerals—involving large-scale operations and international trade, two of BP's strengths. Starting from scratch in 1977, production of coal had reached 17 million tonnes by 1981, and the company has substantial interests in USA, Australia (through its subsidiary Clutha), South Africa and Canada.

BP's major mineral interests are mainly controlled by Selection Trust—purchased for over £400 million—which has worldwide exploration and development expertise, and Kennecott—purchased via Sohio for $1.8 billion—America's largest producer of copper, with interests also in silver, gold and molybdenum.

(*c*) "Step-outs", where BP believes its expertise can be utilised. Largely through acquisitions the company has moved into detergents—a natural progression from petrochemicals—animals feeds and, more recently, foodstuffs for humans.

(*d*) BP Ventures has been established as a home for miscellaneous projects, the emphasis being on high technology. Present projects include solar panels, fluid-bed combustion systems, and the Scicon computer service.

The aim of the diversification programme is to change the distribution of assets along the lines indicated in Table XXIII. The distribution of profits will also change, but the experience of BP and many other companies suggests that there will be a substantial time-lag before some of the new activities are earning profits commensurate with the capital employed. In 1980 coal sales of £383 million yielded a surplus of only £3 million, while minerals made a loss of £3 million.

TABLE XXIII. DISTRIBUTION OF BRITISH PETROLEUM'S ASSETS

Assets	1980 (%)	1990 (%)
Petroleum	83	50
Chemicals	9	10–12
Minerals	3	8
Coal	2½	8
Others	2½	22–24

Diversification and joint ventures

Firms wishing to diversify but being unwilling to enter into a merger may collaborate in joint ventures. Joint ventures were shown in Chapter 10 to enable firms to obtain economies of scale that they could not achieve independently. Many of these joint ventures are concerned with the development of new products and so, by definition, represent diversification.

In some instances collaboration involves the establishment of a company incorporating assets from both parents. For example, in 1940 ICI and Courtaulds established a jointly owned subsidiary, British Nylon Spinners (BNS), to manufacture nylon. ICI had acquired the manufacturing license for the UK from Du Pont, and Courtaulds had long experience in the production of rayon. In 1970 Leyland National was established by the National Bus Company, the country's largest bus and coach operator, and British Leyland, its largest supplier. The assets were jointly owned and the advantages of vertical integration were to be shared.

The formation of a company adds stability to a joint venture, but many such companies subsequently pass under the control of one of the parents. BNS was acquired by ICI following an abortive takeover bid for Courtaulds. In 1981 Bus Manufacturers (Holdings), as Leyland National had been renamed, became a fully owned subsidiary of Leyland Vehicles.

DE-MERGERS

In the late 1970s and early 1980s there was some movement against the dominant tide of growth by merger. There were several reasons for this. First, the economic recession left many companies very illiquid, forcing them to close or sell parts of their business that did not earn adequate profits. Second, the additional assistance made available to small businesses (see Chapter 3) facilitated "management buy-outs", in which senior executives bought from the parent company a part of the business that was unprofitable or did not fit well with the company's major activities. Finally some companies, recognising that the logic of previous mergers was not as strong as had been thought, withdrew from activities that were peripheral to the core. (This often tends to happen following a change of senior management, and especially when this coincides with a worsening of the economic climate.)

This last process is well illustrated by the history of GKN, the large engineering company. The company's steel interests were nationalised in 1967 and the money received in compensation helped to finance a programme of diversified growth. Annual turnover rose from £355 million in 1967 to £1,639 million in 1977, by which time the company was in 120 separate, identifiable businesses.

This was felt to constitute too wide a range of activities to manage effectively under the worsening economic conditions. A divestment programme was drawn up under which the company planned to dispose of about one-eighth of its existing assets. Companies sold or closed in the first two years of the programme included GKN Sankey Plastics and Bumper Divisions, Automotive Fasteners and Firth Cleveland Ropes.

A similar reversal of strategy took place at United Drapery Stores (UDS). In the 1960s and in particular the 1970s it diversified away from its traditional core of ladieswear and menswear shops into mail order, shoe shops, furniture retailing in West Germany, and duty-free shops at Heathrow and Rio de Janeiro airports. This policy appeared to be successful as profits grew from around £2 million in 1954 to a peak of nearly £26 million in 1974–5. However, financing diversification through bank borrowings left the company with heavy interest charges which became even more onerous as the economy turned down.

Moreover, some of the acquisitions proved to be unsuccessful. In 1970 Swears and Wells, the fur and leather chain, was acquired for £4 million but did not earn an adequate profit, and by 1978 all its outlets had been switched to other group stores, mainly Richard Shops ladieswear outlets. In 1971 Myers, a mail order company, was bought for £10.5 million. With around 3 per cent of the market Myers was too small to withstand competition from the market leaders and in 1980 it was sold at a loss to Great Universal Stores. In 1979 Van Allan was bought in an attempt to boost the group's share of the ladieswear market. But the company was making losses when it was purchased and proved to have intractable problems. The solution was again to turn outlets into other group shops.

The group's profits fell in 1980–1 to £12 million, half the level in the previous year. The fall in profits, and the consequent decline in the share price, led, ironically but not unexpectedly, to a (successful) takeover bid for UDS in 1983.

Re-allocation of resources

Companies sometimes divest themselves of some of their activities in order to finance the expansion of the remaining activities. It is possible to effect in this way a distinct change in the "shape" of the company, especially in the case of a smaller concern. For example in the 1970s G. Ruddle and Co, the brewer, achieved a period of substantial growth that proved to be virtually profitless. The company decided that operating as a vertically integrated business, both brewer and retailer, put too great a strain on its resources, financial and managerial. Consequently in 1978 it sold its 38 retail outlets, which at that time accounted for 15 per cent of its sales. It invested the proceeds in new plant. It also increased its marketing expenditure, and by 1982 sales had increased in value by about a half. By emphasising the quality of its beer, Ruddles was able to maintain its prices, despite the intensification of competition, and by 1981 its return on capital employed exceeded 30 per cent.

QUASI-MARKET RELATIONSHIPS

We have discussed market relationships, where firms seek to achieve their objectives by trading with other firms, and non-market relationships, where "trading" activities are internalised. To conclude the chapter we examine two types of quasi-market relationship, licensing and franchising.

Licensing

A firm which develops a new product or process may seek to exploit it entirely from its own resources. Alternatively it may license other firms to produce the product or use the process. The licensor and licensee normally occupy the same place in the chain of production and distribution, i.e. their relationship is usually horizontal. But when they trade in the market for ideas—incorporated in the new product or process—their relationship, as seller and buyer, is vertical.

The choice between going it alone and licensing other producers may be crucial to the well-being of the firm. Two instances in which licensing appears to have been the correct choice are Pilkingtons and Dolby. Pilkingtons decided to license its revolutionary float glass process from the start and although some observers believe that the licence fee was set at too low a level, the firm received massive royalties which were used to develop other new products and processes. Similarly it was probably Ray Dolby's decision to license his pathfinding noise-reduction technology at an early stage which deterred most of the world's tape recorder manufacturers from trying to develop competing processes. The fact that these manufacturers now feature the Dolby system creates both profits and prestige for the originator.

A firm which decided to go it alone, with disastrous consequences, was EMI. It launched the world's first commercial scanner—a brain scanner—in 1972. By 1975 it had received orders for 360 brain scanners out of a world total of 365, and for 40 body scanners out of a world total of 201. However the technological lead established by EMI was gradually whittled away. Indeed, competitive models were introduced that were superior in some respects, e.g. a shorter scan time. Consequently, EMI was unable to withstand the tougher competitive situation that arose when spending on medical equipment was reduced in the USA, the major market. The company's medical electronics division, which made a profit of £14.7 million in 1977, made a loss of £13.2 million in 1978. Further losses followed and eventually EMI was taken over by Thorn, which subsequently withdrew from the scanner market.

There is no doubt that EMI should have sought to license its technology, but this verdict is, of course, given with the benefit of hindsight. It has been suggested that decisions as to whether to sell technology can be improved by applying the concept of the "technology life cycle". Ford and Ryan distinguish six stages of the cycle, at any of which the company might decide to sell its technology.[8]

The first two stages are when the technology is still under development and before it is applied to a new product. In the USA General Electric has established a formal system for marketing technologies that it does not intend to apply to new products, either because it considers the markets too small, or because they lie outside its areas of interest.

The third stage is when the application is first launched. Ford and Ryan forecast a growth in the number of companies whose sole aim is the development of technologies to the "application launch" stage, for sale to other companies.

The fourth stage is when the application is growing within the innovating company, as it was in EMI's case before it attacked the US market. It is at this stage that a decision to sell can be a powerful disincentive to competitors to engage in their own technological development.

The issue of government and industry standards is also frequently vital at this stage, according to Ford and Ryan. The active sale of licences by the originator "will help ensure that its technology is incorporated into the production of as many companies as possible. Different technologies are often incompatible, and thus the first company to have its technology widely adopted may well set the technology standard for everyone." Other factors favouring a sale of technology would be a shortage in the innovating company of cash and marketing resources (both of which contributed heavily to EMI's collapse). On the other hand the existence of spare capacity in the innovating company would militate against the sale of licences.

8. D. Ford and C. Ryan. "Taking Technology to Market". *Harvard Business Review*. Vol. 59 (1981).

In the final two stages of the technology's life cycle, "maturity" and "degraded", Ford and Ryan maintain that markets for the technology will still be found, particularly in the developing world. However they advocate caution: "No producer wants to stumble by accident into the kind of competition that Fiat now faces in its West European car market from its licencees in the Soviet Union and Poland." (*See* Fig. 62, Chapter 10).

Franchising

Franchising describes a situation in which a company establishes a contractual relationship with the owners of separate businesses which operate under the franchisor's name in a specified manner to market the product or service. The relationship between franchisor and franchisee is a vertical one, but franchising also conveys some of the advantages of horizontal integration. The origins of franchising in the UK can be traced back almost two centuries to when the brewers first created the tied-public-house system to guarantee outlets for their beer. During the twentieth century it has developed mainly in the motor trade through franchised petrol stations, car dealers and spare part dealers, and in food retailing through the voluntary groups such as Spar and VG. But in recent years franchised operations have been established in a wider range of markets. Retail sales through members of the British Franchise Association reached almost £400 million in 1981 and were forecast to exceed £500 million in 1983. (This excludes franchises of the major motor manufacturers, the grocery voluntary groups and other large groups such as the brewers, Coca-Cola and Holiday Inns.)

This widening of the scope of franchising reflects its advantage in facilitating the rapid exploitation of a new product or service, in particular by ensuring that capital is contributed by a large number of operators. (The economic recession has made redundancy payments a frequent source of capital.) Expertise is also jointly provided. The franchisor contributes his knowledge of the system (product and process), while the franchisees utilise their experience of local markets.

Of these newer areas for franchising two have proved especially important: fast-food operations such as Wimpy, Kentucky Fried Chicken and Spud-u-Like, and servicing companies such as Dyno-Rod and Prontaprint. Other markets include hairdressing e.g. Steiner, vehicle rustproofing e.g. Ziebart, and self-drive vehicles, e.g. Budget Rent-a-Car.

Franchising is much bigger business in the USA and is continuing to grow there despite the recession. Total sales of all franchised goods increased by over 15 per cent in 1981 to well over £400 billion. The number of franchised outlets is approaching half a million, employing around 5 million people.

The number of markets with franchise operations is, of course, much greater than in the UK but the emphasis tends to be similar, with franchising being especially important in petrol stations, car dealers, soft drink bottlers, and restaurants. The future expansion of franchising is expected to come from professional and other service areas, e.g. dental centres, insurance agents, lawyers and opticians.

QUESTIONS

1. Distinguish between market, non-market, and quasi-market relationships.

2. Discuss the advantages and disadvantages of vertical integration with particular reference to (*a*) brewing, (*b*) steel production, (*c*) the production of cars.

3. Explain the benefits to producers of stability of demand, and discuss the ways in which they might attempt to moderate the impact of fluctuations in sales.

4. What factors might account for the changes shown in Fig. 63?

5. "Diversification is good for management's ego but not for the shareholder's purse." Discuss.

6. How do you account for the trend towards de-mergers?

7. "Licensing and franchising both represent an abdication of the innovator's responsibility for product development." Discuss.

8. A leading pharmaceutical company develops a patented product which assists in the early prediction of cancer. What factors might influence its choice between allowing other firms to manufacture the product under licence and retaining a monopoly of its manufacture?

CHAPTER TWELVE

The Nature and Impact of Technological Change

OBJECTIVES

After studying this chapter the reader should be able to: define and give examples of technological change; distinguish between technical change and product change; explain the relationships between technological change and the choice of production technique; outline the strategic objectives of research and development; construct a check list of the type used in the selection of an R&D portfolio; understand the importance of R&D in modern industry.

INTRODUCTION

Technology can be defined as information concerning what products could be produced and the processes by which they could be produced.[1] Technological change can then be defined as a change in information, a change in awareness concerning the production possibilities (products and processes). This change in awareness sometimes occurs when one person recognises an opportunity that other people have failed to recognise. But more often it arises out of research and development work, whose purpose is by definition to improve awareness of opportunities, to provide information not previously available.

Figure 64 summarises the various elements of technological change. The motive force is research and development, which includes both scientific and marketing research. Scientific research and development is especially important with regard to new techniques or methods of production, for both established and new products. Marketing research is important when new products are produced (whether by new or existing techniques).

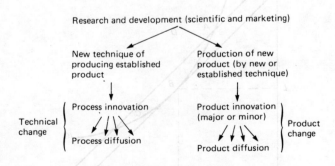

Fig. 64. *The elements of technological change.*

---

1. Other writers have adopted different definitions of technology. For a more detailed examination of technology as information see Hay and Morris, *op. cit.*, pp. 441–2.

Technical change comprises two stages: the first application of a new technique (process innovation) and the subsequent application of this technique by other firms (process diffusion). Product change also comprises two stages. The first is product innovation, which relates to the initial introduction of a new or modified product (major or minor innovation). The second stage, product diffusion, refers either to the introduction of the new (or modified) product by other producers, or to its adoption by other customers.

Technological change refers to new production possibilities that can be exploited in practice, not simply in theory. Technological change occurred, not when it was first realised that supersonic flight was theoretically possible, but when it became possible to build engines with the required thrust, when metals were discovered that could withstand the heat generated in flight, and so forth.

TECHNOLOGICAL CHANGE AND THE CHOICE OF TECHNIQUE

In this section we consider how technological change might affect the production of an established product, i.e. we are concerned with technical change. The initial situation is depicted in Fig. 65, which shows the amount of labour and capital required to produce a given quantity of the product by alternative techniques or methods, given the current technology, the current state of knowledge. The equal-product curve or isoquant IQ contains the most efficient points; it maps the technically efficient frontier. Any point beyond the frontier would require more

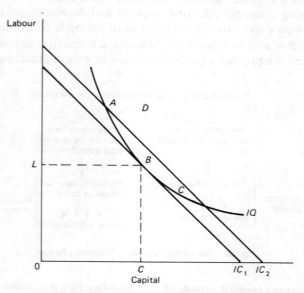

Fig. 65. *Factor costs and the choice of technique.*

labour and/or capital to be employed. For example point D requires more capital than point A (and the same amount of labour), and more labour than point B (and the same amount of capital).

The firm will normally choose the technique that minimises the cost of producing a given output. The isocost curve IC_1 shows the cost of alternative combinations of labour and capital. The technique represented by point B would minimise cost, since IC_1 is tangential to IQ at that point. (L labour and C capital will be employed.) Cost would be higher at all other points on the frontier; for example the technique represented by A would require an outlay IC_2.

The impact of technological change can be illustrated by reference to Fig. 66. The discovery of more efficient methods of production causes the efficiency frontier to shift towards the origin from IQ to IQ'. With the relative price of labour and capital unchanged, the new cost-minimising technique is that represented by point E at which IC_0 is tangential to IQ'. (The parallel shift of the equal-product curve indicates that the technical change is neutral, i.e. gives rise to equal savings in capital and labour. In practice, technical change may be either neutral or biased towards one factor.)

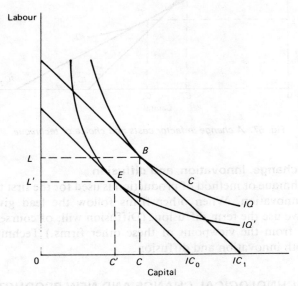

Fig. 66. *Technical change and a change in technique.*

In this example technological change leads directly to a change in the production technique used. Technological change also affects the response to a change in factor prices. In Fig. 67 the initial isocost curve is again IC_1, and B represents the cost-minimising technique. But if the price of labour rises relative to that of capital, as denoted by a shift of the isocost curve to

IC_2, then the new cost-minimising technique is C, where IC_2 is tangential to the equal-product curve. Labour employed falls from L_1 to L_2; capital employed rises from C_1 to C_2. Technique C became apparent as part of technological change in a previous period.

Finally, technological change may encompass both processes described above. Research and development may be undertaken in order to discover more efficient techniques, and in particular techniques which require less of an input whose price has increased, or is expected to increase.

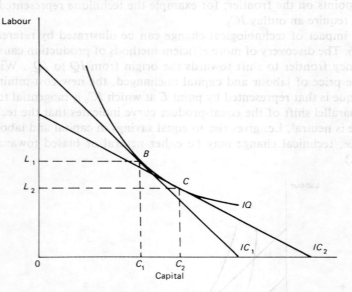

Fig. 67. *A change in factor costs and choice of technique.*

Technical change, innovation, and diffusion

When a technique or method of production is used for the first time we use the term innovation. When other firms follow the lead given by the innovator we use the term diffusion. (Diffusion will, of course, represent innovation from the viewpoint of these other firms.) Technical change includes both innovation and diffusion.

TECHNOLOGICAL CHANGE AND NEW PRODUCTS

As noted in the introduction, technological change includes information relating to the production of new products (which may in turn involve new processes). In some instances the new product may be introduced as soon as possible. In other instances it may be kept "on ice", being introduced subsequently, e.g. to compensate for a fall in demand for some of the firm's existing products.

Product change, innovation and diffusion

Product change comprises innovation and diffusion. Innovation refers to the production of a new or "pioneer" product. As noted above, diffusion sometimes refers to the subsequent introduction of this product by other producers. But it is more often applied to diffusion of use among consumers.

RESEARCH AND DEVELOPMENT AS AN INVESTMENT DECISION

As noted above, research and development expenditure enables the firm to take advantage of opportunities. This is also true of expenditure to enlarge the firm's capacity, and expenditure on market investment, e.g. advertising. Thus R&D has to compete for funds with these other forms of investment. In principle the firm should allocate its expenditure in such a way as to equalise the marginal returns from each form of investment as noted in Chapter 6. But in practice it would be impossible to achieve this, since the returns cannot be accurately estimated. Furthermore, many investment programmes require two or all three forms of expenditure.

The difficulty of estimating the return to investment is particularly acute for R&D which, by definition, is concerned with the exploration of the unknown. (This is especially true of expenditure on basic research.) This may be one of the main reasons why firms often fix their total R&D budgets before specific ideas or projects are identified and assessed, and why the budgets tend to be fairly stable from one year to the next. The firm may have a good idea, based on past experience, as to the total R&D expenditure required to meet its strategic objectives (*see* below), even though it cannot predict the returns from individual projects.

A second reason for stability in R&D spending is the high cost involved in fluctuations in the level of R&D activity. The cost may not be very high in accounting terms. Since staff costs are normally a high proportion of total costs, it is possible to effect a considerable reduction in costs when activity falls (although in the short term the firm might incur heavy redundancy payments). But dismissing staff is likely to have a high opportunity cost. Some redundant staff may find employment with rivals who may thereby obtain valuable commercial information. Furthermore, the productivity of an R&D team is usually enhanced by their experience of working together. Consequently, if the team is disbanded and subsequently another team is built up, some loss of efficiency is to be expected.

Finally there may be a threshold—in terms of either the number of personnel or total expenditure—below which R&D expenditure ceases to be worthwhile. This is more likely to be true if the firm is hoping to make major technological advances than if its aim is a series of small, incremental innovations.

STRATEGIC OBJECTIVES OF RESEARCH AND DEVELOPMENT

The discussion of corporate strategy in Chapter 10 clearly demonstrated the important role played by the introduction of new products and processes. We showed that innovation could be a means of either seizing opportunities or counteracting threats. This corresponds fairly closely to the distinction that is sometimes made between offensive and defensive innovation.

Offensive innovation

Under this heading it is useful to make a further distinction between major and minor innovations. Although in practice it is not always clear where to draw the dividing line, it is easy to identify innovations located at the two ends of the spectrum. An entirely new product is a major innovation, a change in styling is a minor innovation. (If the change in styling is small and cosmetic, i.e. not affecting the product's performance, it would probably not even be classified as an innovation.)

Major innovations

Examples of major innovations are the Polaroid camera, colour television and the Hovercraft. It is interesting to note that despite the importance attached to economies of scale in R&D many major innovations emanate from small firms (although the large-scale commercial development is sometimes undertaken by large firms). Major product innovations are a means by which firms, and especially small firms, can grow quickly, and they often result in substantial changes in market shares.

When an innovation—in product or process—is protected by a patent the innovator may choose to take some of the rewards in the form of licence fees and royalties. When Pilkingtons patented the float-glass process they retained their monopoly of production in the domestic market, but licensed a considerable number of producers in overseas countries. Licensing reduced the development cost incurred by Pilkingtons and produced a more even pattern of cash flow. Many products are made under licence, especially in overseas markets. Markets—both domestic and overseas—can also be developed quickly through the franchise system. The franchise holder pays a fee together with royalties, in return for which he enjoys the benefits of the brand name, central advertising, advice, e.g. on site location, etc.

Minor innovations

Minor product innovations comprise changes in product specifications relating to performance, styling, size etc. All products offer consumers a range of benefits. For example, food can provide nutrition, a pleasant taste, and a pleasant appearance. Different foods offer different combinations of benefits and of the associated costs of purchase and preparation. These different offerings appeal to consumers with different requirements. Many minor innovations are designed to appeal to customers whose requirements are not fully satisfied by existing products. So we have models of cars with numerous permutations of engine size, number of doors, number of gears and various styling features. Toothpaste comes in various colours, detergents are available in various pack sizes, television sets have different sizes of screen. The term "filling the characteristics space" has been applied to this expansion of the range of characteristics offered to the consumer.

In introducing product variations firms hope to increase their sales and hence their profits. This requires customers to be taken away from rival producers—unless the total market expands—and in this sense the innovation is offensive. It is also offensive in the sense that the more of the characteristics space that is filled by one producer the less space is available for other producers, including potential entrants to the market.

The use of minor innovations to deter potential new entrants is especially important where there are economies of scale that make it difficult for new entrants to match the costs, and hence the prices, of existing producers. Faced with a cost disadvantage, entrants will seek unfilled characteristics space; they will search for a niche in the market.

Characteristics space in the car market
As noted above, many car manufacturers now offer a range of alternative versions of a given model in order to fill as much of the characteristics space as possible. Some manufacturers have also expanded their range of models for the same reason, e.g. Ford now competes in the executive class market. But this is a comparatively recent development. In the early post-war years the major manufacturers tended to confine themselves to a few well-defined segments of the market, and this left space which was exploited by smaller manufacturers.

In 1955 BMW produced only a few hundred conventional (i.e. four-wheeler) cars; by 1970 annual production had increased to more than 140,000 (with further expansion since then). The basis of BMW's success was the development of the sports saloon, which combined some of the traditional qualities of the sports car—speed and good roadholding—with the luxury seating and finish found in high-quality saloons. The consumers to whom this particular combination of qualities appealed, and who could afford to pay the appropriate price, were young, successful executives whose spending power was high, and who wished to dissociate themselves from the customs of their elders, including buying large prestige limousines, but who also wished to distinguish themselves from the mass of their less successful brethren. The success of BMW's marketing director, Herr Paul Hahnemann, in identifying and exploiting this gap in the market earned the title of *"Nische-Jäger"* (niche-hunter).

Numerous other manufacturers exploited gaps in the car market. DAF introduced a belt-driven automatic transmission which was much cheaper, simpler and more reliable than the conventional hydraulic automatic transmission, and the first system that could be fitted to low-priced popular saloons. Volvo's expansion in foreign markets was based mainly on the reputation of its car for safety and durability. Saab, Sweden's other car manufacturer, made a similar appeal, with perhaps even more emphasis on safety, although rather less on luxury.

The customer as initiator of innovation

A supplier may be made aware of the existence of a gap or niche in the market by a customer. In fact customers are known to be a very important source of ideas for innovation. In a study of chemical products Meadows found that 9 out of 17 successful innovations (53 per cent) stemmed from ideas generated from customers. In Peplow's investigation of plant processes, process equipment and techniques, 30 out of 48 projects (62 per cent) resulted from direct requests for consumers. Utterbach found that 75 per cent of innovations in the field of scientific instrumentation derived from "need input" and that "when need input originated outside product manufacturer (57 per cent), source was most often customer".[2]

Supplier–customer co-operation

When a customer brings a need to the attention of a supplier this often leads to co-operation in the R&D work required to satisfy this need. Co-operation in R&D may also be initiated by suppliers who need a "test bed" for the results of R&D activity. Gesternfeld's investigation of twenty-two new product launches in West Germany led him to the conclusion that "outside assistance from other firms was used often and was associated with successful projects in nine out of eleven successful innovations." Broadly similar results have been reported for the USA and the UK, as shown in a review paper by von Hippel. This paper "strongly supports the view that, in industrial markets, prospective customers are instrumental not only in aiding the development and modification of existing product concepts via the usual channels of marketing research and test marketing—but additionally in the initiation of potentially innovative concepts."[3]

We have discussed offensive innovation mainly with respect to products, since its effects can be seen most clearly here. Process innovation improves the efficiency with which existing products are made and so is not offensive in the same sense. However, if the innovation enables the firm to reduce its price and so increase its market share then it can be seen as indirectly offensive.

---

2. The studies by Meadows, Peplow and Ulterbach are discussed in: A. L. Minkes and G. R. Foxall. "The Bounds of Entrepreneurship: Inter-Organisational Relationships in the Process of Industrial Innovation". *Managerial and Decision Economics* Vol. 3 (1982)

3. Minkes and Foxall. *Op. cit.*

Defensive innovation

Defensive innovation takes several forms. First it refers to innovation undertaken in retaliation to a prior innovation. Firms whose innovation is defensive can choose between seeking a licence from the "offensive" firm (in which case the initial innovation would be diffused) and trying to counter the innovation independently.

The decision will depend upon several factors. First, would the firm's resources enable it to counter the innovation? This will depend partly, of course, upon the scale and nature of those resources, especially in research and development, and partly upon the nature of the innovation. A differentiated product with a large number of characteristics is easier to imitate without infringing patents than is a new process which is the culmination of years of R&D activity.

The firm must also consider whether its resources would enable it to effectively exploit the licence if granted. Effective exploitation is most likely when the firm has considerable experience with the product or process in question. The dangers that can arise in the absence of experience are illustrated by the problems met by G. and E. Bradley, a subsidiary of Joseph Lucas, when it tried to enter the market for oscilloscopes. To avoid the heavy cost of developing its own product Bradley accepted a licence from a French firm. Unfortunately the instrument had been operated by the licensor in a development version only. Technical problems were revealed as soon as Bradley attempted full-scale production, and Bradley lacked the expertise to "debug" the instrument without outside assistance.[4]

Other very important considerations are how easy it would be to obtain a licence, and what the cost would be. Licences are most likely to be granted to a firm which is not going to compete directly with the innovator. As noted above licences are usually granted more freely in foreign than in domestic markets.

Sometimes innovation is a reaction to a potential or impending threat. The knowledge that a firm is working on a new process or product may stimulate rivals to accelerate their R&D programmes in the hope of being able to patent the process or product. In some industries innovation has become such an important part of the competitive process that each producer believes that it must innovate to survive; the threat is generalised. Commenting on the car industry in the USA, Scherer says: "Auto producers believe they cannot afford not to cover themselves against rival thrusts. Knowledge that others are preparing new models, coupled with uncertainty over the exact character of their plans, compels each firm to sustain its own style change effort."[5]

Innovation is also essential to success in pharmaceuticals. The

---

4. C. Layton. *Ten Innovations.* George Allen and Unwin, 1972.
5. F. M. Scherer. *Industrial Market Structure and Economic Performance.* Rand McNally, Chicago, 2nd Edition, 1980, p. 399.

importance of new drugs can be seen from the fact that of the leading 150 drugs by sales value in 1972, 96 per cent were developed after 1947 and over half after 1963. Of the leading ten firms in 1965 (ranked by total value of sales), only six remained in that group in 1976. The second firm had fallen to nineteenth, and the third firm to thirty-third.[6] In such a situation the distinction between defensive and offensive innovation tends to disappear.

In the discussion so far we have concentrated on innovation undertaken as a response to a threat—specific or general—emanating from within the industry or market. Innovation is also undertaken in an attempt to counter a decline in the total market. The National Coal Board responded to the decline in demand for coal by developing fuel-processing techniques to provide smokeless fuels, and improved blending techniques to allow the use of lower-quality coals. They have also collaborated in the development of more efficient combustion systems and techniques for handling coal and ash, innovations which reduce both the price per therm and the unfavourable non-price attributes such as dirt and inconvenience.[7]

PORTFOLIO SELECTION

In some instances it is clear how the firm should allocate the funds earmarked for research and development. In smaller firms R&D is often concerned with implementing the ideas of the owner or the technical director, who will be clear as to which development should be given priority. When technology is changing very rapidly the potential rewards from one line of approach may be so great that priority in R&D is again determined more or less automatically.

But many firms, especially those with large R&D budgets, have a considerable amount of discretion as to how they should allocate at least part of these funds. In choosing among alternatives, in determining the composition of their R&D portfolios, firms often find it helpful to draw up a check list of the factors that could influence the success of each project. Such a check list might group the factors under a number of headings. For example Betts has suggested five headings, as below.[8]

Market

Does the product meet an unsatisfied market need? This is most likely when the idea comes initially from a customer. What is the growth potential? What is the strength of competition? Even if the growth potential of the overall market is satisfactory it is important to ensure that the firm is able to withstand competition from other suppliers who might enter the market. The failure to do so became known in the USA as the

---

6. W. D. Reekie. "Pharmaceuticals". In: P. S. Johnson, *op. cit.,* p. 155.
7. R. B. Thomas. "Coal". In: P. S. Johnson, *op. cit.*, p. 75.
8. R. J. Betts. *Business Economics for Engineers* McGraw-Hill, London, 1980, p. 147.

"Lestoil syndrome". Lestoil was a small company that pioneered the market for liquid household cleaners. Initially it was very successful, but its success attracted the attention of the giant detergent manufacturers (Procter and Gamble, Lever Brothers and Colgate Palmolive) whose entry decimated Lestoil's market share.[9] The possibility of being able to protect the innovation via a patent is obviously important in this context.

If the market prospects are satisfactory the firm should consider whether the product would fit with the sales patterns of its existing products, and whether it would enhance or detract from the sales of these products.

Marketing

The most important consideration under this heading is probably whether in marketing the new product the firm would be able to build upon its existing reputation. Cadbury's have been able to build upon their reputation as a manufacturer of good-quality chocolate in the marketing of a range of other foodstuffs including hot drinks, biscuits and instant potato. A firm may be unable to build upon its reputation either because it has not yet established a reputation, as would be true of most small firms attempting to enter a market on a national scale, or because the product would be sold in an entirely new market into which the firm's reputation would not carry over. In these circumstances it may be especially important that the product should itself have distinctive "promotable" features.

There are considerable advantages to be gained from introducing a product which can be sold through the firm's existing channels of distribution. If this is not feasible it is necessary to ensure that alternative channels could be used. Finally the firm should make an estimate of the likely price competitiveness of the product. This will be influenced by the factors listed below.

Production

Would the new product use the firm's existing production facilities? As we showed in Chapter 10, a desire to utilise spare production capacity is an important motive for the introduction of new products. Would the product use familiar raw materials and technology? The need to use unfamiliar materials and technology explains some of the more spectacular unsuccessful innovations such as British Rail's Advanced Passenger Train. The risk attached to innovation is also reduced if the new product uses the existing skills of the workforce and company expertise in other areas.

9. C. J. Sutton. *Op. cit.*, p. 162.

Research and development

The discussion under the three previous headings has been based on the assumption that the "shape" of the proposed project was clear, e.g. that the attributes of a product had been identified. But is is often necessary to allocate R&D funds without having so clear an idea of what the technical outcome of the spending will be. In fact the first question to be asked under this heading is: What is the probability of technical success? The answer to this question should be considered together with the answer to another equally fundamental question: What is the likely cost of the project?

The time scale of the project should be assessed since this will affect both its cost and the potential rewards. In general one would expect the potential rewards to be greater the more quickly the innovation is introduced. On the other hand there is evidence to suggest that accelerating the rate of development increases the total cost of development. These two tendencies are illustrated in Fig. 68. The firm should choose the rate of development that maximises the expected excess of benefits over costs.[10] With expected benefits as indicated by B and cost by C, this would be time T.

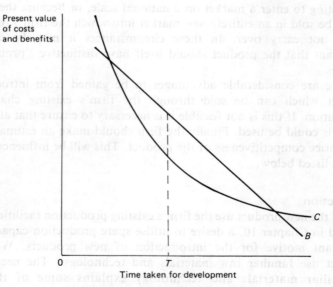

Fig. 68. *Project costs and benefits.*

Where a great deal of uncertainty surrounds the outcome of alternative projects, the firm may institute several alternatives in parallel. These alternatives are followed until enough progress has been achieved to choose one for further development. Parallel development prevents the

---
10. C. J. Sutton. *Op. cit.*, p. 182.

12. THE NATURE AND IMPACT OF TECHNOLOGICAL CHANGE

firm from making a premature commitment to a single route that could eventually have to be abandoned. By reducing the risk that the work will have to be started again from scratch, it may save time.

This is illustrated in Fig. 69. £200,000 is allocated to each of three alternative projects A, B, and C. When this money has been spent, it becomes clear that A is the most promising, and all further work is concentrated on it.

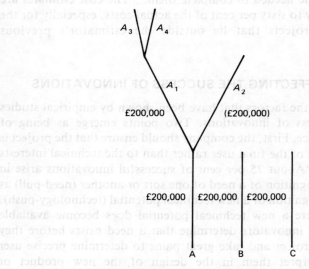

Fig. 69. *A decision tree for expenditure on R & D.*

Figure 69 also illustrates the use of a decision tree. Although A has been chosen, alternative choices for further development exist. These alternatives, A_1 and A_2, which would each cost a further £200,000 to explore, might refer, for example, to the use of alternative materials which would give the final product different characteristics. If the firm feels that it would be wasteful to follow both alternatives it will choose A_1. The opportunity cost of this choice is that A_2 is not pursued. It is possible that at a later stage a further choice between alternatives (A_3 and A_4) will have to be made.

Although the firm is concerned with the payoff of individual projects, it should also consider what further development possibilities may exist. When an aircraft manufacturer considers introducing a new airliner with a given capacity he might also take account of the possibility of introducing a "stretched" version at a later date. A car manufacturer developing a new saloon might take account of the possibility of subsequently introducing an estate version.

Finance

We have already noted that the firm has to assess the likely cost of the project. It must then ensure that this cost is compatible with the firm's balance-sheet objectives and that it fits in with its cash-flow requirements. Many developments have been abandoned because their costs turned out to be higher than anticipated, and outstripped the firm's financial capacity. This was the main reason for the demise of Rolls Royce Ltd. Indeed it seems that firms generally underestimate both the cost of the projects and the time needed to complete them. "The cost estimates are often as low as forty to sixty per cent of the actual costs, especially for the most ambitious projects that lie outside the estimator's previous experience."[11]

FACTORS AFFECTING THE SUCCESS OF INNOVATIONS

Sutton summarises the factors that have been shown by empirical studies to affect the success of innovations. Two points emerge as being of particular importance. First, the company should ensure that the project is related to the needs of the final user rather than to the technical interests of the innovator. "About 75 per cent of successful innovations arise in response to the recognition of a need of one sort or another (need-pull) as opposed to the recognition of a new technical potential (technology-push). In those cases where a new technical potential does become available first . . . successful innovators determine that a need exists before they proceed with the project and take great pains to determine precise user needs and to interpret them in the design of the new product or equipment."[12]

Second, a number of organisational features help to achieve success, the most important being: (a) subjecting the project to independent appraisal at an early stage before it gathers too much organisational momentum; (b) the establishment by management of a clear strategy and a concentration on projects contributing to that strategy, (c) co-operation between R&D staff and operating staff, especially production and marketing personnel. Interviews conducted by Mansfield and Wagner with R&D and operating executives in eighteen US firms suggested "that the overall probability of commercial success might have been fifty per cent greater than it was (that is, 0.5 rather than 0.32 for these firms) if the projects had been appreciated fully, and exploited correctly, by the production and marketing departments."[13]

11. C. J. Sutton. *Op. cit.*, p. 178.

12. R. Rothwell. "The Characteristics of Successful Innovators and Technically Progressive Firms". *R&D Management* Vol. 7 (1977). *See also* the discussion in: C. J. Sutton, *op. cit.*, p. 180.

13. E. Mansfield and S. Wagner. "Organisational and Strategic Factors Associated with the Probability of Success of Industrial R&D". *Journal of Business* Vol. 48 (1975), as quoted in: C. J. Sutton, *op. cit.*, p. 180.

A factor that is assuming increasing importance is the need to take a very long-term view of the returns to research and development expenditure. This is illustrated by results produced by the ICI corporate model. If the introduction of new products ceased, profits would decline only slowly at first; it would be around fifteen years before a sharp decline set in. If then, the danger having been (belatedly) recognised, the rate of innovation could be instantaneously increased to three times what it was before it ceased, it would take another 25 years for profit to recover to the level achieved before the introduction of new products was stopped. In the meantime profit would have fallen to about 60 per cent of its original value.[14]

These figures illustrate the fact that market acceptance of a new product may be slow. This is also illustrated by the results of a study of the reasons for Japan's clean sweep of the world market for video cassette recorders—a Philips–Grundig product excepted—by Rosenbloom and Abernathy. They point out that all the companies which developed video cassette technology tried prematurely to commercialise it in the form of a consumer product, and failed at least once. The American companies withdrew after the failure of their early efforts whereas Sony and Matsushita–JVC were able to maintain a strategic commitment that kept development going in the face of disappointment and failure.[15]

Sony's founder and chairman, Ahio Morita, is on record as saying that the company is prepared to wait over twenty years for a new product development programme to pay off. Sony decided in the mid-1950s that the video recorder would be the next major product after television receivers. The first model developed was a fairly large, quite expensive unit for industrial purposes. It then decided that the general public would be able to use the recorder. The resultant model, the U-matic, was introduced in 1969, well over a decade after development work had first begun. The company's next development was a small video cassette recorder for home use. When the first "Betamax" was introduced in 1975, "people criticised us, saying that no one would need such a machine. We therefore devoted our efforts to spreading our new concept among the public. The task was a great challenge. It required a great amount of investment on the marketing side."[16]

Another illustration given by Rosenbloom and Abernathy of the importance of persistence in apparently adverse circumstances concerns the production of portable monochrome television sets. Sony introduced an eight-inch receiver in 1960, at about the same time as a major piece of market research, commissioned by General Electric, had produced the

14. Address to conference on Design Policy by C. Suckling, former research manager of ICI, as quoted in the *Financial Times*, 5th November 1982.

15. R. Rosenbloom and W. Abernathy. "The Climate for Innovation in Industry". *Research Policy* Vol. 2 (1982).

16. Address to the European Management Forum by A. Morita, quoted in the *Financial Times*, 5th February 1982.

conclusion that "people do not place a high value on portability of the television set." A year later the product was put on mass sale as a luxury item, priced at $250 when some 21 inch sets were available for less than $150. The marketing of these portable sets was so successful that imports of Japanese televisions, negligible in 1960, reached 120,000 in 1962 and a million in 1965. Moreover, in almost completely cornering the market for small-screen sets, the Japanese established a base from which they subsequently expanded to supply larger monochrome sets, colour sets and eventually video recorders. (This extension by Japanese producers of an initial base also occurred in the UK motor cycle market, as recounted in Chapter 10.)

Rosenbloom and Abernathy draw some more general conclusions about the reasons for the Japanese success. The successful companies were companies which persistently pursued "global high-technology strategies"; they looked on the world as their market, and used technology as a prime tool to exploit it. They perceived potential consumer applications of the technology a good fifteen years before the market could actually be tapped and (as noted above), persisted in their development of the technology even in the face of early market failures. They had a highly skilled labour force and they invested heavily in advanced manufacturing.

By contrast the managements of American companies were found to be preoccupied with cost cutting. Product differentiation was sought, not through performance, but in advertising images and product styling. They were more likely to use market research to identify latent market opportunities than to take risks in developing a market for novel products. Moreover the organisational complexity of large, diversified American (and European) companies limited their effectiveness in using new technology, with interdepartmental barriers putting a brake on product development or stopping it entirely. Finally "the managers of American industry have increasingly preferred to make choices based on abstract analysis of seemingly objective considerations, rather than on the insights and judgment of persons seasoned in a business."[17]

Another factor requiring that a long-term view should be taken of the returns to R&D expenditure is the long gestation period between the conception of an idea and its incorporation into a marketable product. This is an especially important consideration in pharmaceuticals, because of the need to ensure, as far as possible, that new drugs are safe. The time spent on scientific research and development for a new drug is twelve years, as shown in Table 24. (Although this table refers to the USA, where controls are especially strict, the position in the UK appears to be very similar.)[18]

17. Rosenbloom and Abernathy. *Op. cit.*
18. This table is based on data in J. R. Virts and F. J. Weston. "Returns to Research and Development in the Pharmaceutical Industry". *Management and Decision Economics* Vol. 1 (1980).

12. THE NATURE AND IMPACT OF TECHNOLOGICAL CHANGE

TABLE XXIV. TIME PERIOD FOR DEVELOPING A NEW DRUG

	Months
Discovery phase	36
Preclinical animal testing	14
Human testing	55
Long-term animal studies	37
Total	142

At any time during this period, the research and development work can yield results which cause the project to be abandoned. The consequences of such a decision are, of course, most serious when adverse results appear at a late stage. For example in 1981 Fisons announced that it had abandoned plans to market Proxicromil, an anti-allergic drug. It had been working on the drug for six years, having spent £12 million, and it had been expected that Proxicromil would account for as much as 50 per cent of the group's profits by the late 1980s.

QUESTIONS

1. Briefly explain the following terms: technology, technological change, process innovation, process diffusion, product innovation, product diffusion.
2. Explain the possible impact of technological change on (*a*) the cost of production, (*b*) the quantity of inputs (factors) employed.
3. "Since research and development enables a firm to take advantage of opportunities, expenditure on R&D should be treated in the same way as other forms of investment." Discuss.
4. How might the idea of characteristics space help to guide R&D activity in firms producing (*a*) cars, (*b*) television sets, (*c*) television programmes, (*d*) computers?
5. "Successful innovation originates in the mind of the consumer, not in the laboratory." Discuss.
6. What factors might firms take into account in determining the composition of their R&D portfolios?
7. What factors are required for successful innovation?

PART FIVE

Implementation of Strategy

CHAPTER THIRTEEN
Price and Output Decisions

OBJECTIVES

After studying this chapter the reader should be able to: list the factors influencing a firm's basic price; explain the relationship between price and other elements of the marketing mix; demonstrate the relative importance of price in purchase decisions; show how a firm might attempt to measure the price awareness and sensitivity of consumers; construct a simple bidding model; describe and evaluate product analysis pricing.

INTRODUCTION

Decisions on price and output featured prominently in the models of firms discussed in Chapters 7 to 9. But these models were inevitably highly simplified, merely outlining the factors influencing pricing decisions. In this and the following chapter we consider pricing policies in more detail. We examine the determinants of the firm's basic price in this chapter, and in Chapter 14 we examine subsidiary pricing decisions.

Basic price denotes the firm's position in the market in relation to other suppliers. We can illustrate this by reference to Fig. 70, which represents two price makers supplying the same market. For firm A price is a major competitive weapon. The firm strives to attain a high level of productive efficiency and spends relatively little on marketing. It adds a modest profit margin to (expected) average cost and sets price P_A. Firm B has higher

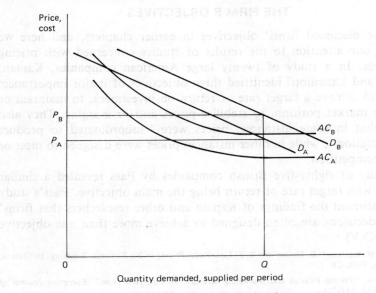

Fig. 70. *Alternative basic prices.*

costs than A, partly because it has a higher level of marketing expenditure, spending more on advertising, employing more salesmen and so forth. This additional marketing expenditure enables the firm to set basic price P_B. (We have assumed for the sake of simplicity that both firms are able to sell Q. Whether this would be so in practice would depend, of course, upon the relative effectiveness of the competitive strategies adopted by each firm.)

Having regard to basic price, we can make a clear distinction between the two firms. Firm A adopts a low-price policy and firm B a high-price policy. But it must be recognised that each firm is likely to have a spread of prices around the basic price, dependent upon the type of customer supplied, the quantity supplied, the time of supply etc. (Deviations from the basic price form the content of subsidiary pricing decisions, discussed in the following chapter.) It is possible that the spread of prices is such that an overlap occurs between the prices of two firms with distinct basic prices. Firm A may sell to some customers at a price above that charged by B to some of its customers.

THE DETERMINANTS OF BASIC PRICE

The basic price set by a firm is influenced by numerous factors, including the firm's objectives, its policies relating to other (non-price) forms of competition, the policies of competitors, the requirements and attitudes of consumers, and legal constraints. We consider each of these factors in the following sections.

THE FIRM'S OBJECTIVES

We have discussed firms' objectives in earlier chapters, and here we confine our attention to the results of studies concerned with pricing objectives. In a study of twenty large American companies, Kaplan, Dirlam and Lanzillotti identified three objectives of major importance: pricing to achieve a target rate of return on investment, to maintain or improve market position, to stabilise prices and/or margins. They also found that in some instances, prices were "subordinated to product differentiation", while in other instances prices were designed to meet or follow competition.[1]

A study of eighty-five British companies by Pass revealed a similar picture, with target rate of return being the main objective. Pass's study also confirmed the findings of Kaplan and other researchers that firms' pricing decisions are often designed to achieve more than one objective (Table XXV).[2]

1. A. D. H. Kaplan, J. B. Dirlam and R. F. Lanzillotti. *Pricing in Big Business.* Brookings Institution, Washington, 1958, Ch. 2.

2. C. Pass. "Pricing Policies and Marketing Strategy: an Empirical Note." *European Journal of Marketing* Vol. 5 (1971).

13. PRICE AND OUTPUT DECISIONS

TABLE XXV. PRICING GOALS OF UK COMPANIES

No. of firms reporting	Principal pricing goal	Target return on capital employed over long run	Maximis- ation of profits over long run	Satisfactory expansion of sales over long run	Maintain- ing or expanding market share	Meeting or following competition	Price stabilisation
				Collateral pricing goals			
41	Target rate of return on capital employed over long run	+	10	28	36	6	24
17	Meeting or following competition	7	3	14	17	+	12
14	Maintaining or expanding market share	8	–	11	+	7	7
9	Maximisation of profit over long run	–	+	5	5	–	1
4	Maximisation of sales over long run	3	–	–	3	1	4

In a study of 728 British manufacturing firms Shipley found the principal pricing objectives to be: target profit or return on capital employed (67 per cent of respondents), prices fair to firm and customers (13 per cent), price similarity with competitors (8 per cent), target sales revenue (7 per cent), stable volume of sales (5 per cent), target market share of sales (2 per cent), and stable prices (2 per cent).[3]

It is important to recognise that the results of these studies are likely to be influenced by the methods adopted by the researcher. "Prices fair to firm and customers" appeared to be a more prominent objective in Shipley's study than in the others. But this reflects the fact that Shipley used a questionnaire in which that objective was listed, whereas the other studies did not.

The fact that the categories sometimes overlap can also influence the results. For example, consider Shipley's conclusion that the size of firm may influence the relative importance of the various objectives. In his study "target return" was given as the principal objective by over 80 per cent of the largest firms as compared to 55 per cent of the smallest. Conversely, "fair prices" was the principal objective of a quarter of the smallest firms but none of the biggest. When a firm determines its rate of return it may be influenced by notions of fairness to customers. In other words apparent differences in the relative importance of these two objectives might have been due partly to differences in the way in which

---

3. D. Shipley. "Pricing Objectives in British Manufacturing Industry". *Journal of Industrial Economics* Vol. 29 (1981).

the firms expressed their objectives, with more large firms using formal criteria (e.g. a return of 20 per cent on capital employed) which could be incorporated into elaborate planning mechanisms. These differences do not necessarily result in different prices being set.

Even if the studies had adopted identical methods we could not expect them to yield the same results, since they were undertaken in different countries, with different samples—in terms of the number and sizes of firms etc.—and at different times. The fact that stable prices was found to be a much less important objective by Shipley than by earlier researchers is no doubt due to the fact that Shipley's study was undertaken in a period of rapid inflation in which very few firms could hope to maintain stable prices. Moreover, as we have shown, many companies have multiple objectives, whose relative importance may change over time.

It follows that it would not be sensible to try to derive a precise measure of the relative importance of the various objectives. However, it is clear that a target rate of return is the most common objective, that firms often set prices with a sales or market-share target in mind, and that a minority of firms feel obliged to meet or follow the prices set by competitors. These objectives were, of course, built into the models discussed in the previous chapter.

THE RELATIONSHIP BETWEEN PRICE AND OTHER ELEMENTS OF THE MARKETING MIX

We noted above that pricing policies should take account of policies relating to other forms of competition. Another way of putting this is that price should be seen as an element of the firm's marketing mix. Since the other elements of the marketing mix are discussed in detail in Chapter 15, they are referred to only briefly here.

Marketing expenditure takes many forms, including spending on advertising, the recruitment and training of salesmen, and packaging. But in every instance the expenditure is justified only insofar as it influences the demand for the firm's products.

Product differentiation

Marketing activities are designed to differentiate the products or brands of one producer from the products or brands of competitors. In Fig. 71 AC_1 represents the firm's average cost when no attempt is made to differentiate its products. Given demand D the firm sets price P at which it sells Q. D is drawn on the assumption that competitors continue to charge P. In the absence of product differentiation demand is highly elastic. (In the models of perfectly competitive markets, considered in Chapter 7, demand is assumed to be *infinitely* elastic at the market price. However, consumers frequently form preferences for particular suppliers, even if these suppliers do not attempt to differentiate their products.) If the firm

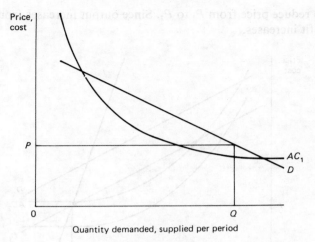

Fig. 71. *Demand in the absence of product differentiation.*

increased its price its revenue and profits would decline. If it reduced its price revenue would increase, but costs would increase more rapidly, and profits would fall. *P* is therefore the profit-maximising price.

If profits are to be increased by product differentiation, this requires that the demand should increase and/or become less elastic. These two effects are shown in Fig. 72. With demand D_1 Q is sold at price *P*. An increase in demand is shown by the shift of the demand curve from D_1 to D_2, a less elastic demand by a shift from D_1 to D_3. (A third possibility is that demand would increase *and* become less elastic.) The firm could take advantage of an increase in demand (D_2), either by increasing the amount sold at price *P* or by selling the same quantity as previously at a higher price (or by an intermediate strategy involving an increase in both price and quantity sold). To take advantage of a less elastic demand (D_3) the firm would have to increase price.

In both cases the increase would, of course, have to exceed the increase in costs (shown by the shift of the average cost curve to AC_2) if profits were to increase. If the firm's primary objective is to increase the volume of sales this obviously requires an increase in demand. A change to a less elastic demand would not contribute to this objective.

Two further points must be made about this basic model. First, the benefits of increased demand may be greater than indicated so far. If higher output gives rise to economies of scale, average cost may not rise as much as shown in Fig. 72. Indeed, average cost may be lower than if additional marketing expenditure had not been incurred. Figure 73 reproduces the cost curves, AC_1 and AC_2, of Fig. 71. AC_3 is the curve pertaining to the increased scale of organisation that is adopted when demand increases from D_1 to D_2. Even with a higher profit margin the firm

V. IMPLEMENTATION OF STRATEGY

is able to reduce price from P_1 to P_2. Since output increases from Q_1 to Q_2 total profit increases.

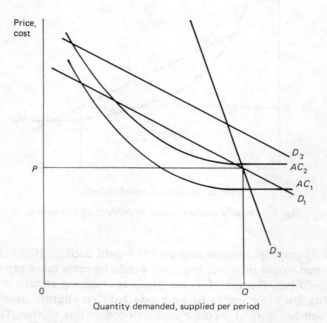

Fig. 72. *Product differentiation and a change in demand.*

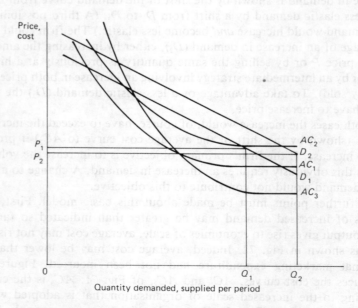

Fig. 73. *Product differentiation and an increase in profits.*

Second, marketing expenditure is sometimes justified as preventing a fall, rather than leading to an increase, in sales and/or profits, i.e. it prevents a shift to the left of the demand curve D_1. Such a shift of the demand curve could result from, and is certainly the objective of, competitors' marketing activities.

A consistent marketing mix

In the previous section we showed how marketing expenditure can give a firm more discretion in its pricing policy. The relationship between price and other elements of the marketing mix may in fact be two-way. If a pricing policy is adopted that leads to higher profits then the firm is able to finance additional marketing expenditure.

Moreover, it is important to ensure that pricing policy is consistent with other aspects of marketing policy. If, by advertising, choice of distribution outlet etc., the firm has acquired a reputation for producing up-market products, a low price would run counter to this reputation or image. If the company's image became less distinct, the result could be to alienate consumers at the top end of the market without a compensating increase in sales to other consumers. More obviously, perhaps, a firm whose existing products appeal to the mass market might be unwise to set a high price for a new product.

When the Parker Pen Co. began the production of ball-point and felt-tip pens, it priced them at the top end of the market. It was able to sustain these prices because of its reputation as a producer of high-quality fountain pens. A lower price would have yielded lower margins on ball-points and felt-tips, and might also have detracted from the company's reputation in the market for fountain pens.

On the other hand when BIC, the French producer of ball-point pens, began the production of other disposable products, such as razors, it extended its initial low-price strategy into the new markets, thus consolidating its reputation as a supplier of cheap, value-for-money products.

THE RELATIVE IMPORTANCE OF PRICE IN PURCHASE DECISIONS

We have shown that firms with strong (non-price) market profiles are usually able to charge higher prices than firms with weaker market profiles. Each producer should try to identify the strength, or weakness, of its market profile and to discover the relative importance in the markets it supplies of price and non-price factors.[4] In the following sections we examine evidence relating to several markets. The evidence takes several forms. In some markets it comprises information on the proportion of consumers for whom given elements of the marketing mix (including

---

4. For an application of this principle see: M. Christopher. "Value-in-use Pricing". *European Journal of Marketing* Vol. 16 (1982).

price) are the most important determinant of the choice of supplier. In other markets it comprises information on the trade-off, as seen by individual consumers, between price and non-price factors.

Groceries

Kenny-Levick asked 554 housewives to name their first-choice grocery shop, and to say why they preferred to shop there. They were asked to give up to four reasons and their answers are summarised in Table XXVI.[5] It can be seen that price was of primary importance to over one-fifth of the respondents. But price is to be interpreted, rather widely, as value for money.

TABLE XXVI. REASONS FOR PATRONISING FIRST-CHOICE GROCERY SHOPS

Reason	Percentage of mentions	
	First	All
Economic (bargains, better value, reasonable prices)	23	21
Personalising (personal service, friendly staff)	11	14
Nearness (it's handy, nearer to work)	14	11
Variety (all under one roof)	9	10
Quickness in shopping (ease/speed in shop)	11	9
Quality (freshness, good food)	4	8
Ethical (support small man)	1	8
Others	27	19

Television rentals

As part of a study undertaken by the present author 523 subscribers were asked the question: "Why did you originally decide to rent from your present company?" It can be seen that, as in the study of the grocery market quoted above, the economic motive ("their terms were the most favourable") is again the most important, accounting for more than one-fifth of the total responses (Table XXVII).[6]

Machine tools

After a detailed study of fifty-one purchase decisions on a range of

---

5. C. Kenny-Levick. "Consumer Motivations: Examples from the Grocery Trade". *British Journal of Marketing* Vol. 3 (1969).

6. F. Livesey. "The Marketing Mix and Buyer Behaviour in the Television Rental Market". *European Journal of Marketing* Vol. 5 (1971–2).

TABLE XXVII. REASONS FOR RENTING TELEVISION FROM PRESENT COMPANY

Reason	Percentage of responses
Terms the most favourable	21
Friend/relative recommended company	19
Showroom was nearest	19
Previous dealings with company satisfactory	11
Company of that size likely to provide good service	10
Advertisement	8
Best choice of sets	5
Other	6

machine tools, Cunningham and Whyte concluded that in the first place "the reputation of the suppliers for delivery reliability, before and after sales service, and of the product for performance and reliability must in most cases be good or very good before the supplier is invited to quote."[7] This implies that an extremely competitive price may not be sufficient to obtain orders and that suppliers would be well advised to concentrate on other competitive weapons. But price cannot be ignored, since it was an important influence on the choice of supplier, once bids were received.

Industrial components and equipment
A detailed study was made by Kelly and Coaker of 112 decisions relating to the purchase of centrifugal pumps, air compressors, liquid-transfer control systems, piping, pressure vessels, etc. This study is of interest in that it shows why the lowest bid may not be accepted, and what additional expenditure purchasers may incur to obtain other benefits. The lowest bid was accepted 66 times (59 per cent). The reasons for accepting a higher bid in the remaining instances are summarised in Table XXVIII.[8] (In some instances more than one reason was given.)

The disadvantages attached to the lowest bid were clearly felt to be substantial in some instances. One company accepted a bid on one item of $2,943 in preference to a bid of $1,866 because of the shorter delivery time. Another company accepted a bid of $362,200 in preference to a bid of $246,500 because the latter involved higher installation costs, a more complex design, and more difficult maintenance.

---

7. M. T. Cunningham and J. G. Whyte. "The Behaviour of Industrial Buyers in their Search for Suppliers of Machine Tools". *Journal of Management Studies* Vol. 11 (1974).

8. J. P. Kelly and J. W. Coaker. "The Importance of Price as a Choice Criterion for Industrial Purchasing Decisions". *Industrial Marketing Management* Vol. 5 (1976).

TABLE XXVIII. REASONS FOR NON-ACCEPTANCE OF LOWEST BID

Reason	Times mentioned
Did not meet specifications	18
Not interchangeable with existing equipment	18
Longer delivery time	9
Vendor unacceptable from past experience	7
More costly to operate	6
Spare parts not available in-house	6
Others	6
Total	70

Computers

On the basis of a study of prices of computers in 1964, 1967 and 1971, Ratchford and Ford concluded that there were large and statistically significant price differences between IBM and its competitors: "Holding machine characteristics and age constant, it appears that this differential was, on average, 40–50 per cent."[9] But this price differential did not prevent IBM from expanding its share of the world market during this period. It must be concluded that this differential indicates the premium that buyers were willing to pay in order to enjoy other benefits offered by IBM: "Though precise evidence on the nature of IBM's non-hardware superiority is scarce . . . there is some survey evidence that computer users generally rate the quality of IBM after-sales service, product reliability, and support better than competition."

PRICE AWARENESS AND SENSITIVITY OF CONSUMERS

The studies reported above were concerned with the relationship between price and non-price factors, as incorporated in the offers of rival firms. Further evidence on the relative importance of price is provided by studies relating to the price awareness and sensitivity of consumers.

Price awareness

In their study of machine tool purchases, Cunningham and Whyte found that in 15 out of 51 purchase decisions only one supplier was considered, while in a further 19 instances only two or three quotations were obtained.[10] The limited degree of price awareness implied by these figures

---

9. B. T. Ratchford and G. T. Ford. "A Study of Price and Market Shares in the Computer Mainframe Industry". *Journal of Business* Vol. 49 (1976).

10. Cunningham and Whyte. *Op. cit.*

is consistent with the secondary role of price in this market, noted above.

A limited degree of price awareness has been identified in other studies. Bayliss and Edwards found that of 361 companies engaged in the purchase of freight transport services only 120 were aware of the prices of alternative modes of transport, and of these only 90 could actually quote prices.[11] Kettlewood found that only 23 out of 43 companies had obtained alternative quotations for freight transport services over the previous ten years.[12] (It must be remembered that economic conditions were more favourable at the time that these studies were undertaken. One would expect to find a higher level of price awareness in the more difficult circumstances ruling in the 1980s.)

In an early study of consumers' awareness of the price of groceries, Gabor and Granger found a "remarkable dispersion" of price awareness among different products. The percentage of respondents claiming to remember the price of fifteen grocery products bought within the previous seven days ranged from 95 for tea and 93 for eggs to 70 for breakfast cereal and 63 for flour. When the estimated prices of seven products were checked against the actual prices, the percentage of correct responses again varied considerably, from 79 for tea to 35 for breakfast cereal.[13]

Price sensitivity
There are various alternative methods of estimating consumers' price sensitivity. Statistical methods, and in particular regression analysis, have been used to estimate the price elasticity of demand for a wide range of products. Such estimates, relating to the market as a whole, may be useful when producers are able to co-ordinate their pricing decisions. (Although estimates based on past data must always be treated with caution.) But a producer is usually more interested in the consumers' sensitivity to any price change that he might make, than in more aggregate estimates. In the following sections we discuss some of the methods used in an attempt to measure sensitivity to individual price changes.

Price experimentation
The producer of a well-established product may change the price for a limited period and compare sales in this period with sales in previous and subsequent periods. The producer should try to ensure that normal trading

11. B. T. Bayliss and S. L. Edwards. *Industrial Demand for Transport.* HMSO, 1970, Ch. 14.

12. K. Kettlewood, *The Marketing of Freight Transport Services with particular reference to Buyer Behaviour.* MSc Dissertation, UMIST, 1971.

13. A. Gabor and C. W. J. Granger. "On the Price Consciousness of Consumers". *Applied Statistics* Vol. 10 (1961).

conditions prevail during the experimental period, e.g. seasonal influences should be minimised and a price reduction should not be promoted as a "special offer".

Even if the price reduction is not promoted, consumers may see it as a promotion and hence increase their purchasing rate above the long-term level. Conversely, when price is raised again the reduction in sales may be greater in the short than in the long run (partly because of the earlier build-up of consumers' stocks). Such changes in the rate of purchasing can lead to incorrect deductions being drawn from the test results. Changes in the activities of competitors during the test period can have the same effect. In fact competitors sometimes deliberately change their policy, e.g. by giving a short-term boost to advertising, in order to prevent a firm from acquiring accurate estimates of consumers' price sensitivity.

An alternative approach is to set different prices in outlets located in different areas. The sales in the various areas may give an indication of price sensitivity, especially if the producer is able to correct for any differences between the areas in terms of (a) consumer characteristics, e.g. income, (b) competitive activity.

Despite the difficulties that may arise in creating a satisfactory experimental framework, successful experiments have been reported in the literature (and many more are no doubt contained in company files). In the USA the Parker Pen Co. was selling Quink ink at 15 cents, a price comparable to other inks but at which Parker was making a loss. The experiment consisted of increasing the price to 25 cents in a sample of outlets and comparing sales in these and other outlets. At the higher price the volume of sales fell slightly, but revenue and profits increased significantly. Parker adopted the higher price throughout the market, and several competitors subsequently followed.[14]

When the Princess telephone was introduced in the USA different prices were set in two test areas: an installation charge of $8.50 plus a monthly charge of 65 cents, and an installation charge of $29.50 plus a monthly charge of 50 cents. The first price was the most acceptable to consumers and was adopted as the basis for the company's national pricing policy.

Another experiment reported by Dean was designed to identify the extent to which a price premium could be justified on the basis of a brand name. Identical mattresses, some bearing the Simmons brand and others an unknown brand, were offered for sale with varying price differentials. When prices were equal the Simmons brand outsold the unknown brand by fifteen to one, whereas when the Simmons brand was sold at a 25 per cent premium sales were equal.

---

14. This and other studies are reported in: J. Dean. *Managerial Economics*. Prentice-Hall International, London, 1961, pp. 180ff.

Simulated shopping situations

Another method of estimating consumers' price sensitivity is to create a simulated shopping situation. A mobile caravan or a hall is fitted out to resemble a section of a shop. Shoppers are invited to make the choices that they would make if they were faced by the prices marked on the products.

The advantage of this method is that it allows for far more manipulation of prices than with "real-life" experiments. The obvious disadvantage is that consumers are not asked to back their preferences by spending money. (The results of one such experiment are discussed below.)

Hypothetical shopping situations

This method involves asking potential customers whether they would be likely to buy a product or brand at various prices. If the product is familiar to consumers it may simply be named. If it is not, the consumer may be given a verbal or pictorial description or, more rarely, be shown the actual product.

This method shares with simulated shopping situations the disadvantage that the consumer is asked merely to express an opinion, not to spend his or her money. On the other hand it does allow a large number of consumers to be involved at a relatively low cost, and it is claimed to give useful guidance for pricing decisions.

Much of the fundamental research in the UK was conducted by the Nottingham University Group under the leadership of Gabor and Granger. The method they adopted was to ask a large (preferably at least 1000) representative sample of consumers whether they would buy the product at a given price. Those replying in the negative were asked whether this was because the price was too low or too high. The answers to these questions guided the prices used in the next round of questioning. For example a person replying that she would not buy at a price of 15p because it was too expensive, would be asked whether she would buy at 14p; someone who would not buy at 15p because it was too cheap (see below) would be asked whether she would buy at 16p. Each person would typically be presented with about six prices, so that a sample of 1,000 respondents would yield 6,000 responses. From these responses a buy-response curve was derived, indicating the percentage of consumers who would buy the product at alternative prices.

The application of statistical theory to the results of the early studies suggested that all buy-response curves are essentially identical, and that a generic "norm curve" could be derived which closely approximates to a log–normal curve in its central part (Fig. 74).

Although the buy-response curve indicates how many consumers would buy at the various prices, it does not show how many items each consumer would buy at the acceptable prices. Consequently the buy-response curve cannot be translated directly into a demand curve. It has, nevertheless,

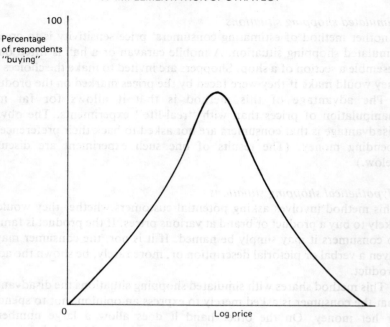

Fig. 74. *A generic buy–response curve.*

strong implications for the shape of the demand curve. Above a certain point an increase in price is likely to lead to a reduction in the quantity purchased. This reaction can be explained in terms of traditional economic theory, involving income and substitution effects. But, second, below another point a decrease in price is likely to lead to a reduction in the quantity purchased. This reaction is to be explained by the fact that consumers see the price of a product (and more especially the price of a brand) as an indicator of its quality. (This point is discussed further below.)

These findings might in themselves be useful to pricing executives, in particular by encouraging a cautious attitude towards price reductions. But if buy-response analysis is to be fully effective, data on consumers' attitudes towards price has to be supplemented by other information.

In Fig. 75 the buy-response curve $B(P)$ can be compared with the curve *PLP* showing the prices last paid for the product. (The relationship between the two curves shown in Fig. 75 is, of course, only one of many possible relationships.) There is a strong presumption that many consumers considered that the articles that they last bought were overpriced, and that they would not have distrusted the quality of articles priced at, say P rather than Q.

This suggests that there is a gap in the market that could be filled by a new brand, or that a reduction in price would lead to a substantial increase

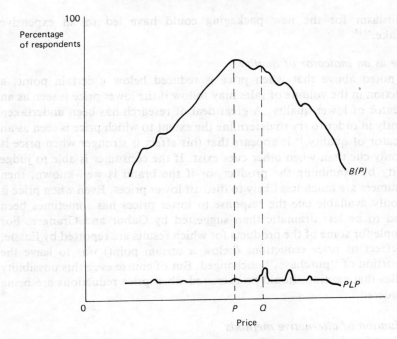

Fig. 75. *Buy-response and price-last-paid curves.*

in the sales of an existing brand. But the profit margin per unit sold would, of course, be lower unless higher sales led to a fall in average cost. Moreover, the introduction of a successful cheaper brand might destabilise the price structure, the prices of competitive brands being reduced in retaliation.

Another use of buy-response analysis is reported by Richard Eassie. A new form of packaging was developed which was found in testing with a sample of 250 housewives to be well received. (Table XXIX). However, buy-response analysis showed that for the 1 lb size of the product the new pack could command a premium of only 1p, whereas the cost of the new pack would require a price rise of 3p to maintain profit margins. "Once one had looked at the pricing research results, the decision to abandon the new pack was obvious. But without the buy-response's down-to-earth examination of what people would pay, the consumers' superficial

TABLE XXIX. REACTIONS TO A NEW PACK (PER CENT)

	Agree	Disagree	Don't know
New pack has better appearance than old one	88	11	1
New pack is easier to open than old one	82	16	1

enthusiasm for the new packaging could have led to an expensive mistake."[15]

Price as an indicator of quality

We noted above that when price is reduced below a certain point, a reduction in the volume of sales may follow if the lower price is seen as an indicator of lower quality. A great deal of research has been undertaken recently in order to try to determine the extent to which price is seen as an indicator of quality.[16] It appears that this effect is stronger when price is the only cue than when other cues exist. If the consumer is able to judge quality by examining the product, or if the brand is well known, then consumers are much less likely to distrust lower prices. Even when price is the only available cue the response to lower prices has sometimes been found to be less dramatic than suggested by Gabor and Granger. For example for some of the products for which results are reported by Eassie, the effect of price reductions (below a certain point) was to leave the proportion of "purchases" unchanged. But of course even this possibility implies that caution should be exercised when price reductions are being considered.

Evaluation of alternative methods

In choosing from among the various methods described above, pricing executives should take account of (*a*) the feasibility of the methods in the relevant markets, (*b*) their relative costs, (*c*) the validity of the results. We have already discussed the first two factors at various points. In this section we summarise the results of two studies which compared the results obtained by alternative methods.

Professor Stout used three methods to assess the price elasticity of demand for four food products: price (in-store) experimentation, a simulated shopping situation using a mobile trailer, and a hypothetical shopping situation using personal interviews. The results of the three methods are shown in Table XXX.[17] It can be seen that the three methods yield quite different results. One cannot say that any one set of results is correct. However the application of a t-test revealed that "only the in-store experiment provides estimates that were significantly different from zero. In other words, they are the only stable relationship established."

15. R. W. F. Eassie. "Buy-response Analysis: A Practical Tool of Market Research". *European Journal of Marketing* Vol. 13 (1979). For a more sceptical view of studies in this area, see: P. Bowbrick. "Pseudo Research in Marketing: The Case of the Price/Perceived-Quality Relationship". *European Journal of Marketing* Vol. 14 (1980).

16. *See*, for example: J. J. Wheatley and J. S. Y. Chiu. "The Effects of Price, Store Image, and Product and Respondent Characteristics on Perceptions of Quality". *Journal of Marketing Research* Vol. 14 (1977); K. B. Monroe. "Buyers' Subjective Perceptions of Price". *Journal of Marketing Research* Vol. 10 (1973).

17. R. G. Stout. "Developing Data to Estimate Price–Quantity of Relationships". *Journal of Marketing* Vol. 33 (1969).

TABLE XXX. ESTIMATED PRICE ELASTICITIES

Product	In-store experiment	Trailer simulation	Personal interviews
A	−1.57	−1.25	−0.33
B	−1.27	−0.64	0.71
C	−1.58	−0.76	−1.86
D	−1.74	1.13	0.35

Gabor, Granger and Sowter compared the results of the hypothetical shopping situation with price experimentation. They found that the two methods gave similar results for two household cleansing products. But in the case of instant coffee the hypothetical shopping situation implied that price differences had considerably stronger effects on market shares than evidenced in the price experiments. The conclusion that they drew from this was that where brand loyalty is relatively high, it becomes particularly important to call customers' attention to prices in the shops.[18]

LEGAL CONSTRAINTS

In the UK pricing decisions have been subject to legal constraints from two sources. Direct controls on a wide range of products have been imposed on prices from time to time under legislation implementing prices and incomes policies. Direct controls have also been imposed on a few products under competition policy. But the main impact of competition policy has been less direct. It has caused firms to consider whether certain pricing policies would incur the displeasure of the authorities. A very aggressive policy which forced competitors out of the market might bring a firm within the scope of legislation relating to monopoly. Price discrimination (discussed in the next chapter) has frequently been criticised by the Monopolies Commission.

At the end of 1982 there was no general price control in the UK. But British exporters (together with other suppliers) faced controls in some overseas markets. For example in Austria the Price Regulation Law enabled the maximum price of various products to be fixed. In the Netherlands price controls applied to all parts of the economy, with the exception of prices reached at auctions. In Belgium price increases for most product categories had to be approved by the Price Control Commission on the basis of a very detailed price analysis.

18. A. Gabor, C. W. J. Granger and A. P. Sowter. "Real and Hypothetical Shop Situations in Market Research". *Journal of Marketing Research* Vol. 7 (1970).

THE IMPLEMENTATION OF PRICING POLICIES

Having examined the main factors influencing decisions on basic price, we conclude by presenting some short case histories of the implementation of pricing policy. We introduce some additional variables into the analysis, and also show how the various factors considered above may interact. Much of this section is based on the findings of Kaplan, Dirlam and Lanzillotti and it is therefore appropriate to begin with a quotation from these authors that emphasises the complexity of pricing policies: "The company history and the dominant personalities that served to shape general company policy have also helped to determine the pricing policies of their companies. The legacy of the past tends to accumulate in the big enterprise, what might be termed the collective company personality: a complex mixture of organisation and dominant personalities, anti-trust suits and marketing methods rooted in tradition."[19] In addition to the company personality Kaplan and his colleagues found a number of other factors to be of major importance in the implementation of pricing policy.

Character of the product

In some instances the physical attributes of the product were of particular importance. Although Swift and Co. had a dominant position in meat canning their influence on price was negligible, because the primary product, fresh meat, is perishable and subject to unpredictable output and shipments. Producers of a durable product with controlled raw material output, such as steel, were able to maintain a much greater measure of price stability. (This has, of course, been less true in recent years as the recession has led to a fall in demand for steel and increasingly competitive market conditions.)

New products provide opportunities for pricing discretion not generally available in standardised goods. (How producers might use this discretion is discussed in greater detail in the following chapter.) Large producers of established standard products such as heavy chemicals, flour and metals, were aware—often as a result of their own past experience—of the general unprofitability of price wars conducted with similarly large and resourceful competitors. Hence they usually tried to maintain stable margins and to increase sales by non-price competition, such as the provision of a quick and efficient service.

Alcoa, the dominant producer of aluminium, initially set prices designed to penetrate the markets held by copper and other metals. Kaplan and colleagues at the time of that investigation found that "Its technical development in a capital-intensive form with integrated production and standardisation of finished product now tends to assert itself; so that while product promotion remains vigorous, pricing in the basic aluminium lines is showing resemblances to steel's pattern of base prices and extras."[20]

19. Kaplan, Dirlam and Lanzillotti. *Op. cit.*, p. 252.
20. Kaplan, Dirlam and Lanzillotti. *Op. cit.*, p. 255.

(More recently, however, the producers of aluminium have reverted to a more aggressive pricing policy. This resulted in an increase in aluminium's share of the UK beverage can market from 12 per cent to 50 per cent in the three years to 1982. In the USA this process has gone even further; nearly 90 per cent of beverage cans are made of aluminium, representing an annual loss of around 1 million tonnes of tinplate sales.)

The type of use to which the product was put influenced pricing policies. Price competition was relatively unimportant when the price of the product represented a small part of the final cost of the product into which it was incorporated, e.g. special electrical equipment and industrial gases.

Production and cost characteristics of the main product played a primary role in conditioning the pricing policies adopted by several companies interviewed by Kaplan and his colleagues. For example they found that in the long run the producers of tin cans "become transmission belts for passing material and labour costs on to consumers with an inelastic demand."[21]

Interdependence of the product mix

Kaplan and his colleagues found that the pricing of an individual product was frequently affected by the place it occupied in the company's product mix: "Enjoyment of a dominant position in one line may alter market tactics elsewhere. Profits or losses in one area may help to explain an intensification or moderation of marketing effort in another field."[22]

They also found that homogeneity of product line made for standardisation of pricing policies and procedures, with authority at a high level, while wide diversification tended to vest pricing authority at the level of the product division: "Firms that can focus on one product or which obtain their chief revenues from one product, such as National Steel, or from products performing the same function, such as American Can's containers, naturally tend to have more consistent pricing than is to be found in a firm, such as Union Carbide, whose products range from flashlight cells to industrial oxygen, or one, such as General Mills, that is selling airplane controls as well as Wheaties".[23]

Market objectives reflected in price

The term market objectives refers to the overall offer that the company makes to the consumer, the company's desired market profile. This profile may vary substantially from one market to another: "Du Pont points out that, while heavy chemicals may sell mainly on a price basis, it is the missionary work with dealers and first-hand demonstrations to farmers that permit the company to compete effectively in the sale of agricultural chemicals, insecticides and fungicides".[24]

21. Kaplan, Dirlam and Lanzillotti. *Op. cit.*, p. 256.
22. Kaplan, Dirlam and Lanzillotti. *Op. cit.*, p. 257.
23. Kaplan, Dirlam and Lanzillotti. *Op. cit.*, p. 257.
24. Kaplan. Dirlam and Lanzillotti. *Op. cit.*, p. 261.

A similar point was made more recently by Dr Kaya Naprstek, ICI's chief planner. Dr Naprstek was commenting on the temptations facing commodity chemical companies to move into chemical specialities. The apparent attractions included higher added-value than bulk chemicals, less capital and energy intensity, and less intense competition. However, "if you are only used to commodities, moving into specialities is very dangerous." Although an apparently related business area, "it is quite a different culture, requiring very different skills . . . away from a prime focus on fixed assets and towards human resources."[25]

Price leadership

In the previous chapter we showed that price leadership can be used to stabilise prices and/or to obtain higher prices than would exist in the absence of co-ordination. Kaplan concluded that the former motive was more important in the firms studied: "The steel and oil companies, and General Motors, Alcoa and Goodyear, among others, forsook short-term profits that they could easily have obtained immediately after the Second World War by allowing prices to rise to match the demand".[26]

PRICING IN BID SITUATIONS

The importance of the bidding process has been described by Arleigh Walker, a product sales manager with an American manufacturer, as follows: "Great segments of industry buy and sell through the process known as the inquiry/bid system. This bidding process is used not only for custom-engineered products but for standard manufactured items. . . . Bidding is a continuous process for most industrial companies. Batteries of engineers, estimators, and salesmen are constantly occupied with the search for new business and handling the flow of inquiries received from companies and governmental units wishing to purchase manufactured items."[27]

Walker goes on to point out that "bids from different companies for identical items will vary, even when internal costs are essentially the same for all competitors. The market level is therefore not a specific value for a given item, but rather a band, or spectrum, of prices."

It follows that we cannot describe firms as following a high- or low-price strategy in the same way as in the earlier sections. However, each bidder has to take account of the prices that it *expects* other bidders to make (and also the various non-price factors discussed above). Various techniques and models can be used to reduce the degree of uncertainty surrounding competitors' prices.

25. *Financial Times*, 24th November 1982.
26. Kaplan, Dirlam and Lanzillotti. *Op. cit.*, p. 269.
27. A. W. Walker. "How to Price Industrial Products". *Harvard Business Review* Vol. 45 (1967).

A simple bidding model

In this first model we assume that there are only two competitors and that data is available on past bids. Firm A is thus able to examine the relationship between firm B's prices and A's estimated *cost* (Table XXXI). This examination reveals that on five occasions (5 per cent of the bids) B quoted a price equal to A's cost, on 10 occasions B quoted a price 10 per cent above A's cost, and so forth.

TABLE XXXI. PRICE–COST RELATIONSHIPS

Ratio of B's price to A's cost	No. of times occurring
1.0 : 1	5
1.1 : 1	10
1.2 : 1	15
1.3 : 1	20
1.4 : 1	40
1.5 : 1	10
	100

If this relationship holds in the future, A can calculate the probability of winning a bid at any price. If, for example, A set a price 49 per cent above cost, the probability of success would be 0.1, since B has set a price 50 per cent above cost on one occasion in ten.

The probability of success having been estimated, it is easy to calculate the expected profit at various prices. This is shown in Table XXXII, where a cost of £100,000 is assumed, and the probability of success is as in Table XXXI. It can be seen that in order to maximise its expected profit, A should enter a bit of £129,000.

TABLE XXXII. BID PRICES AND EXPECTED PROFIT

A's bid	Profit	Probability of success	Expected profit
£ 99,000	£ –1,000	1.0	£ –1,000
109,000	9,000	0.95	8,550
119,000	19,000	0.85	16,150
129,000	29,000	0.70	20,300
139,000	39,000	0.50	19,500
149,000	49,000	0.10	4,900

This model assumes that the contract is awarded solely on the basis of price. If it is felt that non-price factors work in favour of one or other of the firms then the probability of success should be modified accordingly.

An extension of the model

In practice a bidder is likely to face more than one competitor. This makes the analysis more complex, but the same principles can be applied provided that data is available on the bids submitted by each competitor. The first step is to calculate, from this data, the average success probability. This is shown in Table XXXII, where firm C has set the same prices as B (above), D has set lower prices, and E higher prices.

TABLE XXXII. PRICE AND AVERAGE SUCCESS PROBABILITY

A's bid	Probability of success if competing against				Average success probability
	B	C	D	E	
£ 99,000	1.0	1.0	0.95	1.0	0.988
109,000	0.95	0.95	0.90	1.0	0.950
119,000	0.85	0.85	0.75	0.90	0.838
129,000	0.70	0.70	0.60	0.80	0.700
139,000	0.50	0.50	0.30	0.60	0.475
149,000	0.10	0.10	0.10	0.20	0.125
159,000	0.00	0.00	0.00	0.10	0.025

The average success probability indicates the probability of success if A faced any one competitor drawn at random. If there are two or more competitors, joint probabilities must be calculated, as shown in Table XXXIV.

TABLE XXXIV. JOINT SUCCESS PROBABILITIES

A's bid	Two competitors	Three competitors	Four competitors
£ 99,000	0.975	0.963	0.951
109,000	0.903	0.857	0.814
119,000	0.701	0.587	0.492
129,000	0.490	0.343	0.240
139,000	0.226	0.107	0.051
149,000	0.016	0.002	0.3×10^{-3}
159,000	0.001	0.16×10^{-4}	0.4×10^{-6}

The joint probabilities can be used to calculate expected profit at each price. If the profit data given above is applied to the joint probabilities it will be found that the profit-maximising price can change as the number of competitors changes. It is therefore important to estimate the number of bids being submitted. It is, however, not always possible to make such an estimate with any degree of accuracy. But even here probability theory can be applied, as shown in the following section.

A statistical model

When data on a large number of bids, successful and unsuccessful, is collated it is sometimes found that the distribution around the mean price approximates to a normal curve. It is then reasonable to assume that for a future contract the bids will be normally distributed around the most likely price, as estimated by the bidder, *ML* (Fig. 76). (In making its estimate the bidder will take account of the bids on past contracts, changes in costs since then, changes in competitors' capacity utilisation etc.) The bidder should also be able to estimate the "minimum" price *MN* (in the sense that there is only a 2½ per cent probability of a lower price being quoted) and the "maximum" price *MX* (in the sense that there is only a 2½ per cent chance of a higher price being quoted. In Fig. 76 each shaded area contains 2½ per cent of the total area under the curve.)

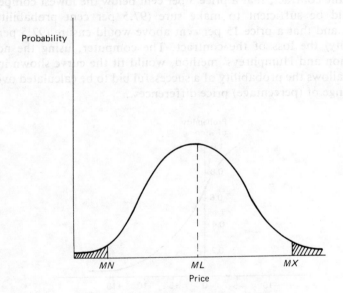

Fig. 76. *Estimated distribution of bids.*

This information allows the probabilities associated with specific prices to be calculated. (This can be done very easily using a computer package.) Thus if *ML* = 50, *MN* = 45, and *MX* = 55, the probabilities are as shown in Table XXXV. (If *ML* minus *MN* does not equal *MX* minus *ML*, i.e. if the distribution is skewed, a technique proposed by G. Humphreys can be used to work out the probabilities or likelihood of the various prices.)

This data can be used in conjunction with cost data to give expected profits at each price. Alternatively it can be used to identify the bids that should be submitted in order to obtain a given market share.

In each case adjustments may be required to take account of the impact of non-price factors. Assume, for example, that firm A believes that

TABLE XXXV. PRICE PROBABILITIES

Price	Probability	Price	Probability
44	0.014	51	0.146
45	0.022	52	0.116
46	0.045	53	0.078
47	0.078	54	0.045
48	0.116	55	0.022
49	0.146	56	0.014
50	0.159		

matching the lowest competitive bid would give it a 60 : 40 chance of winning the contract, that a price 5 per cent below the lowest competitive bid would be sufficient to make sure (97.5 per cent probability) of winning, and that a price 15 per cent above would ensure (97.5 per cent probability) the loss of the contract. The computer, using the normal distribution and Humphreys' method, would fit the curve shown in Fig. 77. This allows the probability of a successful bid to be calculated over the whole range of (percentage) price differences.

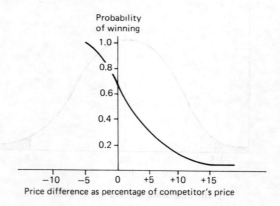

Fig. 77. *Probability of successful bid.*

An illustration of the potential for improved bid pricing is given by Edelman. The Radio Corporation of America compared the prices emanating from a bidding model with those suggested by marketing managers given identical information. A comparison of columns 4 and 5 of Table XXXVI shows that given an objective of maximising the profit contribution for each bid, the model performed better on six out of seven occasions.

Even when a model performs as well as this, it is necessary to ensure that the environment is constantly monitored in order that the model is improved and updated as required. It may also be necessary to modify the

TABLE XXXVI. THE PERFORMANCE OF A BIDDING MODEL

Test	Bid without model (1)	Bid with model (2)	Lowest competitive bid (3)	$(1 \div 3)$ $\times 100$ (4)	$(2 \div 3)$ $\times 100$ (5)
A	$44.53	$46.00	$46.49	95.8	98.9
B	47.36	42.68	42.93	110.3	99.4
C	62.73	59.04	60.76	103.2	97.2
D	47.72	51.05	53.38	89.4	95.6
E	50.18	42.80	44.16	113.7	96.9
F	60.38	54.61	55.10	109.6	99.1
G	39.73	39.73	40.47	98.2	98.2

model's predictions in the light of management's knowledge of a particular situation. As Edelman says: "Not only is the quality of the input information the ultimate determinant of the usefulness of the results, but the value of the entire approach is firmly based on the simple fact that the results are contributing, rather than deciding, factors in the decision which executives must make."[28]

PRODUCT ANALYSIS PRICING

The absence of a clearly defined market price also characterises the markets for jobbing firms, such as the manufacturers of small engineering products. However these markets have two other characteristics which make it very difficult to apply the models discussed in the previous section. First, the number of quotations required is often very large, perhaps hundreds or even thousands a week. Second, many of the quotations are for products that are unique in one way or another.

If it is impossible to obtain even an approximation to the ruling level of prices, there may be a temptation to use a rigid cost-based pricing system. But the proponents of Product Analysis Pricing (PAP) would see this as a counsel of despair. They suggest that price should be related to the value of the product to the purchaser; in the absence of an external market-indicator of this value, PAP is intended to generate a series of internal indicators.[29]

The central concept of PAP is the *target price,* which consists of three elements:

(a) *The total bought-out value,* which comprises (i) material value, defined as the quantity of material embodied in the product, valued at the customer's perception of current market price, plus a material-policy

---

28. F. Edelman. "Art and Science of Competitive Bidding". *Harvard Business Review* Vol. 43 (1965).
29. For a fuller explanation *see*: W. Brown and E. Jaques. *Product Analysis Pricing.* Heinemann, 1965; L. Symons. "Product Analysis Pricing". In: G. Wills and B. Taylor (eds). *Pricing Strategy.* Staples, 1969.

percentage, determined in the light of competitors' normal input–output ratios, (*ii*) bought component value, defined as the cost to the purchaser if it bought the components itself and gave them to the producing firm to assemble, plus a bought-component policy percentage (the customary handling charge in that industry).

(*b*) *Net standard value,* the calculation of which is rather complex. The first step is to divide the firm's range of products into categories, in each of which the products differ in one important dimension, usually size, e.g. the surface area of bearings or the horsepower of motors. A sample of recent prices is selected covering the entire size range of a category, and from these prices the bought-out values ((*a*) above) are subtracted, giving the net standard values. The net standard value is disaggregated into feature values—such as those conferred by special finishes—and property values.

These various values are then related in a formula (chosen to give the best fit) which is used to calculate the net standard values and (via the addition of the total bought-out values) the standard values for future orders.

(*c*) *Market percentage.* The above procedure should yield a price structure for each product category that reflects the relative values to purchasers of the features (including size) of the various products in that category. But there is no guarantee that the *level* of prices thus derived is the most appropriate. The prices included in the sample might have been too low, yielding inadequate margins, or too high, yielding an inadequate flow of orders. Moreover, even if the initial prices were adequate, they might not have remained so in the light of subsequent changes in costs and/or market conditions.

Consequently, an adjustment mechanism is provided in the form of the market percentage. This is a percentage (plus or minus) of the net standard value, and is applied across a given product category. The market percentage is the key strategic variable and is subject to decision at the highest level.

The proponents of PAP are "confident that its underlying rationale will be of value to any company which sells goods or services to customers."[30] But differences between markets may limit its application. Some textile markets have features in common with the market for jobbing engineers, e.g. firms have to deal quickly with a large number of orders for a wide range of products for which there are no price lists, or at least where the price lists become a basis for negotiation. But in textile markets bargains are often struck on the spot, ruling out reference back to the "pricing analyst" who administers PAP.

Moreover "size" may be a much less appropriate dimension by which to distinguish between different members of a product category. For example the amount of yarn in a piece of cloth depends upon not only the length

30. L. Symons. *Op. cit.,* p. 345.

and width of the cloth, but also the closeness of the weave, and this may not be reflected in price in a consistent way. Fashion may decree that a close weave is either more or less desirable than an open weave. Even if closeness of weave is treated as a feature value rather than a property value, it remains difficult to quantify.

QUESTIONS

1. Discuss the factors that influence a firm's basic price.
2. What factors would influence the relative importance of the pricing goals listed in Table XXV?
3. Show how product differentiation might affect decisions on price and output.
4. What factors might influence the relative importance of price in patronage decisions?
5. How might a firm attempt to estimate consumers' price sensitivity for: (*a*) baked beans canned in a new type of sauce, (*b*) a personal computer designed for use by small businesses, (*c*) seats in a new theatre?
6. "You can only measure consumers' price sensitivity by requiring them to put their money where their mouth is." Discuss.
7. Discuss the implications for pricing policy of the fact that price may be seen as an indicator of quality.
8. Explain how information on past bids can assist a firm in preparing a bid for a current contract.
9. Discuss the advantages and limitations of Product Analysis Pricing.
10. "Pricing policy should be consistent with other elements of marketing policy." Discuss.
11. The following information (abstracted from: A.R. Oxenfeldt. "A multi-stage approach to pricing". *Harvard Business Review* Vol. 38, 1960) relates to a number of US companies in their early days as manufacturers of television sets.

Zenith Radio
This company had extensive experience in the manufacture of car radios, which had resulted in the accumulation of substantial production expertise and a healthy liquidity position. But the company's outstanding resource was probably its widespread distribution network in a market in which retailers have considerable influence on consumers' decisions. In addition the company had built up a considerable degree of customer loyalty, reflecting the very high reputation of Zenith's radios.

Columbia Broadcasting Corporation
This company had a very different set of assets from Zenith. Its expertise mainly related to the management of entertainers and the production of

television programmes. It had some manufacturing facilities, but these were of poor quality. Moreover it had no suitable distribution facilities. However it did have great prestige as a producer of television programmes, and it also had substantial low-cost advertising facilities at its disposal.

Emerson

This was one of a number of companies which were under strong pressure to cultivate customers who put heavy emphasis on price, either because the company lacked the financial resources needed to convey a quality image or because its previous experience in the manufacture of consumer durables was with products of below average price. The chief asset of Emerson was a very efficient manufacturing organisation, geared to high-volume, low-cost production.

Indicate, for each of the three companies, what you think would be the most appropriate policies in terms of pricing, product development, sales promotion and the choice of distribution channels.

12. *Case Concrete Products*

Prior to 1956 this firm's principal product was concrete burial vaults, other products including lintels, patio stones and bird baths. In all of these products the firm enjoyed a local monopoly. There was competition from metal burial vaults; however the price differential was large enough to reduce the importance of price competition.

The basis on which these products were priced was full cost plus markup. The full cost estimates were determined as follows: labour and materials were added together, and to their combined cost was added a 10 per cent markup to cover overhead; to the resulting figure was added a 100 per cent markup.

The firm spent a great deal of time revising the cost estimates as costs changed. For example when a wage increase was granted the cost estimates, and therefore the prices, of all products were raised. However the firm did not have a job-order cost-accounting system which would accumulate the cost of each product; instead the cost estimates were checked only periodically against actual costs. Moreover the firm had never verified that overhead cost was actually 10 per cent of direct cost. It had simply accepted this figure when it was put forward at a trade association meeting.

In 1956 the firm was contemplating the manufacture of a new product, concrete septic tanks, which was well suited to the existing production facilities. There was only one producer of septic tanks in the city in which Case was located, and the firm believed that the building boom was creating a market large enough to support two producers.

In order to arrive at some estimate of costs, the firm manufactured a pilot model. The cost estimate was:

material	$26.85
labour	9.00
overhead	3.60
	$39.45

Applying the same pricing policy as was used on the other products would result in a price of $78.90. However the established producer's price was only $65. Case decided that its initial price should be the same as its competitor's. The competitor did not retaliate by lowering its price. Later, however, it did initiate discounts for certain customers. Case did not grant discounts, partly because the volume of sales was "satisfactory" and partly because it feared that if it were too aggressive, the competitor might begin producing concrete burial vaults. (The above information is based on an interview reported in W.W. Haynes, *Pricing in Small Business*, University of Kentucky Press, 1962.)

Evaluate Case's pricing policy.

13. In 1975 the retail petrol market was characterised by price cutting on a scale not previously encountered—some garages sold petrol at 12p a gallon below the recommended price. Eventually, following talks with the Minister for Prices and Consumer Protection, the major oil companies agreed to reduce the discounts they had been granting to some retailers, one of the sources of the reductions in retail prices. (Subsequently the majors successfully applied to the Price Commission for an increase in the recommended retail price.)

However in January 1976 Esso announced that they were re-introducing major discounts to selected retailers in certain areas, mainly in North and East England. The lead given by Esso was followed almost immediately by the other major oil companies. Esso stated that they had been forced to re-introduce these special discounts because of competition from three sources: (*a*) garages selling petrol imported from continental refiners at low prices; (*b*) garages selling petrol obtained from ICI who produce petrol as a by-product of chemical processes; (*c*) garages owned by ASDA, a prominent supermarket chain, and located on supermarket sites. While competition from these sources certainly existed, the fact that the other major companies followed Esso's lead so quickly was seen by certain commentators as an indication of a concerted effort by the majors to force the smaller independent producers out of the market.

(*a*) Why do you think ICI (*i*) was able and (*ii*) decided to sell petrol so cheaply? (*b*) Why do you think ASDA (*i*) was able and (*ii*) decided to sell petrol so cheaply? (*c*) Would you agree that the fact that all the other majors followed Esso so quickly in re-introducing special discounts was an indication of a concerted strategy? What alternative explanation of this policy might be advanced? (*d*) In 1975 the majors withdrew special discounts after discussions with a government minister. This implies that the public might suffer some disadvantages as a result of these discounts. What might these disadvantages be?

CHAPTER FOURTEEN

Subsidiary Pricing Decisions

OBJECTIVES
After studying this chapter the reader should be able to: distinguish between price differentials and price discrimination; describe the conditions under which price discrimination increases profitability; list the ways in which markets may be subdivided; understand the principles governing discount structures; explain the requirements for successful promotional pricing; understand the relationship between the product life cycle and pricing decisions; list the factors taken into account in product line pricing; define transfer pricing and discuss its significance.

INTRODUCTION

Having discussed the factors influencing the firm's basic price we now examine subsidiary pricing decisions. The term subsidiary does not imply that these decisions are of minor importance. In fact much of the time of pricing executives is devoted to such decisions, and they are often a critical determinant of sales and profitability. The term simply denotes the fact that these decisions follow from decisions on basic price, or to put it slightly differently, they lead to modifications of the basic price.

In some instances these modifications give rise to price differentials, a spread of prices around the basic price, at a given point in time. In other instances they give rise to price differentials over time. The rationale of both sets of differentials is a perceived difference in the price elasticity of demand.

ELASTICITY OF DEMAND AND PRICE DIFFERENTIALS

A basic model demonstrating the importance of price elasticity is presented in Fig. 78. D_A and D_B represent the demand for the firm's products in two markets (or sub-markets). If the firm sets price P it sells Q in both markets. But since elasticity differs between the two markets, profitability can be increased by the introduction of price differentials.

Price is reduced in market A, where demand is elastic, and increased in market B, where demand is inelastic. To simplify the analysis we assume changes in price which leave the quantity sold unchanged, i.e. Q_BQ equals QQ_A. If the unit cost of supplying the two markets is the same, total cost is unchanged, and a change in revenue implies a change in profitability. In market A the change in revenue is FGQ_AQ minus $PDFP_A$. In market B the change is P_BCEP minus $EDQQ_B$. In both markets revenue increases.

Turning to the situation where an increase in output is feasible (Fig. 79), we again start from a position where price P and the quantity sold Q are identical in the two markets. We make the further assumption that within the price range P–P_L demand is elastic in A and inelastic in B. If the firm's

14. SUBSIDIARY PRICING DECISIONS

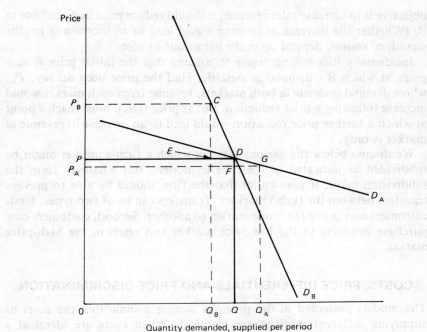

Fig. 78. *Price discrimination with constant output.*

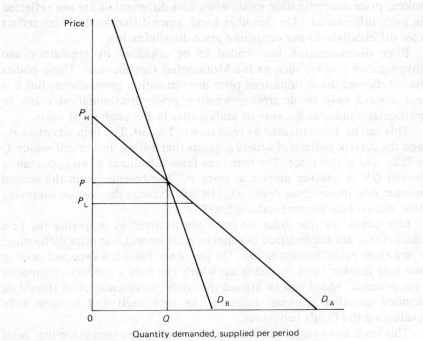

Fig. 79. *Price discrimination with increased output.*

objective is to increase sales revenue, it should reduce price in A, but not in B. (Whether the increase in revenue would lead to an increase in profits would, of course, depend upon the behaviour of costs.)

Incidentally it is not necessary to assume that the initial price is at a point at which B's demand is inelastic. Had the price been at, say, P_H, where demand is elastic in both markets, revenue from each market would increase following a price reduction. But as price falls it must reach a point at which a further price reduction would lead to an increase in revenue in market A only.

We discuss below the various ways in which a firm's market might be subdivided as indicated in these basic models. But whatever form the subdivision takes, it is essential that the firm should be able to prevent transfers between the (sub-) markets. Transfers can be of two types. First, customers may move from one market to another. Second, customers may purchase products in the low-price market and resell in the high-price market.

COSTS, PRICE DIFFERENTIALS AND PRICE DISCRIMINATION

The models presented in the previous section assume that the costs of supplying different markets are identical. When costs are identical a system of price differentials constitutes price discrimination. By the same token, price discrimination exists when cost differentials are not reflected in price differentials. On the other hand, price differentials which reflect cost differentials do *not* constitute price discrimination.

Price discrimination has tended to be criticised by regulatory and investigative bodies, such as the Monopolies Commission. These bodies have followed the definition of price discrimination given above. But it is not always easy to determine whether price discrimination exists in particular situations because of ambiguities in the analysis of costs.

This can be demonstrated by reference to Fig. 80. The firm sets price P_1, and the current pattern of orders suggests that during the current season Q will be sold at this price. The firm then takes advantage of an opportunity to sell QR in another market at price P_2. The revenue from the second market (the incremental revenue), $QWVR$, exceeds the cost of supplying that market (the incremental cost), $QTSR$.

One could say that since no costs are incurred in supplying the first market that are not incurred in supplying the second, the price differential constitutes price discrimination. On the other hand the expected sales in the first market form the basis on which the firm's productive capacity was planned, and it can be argued that only incremental costs should be applied to other markets, both by the firm itself and by any body evaluating the firm's behaviour.

This leads us to reconsider our earlier simplifying assumption that costs do not change as a result of price discrimination. It is clear that if, as is

14. SUBSIDIARY PRICING DECISIONS

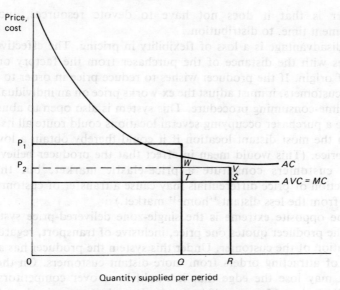

Fig. 80. *Incremental cost and price differentials.*

likely, price discrimination leads to an increase in the total volume of sales, then average cost may fall. This is especially likely if the increase in output enables the firm to obtain additional economies of scale.

THE SUBDIVISION OF MARKETS

Markets may be subdivided in various ways. In the following sections we discuss subdivision by space, time, the functional role of the customer and the personal characteristics of the customer. Other writers have adopted different classifications. For example Oxenfeldt distinguishes five bases for pricing differentials: geographical (corresponding to our space), temporal (time), vertical (functional role of customer), horizontal (partly functional role of customer) and internal (discussed below under product line pricing).[1]

THE SUBDIVISION OF MARKETS BY SPACE

Domestic markets
The basic choice facing suppliers is between setting ex-works prices and setting delivered prices. When a product is sold ex-works,[2] the buyer chooses and pays the costs of transportation. The advantage to the

---
1. A. R. Oxenfeldt. "The Differential Method of Pricing". *European Journal of Marketing* Vol. 13 (1979).
2. Or free on board (f.o.b.) origin or mill.

producer is that it does not have to devote resources, including management time, to distribution.

The disadvantage is a loss of flexibility in pricing. The effective price increases with the distance of the purchaser from the factory or other point of origin. If the producer wishes to reduce price in order to attract distant customers, it must adjust the ex-works price on an individual basis, a very time-consuming procedure. This system is also open to abuse. For example a purchaser occupying several locations could route all its orders through the most distant location if it could thereby obtain a lower ex-works price. (This would mean in effect that the producer believes that distant customers constitute a price-elastic market, but that the introduction of price differentials may cause a transfer of custom to this market from the less distant "home" market.)

At the opposite extreme is the single-zone delivered-price system, in which the producer quotes one price, inclusive of transport, regardless of the location of the customer. Under this system the producer has a better chance of attracting orders from more distant customers. On the other hand it may lose the edge that it would have over competitors in its "home" market. Moreover if its total sales volume remained unchanged its profits would fall, since the provision of transportation means that it costs more to supply distant customers than those located nearby. (If the producer increases his total sales, he may reduce average costs and so maintain his competitive edge in the home market.)

Under a multiple-zone delivered-price system the producer sets prices which are uniform within each of two or more zones. This system comes midway between the other two.

The use of delivered prices to extend and consolidate the producer's market has been described by the chairman of the London Brick Company in a statement circulated to shareholders: "Before the war when London Brick was seeking to expand its markets throughout the country, a policy was adopted of seeking a lower return on the price of bricks delivered longer distances from the works from those delivered nearer home. This was unashamedly designed to establish wider markets for the fletton brick at a time when the 'fletton' was not nationally accepted and when a few pence off the price could mean the difference between winning or losing an order. Those days have long since gone and for some years the sale of LBC bricks has been firmly established throughout the country at prices considerably below those of its competitors. The practice however of accepting some lower margin on bricks delivered over longer distances and balancing this by rather higher margins on bricks delivered nearer home has been maintained for rather different reasons. It was believed that, as fletton bricks are a basic material for building and particularly used in low-cost housing, it was in the interest of both our builder and local authority customers engaged in brick construction to apply some element of levelling in the prices charged throughout the country. Secondly it was felt that through maintaining a large volume of business at distant points we would gain the same additional benefit of economy of scale, both in our production and perhaps more important in our methods of distribution."

International markets

The barriers created by space are greatest when firms supply two or more countries, and there is evidence that despite some reluctance to "subsidise the foreigner",[3] profit margins tend to be lower in export than in domestic markets. In a study of 41 products made by 29 British engineering firms, Rosendale found virtually no difference overall between domestic and export prices. But profitability was lower in export markets for over half the products (Table XXXVII).

TABLE XXXVII. RELATIVE PRICES AND PROFITABILITY IN EXPORT MARKETS

Export prices relative to home prices	Profitability of export markets relative to home market			
	Greater	Equal	Less	Total
Greater	7	3	—	10
Equal	1	7	14	22
Less	—	1	8	9
Total	8	11	22	41

Rosendale found that most firms were emphatically opposed to the setting of prices in the home market which did not fully cover direct costs plus a full contribution to overheads. But "in export pricing, nine firms were prepared to consider and if necessary accept such prices".[4]

More recent studies have suggested a greater flexibility in export pricing, probably due to an intensification of international competition. Piercy found that of a sample of over one hundred exporters, more than two-thirds charged different prices in export and home markets, and that further variations occurred between one export market and another (Table XXXVIII).[5]

---

3. A widespread feeling to this effect was reported in H. G. Hunt, J. D. Froggatt and P. S. Hovell. "The Management of Export Marketing in Engineering Industries". *British Journal of Marketing* Vol. 1 (1967).

4. P. B. Rosendale. "The Short Run Pricing Policies of Some British Engineering Exporters", *National Institute Economic Review* No. 65 (1973).

5. N. Piercy. "British Export Market Selection and Pricing". *Industrial Marketing Management* Vol. 10 (1981). *See also: How British Industry Prices.* Industrial Market Research Ltd, 1976; F. Suntook. "How British Industry Exports." *Marketing* Vol. 7 (1978); ITI Research, *Factors for International Success*, Barclays Bank International, 1979.

TABLE XXXVIII. EXPORT PRICE BASES AND DISCRIMINATION

		%
Are ex-works prices the same for export as for the UK?	Yes	31
	No	69
Are ex-works prices the same in all export markets?	Yes	27
	No	73

A major reason for price differentials appeared to be that they allowed suppliers to tailor their prices to the competitive conditions in each market. Piercy found that almost two-thirds of the firms adopted market-based pricing methods ("pricing by reference to competitors' prices, pricing by investigation of customer reaction, judgment of what the market will bear").

In order to implement a market-based pricing policy firms should price goods in the local currency. But a majority of exporters in Piercy's study (and in other studies) priced in sterling. This appeared to be due mainly to "exporters' wishes to avoid the risks they perceive in local currency dealing and to maintain stable sterling income and prices, together with the attractions of administrative simplicity and convenience of single-currency operations."

The pricing policies of the multinational car manufacturers have received considerable attention. In a recent study the Institute of Fiscal Studies found that on average prices in Belgium were more than 11 per cent below the prices of comparable models in the UK. The median discount figures ranged from 2.3 per cent on the BMW 528 to 16 per cent on the BL Maxi.[6]

THE SUBDIVISION OF MARKETS BY TIME

In this section we are concerned with situations in which there is a regular cycle of price differentials. Changes in price over the life cycle of a product are discussed later. The subdivision of markets by time is more common in services than in manufacturing. This is due to the combination of demand and supply conditions found in many service industries.

Many services are subject to severe peaks in demand. Far more telephone calls are made during the day than at night. The greatest demand for passenger transport facilities arises when people are travelling to and from work. Many leisure activities are subject to heavier demand in the evening than during the day.

Considerable difficulties can arise in trying to match supply to this

---

6. *Differentials Between Car Prices in the UK and Belgium.* Institute Fiscal Studies, 1982. Commenting on the IFS's findings, industry spokesmen pointed out that Belgian prices are subject to price controls, and that the differentials quoted are less in most other countries.

pattern of demand. Since services cannot be stored for future consumption, a perfect matching of supply to demand would imply a very erratic work-pattern for the labour force, involving early starts, late finishes and split shifts. Moreover it is impossible to make major adjustments in such capital inputs as buildings and machinery. Since many of the costs attaching to these inputs are incurred even if the inputs are not utilised, producers may install less capacity than is needed to meet the peak demand.

Consumers are unable to store services for future consumption. Consequently a restriction of supply results in the formation of queues, either literally, as at bus stops, or metaphorically as when telephone services become overloaded so that numbers are obtained less quickly. The reverse applies in off-peak periods; supply exceeds demand and buses, trains, cinemas etc. have room to spare.

There are several factors that suggest that in such situations price should be higher in peak than off-peak periods. Since the capacity of the supplier is determined by the level of peak demand, the costs incurred in extending capacity beyond that required to meet off-peak demand should be recovered from peak-period customers. On the demand side, differential pricing is suggested if, as is likely, demand is less elastic in peak than non-peak periods. Price differentials may cause some transfers between markets, especially in the longer term. But the loss of revenue may well be balanced by a reduction in capacity costs.

These considerations explain why price differentials exist in so many service markets. The differentials may have a daily basis, e.g. telephone calls. They may relate to a period of days or weeks, e.g. railway travel. They may have a seasonal basis, e.g. in the holiday industry where winter rates are often much cheaper than summer rates.

Regular time differentials are much less important for manufactured goods, mainly because producers and consumers can store goods. (Many retailers have regular sales, and these sometimes involve the granting of discounts by manufacturers.)

THE SUBDIVISION OF MARKETS BY THE FUNCTIONAL ROLE OF THE CUSTOMER

In this section we discuss the relationship between the prices at various stages in the vertical chain of production and distribution: manufacturing, wholesaling, retailing (and consumption). (Oxenfeldt uses the term vertical differentials to describe this series of relationships.) We concentrate our attention on the decisions facing manufacturers, beginning with those relating to discounts to distributors.

Distributor discounts

In some markets manufacturers sell to distributors (wholesalers and/or retailers) in accordance with a conventional discount structure. A manufacturer may challenge this structure by offering a discount which is either smaller or bigger than usual.

If a manufacturer offering a lower than conventional discount is to achieve adequate distribution he must offer distributors a compensating advantage. A manufacturer would therefore be unwise to adopt such a strategy unless he had a technological or product advantage over competitors or is willing to spend more on advertising. He might then be able to charge a higher price so that a smaller percentage discount yields the distributor an absolute margin as big as on competitive products. Alternatively or additionally the demand for his products might be so high that the distributors' rate of stock turn is higher than on competitive products. Cadbury's used the high reputation of their products as a justification for offering retailers a margin that was conventional for chocolates but lower than usual for sugar confectionery when they entered the latter market.

A manufacturer lacking such advantages is more likely to accept the conventional discount structure. Indeed if he wishes to enlarge his distribution network he may offer an above-average discount. However this will, of course, mean either a lower margin for the manufacturer or a higher price to the consumer.

When there is not a conventional discount structure, a manufacturer has to consider what incentive is required to persuade sufficient distributors to perform the functions that he wishes them to perform. It is helpful if the manufacturer can estimate the costs incurred in performing those functions and the distributors' target profit.

The situation facing the manufacturer becomes more complex when—as happens in many markets—distributors differ in terms of both their cost structure and their target profit. It may then be necessary to choose between offering a low discount that satisfies a smaller number of distributors (those with high efficiency and/or low target-profits) and a higher discount that will satisfy a larger number of distributors.

A manufacturer may wish to limit the number of distributors for two reasons. First, it reduces the manufacturer's costs of distribution (and especially of transportation). Second, by giving each distributor a larger share of the market it offers him the prospect of higher total profits. If these profits are ploughed back and thus lead to greater efficiency on the part of the distributors, the manufacturer's total sales may rise. This is one of the reasons why a number of car manufacturers have reduced the size of their dealer networks in recent years.

Given the efficiency and target profitability of the distributor, the more resources he devotes to reselling the product the higher the discount likely to be offered by the manufacturer. In some instances the use of more resources enables the distributor to perform a given range of functions more intensively ("pushing" the product hard). In other instances the distributor is able to undertake a wider range of functions. Dean quotes the example of the manufacturer of building materials who gave a discount of 5 per cent to wholesalers who resold in container-load lots shipped directly from the manufacturer to the retailer, and a 12 per cent discount on shipments that were warehoused by the wholesaler and subsequently sold by him in smaller lots.[7]

Lucas defined several categories of stockists of vehicle components in terms of the facilities provided and the support given to the product. The highest rates of discount, 35 to 45 per cent, were given to wholesale electrical agents and motor distributor agents who were expected to offer a specialised service in electrical equipment, to carry adequate stocks (particularly of spare parts for repairs), to diagnose faults and to undertake repairs and testing. Factors who offered a less comprehensive service were given discounts of 32½ to 42½ per cent, while electrical stockists who specialised in motor electrical equipment, and had been appointed service agents of *other* manufacturers, were given discounts of 30 to 40 per cent.[8]

Discounts to retailers
Differences in the range of functions performed by the retailers of various types of product are reflected in differences in rates of discount (gross margins) as shown in Table XXXIX. High discounts are required in the fashion trades such as shoes and clothing, because of the labour-intensive nature of the operation and the risk of high stock-losses. Low discounts are given to retailers selling low-value, frequently purchased items with a low labour content, e.g. groceries sold by self-service.

TABLE XXXIX. GROSS MARGINS IN RETAILING, 1980

Kind of business	*Gross margin (% of turnover)*
Grocery retailers	17.0
Greengrocers, fruiterers	24.1
Chemists	24.3
Cycle and perambulator retailers	28.4
Toys, hobbies and sports goods retailers	29.4
Furniture retailers	32.3
Men's and boys' wear retailers	39.7
Footwear retailers	42.0

Source: *Business Monitor SDA 25*

7. J. Dean. *Op. cit.,* p. 521.

8. Monopolies Commission. *Report on the Supply of Electrical Equipment for Mechanically Propelled Land Vehicles.* HMSO, 1963, Ch. 9.

Own labels

Retailers are also able to obtain better terms from manufacturers by having products made under the retailer's own label. Manufacturers are prepared to sell at low prices for several reasons.

First, for producers of manufacturers' brands, the addition of own-label production can reduce unit costs, by enabling economies of scale to be further exploited and/or excess capacity to be utilised.

Second, retailer brands can usually be produced at a lower cost than manufacturer brands. Cost reductions can be obtained in the formulation of the product, packaging, advertising, and selling. (But *see* below.)

Third, own-label business may provide a basis for the expansion of the firm. Firms such as Northern Foods, Avana, Ruddles and Nottingham Manufacturing have grown by supplying own-label products to Marks and Spencers, Sainsburys and other large retailers. Some manufacturers are able to enter, or survive in, a market only by virtue of own label business. Faced with Kelloggs' monopoly in the market for corn flakes, Viota began supplying own labels to Tesco, and then to other multiple retailers. Some Italian manufacturers of refrigerators and other consumer durables used own-label contracts as a means of entering the UK market.

Finally, production of manufacturers' and retailers' brands may provide a means of price discrimination. The scope for this is greatest when there is substantial product differentiation among manufacturers' brands. However, some manufacturers with a strong image, e.g. Heinz, have been reluctant to produce own labels.

We noted above that own labels are usually cheaper to produce than manufacturers' brands. But a firm which produces a manufacturer's brand may find that extending production to own labels would increase average costs. Whether this is so depends partly upon the nature of the difference between the manufacturer and the retailer brand, and partly upon the relative size of the business. Baden-Fuller states that "Differences between domestic appliance brands are moderately easy to generate so long as the box or casing remains the same. For vacuum cleaners the differences may be in the colour and position of dust bag or the shape of the front; for refrigerators different shaped interiors or different knobs are used; for washing machines and cookers the fascia panel may be different."[9] Baden-Fuller estimated that in the case of refrigerators or vacuum cleaners moulds for the plastic parts involved in brand differentiation might cost from £5,000 to £35,000. For an order of 100,000 units this would increase unit costs by only a few pence for each mould change. Even with an order of as few as 20,000 units, costs would be increased by only 50p to £2 a unit.

When UK and US appliance producers were asked "What is the smallest economical order for a brand line?", most thought that 10,000 to 20,000 units a year would be a satisfactory order, although a few quoted a lower

9. C. Baden-Fuller. PhD Thesis, University of London, 1980.

figure. But "all producers pointed out that should a trade buyer require a machine with a different-sized box, or some other major difference in styling, then no order of less than 50,000 would be considered because such an order would require extensive retooling in the plant."

Although retailers normally pass part of their saving on own labels on to the consumer, gross margins are usually higher on own labels. An estimate by the Economist Intelligence Unit of margins on a typical grocery product are shown in Table XL. Moreover, store audits by A.C. Nielsen have revealed that stock turn is often faster on own labels, increasing their overall profitability to the retailer. Furthermore, consumers attacted to a store by own labels are likely to buy manufacturer brands of other products, especially in stores with a wide product-range.

TABLE XL. ESTIMATED MARGINS AND PRICES

	Own label	Manufacturer brand
Manufacturer's cost	100	112
Manufacturer's margin (%)	15	15
Price to retailer	115	129
Retailer's margin (%)	25	20
Price to consumer	144	155

The grocery market in the USA has been characterised for many years by a two-tier price structure for own labels. In the depressed trading conditions of the early 1980s the first distinct sign of a similar trend was seen in the UK with the introduction of generics. These basic products, simply packaged and with minimal marketing support, are much cheaper than both manufacturer brands and the retailers' main own labels (Table XLI). Fine Fare attribute much of their growth in the early 1980s to generics, sales of which accounted for about 5 per cent of turnover in 1982.

TABLE XLI. PRICE DIFFERENTIALS ON GENERICS

Company	No. of product classes	% below own labels	% below manufacturer brands
Presto	5	29	46
Carrefour	13	–	26
Fine Fare	13	17	39
International	14	–	30
Tesco	13	23	45

Source: A.C. Nielsen Co.

Pricing to other manufacturers

In deciding what prices to charge for materials, components etc. sold to other manufacturers, account must be taken of the fact that these manufacturers are likely to have a better idea than distributors of the costs involved in manufacturing the products in question. Moreover they are often in a better position to begin the manufacture of the products themselves, should they consider the price too high.

Furthermore, in certain markets sales to manufacturers may aid future sales through distributors. If, for example, an automotive component is designed for a particular model of vehicle in such a way that no rival manufacturer is able to offer a substitute, the supplier may expect to earn high margins on his replacement business, especially from sales made to wholesalers and retailers. Even where substitutes are available consumers may express a preference for the original brand, allowing the manufacturer to charge a premium price.

The Monopolies Commission found that in the market for automotive electrical equipment the Lucas group earned on average a profit rate on sales of 13 per cent on replacements, as compared with a rate of 6.1 per cent on initial equipment. Chloride's profits on automotive batteries were found to be 1.6 per cent on sales (or 3.2 per cent on capital employed) for original equipment as compared with 14 per cent on sales (31 per cent on capital employed) for replacement equipment.[10]

Too wide a differential between the two markets carries the danger that rival manufacturers may be established purely to supply the more lucrative replacement market. By offering lower prices they are able to counteract consumers' brand preferences. In the UK the replacement market was the basis of the growth of such firms as Quinton Hazell, Wipac and Park Bros.

QUANTITY DISCOUNT STRUCTURES

In many instances decisions on quantity discount structures take account of the functional role of the customer. But in this section we confine our attention to principles that apply regardless of the type of customer.

Quantity discounts are mainly designed as a means of, first, influencing the pattern of orders, so that a given volume of orders can be met at minimum cost, and, second, increasing the volume of orders, or at least preventing the loss of orders to competitors. Some types of discount structure contribute more to the first objective, others to the second.

The discount may be related to either (*a*) the amount of an individual product purchased or (*b*) the amount of all products purchased,

---

10. Monopolies Commission. *Op. cit.,* Ch. 18. A similar picture was revealed in the Commission's *Report on Clutch Mechanisms for Road Vehicles*, HMSO, 1968.

aggregated together. (In single-product firms the second does not apply, of course.) Further, "amount" can be measured in terms of (*i*) volume or (*ii*) value.

Alternative (*a*) is more likely to encourage a pattern of ordering leading to longer production runs, with consequent economies in production. (*a*) (*i*) has the additional advantage of enabling the producer to offer incentives for the purchase of full case-loads, which may lead to savings in packaging and handling costs.

Alternative (*b*) encourages purchasers to amalgamate their orders for different products, thus allowing economies in order-processing costs. It may also help a producer with a dominant position in one market to extend its sales in other markets. But this policy can result in a fall in the effective price of the major product without an increase in its sales. Whether this is acceptable depends upon the importance attached by the firm to diversification and a wide mix of products.

In some instances alternative (*b*) (*i*) is ruled out because it is impossible to find a meaningful method of aggregating the volume of purchases of different products. But when a value measure, whether (*a*) (*ii*) or (*b*) (*ii*) is used, it must be carefully monitored. As the price of the product increases, the absolute discount may increase even if the volume purchased remains unchanged. This can lead to a squeeze on the producer's profit margins if all prices, including input prices, rise.

A further choice has to be made between a non-cumulative system, in which the discount is based on the size of a given order, and a cumulative system, in which it is based on the total amount purchased in a given period. The non-cumulative system encourages large individual orders, and hence leads to savings in manufacturing, handling, and order-processing costs. On the other hand, cumulative discounts can help to "tie" the purchaser to a supplier. But although cumulative discounts discourage divided accounts or dual sourcing, it cannot be said which producer will benefit and which will lose. Consequently, before instituting a cumulative system a producer should carefully analyse the benefits that it can offer to purchasers, *vis-à-vis* other producers. Moreover, bodies such as the Monopolies Commission often look unfavourably upon such systems, and have sometimes recommended that they be discontinued.

A further important dimension of a discount structure is its width, i.e. the size of orders (however defined) which qualify for the minimum and maximum discounts. A large proportion of a firm's sales are often accounted for by a small proportion of its customers (the 80 : 20 ratio). If it is felt that a multiplicity of small orders is raising unduly the costs of production, handling and order processing, it may be desirable to raise the point at which a discount becomes available, i.e. to narrow the structure.

The final, very important dimension of a discount structure is its depth, i.e. the size of the discount for given purchase quantities. Each producer has to take account of the discounts offered by competitors, although it appears that there is sometimes a considerable diversity within a given market.[11] Moreover a producer may face some very powerful purchasers whose business can be obtained only on better terms than those in the formal discount structure. The pressure that can be exerted by large purchasers is well documented in two reports of the Monopolies Commission.

In its report *Metal Containers*[12] the Commission showed that Metal Box, the dominant producer, had established a structure which related prices to the underlying costs of supply and which encouraged the full utilisation of highly automated machinery. For processed food cans the discount rate ran from 1 per cent on annual purchases of 10 million to 3 per cent on annual purchases of 50 million. Additional discounts, relating to the combined purchases of food and beverage cans, of up to 3 per cent were available for purchases up to 200 million a year. Additional rebates were also given relating to the quantity of any one kind of can purchased in one year. Finally, additional rebates were given to customers purchasing all their requirements from Metal Box.

But even a company with such a dominant market position (more than three-quarters of home sales at the time of investigation) and so elaborate a discount structure felt it necessary to go outside the structure when negotiating orders with very large customers, in order to meet competition, not only from other can manufacturers, but also from customers who made, or might make, cans themselves. The Commission noted that "Metal Box says that in many cases terms have been negotiated at the insistence of large customers, whose bargaining power is considerable, and they represent the best terms the company could get." Of the company's 624 customers, only 45 bought at special prices or under specially negotiated agreements. However these customers accounted for 88 per cent of total net sales.

In its report *Discounts to Retailers*[13] the Monopolies and Mergers Commission gave figures showing the total cost of special terms given by 15 major manufacturers to the three largest and most rapidly expanding multiple grocery chains (Table XLII). In addition to special prices and discounts these special terms included contributions to retailers' advertising, the provision of shop equipment, and the provision of sales staff.

---

11. *See*, for example: J. Crowther. "The Rationale of Quality Discounts". *Harvard Business Review* Vol. 42 (1966). Crowther also makes the point in this article that the buyer may not need to be offered an incentive to increase the size of this order until his purchases reach the economic order quantity, and he suggests a strategy for setting discounts at points beyond this size.
12. HMSO, 1970.
13. HMSO, 1981.

TABLE XLII. SPECIAL TERMS RECEIVED BY LARGEST MULTIPLE CHAINS

	Total of 15 manufacturers' sales of national brands (£000)	Cost to manufacturers of special terms to retailers (£000)	(% of sales)
Tesco	87,045	7,270	8.35
Sainsbury	21,431	1,666	7.77
Asda	49,774	3,518	7.06

THE SUBDIVISION OF MARKETS BY THE PERSONAL CHARACTERISTICS OF PURCHASERS

The most common permanent basis of differentiation is age, with lower prices being charged for children and, less frequently, for elderly people than for adults of working age. These reductions are most frequently found in service industries, e.g. in transport, entertainment and personal services such as hairdressing. Since these services are normally consumed in public, often at the point of sale, the possibility of transfers occurring between the two price segments is minimised.

These price differentials can often be justified in terms of differences in price elasticity, arising from differences in incomes. But social considerations are also important, especially with respect to essential services such as transport; allowing children to travel at half price during peak periods can make little sense economically.

Occasionally different prices are charged for males and females. Some discos allow free entrance for females on certain days. In the past British Rail has offered ladies' tickets on some Inter-city routes.

PROMOTIONAL PRICING

We define promotional pricing as the setting of a price *on a temporary basis* below the price normally charged. Promotional prices are often set when new products are introduced to the market in an attempt to persuade consumers to make trial purchases. (As we show in the next chapter promotional prices are sometimes more effective than advertising in this respect.) Distributors may also be offered additional discounts as an inducement to stock the product. Thereafter firms may make regular price promotions an integral part of their overall pricing strategy. This implies, of course, a reduction in the average price. It is important therefore to identify the price reduction required to generate the desired increase in sales.

There is evidence that this requirement is not always met. A study of the sales pattern of 65 products suggested that in a significant proportion of promotions, money was given away to consumers to little or no purpose. Of the 65 promotions, 16 offered price reductions of less than 10 per cent. However "even a casual glance at the record for the 16 brands indicated that the response to this range of discounts was not significant in terms of the job to be done," i.e. to gain an increased market share during the period of the promotion.[14]

Larger reductions usually elicited short-term gains in brand share; particularly effective were larger reductions on a smaller quantity of merchandise, especially by concentrating the promotion on a giant pack-size. But even here permanent gains in brand share were very rare, since this type of promotion appealed mainly to established users of the brand.

Research into housewives' attitudes towards price reductions by Harris International Marketing Ltd also suggests that promotions have a very limited effect on brand switching. Of more than a thousand housewives questioned in February 1974 only 8 per cent said that they looked for price cuts, while of 495 housewives questioned in the following month, the majority said that they would buy cut-price goods only if they were their usual brands. Subsequent enquiries produced similar results.

Promotional pricing by retailers

Promotional pricing by retailers has been justified on the grounds that since the cost of search makes it difficult for consumers to judge whether the overall level of prices is lower in one store than another, they evaluate relative price levels on the basis of a small sample of goods. Consequently the retailer should cut heavily the price of a limited range of goods.

This policy was adopted by the multiple grocery chains such as Tesco that grew very rapidly in the 1960s and early 1970s. But since then more rapid growth has been achieved by retailers, such as Asda, following an alternative strategy of more modest price reductions on a much wider range of products. The success of this alternative policy is probably due at least in part to the increasing sources of information on the average price levels in different shops. Also, the rapid inflation experienced in the 1970s reduced the impact of promotional pricing.

The cost of retailers' promotional prices is often met, at least partly, by manufacturers. In some instances assistance is sought by retailers. But frequently manufacturers take the initiative. The Monopolies and Mergers Commission found that of the total cost to manufacturers of special terms, expenditure on special promotions accounted for 30 per cent in biscuits, and 24 per cent in cakes.[15]

PRICING AND THE PRODUCT LIFE CYCLE

It is generally believed that the critical decisions concern the pricing of new

14. A. C. Nielsen Co. Ltd. "Money-Off Promotions". *Nielsen Researcher*, 1964.
15. Monopolies and Mergers Commission. *Discounts to Retailers. HMSO, 1981.*

or pioneer products, and it is to these decisions that we give most attention.

The pricing of pioneer products
The classic distinction, first made by Joel Dean, is between a skimming and a penetration price, and although many firms adopt an intermediate strategy, the distinction remains useful as a means of exploring the implications of alternative strategies. A skimming price policy involves a high initial price (to skim the cream off the market) followed by a reduction of price, often in a series of steps, in order to expand sales. A penetration price policy involves a low initial price, perhaps below full cost, designed to penetrate the market as quickly as possible. As sales increase, profit margins improve. In choosing between these alternatives the producer should take account of several factors.

The rate of market growth
The first factor to take into account is the rate of growth of the market as a whole. A skimming price policy is more likely to be adopted if the rate of the market growth is limited by the need for an extended programme of consumer education concerning the merits of the product, or by the need to establish an extensive distribution network. (It is interesting to note that these needs still exist in the UK in the market for electric waste-disposal units, a product suggested by Dean in 1951 as being suitable for a skimming price policy in the USA.) New drugs often have a wide range of potential uses, but have an advantage over other drugs for only some of these uses. Producers usually adopt a skimming price policy, accepting that sales will initially be limited to users whose needs cannot be met satisfactorily by existing drugs.

A fast rate of market growth can be expected when it is possible to demonstrate clearly the advantages of a product by means of laboratory or engineering tests; this is particularly important for industrial products. Rapid acceptance can also occur when a high proportion of sales is made to a relatively few buyers, perhaps half a dozen in the vehicles industry, for example. Fast market-growth is conducive to a penetration price policy, since the period of low margins is less likely to be prolonged.

The erosion of distinctiveness
Even if the producer of a pioneer product enters a market with a potentially rapid rate of market growth he may adopt a skimming price policy if he is confident that his product's distinctiveness can be maintained over a long period. A product's distinctiveness is least likely to be eroded when it is built on extensive research and development work, and especially when the results of this work are protected by patents. But distinctiveness can also be achieved by marketing activities, and especially by advertising and branding.

Du Pont was described as "one of the classic skimmers" in an article in the journal *Business Week*. When Du Pont introduced Quiana, a synthetic fibre with the look and feel of silk, it was launched into the high-fashion prestige market with a price range of $5.95 to $8.95 per lb (above that of other synthetics) compared with $8 to $10 for silk. "You get it into the very highest prestige garments to build a reputation and identity for it. We got the biggest designers and biggest names (Dior, Cardin and Givenchy, for instance) to develop this identity". Subsequently as volume builds up and cost fall, "to broaden your market you go into the next lower price category."[16] (For example, five years after Quiana's introduction the price was cut by 35 per cent.)

The length of time over which distinctiveness can be maintained should be set against the expected life of the product. Production of items with a high fashion content, e.g. some clothing and footwear, may continue for only a couple of years. Maintaining a product's distinctiveness for, say, twelve months, might justify the adoption of a skimming price policy.

Cost structures

The third major factor to be considered is the cost structure of the firm and of (existing or potential) competitors. As shown in Chapter 5, average cost can be reduced by operating on a large scale and also as a result of an increase in cumulative output (the experience or learning effect). The greater the effect of higher output on cost the more profitable a penetration price policy is likely to be. This is partly because the higher output enables the pioneer producer to reduce its unit costs. But more important, by denying sales to competitors, the pioneer producer is able, by virtue of the experience effect to maintain the initial advantage gained over these competitors.

This is illustrated in Fig. 81. Reductions in unit cost are passed on in the form of lower prices. Having a lower cumulative volume of output, competitors have higher unit costs. If, in order to compensate for their higher costs, they set higher prices, their volume of sales will be lower, and hence they become at an even bigger disadvantage. Alternatively, if they match the price of the low-cost producer their profit margins are squeezed and they are denied the cash required to finance the investment required to obtain a competitive advantage. (*See* Chapter 10.)

The alternative policy is illustrated in Fig. 82. As the firm's profit margin is allowed to widen, it provides a price umbrella for competitors. These competitors can now more easily obtain the volume of sales required to reduce their costs to a competitive level. When this happens the price structure comes under pressure and eventually collapses. (The point of collapse is indicated by the kink in the curve.)

---

16. "Pricing Strategy in an Inflation Economy". *Business Week*, 4th April 1974, reprinted in: I. R. Vernon and C. W. Lamb. *The Pricing Function*. D. C. Heath, 1976, Ch. 3.

14. SUBSIDIARY PRICING DECISIONS

A similar situation can arise when price is allowed to follow cost down, as in Fig. 81, but the initial profit margin is so high that it allows competitors to enter and build volume.

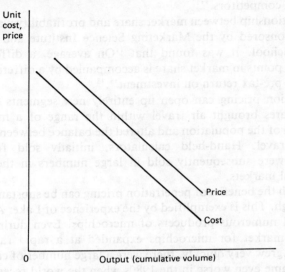

Fig. 81. *Pricing down the experience curve.*

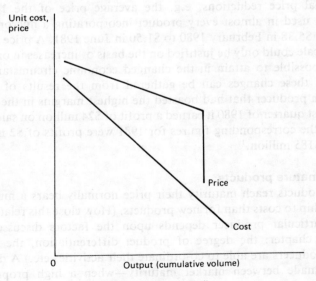

Fig. 82. *A price umbrella.*

Probably the best-known advocates of a penetration price policy are the Boston Consulting Group. They argue that "the basic objective in pricing a new product should be to prevent competitors from gaining experience and market share before the new product has achieved major volume. If this is done, it is possible to achieve a cost advantage over competition which cannot ever profitably be overcome by any normal performance on the part of competitors."[17]

The relationship between market share and profitability was explored in a study sponsored by the Marketing Science Institute and the Harvard Business School. It was found that "On average, a difference of 10 percentage points in market share is accompanied by a difference of about 5 points in pre-tax return on investment".[18]

Penetration pricing can open up entirely new segments of a market. Low air fares brought air travel within the range of a much-enlarged proportion of the population and altered the balance between business and pleasure travel. Hand-held calculators, initially sold for industrial purposes, were subsequently sold in large numbers in the leisure and educational markets.

Although the benefits of penetration pricing can be substantial, the risks are also high. This is exemplified by the experience of Laker Airways in air travel, and numerous producers of microchips. Even during the 1970s, when the market for microchips expanded at a rapid rate and some companies grew very quickly, there were a large number of casualties. But things became even worse in the 1980s when the world recession checked the rate of market growth. The emergence of excess capacity led to substantial price reductions, e.g. the average price of the 16K RAM memory, used in almost every product incorporating a microprocessor, fell from $5.38 in February 1980 to $1.50 in June 1981. A price reduction on this scale could only be justified on the basis of increases in output that were impossible to attain in the changed economic circumstances. The effect of these changes can be gathered from the results of Intel, an American producer that had boasted the highest margins in the industry. In the first quarter of 1980 it earned a profit of $24 million on sales of $204 million; the corresponding figures for 1981 were profits of $2 million on sales of $185 million.[19]

Pricing mature products

When products reach maturity their price normally bears a much closer relationship to costs than for new products. (How close this relationship is for a particular producer depends upon the factors discussed in the previous chapter: the degree of product differentiation, the extent to which producers are able to co-ordinate their activities etc.) A distinction can be made between market maturity—when a high proportion of potential purchasers have become actual purchasers—and product or

---

17. Boston Consulting Group. *Op. cit.*, Ch. 8.
18. R. D. Buzzell, B. T. Gale and R. G. M. Sultan. "Market Share–A Key to Profitability". *Harvard Business Review* Vol. 53 (1975).
19. *Financial Times*, 17th June 1981.

technological maturity. Once maturity in both respects has been achieved, pricing tends to become a much less important competitive weapon, since producers realise that few gains can be expected from further price reductions. Conversely, more attention is given to other forms of competition such as advertising and the provision of service.

Pricing products in decline

The passive role of pricing for mature products is often continued when sales begin to decline. But in certain circumstances a more aggressive pricing policy may be adopted. The product may be reformulated so as to reduce costs and hence permit a price reduction. The saturation of the market for a hard-back edition of a book is often the sign for the introduction of a soft-back version. The withdrawal of marketing support may also enable price to be reduced, so that the product can be sold to customers who respond to a different marketing mix. Finally, in times of inflation prices may be held stable, or raised less than prices in general, in order to moderate the rate of decline of sales.

PRODUCT LINE PRICING

In this section we discuss the factors influencing internal price relationships, to use Oxenfeldt's term. Most firms produce more than one product, or more than one model or version (size, colour etc.) of a single product. If there are market or production interrelationships between these products or models, the firm must take account of factors additional to those considered above.

Substitution

The various products or models may be seen by consumers as substitutes for each other. Consequently, when the firm is considering changing the price of a model (or product) it should take account of the impact of the price change on the sales and profitability of other models. If BL reduced the price of the Mini in order to extend its product life, this might cause sales of the Metro to fall. If it raised the price of the Triumph Acclaim, some purchasers who were unable to afford the Acclaim might buy a Metro. It is obviously easier to take account of internal cross-elasticities when pricing authority is centralised than when it is devolved among a number of product or brand managers.

Consistency

A firm's price structure is said to be consistent when the relative prices are seen to be fair by consumers. In fact fairness is not a straightforward concept. For example, consider a manufacturer selling a range of men's suits of a given quality through a given type of store. If a higher price is charged for a larger size this will probably be accepted as fair by consumers since additional expense (material cost) is incurred. On the other hand it may be considered unfair if more is charged for a colour of suit that is in less demand, even though average cost may be higher due to the shorter production run.

If the producer is willing to supply a higher-cost model only at a higher price he will try to avoid such unfavourable reactions. For example when the product is made to order, the list price may refer to the standard model, with higher prices being quoted for "special" versions, implying that for the extra money the buyer can obtain a certain degree of prestige or exclusivity. (In many instances, e.g. cars, the producer is able to set a price premium in excess of the cost differential.)

Coverage

The extent to which a producer's price range covers the market often depends upon its product policy. But consumers' reactions to the price structure can lead to a modification of the product policy. In the United States Shwayder Brothers, makers of Samsonite luggage, decided to concentrate on medium-price models, ignoring both the expensive leather and the cheap paperboard segments of the market. In 1965 the company had two principal lines, the Streamlite, wood-frame models selling for between $14.95 and $26.95, and the Silhouette, magnesium-frame models, selling for between $27.95 and $55. This structure appeared to cover the target market adequately, there being no obvious gaps. However consumer reaction suggested that the structure was less than fully adequate.

Many customers started with a cheap line and subsequently traded up; but the jump in price between the two ranges was such that many Shwayder customers traded up to a competitive brand. To overcome this problem, the firm introduced an intermediate range, the Contoura, selling for between $19.95 and $36.95. It also extended the line downward with the introduction of the Royal Traveller models, sold through discount stores at 25 to 30 per cent below the prices of the "regular" models. By restricting the distribution of this model to a particular type of outlet the firm reduced the risk that consumers would substitute the cheaper models for the more expensive alternatives that yielded higher margins.[20]

There are many examples in the tyre industry of producers introducing more expensive models in an attempt to widen their margins. In the USA in the early 1960s cross-ply tyres selling at about $30 dominated the market. In 1965 Goodrich launched a radial at $50. But the price jump proved to be too great. Consequently an intermediate product, the bias-belted tyre, was introduced at about $40. This became the most popular tyre and subsequently many consumers made the step up to radials. A further extension to the product range occurred when Goodyear introduced, at a 5 per cent price premium, a radial using a synthetic tyre

20. "Samsonite: On Land, in the Air, and on the Sea". *Business Week*, February 1965.

cord instead of steel. The UK market followed a similar pattern in the 1970s, but one innovation, the run-flat tyre, pioneered by Dunlop, has still found very limited acceptability at the time of writing.

Complementarity
Complementarity exists when an increase in the sales of one product leads to an increase in the sales of a second product. Until it ran foul of the antitrust authorities, IBM tied the sales of peripheral equipment and software to sales of its computers, either by means of technical specifications or via contracts. A weaker form of complementarity exists where consumers associate two products. For example a purchaser of a Dunlop tennis racquet may be thereby encouraged to buy Dunlop tennis balls. However it is doubtful whether this weaker form of complementarity would often justify a substantial price reduction in the price of the "leading" product.

The use of joint facilities
When different products compete for the use of common production facilities, the producer must bear in mind the possibility that a price reduction that caused an increase in the sales of one product could lead to a restriction of the facilities available for another product. Any profit forgone on the other product (the opportunity cost) should be offset against the increased profits resulting from the price change.

Competitive market relationships
Figure 83 refers to a situation in which two companies, A and B, both supply markets 1 and 2. (The areas of the circles indicate the respective sales values.) A, the dominant producer in market 2, may decide to use the cash generated in this market to increase its sales in market 1. B may choose to fight it out in market 1. Alternatively, B may adopt the "cash cutting gambit", lowering its price in market 2, forcing A to cut its price

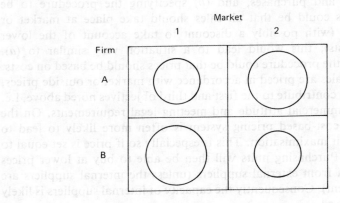

Fig. 83. *Cash-cutting gambit.*

and thus cutting off the cash needed by A to finance its offensive in market 1.

TRANSFER PRICING

In this section we discuss the pricing of products that are sold by one unit (firm, division, etc.) to another unit within the same organisation (firm or group). Although internal sales take place within many firms selling within a single country, transfer pricing policy assumes more significance when these sales take place across international boundaries. However, we first examine the factors influencing transfer pricing policy, whatever its geographical scope, beginning with company objectives.

Company objectives and transfer pricing systems

The most important objectives influencing transfer pricing systems are:

(*a*) To foster in those responsible for the performance of a profit centre (e.g. a firm, division) a commercial attitude, i.e. one which focuses on profitably meeting the demands of customers rather than on narrower considerations such as cost reduction or meeting engineering specifications. This implies a long-term view of profitability, with an emphasis on the development of managerial ability.

(*b*) To maximise short-run profits. Especially important in this respect is the optimum utilisation of the existing (and particularly the physical) assets of the firm.

(*c*) To meet legal requirements. This objective assumes great importance in the multinational enterprise.

Transfer pricing systems

The basic choice is between (*a*) allowing the individual units to trade at arm's length, giving them the same freedom as they have with respect to external sales and purchases, and (*b*) specifying the procedure to be followed. This could be that all sales should take place at market or outside prices (with possibly a discount to take account of the lower marketing costs); this would lead to a situation very similar to (*a*). Alternatively, the procedure could be that prices should be based on costs.

If internal sales are priced in accordance with market or outside prices, the system will contribute to the first and third objectives noted above, i.e. fostering a commercial attitude and meeting legal requirements. On the other hand a cost-based pricing system is often more likely to lead to short-run profit maximisation. This is especially so if price is set equal to variable cost. Purchasing units will then be able to buy at lower prices internally than from external suppliers (unless the internal suppliers are highly inefficient). Consequently the capacity of internal suppliers is likely to be well utilised.

Cost-based pricing systems obviously influence the distribution of profits within the firm or group. In the above example, with prices set equal to variable cost, all the profits accrue to the purchasing units. The profits of the supplying units are zero in the short run and negative in the long run. An alternative basis, e.g. that prices should equal full (total) cost plus a profit margin, would lead to a different distribution of profits.

The implications for MNEs are clear. By varying the transfer pricing system it is possible to affect the geographical distribution of profits and hence, if rates of corporate taxation vary from one country to another, total after-tax profits. (MNEs can influence the distribution of profits by *ad hoc* decisions on transfer prices, but this is far more cumbersome than establishing a routine procedure unless the transfers are few in number and high in value.)

MNEs may also wish to influence the distribution of profits for other reasons. They may wish to maximise the profits earned in a country in order to gain the approval and support of the government of that country. On the other hand they may wish to minimise the profits earned in a country if the political climate is unstable or hostile, e.g. if there is a danger that foreign-owned assets will be appropriated, or if it is believed that the currency is likely to depreciate.

In view of the possibilities that exist for manipulating profits and hence affecting government revenue, it is not surprising that MNEs have come under pressure to adopt arm's-length pricing. An increasing number of countries have introduced procedures to ensure that internationally traded goods are valued at market prices for fiscal purposes regardless of the procedures adopted for internal purposes by the MNE.

Many countries, including all the members of the EEC, have accepted the Convention on the Valuation of Goods for Customs Purposes together with the various recommendations made by the Customs Co-operation Council. These regulations lay down that the normal transfer price should be the market price as arrived at by an independent buyer and seller. If a market price does not exist, and no comparable goods can be found, a sales-minus approach should be adopted, i.e. one arrives at a valuation by taking the market price of the final product minus the expenses incurred in the importing country, and minus a reasonable profit-margin for the importer. However it has been observed that "when an obvious market price is not available, the process often degenerates into bargaining between the importer and the customs authorities with no real reference to the value of the goods."[21] Another approach is to take the cost of production and add a profit margin. But there is again considerable scope for bargaining about both cost and profit. For example the UK Inland Revenue has sometimes accepted a transfer price below full cost where the

---

21. R. B. Flavell. "Divisionalisation and Transfer Pricing: A Review". *Omega* Vol. 5 (1977).

company is trying to break into the market, trying to sell a complete range, or selling an item related to its main line of business as a loss-leader.

In many countries, including the UK and the USA, the authorities have the right to reallocate profits if they believe that transfer prices have not been set in accordance with the arm's-length principle. Section 482 of the US Internal Revenue Code states that: "In any case of two or more organisations, trades or businesses . . . owned or controlled directly or indirectly by the same interests, the Secretary may distribute, apportion, or allocate gross income, deductions, credits or allowances between or among such organisations, trades or businesses, if he determines that such distribution, apportionment, or allocation is necessary in order to prevent evasion of taxes or clearly to reflect the income of such organisations, trades, or businesses."

The attraction of such legislation to the authorities is clear. They are able to enhance government revenue without being involved in prolonged negotiations relating to a long series of transactions. The danger to companies is that the authorities will use their power in an arbitrary manner. This danger was illustrated by the proposal of several states in the USA to apply unitary taxation to foreign multinationals.

Under the proposed method, an MNE would be taxed on the basis of its worldwide profit rather than the income earned in an individual state or country. The taxing authority decides what proportion of a MNE's operations falls within its area, and taxes that proportion of the company's worldwide profits regardless of whether or not a profit was made within its jurisdiction. The system becomes arbitrary when different authorities use different bases. There would, of course, be a strong temptation for each authority to choose a basis favourable to itself. For example, California, a high-wage area, has inserted a labour content into its formula whereas a low-wage country would probably not do so.

QUESTIONS

1. Distinguish between price differentials and price discrimination.
2. Explain the conditions required for profitable price discrimination.
3. Why may it be difficult to determine whether a firm is practising price discrimination?
4. Discuss the various ways in which a firm may attempt to subdivide its markets.
5. Explain why price discrimination has sometimes attracted criticism, and say whether you believe this criticism to be justified.
6. Why is the subdivision of markets by time more feasible for services than for goods?
7. What factors should a manufacturer take into account when deciding what discounts to offer to distributors?

8. How would you explain the differences in gross margin shown in Table XXXIX?

9. Under what conditions is a firm most likely to begin manufacturing products under a retailer's label or brand?

10. "A quantity discount schedule is always a compromise between the aims of the producer and those of his customer." Discuss.

11. Define the terms "skimming" and "penetration" price policies, and explain the circumstances under which each policy is likely to be most successful.

12. What factors must be taken into account when a firm produces several products (or several versions of a product) which do not apply to a firm which produces only a single version of one product?

13. Explain which transfer pricing system is likely to be most appropriate when the firm's main objective is (a) to develop the ability of its managers, (b) to maximise short-run profits.

14. Discuss the factors which might influence the transfer pricing system adopted by a multinational enterprise.

15. *The Variety Press*

The Variety Press is a small job-printing shop employing ten persons. The firm's general pricing policy is full cost plus a 20 per cent markup. The management obtains cost estimates from a nationally published manual, which provides regional breakdowns, but it checks these estimates against its own experience.

For regular customers the firm usually does not quote a price in advance, but instead bases the final charge on the actual costs that have been accumulated on the order, plus the 20 per cent markup. In such cases the management protects customer goodwill by carefully checking the actual costs. If the actual costs are found to be high, the markup may be reduced.

One clear exception to the usual policy is the pricing of envelopes and letterheads, on which the markup is only 10 per cent. A higher markup would lead to a loss of this business. The managing director believes that the company must maintain this line as a part of its service to its customers, many of whom prefer to place all their printing with one firm.

With this exception, the managing director believes that prices either above or below those provided by the 20 per cent markup are usually unsound. He is firmly opposed to pricing below full cost, stating that "profitable plants make a profit on every job." He has apparently given little direct attention to demand elasticities. However he faces competition from at least 20 similar firms in the vicinity, and he believes that this competition limits his ability to raise prices.

The basis of the cost estimates is the machine time required by the job. The hourly machine rates include labour and overhead costs. Electricity, heat and rent are allocated to particular machines on the basis of floor space occupied. In calculating the depreciation element of the hourly charge, an allowance is made for idle time. For example, if it appears that a machine is normally idle 30 per cent of the time, the hourly charge is higher by 43 per cent $((100/70) \times 100 - 100)$ than it would be otherwise. However the managing director stated that it would be unreasonable to use this principle on a machine that is idle most of the time, for the result would be charges that would price them out of the market.

Indeed if there is some equipment that is chronically idle, the firm will replace it with other equipment needed to handle the kind of business it can sell. For example it has recently sold a press which can take care of large pages because the volume of such business does not justify such a machine. Any future orders received for this type of business will be farmed out to other firms. Similarly the firm has given up some types of business that require too much time for quoting and servicing. (The above information is based on an interview reported in W.W. Haynes, *Pricing in Small Business*, University of Kentucky Press, 1962.)

(*a*) Comment on the statement that "profitable plants make a profit on every job."

(*b*) Evaluate the policy of putting a lower markup on envelopes and letterheads than on other products.

(*c*) Discuss the method of calculating the depreciation element used in cost estimation.

CHAPTER FIFTEEN

Non-price Competition

OBJECTIVES

After studying this chapter the reader should be able to: understand the aims of non-price competition; list the forms of non-price competition; explain how non-price competition can enable a firm to develop and protect its markets; list the factors which influence the level of advertising expenditure; rank advertising media in terms of expenditure; explain changes in the relative importance of the various media; list the forms of sales promotion; give examples of marketing communication in different industries; demonstrate the importance of new product introductions; list the factors that influence the success of new products; explain the role of packaging; understand the importance of service as a form of competition; list the factors influencing a supplier's choice of distribution channels; understand the importance to firms of market information.

INTRODUCTION

Having discussed pricing policies in the previous two chapters, we now examine other forms of competition, most of which involve marketing expenditure. We have already shown that non-price competition may have two aims: (*a*) to increase demand; (*b*) to make demand less price-elastic. These two effects are summarised in Fig. 84, in which D_1 is the firm's demand curve when it does not undertake non-price competition. It can be seen that the firm can expect to benefit in terms of a higher sales volume, and/or a higher price. (These benefits must, of course, be weighed against the costs incurred in non-price competition.)

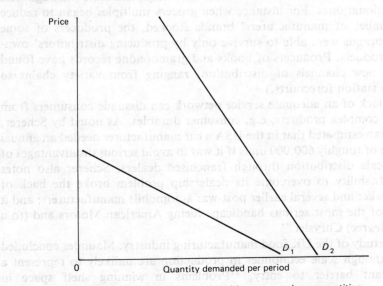

Fig. 84. *Demand curves with and without non-price competition.*

Even if it cannot be demonstrated that the firm has benefited in one or other of these ways, non-price competition may still be justified, since it may prevent a fall in sales volume and/or price, that would otherwise have resulted from the activities of (existing and potential) competitors. In other words, non-price competition can contribute both to the development and the protection of the firm's markets.

THE DEVELOPMENT AND PROTECTION OF MARKETS

It is possible to distinguish three ways in which non-price competition can enable a firm to develop and protect its markets.

First, by branding its product—and successful branding involves appropriate policies relating to advertising, product development, packaging etc.—a supplier creates an image in the mind of the consumer that cannot be replicated by competitors; i.e. it differentiates the product from that offered by other suppliers. Product differentiation reduces the price elasticity of demand. It also increases demand insofar as the brand occupies a position in characteristics space that is then denied to other brands.

Second if, as a result of marketing expenditure, a firm's products occupy space in the channels of distribution, this space is denied to competitive products or brands. There is often a fairly rigid limit—at least in the short term—to the total "width" of distribution channels, a limit set by the number of distributors able and willing to stock a given type of product, and the physical resources of these distributors. Consequently, denying space to rivals can be a very powerful competitive weapon. (Firms denied access to conventional channels may distribute through less conventional ones. For instance when grocery multiples began to reduce the number of manufacturers' brands stocked, the producers of some minor brands were able to survive only by producing distributors' own-label products. Producers of books and gramophone records have found several new channels of distribution, ranging from variety chains to railway station forecourts.)

The lack of an adequate service network can dissuade consumers from buying complex products, e.g. consumer durables. As noted by Scherer, Pashigian estimated that in the USA a car manufacturer needed an annual volume of roughly 600,000 units if it was to avoid serious disadvantages of small-scale distribution through franchised dealers. Scherer also notes that "Inability to overcome its dealership problem broke the back of Studebaker and several earlier post-war automobile manufacturers; and it is one of the most serious handicaps facing American Motors and (to a lesser degree) Chrysler."

In a study of the UK food manufacturing industry, Maunder concluded that although scale economies in production are unlikely to represent a significant barrier to entry, "Problems in winning shelf space in supermarkets and the level of marketing expenses incurred in support of new brands present more formidable problems for entrants to many new food markets." It is therefore not surprising to find that "Where entry involving nationally branded goods does occur it is usually by established rather than new firms." Maunder quotes the examples of the expansion of Golden Wonder crisps from a small Scottish-based firm to the second largest national concern, estimated to have cost Imperial Tobacco £10 million between 1961 and 1965, and of Bovril's estimated marketing expenditure of £3 million (compared with expenditure on plant and equipment of £2½ million), in developing a granulated meat cube to challenge Oxo, the market leader. He also notes that "Even large food firms may find that despite heavy promotional expenditure they have developed an inadequate brand image and have only a low market share." Walls pulled out of the yogurt market in 1970 and Unigate stopped producing canned puddings in 1978. "Both did so having incurred heavy losses in unsuccessful attempts to compete with market leaders in these products."

Third, it is sometimes argued that economies of large-scale promotion make it difficult for potential entrants to compete with existing suppliers. This argument is most frequently advanced with respect to advertising, since it is suggested that it may be necessary to attain a threshold of advertising messages before maximum effectiveness is reached, i.e. returns to advertising increase, up to a point, as shown by A in Fig. 85.

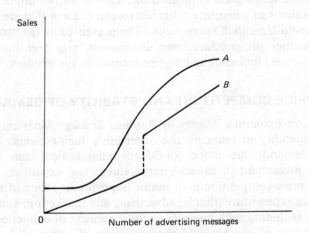

Fig. 85. *The response of sales to advertising.*

Alternatively, potential entrants may be at a disadvantage because the sales advertising relationship may have a discontinuity, as shown by B.

If potential entrants are unable to match the advertising expenditure of existing producers—as happens in many instances, as noted by Maunder—then increasing returns to advertising may constitute a barrier to entry. If they are able to match the spending of existing producers, increasing returns do not in themselves constitute an entry barrier. But even here a barrier will exist if, as is likely in many instances, the effectiveness of a given number of messages is inversely related to the time period over which these messages are delivered, as shown in Fig. 86. In such circumstances a potential entrant is unable to match the (cumulative) impact achieved by an existing supplier.

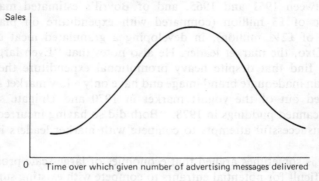

Fig. 86. *Advertising, time and sales.*

This means that, insofar as advertising influences demand, the potential entrant would have to operate at a lower output than existing suppliers. If there are economies of scale in production, a lower output implies higher unit costs, which can constitute a barrier to entry. Even if there is not a significant cost differential, entry may still be prevented by the prospect of low sales; neither the producer nor distributors may feel justified in devoting resources, including management time, to the product.

NON-PRICE COMPETITION AND STABILITY OF DEMAND

In his book *An Economic Theory of Business Strategy* Moss emphasises the role of stability in reducing the uncertainty facing firms. The less volatile is demand, the more confidence management can have in undertaking investment in capacity replacement and expansion. In this context non-price competition is of major importance: "One of the aims of both selling expenditure (that is, advertising and marketing) and quality competition, including such qualities as the timeliness of deliveries as well as differentiation of the physical characteristics of commodities, is not only to attract new customers but—and this is probably more important—to keep existing customers. This stable relationship between buyer and seller is called goodwill by businessmen."[1]

Moss considers the possibility that certain forms of non-price competition may increase the uncertainty facing rivals, but concludes that

1. S. Moss. *Op. cit.*, p. 83.

this is unlikely. He argues that "quality competition will result in segmented rather than unstable markets." While conceding the possibility that competitors may engage in an advertising war, Moss puts forward two reasons why advertising is less likely to lead to an all-out advertising war than a price-cut is to a price war.

First, "secret advertising is inconceivable, while secret price cuts in an uncertain climate are always to be watched for. . . . Competitors can never feel that they have completely reliable information even when price cuts are announced, but they will know with complete confidence the precise extent of competitors' advertising. Thus, while a price cut can increase uncertainty without limit, a more intensive advertising campaign will only involve uncertainty as to the response of one's competitors."[2]

Second, advertising competition is likely to be less volatile than price competition because there is an upper limit to advertising expenditure. This upper limit appears because of (a) the onset of diminishing returns, (b) the loss of goodwill that would arise if the firm were unable to supply the additional demand created by advertising. Overall, Moss concludes, "price competition generates uncertainty and tends to destabilise markets; goodwill competition tends to stabilise markets . . . while generating only limited uncertainty and then in uncommon circumstances attendant, for example, upon periods of significant product innovation."[3]

The destabilising effects of price competition, leading to a preference for non-price competition, is also emphasised by Koutsoyiannis.[4] Another cause of increasing non-price competition to which she draws attention is the rapid rate of technological progress in recent years which has resulted in greatly improved or completely new products.[5] This increased variety of available products has met the demands of an increasingly affluent buying public, greater affluence again tending to be associated with a dampening of price competition.

THE RELATIVE IMPORTANCE OF ALTERNATIVE FORMS OF COMPETITION

There have been a considerable number of studies, some of which have been referred to in earlier chapters, of the relative importance of various forms of competition. The results of four such studies, which covered roughly comparable policy areas, are presented in Table XLIII.[6]

---

2. S. Moss. *Op. cit.,* p. 87.
3. S. Moss. *Op. cit.,* p. 88.
4. A. Koutsoyiannis. *Non-Price Decisions.* Macmillan, 1982, p. 2.
5. The introduction of new products may, of course, destabilise the demand for existing products.
6. H. A. Said. *The Relevance of Price Theory to Pricing Practice.* PhD Thesis, University of Strathclyde, 1982. J. Udell. *Successful Marketing Strategies of American Industries.* Mimer, Madison, 1972. C. Pass. *Op. cit.*

V. IMPLEMENTATION OF STRATEGY

TABLE XLIII. THE RELATIVE IMPORTANCE OF FORMS OF COMPETITION

	Said (1980)	Robicheaux (1975)	Pass (1970)	Udell (1964)
Pricing	1	1	6	6
Customer services	2	2	4	5
Product R&D	3	4	1	1
Product services	4	–	3	–
Sales management	5	3	7	3
Physical distribution	6	6	8	11
Advertising, sales promotion	7	9	5	4
Marketing research	8	7	2	2
Marketing cost; budgeting, control	9	5	11	9
Distribution channels control	10	10	9	8
Extending customer credit	11	11	12	10
Public relations	12	12	13	12
Organisational structure	–	8	10	7

Although our main concern in this chapter is with non-price competition, the importance attached to price competition in the later studies deserves mention. The fact that pricing is ranked first in these studies does not, of course, mean that firms prefer to compete on price, but that pricing policy is seen as an important determinant of a firm's success or failure. The increase in the importance attached to price over time is probably due to the slackening in the rate of economic growth in the 1970s and the emergence of excess supply in many markets.

Turning to non-price competition, two policy areas were given a consistently high ranking: service and product R&D. At the other end of the scale, consistently low rankings were given to public relations, customer credit and distribution-channels control. The ranking of the remaining policy areas was less consistent.

One would not, of course, expect to find fully consistent rankings, given the differences between the studies in terms of the date, size of sample, type of product manufactured, etc. The influence of the type of product can be illustrated by reference to Said's study. Physical distribution was ranked fifth by producers of non-durable goods, but only tenth by producers of durable goods. Product services was ranked fourth by producers of industrial goods and seventh by producers of non-durable goods.

We now examine policy relating to several forms of non-price competition. We begin by considering advertising, the main way in which many suppliers communicate with actual and potential purchasers.

ADVERTISING

It can be seen from Table XLIV that there has been no clear trend in advertising expenditure in recent years. Total expenditure (at constant prices), and expenditure as a proportion of GNP, increased year by year between 1975 and 1980. But this represented only a partial reversal of a previous decline, and expenditure was less in 1980 than in 1973.

TABLE XLIV. ADVERTISING EXPENDITURE

	At current prices (£m)	As % of GNP	At constant prices (£m)
1970	554	1.27	554
1971	591	1.20	544
1972	708	1.28	608
1973	874	1.36	716
1974	900	1.21	667
1975	967	1.03	565
1976	1188	1.07	567
1977	1499	1.19	604
1978	1834	1.27	645
1979	2137	1.30	651
1980	2562	1.34	628

Source: *The Advertising Association*

THE DEMAND FOR ADVERTISING

Reekie has suggested that consumers' demand for advertising is influenced by the following six characteristics, relating to either the product or the consumer.[7]

(a) *Product complexity*. Within a given product group, the more complex the product is to use or maintain, the greater is the amount of information, and hence advertising, required. More information is required about the operation and performance of washing machines than refrigerators, about power mowers than manually operated machines, about foreign holidays than holidays at home.

(b) *Changes in the conditions of sale*. The more frequently changes—in styling, price etc.—are made in existing products, and the more rapid the rate of new product introductions, the greater the consumer's need for advertising. Reekie suggests that this may partly explain trends in promotion in the soap powder market. "In 1954, the year of the introduction of the new synthetic detergents, Unilever's selling expenses

---
7. W. D. Reekie. *The Economics of Advertising*, Macmillan, 1981, p. 84.

were equal to 36 per cent of sales turnover. This was double the 1952 figure and well above the normal level of around a quarter of sales value thereafter."[8]

(c) *The experience of the purchaser*. The more frequently a purchase decision is made the more knowledgeable the consumer becomes about conditions in the market-place. Less information about current market conditions is required by the firm purchasing standard components or the housewife purchasing chocolate bars, than by the firm purchasing a machine to replace one bought five years previously or a housewife purchasing a new cooker.

However, Reekie suggests that this conclusion applies only to the "intensity" and "data variety" dimensions of advertising, and does not necessarily apply to the "data style" dimension. "There is no reason to suppose, for example, that the businessman who gets pleasure from expensively styled adverts in the weekend colour supplements will not prefer similarly styled advertisements for, say component parts in his appropriate trade journal."[9]

(d) *Buyer-population stability*. The more new consumers enter a market, due to either market growth or membership turnover, the more advertising will be demanded. This will be especially true of the data variety dimension, since new buyers demand a wider variety of data than experienced buyers, but advertising intensity may also increase with a high level of buyer mobility. Reekie quotes the example of the teenager receiving his first wage packet who may have little understanding of the advantages of having a bank account. "As a result, the new entrant's threshold of awareness to advertising may well be higher than in the case of established and frequent product purchasers. To get over this threshold, advertising intensity must be raised to a relatively high level."[10]

(e) *Product differentiation*. It is clear that the wider the range of similar product types, the greater will be the demand for "data variety" advertising. However it does not follow that greater intensity or a costlier style of advertising should be demanded.

(f) *The price–income ratio*. The price–income ratio indicates the proportion of consumer income a particular purchase would absorb. Convenience goods such as foodstuffs usually have a low ratio while consumer durables usually have a high ratio. "It can be postulated that the higher is the ratio then the greater is the consumer awareness of the value of advertising to aid choice. . . . High consumer awareness of the value of advertising when the price–income ratio is high implies that the threshold level of intensity required for advertising to be noted is low." This argument is "in agreement with those studies which have shown that low-

---

8. W. D. Reekie. *Op. cit.*, p. 85.
9. W. D. Reekie. *Op. cit.*, p. 86.
10. W. D. Reekie. *Op. cit.*, p. 87.

priced consumer goods tend to have a higher advertising-sales ratio than higher-priced goods."[11]

Reekie's arguments are summarised in Table XLV. Because for each characteristic the effect on at least one dimension is indeterminate, no firm conclusions can be drawn about the relationship between a characteristic and the quantity of advertising demanded. But it seems highly likely that, with the exception of a high price-income ratio, each characteristic listed is associated with a high demand for advertising.

TABLE XLV. MARKET CHARACTERISTICS AND THE DEMAND FOR ADVERTISING

	Quantity dimension		
Market characteristic	Advertising intensity	Data variety	Advertising style
Complex products	Indeterminate	Directly	Indeterminate
Variable conditions of sale	Directly	Directly	Indeterminate
Inexperienced purchasers	Directly	Directly	Indeterminate
Mobile buyer population	Indeterminate	Directly	Indeterminate
Product differentiation	Indeterminate	Directly	Indeterminate
The price-income ratio	Inversely	Directly	Indeterminate

THE SUPPLY OF ADVERTISING

Table XLV refers to the demand for advertising in a market as a whole. It does not follow that the decisions of individual firms will lead to the total supply of advertising being equal to the quantity demanded. (The fact that advertising is supplied at zero price means that the usual market-clearing mechanisms do not operate.) For example each supplier may increase the advertising style dimension because he believes that this is necessary if his product is to receive attention from consumers. This leads us to consider the functions that suppliers expect advertising to perform.

We have said that advertising is intended to increase demand and/or make demand less elastic. But a more detailed set of objectives is usually required for planning an advertising campaign and monitoring its effectiveness. For example Colley has suggested that purchasers may have any of the mental sets shown in Fig. 87, and that "Advertising's function is to move the consumer, step by step, closer to buying-conviction and, finally, to buying-action."[12]

11. W. D. Reekie. *Op. cit.*, p. 88.
12. R. Colley. *Defining Advertising Goals for Measured Advertising Results.* Association of National Advertisers, New York, 1961; quoted in: G. R. Foxall. *Strategic Marketing Management.* Croom Helm, 1981, 9. 116.

Fig. 87. *Potential purchasers' mental sets.*

The effectiveness of an advertising campaign can obviously be increased if the distribution of purchasers among the categories in Fig. 87 can be estimated. For example if a high proportion of consumers are purchasers of the product it may be appropriate to have a series of very short television commercials at peak periods to keep the product before the public's eyes. On the other hand if a high proportion of consumers are unaware of the product or are not familiar with its advantages, a series of more "educative" advertisements, e.g. in magazines, may be required.

Advertising themes

In attempting to move consumers closer to buying-action, advertisers frequently conduct research to try to identify the information that will influence purchasing decisions. This information becomes the theme of advertising. It is necessary to conduct research because the value of particular pieces of information, the impact of particular advertising themes, may change over time.

During the 1970s the advertising theme of most toothpastes changed form the cosmetic to the therapeutic. Fulop has shown that "Whereas the emphasis in the advertising of Maclean's toothpaste had in the 1950s been on the benefit of cleaning teeth with toothpaste, leading to healthy teeth and white teeth, and in the 1960s the stress was almost entirely on the whiteness, with the inclusion of fluoride in Macleans toothpaste and Aquafresh the emphasis changed to the value of toothpaste in preventing tooth decay." Subsequently there was a partial return to the earlier emphasis: "In 1980, however, since the value of fluoride is generally accepted and included in all toothpastes, Aquafresh is once more being promoted on a freshness claim, while Macleans toothpaste has been re-introduced with an improved fluoride (which has been patented) that gives more protection against decay and helps to remove plaque, which is of concern to consumers."[13]

When Persil Automatic washing powder was introduced, the advertising had a strong educational theme, explaining why it was especially suitable for the front-loading washing machines that were taking an increasing share of the market. This theme was also emphasised on the pack. In addition "a contract was negotiated with washing machine manufacturers to supply a sample with every front-loading machine. This was to ensure that it would be the first brand tried by the housewife in her newly

---

13. C. Fulop. *Advertising, Competition and Consumer Behaviour.* Holt, Rinehart and Winston, Eastbourne, 1981, p. 60.

acquired machine as the market expanded and encouraged the entry of competitive products."[14]

It has been suggested that "Reviewing Heinz commercials (for baked beans) since they began 30 years ago, is a lesson on the changing market place."[15] The advertising themes have included the competent caring mother (1950s and 1960s), quality (early 1970s to counteract competition from other brands), wholesome goodness for children (1976 to draw attention from rising prices of beans), value for money (1976 to counteract competition from own labels), quality, associating beans with quails' eggs etc. (1977 as market became more buoyant), good value—"Every penny spent on Heinz baked beans is a penny wisely spent." "Penny for penny Heinz baked beans give you more protein than meat or fish." (1982, economic recession.)

In the synthetic-fibres industry the manufacturers advertised heavily in the 1950s and 1960s in order to establish the brand names of their products, as well as to promote the demand for synthetic fibres by final consumers. However in the 1970s this emphasis became less appropriate for several reasons. "Fabric and garment labels now have to specify generic product type (e.g. polyester) rather than brand names, and many retailers also have emphasised generic rather than brand names in their promotional activities. Also—and partly because of this—consumers have become more knowledgeable about the properties of individual fibres, and thus the power of the manufacturer's brand name has declined, thus reducing the value of actively promoting it."[16]

Media planning and selection

Having decided what functions advertising is intended to perform, suppliers must decide which media will enable these functions to be performed most cost-effectively. Reekie notes that in the last decade quantitative tools have increasingly been applied in this area, one of the most frequently used techniques being linear programming. However, as Reekie points out, to use linear programming it is necessary to make a number of assumptions which will usually be false.[17] These are:

(a) The sales response to a medium insertion is constant, i.e. the possibility of economies of scale is denied.

(b) The time factor is not relevant, i.e. the positive impact of replication and the negative impact of forgetfulness are ignored.

(c) Sales response per insertion is known.

14. C. Fulop. *Op. cit.*, p. 82.
15. F. McEwan. "Behind the Heinz Advertising Beano". *Financial Times* 28th October 1982.
16. R. W. Shaw and S. A. Shaw. "Synthetic Fibres". In: P. S. Johnson, *op. cit.*, p. 216.
17. W. D. Reekie. *Op. cit.*, p. 63.

(d) Costs of media insertions are constant, i.e. the existence of quantity discounts is ignored.
(e) There is no media interaction.
(f) The number of insertions is a continuous variable.

Speaking more generally Reekie notes that because of the difficulties involved in predicting the sales response to advertising, media scheduling "is often solely a matter of managerial intuition, albeit based on close and intimate knowledge of the product, the market and the available media."[18]

The product and the market
We have described above the advertising of individual products, and further illustrations are given below. Table XLVI presents data at a more aggregated level.[19] It can be seen that the advertising-to-sales ratio varies considerably from one product group to another, suggesting that advertising is considered a more effective use of resources in some markets than others.

TABLE XLVI. ESTIMATED UK ADVERTISING-TO-SALES RATIOS (PER CENT) BY PRODUCT GROUP 1969–80

Product group	1969	1973	1977	1980
Food	1.06	1.04	0.89	0.98
Clothing and footwear	0.52	0.31	0.28	0.31
Automotive	0.92	0.74	0.72	1.02
Drink and tobacco	1.18	1.19	1.08	1.33
Toiletries and medical	7.32	6.52	6.00	5.07
Household and leisure	1.97	1.69	1.71	1.92
Publishing, books	2.23	2.55	2.09	2.32
Tourism, entertainment, foreign	0.89	0.79	0.63	0.70
Nationalised industries, government	0.36	0.37	0.22	0.29
Retail trade	0.38	0.55	0.68	0.74
Savings, financial	1.09	0.65	0.55	0.41
Industrial	0.51	0.50	0.46	0.60

Source: *Advertising Association*

These figures reflect the factors influencing the demand for advertising, discussed above. For example there is a rapid rate of product introduction and a high level of product differentiation in the markets for toiletries and medical products. Buyers of foodstuffs are experienced and the price–income ratio is low.

18. W. D. Reekie. *Op. cit.*, p. 61.
19. M. J. Waterson. "Advertising Sales Ratios in the UK, 1969–80". *Journal of Advertising* Vol. 1 (1982).

However, although there are clear differences in the advertising–sales ratio, the situation is not static. Retailers have increased their advertising substantially during the period covered by Table XLVI, the ratio having doubled. On the other hand the ratio has declined in toiletries and medical products.

Table XLVII lists the companies and brands with the largest advertising expenditure in 1981. The left-hand column demonstrates the importance of advertising to the manufacturers of low-value, frequently purchased items such as confectionery and detergents. The right-hand column demonstrates the importance of advertising to large retailers. (It is, of course, unusual to define retailers as brands. The justification for this is that a retailer's advertising budget is often determined centrally, in the same way as that for an individual brand.)

TABLE XLVII. TOP ADVERTISERS 1981

Company	£m	Brand	£m
1. Procter & Gamble	25.0	1. F.W. Woolworth	10.2
2. Mars	20.8	2. MFI	9.6
3. Cadbury Schweppes	19.2	3. Boots	9.4
4. Rowntree Mackintosh	18.9	4. Co-op	9.1
5. Lever Bros	14.0	5. Tesco	7.1
6. Nestle	13.7	6. Asda	6.5
7. Kelloggs	13.6	7. Currys	6.2
8. Electricity Council	13.0	8. Debenhams	6.0
9. Van den Berghs	13.0	9. Dulux	5.8
10. John Player	12.4	10. Guinness	5.6

Source: *MEAL*

TABLE XLVIII. DISTRIBUTION OF TOTAL EXPENDITURE BY MEDIA (PER CENT)

	Newspapers	Magazines	Television	Radio	Cinema	Posters/Transport
1970	49.5	22.7	22.6	0.2	1.1	4.0
1971	48.5	22.2	24.2	0.2	1.0	3.9
1972	49.3	21.0	24.9	0.1	1.0	3.7
1973	51.4	20.0	24.0	0.2	0.8	3.5
1974	52.1	20.0	22.6	0.7	0.9	3.8
1975	49.6	20.6	24.4	1.0	0.7	3.6
1976	47.6	20.5	25.8	1.5	0.7	3.6
1977	46.5	21.0	26.6	1.7	0.6	3.6
1978	46.0	21.4	26.3	1.9	0.7	3.7
1979	47.8	22.6	22.0	2.4	0.8	4.4
1980	45.1	20.6	27.0	2.1	0.7	4.5

Source: *Advertising Association*

The media
Table XLVIII shows how advertising expenditure was distributed across the media. It can be seen that despite the expansion of advertising by television and radio, in 1980 the press remained the major advertising vehicle, accounting for almost two-thirds of total expenditure.

Newspapers

The existence in Britain of several newspapers with national circulations means that the press can be used to advertise products for which widespread coverage is required. The fact that there are significant differences in the readership profiles between say, the *Sun* and the *Daily Telegraph*, enables the national market to be segmented, and this helps in targeting advertisements.

Regional and local newspapers are especially suitable for use when suppliers wish to reach a more limited geographical market, or when there are geographical differences in tastes and spending patterns, e.g. lager has a higher share of the beer market in Scotland than in England. In total, regional and local papers attract about 50 per cent more advertising than national newspapers. However, they have been particularly hard hit by the recession which has resulted in a very sharp decline in classified advertising, which has traditionally accounted for up to half of their advertising revenue. Local papers have also been hit by the increase in free distribution newspapers (freesheets), which numbered about 470 by the beginning of 1983. The high cost-effectiveness of some freesheets has enabled them to attract national as well as local advertisers, and in 1981 their revenue increased by a quarter to over £100 million.

Photographs and sketches often reproduce badly, making newspapers unsuitable for products where appearance is important, e.g. cosmetics. However an exception to this rule is the colour supplements included in a number of Sunday newspapers. The standard of reproduction is often akin to that in the best magazines, being so high that these publications have attracted a considerable amount of up-market advertising. (The readership profiles also help in this respect.)

Since newspapers are quickly discarded, advertisements must make their point quickly. It is therefore unusual to find newspaper advertisements with dense text. (Another disadvantage of such an advertisement would be poor differentiation from other, non-advertising, material.)

Magazines

The two main types of magazine, consumer magazines and trade journals, each account for almost one-tenth of total advertising expenditure. The readership can vary widely. For example, in consumer magazines *Reader's Digest* is a general-interest magazine that attracts both male and female readers, *Woman's Own* is a general-interest magazine that attracts female readers, while *Chess* and *The Gramophone* have a much more specialist appeal. Trade magazines tend to have more specialised readerships, e.g. *Architectural Review*, the *Journal of the Institute of Heating and Ventilating Engineers*, although some, e.g. *Management Today*, have a more general appeal.

The varied nature of the readership means that magazines as a whole accommodate a wide range of types of advertisements, from the strictly "educational" to the "reminder". (The fact that magazines are discarded less quickly, and often read at a more leisurely pace, than newspapers makes them more suitable for educational advertisements.)

Television
Television accounts for over one-quarter of total advertising expenditure in Britain. The advent of Channel 4 and breakfast television is likely to give a boost to television advertising. On the other hand the spread of video recorders may reduce the viewing of television advertisements and lessen the attractiveness of the medium to advertisers.

Television advertising has many advantages. There are the obvious advantages of bringing movement, sound and colour into the homes of potential customers. The regionally based networks allow geographical flexibility, and there is also considerable flexibility in time, increased as total broadcasting hours are extended. Advertisers can choose a spot which they hope will give the target number of viewers in total and/or of specific types, e.g. advertisements aimed at children are concentrated between four and five o'clock, advertisements aimed at men are broadcast on Saturday afternoons when horse racing is featured. (But *see* below.)

The main disadvantage of television advertising is, of course, its high cost. This means that most advertisements are brief and can put over little detailed information. A way of trying to overcome this disadvantage that has found increasing favour is to invite viewers to telephone or write for additional information, e.g. to request holiday brochures.

Another disadvantage arises from the fact that in Britain individual programmes are not sponsored. Since the number of people seeing an advertisement depends upon the number viewing the programmes with which the advertisements are interspersed, and since the content and quality of these programmes are outside the control of the advertiser, there is often considerable uncertainty concerning the numbers that will view any advertisement. (When a high viewing figure can be virtually guaranteed, as for "Coronation Street", the tariff is, of course, set at a correspondingly high level.)

Commercial radio
At present there are less than forty commercial radio stations in the UK, as compared with eight thousand in the USA, and radio accounts for only 2 per cent of total advertising expenditure. However, it is planned to double

the number of stations by the end of the decade, and an increase in market share seems likely.

As the network expands radio might expect to attract more national advertising. But since it is organised on a regional basis, it will continue to be suitable for local advertising. A major advantage of commercial radio is the flexibility in time offered to advertisers. A retailer can advertise special offers to housewives who are doing the washing up before going out to do the shopping. A manufacturer of a chocolate bar aimed at children can advertise around tea-time.

It is, of course, normally much cheaper to advertise by radio than television. But as the total supply of television transmission time increases, price competition is likely to become keener. In the early months of Channel 4 a 30 second spot on Granada cost only £200 at the lowest rate, and commercial radio might be particularly susceptible to this competition.

Posters and Transport

In the 1960s there were about 700 poster contractors, many of which were small businesses controlling sites in a single town or part of the country. Since then there has been considerable rationalisation, and today about 70 companies are responsible for some 180,000 sites. This rationalisation has made it much easier to conduct a national advertising campaign, and posters are frequently used by the manufacturers of such nationally distributed goods as cigarettes, beer and cars. Posters give the benefit of repetition at low cost. But the need for immediate impact means that the message conveyed must be simple.

Cinema

Cinema shares the advantages of television advertising in terms of sound, colour and movement. It can also be used for both national and local advertising. However, cinema's share of the advertising market has declined as audiences have dwindled in the face of growing competition from television and other leisure pursuits. Cinemas now account for less than one per cent of total advertising expenditure, and a further decline is likely as more households acquire video recorders.

Direct mail

A recent survey of advertising in Europe found that television advertising appears to have the greatest impact not on the press, but on direct-mail advertising (excluded from Table XLVIII.) In countries where television advertising accounts for 10 per cent or more of the total, direct mail rarely exceeds 10 per cent. On the other hand, in those Nordic countries where there is no television advertising, direct mail has soared to "unproportional volumes", e.g. 40 per cent in Sweden. In Netherlands and Switzerland, where television advertising accounts for less than 10 per cent of the total, direct mail accounts for 30 per cent and 18 per cent respectively.[20]

It seems likely, then, that the extension of television advertising may hit direct mail in the UK. On the other hand recent developments in direct mail have increased its effectiveness. An indicator of the growth of direct-mail activity is the increase in the number of business reply–freepost items handled by the Post Office from 97 million in 1971 to an estimated 305 million in 1980. Moreover information systems such as Prestel Viewdata will make home-shopping even easier, especially if linked with interactive home computer terminals.

The scope for direct-mail advertising has been increased by the "Consumer Location System", developed recently by the Post Office in conjunction with Billett and Company. The system makes use of the Target Group Index (TGI) which analyses, on an annual basis, the responses of 24,000 people to a questionnaire concerning purchasing habits in over 500 product fields. The British Market Research Bureau have fitted their TGI results into ACORN neighbourhood types. Each neighbourhood type comprises a set of areas shown by census data to have similar demographic and social characteristics and hence, it is assumed, sharing common lifestyle features and presenting similar potential for the sales of any product. ACORN ("*A Classification of Residential Neighbourhoods*") defines and locates these different sorts of areas.

For any brand or product whose purchases are reliably measured by TGI, it is possible to estimate the proportion of the market accounted for by any of the thirty-six ACORN neighbourhood types. This information can be used by media planners in deciding the types of neighbourhood at which to direct their advertising. The choice of media is assisted by the data on exposure to media provided by TGI. It is known, for example, that in certain neighbourhood types the readership of the "quality" Sunday papers is well above the national average. If these neighbourhood types account for a high share of the market for the product in question then advertising in these papers is likely to be effective.

The use of this data for direct mail has been made much easier recently by the computerisation of the electoral register. An advertiser can now obtain a comprehensive list of names and addresses in any ACORN type in any geographical area. These can be produced on magnetic tape, as "personalised" letters or on sticky labels. The Post Office has also developed a range of techniques for producing personalised mailings in large quantities.

To illustrate the information available to media planners, take the example of an advertiser who wishes to reach people classified by TGI as

---

20. C. Byoir, as quoted in: "Television Advertising—A Threat to the Daily Press?" *Financial Times*, 2nd December 1982.

"heavy drinkers of table wine". It is estimated that a mailing of 454,000 would reach 2.5 per cent of the market, a mailing of 10,100,000 would reach 42.4 per cent, and so forth. (Similar estimates can be made for other advertising media.)

SALES PROMOTIONS

As noted above, advertising is only one of several ways in which suppliers attempt to communicate with purchasers. Many of the other forms of communications are grouped under the heading of sales promotions.

Kotler defines sales promotions, or "below the line" advertising, as "those marketing activities, other than personal selling, advertising and publicity, that stimulate consumer purchasing and dealer effectiveness."[21] These activities are said to account for more than half of firms' total expenditure on marketing communications in both the UK and the USA. However this includes the cost of various forms of promotional pricing, discussed in the previous chapter.

The main objectives of sales promotions, and the types of promotion best suited to each objective, have been listed by Morgan (Table XLIX).

Fulop gives a number of specific illustrations of the use of promotions. For example the promotions for Persil Automatic were designed not only to provide the consumer with an incentive at the point of sale to purchase the product, but also to encourage retailers to feature the brand, which may involve providing a prime display spot in the store or the provision of additional display space.

Competitions have sometimes featured as prizes the products of firms which also manufacture washing machines, emphasising the link between Persil Automatic and front-loading washing machines. Competitions have also incorporated other Lever Bros products, e.g. the offer of a "free" rail ticket voucher in exchange for three tokens from one or more of six Lever Bros products. (In the year 1980-81, an estimated 3.5 to 4 million vouchers were issued.) Other promotions have been tailored to the requirements of a particular retailer, Persil Automatic being included in that retailer's own promotions and advertising.

As competition has increased and consumers have become more price-sensitive, a higher proportion of promotional expenditure has taken the form of price promotions. "These have been found to be effective in encouraging the most price-sensitive consumer, namely the purchaser of distributor own labels, and the shopper who shows little loyalty to any manufacturer brand, to try Persil Automatic."[22]

---

21. P. Kotler. *Marketing Management: Analysis Planning and Control.* Prentice-Hall, Englewood Cliffs, 4th Edition, 1980, p. 337.

22. C. Fulop. *Op. cit.,* p. 84.

TABLE XLIX. PROMOTIONAL AIMS AND METHODS

Purpose	Free with pack	Money-off voucher	Money-off offer	Sampling	Collectable items	Competitions	Free mail-in	Self-liquidating promotion	Continuous self-liquidating promotion	Continuous free mail-in promotion	Household stock reward scheme	In-store/shop floor	Trading stamps	Free gifts
To get trial		x	x	x		x	x					x		x
Obtain repeat purchasing	x	x			x								x	
Long-term loyalty					x					x			x	
Increased frequency/quantity	x				x	x		x	x				x	
Move high stocks			x			x	x	x						
Get consumers to visit store	x	x				x						x	x	x

Source: A. Morgan, *A Guide to Consumer Promotions*. Ogilvy, Benson and Mather, 1977

OTHER FORMS OF MARKETING COMMUNICATION

In some instances the nature of the product or the market gives scope for forms of communication additional to those considered so far. Since doctors have a very considerable influence on the purchases of medical products it is not surprising to find that expenditure on medical representatives accounts for roughly half of total promotional activity on pharmaceuticals. The need for representatives to visit doctors regularly is increased by the rapid rate of introduction of new or improved products.[23]

The sales of Sensodyne, a toothpaste which caters for a semi-clinical condition of sensitive teeth, depend more on the personal recommendation of dentists than on advertising, again implying a bigger role for personal selling.

The Institute of Public Relations defines public relations as "the deliberate, planned and sustained effort to establish and maintain mutual understanding between an organisation and its public." This encompasses a wide range of activities, from the attempt by companies to dissuade government from extending or implementing a programme of nationalisation, to the postal advice bureaux operated by manufacturers of washing powders and detergents.

THE INTRODUCTION OF NEW PRODUCTS

Toothpaste

As noted in Chapter 12, a firm introducing a new or modified product hopes to occupy a part of characteristics space that is sparsely inhabited or—in the case of a pioneer product—uninhabited.[24] In the toothpaste market Beechams, once the major producer, was overtaken in the 1950s by Colgate. In trying to regain market leadership Beechams introduced in 1967 a second flavour of Macleans toothpaste—spearmint—in addition to their original mild mint flavour. Both were intended to appeal to the section of the market that preferred a mild flavour. By 1973 Macleans Spearmint had attained a 6.5 per cent share of the market. But this appeared to be mainly at the expense of Macleans Fresh Mint, whose market share had fallen from 20.6 per cent in 1966 to 13 per cent in 1975.[25] This was, perhaps, not surprising given that both varieties appealed to the same sector of the market (they overlapped substantially in characteristics space). Consequently in 1973 the development work which had been carried out on a blue-and-white striped gel led to the launch of Aquafresh, designed to appeal to the desire for mouth freshness (and hence located in a different area of characteristics space). The introduction of this second

---

23. W. D. Reekie. "Pharmaceuticals". In: P. S. Johnson, *op. cit.*, p. 116.
24. This refers in particular to offensive innovation. Defensive innovation may involve placing a product in, or close to, an area already occupied.
25. C. Fulop. *Op. cit.*, p. 58.

brand raised Beecham's total share of the market from 20 per cent in 1972 to 27 per cent in 1975 (Aquafresh accounting for 7.6 per cent).

Other innovations have included the fluoride toothpastes produced by all the major manufacturers—the initial offensive innovation giving rise to considerable defensive innovation—and the specialised toothpastes appealing to particular types of consumer, e.g. children, smokers, produced by minor manufacturers.

Custard

The total market for toothpaste has shown steady growth at one to three per cent a year, and the main impact of new products has been on the market shares of individual brands. By contrast new types of custard have reversed a long-term decline in the total market (due to competition from a wider range of sweets, the preference on the part of an increasing number of working housewives for convenience desserts, and a change in taste towards lighter sweets).

The introduction of canned custard, by Ambrosia and Heinz in 1969 and by Birds in 1975, stimulated an expansion of the total market (Table L).[26] In 1978 the introduction nationally of Batchelors Quick Custard and Brown and Polson's Instant Custard offered consumers a product with yet another set of characteristics. Quick Custard was cheaper than canned custard, did not require a saucepan to make hot custard, had lighter packaging, and enabled the housewife to be involved in the preparation of the custard and determine the degree of thickness required by varying the quantity of water added. The attraction of this set of characteristics can be judged from the data in Table LI.

TABLE L. VALUE OF CUSTARD MARKET (CONSTANT PRICES)

Year	£ million	Market Share (%) Powder	Canned
1969	13	90	10
1977	16	66	34

TABLE LI. SHARE OF CUSTARD MARKET BY VALUE, JULY TO DECEMBER 1978

	%
Custard powder	53
Canned custard	22
Quick + instant custard	25

Source: *Trade Estimates (quoted by Fulop)*

26. C. Fulop. *Op. cit.*, p. 87.

Yogurt

The benefits to be gained from introducing varieties to a basic product is well illustrated by the growth in sales of yogurt.[27] In the early 1960s most yogurt was sold plain, and was seen as a health food rather than as an appetising dessert. Believing that this was a limited appeal the producers began to change the content and develop the image of the product.

In the mid 1960s real fruit, rather than fruit flavouring, was added to yogurt, a move that gave Ski and Eden Vale market leadership, a position retained to the present day. An increase in total sales of yogurt from 206 million pots in 1970 to 682 million in 1980—giving a retail value of over £100 million—was due to several factors. The increase in the number of working housewives, more television viewing and greater emphasis on other leisure activities led to an increased demand for convenience foods. Moreover, there was an increased demand for "natural" foods. But the producers of yogurt also played a part, partly by increasing their advertising expenditure, especially that aimed at children, e.g. Eden Vale's Prize Guys and Ski's Munch Bunch, and partly by introducing further product variations, e.g. yogurt with such exotic fruit as passion fruit, aimed mainly at adults.

New product failures

Most of the new product introductions discussed above have been successes, contributing to increased sales and/or profits. But it is known that many new products do not succeed. A study by John Madell found that over the period 1969 to 1978, 730 new fast-moving food products were launched. Fifty-two per cent had survived to the end of the period, although the percentage of survivors naturally increases as the time scale grows shorter; only 15 of the 53 brands launched in 1969 were still alive in 1978, against 33 of the 53 launched in 1975.[28]

Twenty-four per cent of the new products failed within the first year, many not progressing beyond an area test. The failure rate was also high in the fourth year, a finding which ties in with other research, which reveals that many new products begin to show a profit only five years after their introduction. Presumably the products abandoned in year 4 did not offer the prospect of crossing the line from loss to profit.

If success is defined as an annual retail turnover of at least £4 million—a figure which Madell suggests most major fast-moving packaged-goods manufacturers would regard as the minimum necessary to justify continued marketing support—only 4 per cent of the new products succeeded. Moreover, for manufacturers diversifying out of their main field of activity, Madell estimated the chances of success to be only 5 in 1,000.

27. This section draws on D. Churchill, "Prize Guys Battle For Their Just Desserts". *Financial Times*, 1982.
28. "How the Odds are Loaded". *Financial Times,* 13th March 1980.

Foxall quotes an average failure rate in consumer markets, based on the results of several studies, of 70 per cent, and notes that a study by A.C. Nielsen found that the product and its package accounted for 67 per cent of product failures (as compared with the 15 per cent of failures due to price–value problems and lack of trade acceptance). The overall conclusion was that "the new (failed) products had no demonstrable advantage to offer compared with existing brands."[29]

New product failure can be very expensive, and the fact that so many new products were launched which did not offer a clear advantage over existing products may indicate a belief by producers that few gains are to be made through other marketing activities.

The timing of new product introductions
Even when a new or improved product offers a clear advantage over existing products, it may fail if launched at the wrong time. We noted in Chapter 8 that the public came to accept only slowly the benefits of fluoride toothpaste. Three of the four major manufacturers introduced a fluoride toothpaste in the 1960s, but all were unsuccessful and were withdrawn. In the 1970s, on the other hand, fluoride toothpastes were commonplace. Indeed Crest, launched in 1973, achieved brand leadership by 1978.

The development of the microchip has faced the manufacturers of a wide range of products with the question as to what is the appropriate rate at which they should incorporate micro-electronics into their products. It is not at all clear when consumers in general will be prepared to pay for the advantages of electronic control of car engines, air and fuel supplies, for electronic devices in washing machines, giving more choice over washing programmes, spin speeds, and temperature, for the benefits of electronic controls in hairdryers, electric irons, food mixers etc.

PACKAGING

Expenditure on packaging materials amounts to more than 2 per cent of gross domestic product, which might suggest that packaging is of roughly equal importance to advertising. Some expenditure on packaging is, of course, required to protect products as they are transported through distribution channels to consumers. But there is also an important discretionary element in expenditure, and expenditure on packaging should be viewed in the same way as on other forms of non-price competition, i.e. the costs should be balanced against effectiveness in persuading consumers to buy the product.

Packaging as a form of marketing communication
This role of packaging is influenced by other changes in the market. This

29. G. Foxall. *Op. cit.*, p. 95.

can be seen most clearly in the market for foodstuffs and other essential household products.[30] In the nineteenth century many manufacturers supplied local markets and consumer choice was influenced by the visible qualities of products. Then increased industrialisation and improvements in transportation allowed economies of scale to be enjoyed by manufacturers supplying wider, perhaps national, markets. Pre-packaging became important in the transport and storage of goods. Moreover in building wider markets manufacturers branded their products, the brand name being prominently displayed on the packet. Subsequently, as the range of product varieties supplied by given manufacturers increased, product names became a prominent feature on the package, frequently aided by an illustration of the contents.

The growth of supermarkets and self-service gave added importance to packaging. To be effective in self-service stores, packaging must first enable consumers to locate the product and then persuade them to buy it. The first requirement has led to changes in packaging materials, e.g. transparent packs have made it easier for producers to obtain store display space. Consumers can be persuaded to buy by changes in pack size and shape, as well as in materials. Giant packs, as in detergents and breakfast cereals, yield savings to consumers in purchase and/or transactions (e.g. transport) costs. Small packs encourage multiple purchase, e.g. one pack of facial tissues may be purchased for use in the home, one for the office, one for the car, etc. Many food items are now packed in rectangular cartons which facilitate storage in the domestic refrigerator or freezer.[31]

Packaging and the product life-cycle

When products have reached maturity, changes in packaging may be used to delay the onset of the decline stage of the product life-cycle. The change may take the form of added convenience, e.g. ring-pull cans for soft drinks, aerosols for hair-sprays and deodorants.[32] Cheaper packaging may enable a new market segment to be tapped as when plastic pots are substituted for glass pots in cosmetics. Multi-packaging of low-profit-margin mass-consumption products allows more worthwhile price reductions to be made.

As noted above, producers should balance the costs of packaging against the benefits. We have discussed benefits mainly in terms of increasing sales. Another benefit may be a reduction in distribution costs. Stronger packaging can reduce damage and pilfering, and can facilitate the use of pallets. New materials can extend the shelf life of a product and so make it feasible to deliver less frequently. For example when Golden Wonder Crisps were sold in a plastic-film bag instead of the conventional

---

30. R. N. Theodore. "Packaging as a Marketing Tool". In: M. Rines (ed.). *Marketing Handbook*. Gower, Aldershot, 2nd Edition, p. 185 ff.

31. G. Foxall. *Op. cit.*, p. 203.

32. R. N. Theodore. *Op. cit.*, p. 190

glassine paper bag, shelf life was extended to a period of weeks rather than days.

Continuous competition between the suppliers of packaging materials means that manufacturers must constantly monitor the relative advantages of different materials. This competition is exemplified by innovations in bottles, cans and plastic containers. Some innovations have reduced manufacturers' costs, e.g. the use of thinner materials. Others have been of direct benefit to consumers, e.g. by offering increased convenience.

Among the more notable recent developments have been the following. The introduction of the ring-pull can enabled cans to take sales away from bottles. Subsequently the introduction of wide-necked bottles helped to reverse this trend. In 1975 bottles of carbonated drinks in a new plastic, PET (polyethylene terephthalate), were test-marketed; within five years sales had grown to 2.5 billion units. (This can be compared with estimated sales of cans for beer and soft drinks of 2.7 billion units in 1982.) An increasing proportion of fruit-juice sales are in the form of cartons made of laminated plastic, paper and foil. Increasing quantities of wine are being sold in the bag-in-the-box (a plastic sack inside a corrugated case), although recent taste-tests conducted by consumer bodies have suggested that the quality of the wine deteriorates. Several producers of food have substituted metal pouches for cans, although this can still be said to be at the experimental stage.

SERVICE

Service is so ubiquitous a form of competition that it is impossible to do it justice in the space available. We have already noted in Chapter 13 the results of several studies demonstrating the importance of service in industrial-goods markets. In another study Buckner investigated, by means of a postal questionnaire, attitudes in firms which purchased plant and equipment. Buckner concluded that, of the factors considered by the production engineers responsible for purchase decisions, service was second in importance only to technical specifications, and ahead of price.[33]

For manufacturers of consumer goods the service that they provide to retailers and other distributors may strongly influence the chances of their product being stocked. Cunningham and Whyte found that retailers were most influenced by the following five service elements (ranked in order of importance): reliability of delivery, call/delivery frequency, availability of stock, personal relationships with salesmen, provision of information.[34]

In many consumer goods the manufacturer provides virtually no service

---
33. H. Buckner. *How British Industry Buys*. Hutchinson, 1967, p. 34.
34. M. T. Cunningham. "Innovation in Sales and Distribution Systems in *Marketing and Innovation*". Strathclyde University, 1973.

to the ultimate customer, and attention is focussed on the service provided by the retailer (see below). However there are some consumer goods whose manufacturers do supply services either directly or through a system of approved agents. The penetration of the US car market by Volkswagen and Mercedes Benz was based on highly efficient service networks. On the other hand, in Britain the deficiencies of the service networks of domestic appliance manufacturers received so much critical comment in the past that the Director of Fair Trading sought assurances that these deficiencies would be remedied.

Helen Smith identified no fewer than 21 aspects of service in grocery retailing. The relative attractiveness of these factors is indicated in Table LII. (The sample comprised 261 housewives, and a low score indicates that a high priority is attached to the factor.)

TABLE LII. IMPORTANCE OF SELECTED SERVICE FACTORS

Service Factor	Average Score
No queuing/waiting	7.22
Helpful efficient assistants	7.91
Wide choice of brands	7.92
Quick service from assistants	8.12
Easy to find goods	8.17
Friendly courteous staff	8.65
Plenty of space	9.11
Open in lunch hour	9.25
Open late one night a week	9.79
Delivery service	9.90
Good lighting	10.07
Sell other things besides groceries	10.86
Facilities for children	10.99
Accept telephone/written orders	11.21
Car park	11.55
Seating for customers	12.18
Accept cheques	12.47
Give credit	13.92
Trading stamps/dividend	14.06
Background music	15.19

Source: H. Smith: *The Retail Customer, What Kind of Service? (Unpublished)*

The quality of sales assistants—helpful, efficient, friendly etc.—was found by Smith to be of considerable importance. An interesting illustration of the effect of a salesperson's expertise is provided by an experiment conducted by Woodside and Davenport.[35] A salesperson attempted to induce purchase of a product innovation—a head and capstan cleaner kit, for use with a tape recorder—in a music shop. The only difference in the approach made to potential customers was in the oral information given by the salesperson. Two alternative messages were given, one conveying a high level of expertise (expert) and the other a low level (non-expert). This resulted in a highly significant difference in purchasing behaviour; 57.5 per cent of the customers receiving the expert message made a purchase, as compared to only 27.5 per cent of those receiving the non-expert message.

Another interesting result emerged when purchases at various prices were compared. Customers receiving the expert message behaved in the "normal" way, with sales declining as price increased. However sales to customers receiving the non-expert message were higher at $3.98 and $2.98 than at $1.98. This suggests that these customers saw price as an indicator of quality—see Chapter 13—and distrusted the lowest price. This distrust was, however, overridden by the reassurance received by the other customers from the expert salesperson, as shown in Table LIII.

TABLE LIII. PURCHASING BEHAVIOUR BY PRICE AND SALESPERSON'S EXPERIENCE

Price ($)	Percentage purchasing	
	Expert	Non-expert
1.98	80.0	30.0
2.98	70.0	36.7
3.98	66.7	40.0
5.98	13.3	3.3

CREDIT

The provision of credit has become an increasingly important competitive weapon. In international trade the provision of cheap and extended credit—often provided indirectly by governments—has been crucial in gaining some very large orders. An indication of the official importance attached to credit in international trade is the growth of support payments from the Export Credits Guarantee Department in respect of export finance supplied by banks (Fig. 88).

At the other end of the spectrum, there has been a large increase in the forms of credit available—from both financial and non-financial institutions—to consumers. A consumer can now supplement a bank loan or hire-purchase agreement by purchasing with the aid of a range of credit cards. (Table LIV).

35. A. G. Woodside and J. W. Davenport Jun. "Effect of Price and Salesman Expertise on Customer Purchasing Behaviour". *Journal of Business* Vol. 49 (1976).

V. IMPLEMENTATION OF STRATEGY

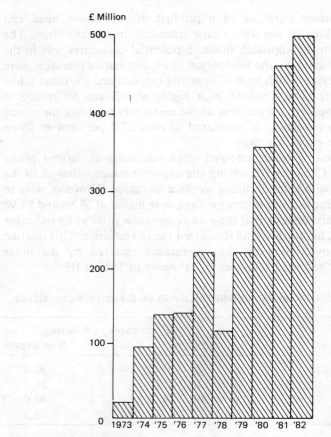

Fig. 88. *Interest support payments (estimate; year end March).*

Source: *ECGD.*

TABLE LIV. UK CREDIT CARD MARKET, END 1981

	No. of cards (million)	No. of retailers accepting
Barclaycard/Visa	6.1	169,000
Trustcard	1.5	
Access	5.4	175,000
Amex	0.6	53,000
Diners Club	0.3	41,000
Store cards	4.5	

Source: *Banking Information Service*

Of total consumer credit of £13.3 billion outstanding at the end of 1981, the banks accounted for just over two-thirds, finance houses for over one-quarter, and retailers for over one-tenth.

CHOICE OF DISTRIBUTION CHANNELS

All the elements of the marketing mix are designed to facilitate a product's progress from producer to consumer. In many instances there is a considerable diversity of channels through which the product can be distributed, and the choice of distribution channel is often an important strategic decision.

Figure 89 illustrates the various channels that a manufacturer of antiseptic washing-up liquid might use.[36] In making his decision the manufacturer has to answer many questions, including the following: Do I wish to sell to final users (via chemists and grocers) or to intermediaries (hospitals and catering establishments)? Do I wish my product to have a specialist, up-market image (sales via chemists rather than grocers)? Do I wish to sell small packages (especially chemists and grocers) or in bulk (hospitals and catering establishments)? Do I wish to take full responsibility for delivery to retailers (multiple chemists and grocers) or to sell via wholesalers? Even this small sample of questions is sufficient to demonstrate that decisions concerning the choice of distribution channel should be closely integrated with decisions concerning other elements of the marketing mix.

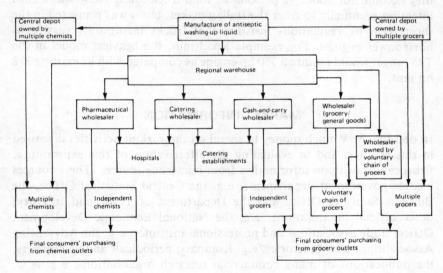

Fig. 89. *Channels of distribution for antiseptic washing-up liquid.*

When Leyland Vehicles launched its T45 range of heavy trucks in 1981 it had to decide how many European countries it should initially supply. It decided to confine its initial overseas selling operations to only six European countries: Belgium, Denmark, Holland, Spain, Portugal and

---

36. This figure, which is based on the work of C. Magrill, first appeared in: B. Lowes and J. R. Sparkes. *Modern Managerial Economics.* Heinemann, 1974, p. 211.

France. It was felt that to have tackled more countries might have put too great a strain on its resources. The main factor determining the choice of country was that Leyland already had its own distribution company in each country with the exception of Portugal. In Portugal Leyland was established as a supplier of heavy trucks in kit form, to be assembled by a Portuguese company, and as a supplier of light trucks in its own right. Imports into both Portugal and Spain are strictly controlled by a licensing system, but it was anticipated that these markets would become more accessible when the two countries entered the EEC.

France was seen as the key market for the initial push into Europe. It ranks as the third-largest European market, after West Germany and the UK, and Leyland already had—in addition to its own distribution company—a sizeable dealership network: 12 dealers selling Leyland vehicles exclusively, 12 selling Leyland vehicles alongside other makes, and 12 equipped to service Leyland vehicles. Moreover it was felt that the rationalisation of dealer networks by other groups would leave some dealers anxious to acquire a Leyland franchise.

The decision not to enter West Germany at this stage was mainly due to the very firm hold the German manufacturers have on their home market: they account for about 92 per cent of total truck sales. There was a firm intention eventually to enter the Italian maket, but it was protected in the short term by regulations insisting that trucks incorporate very-high-horsepower engines. For example Roadtrain, the heaviest model in the T45 range, would require a 350 hp engine as compared with its existing 272 hp unit.

MARKET INFORMATION

In deciding how much money to spend on the various activities discussed in this chapter, and in evaluating the effectiveness of this expenditure, firms can draw upon information from numerous sources. These sources include government departments, e.g. the Central Statistical Office, the Business Statistics Office and the Department of Trade and Industry; other official organisations, e.g. the National Economic Development Office; trade associations and professional institutes, e.g. the Advertising Association; trade directories, e.g. Kompass; periodicals and newspapers; the publications of many commercial research organisations, e.g. A.C. Nielsen, Mintel and AGB Research Ltd.

Ian Maclean has suggested that information obtained from these various sources can be grouped under five main headings:[37]

(*a*) The size of the market.
(*b*) The segmentation of the market by end-use industries, regions and size range of customers.

37. I. Maclean. *Marketing Data*. In: M. Rines, *op. cit.* p. 75ff.

15. NON-PRICE COMPETITION

(c) Growth or decline of end-use sectors, due to changes in the use of products and particular applications.

(d) Factors influencing the share of a market held by a company.

(e) Individual companies, both customers and competitors.

Broadly speaking, official statistics are most useful for the earlier headings, trade sources for the middle headings, and specific enquiries undertaken by, or on behalf of, the individual firm for the later headings.

QUESTIONS

1. Discuss the ways in which the following firms might attempt to protect and develop their markets: (a) a biscuit manufacturer, (b) British Telecom, (c) a manufacturer of high-quality woollen yarn, (d) a firm which owns a chain of bingo halls, (e) an owner of a racecourse.

2. Discuss the relationship between competition and uncertainty.

3. In what circumstances is advertising likely to be most effective?

4. Why might an advertising theme for a product be changed even though no change occurs in the product itself?

5. What factors might account for (a) differences in the advertising-to-sales ratio for different product groups, (b) changes in the ratio for given groups? Illustrate your answer by reference to Table XLVI.

6. Comment on the distribution of advertising expenditure by media, shown in Table XLVIII.

7. Discuss the suitability of alternative media for advertising the following products: (a) double glazing, (b) a multi-purpose machine tool, (c) a new type of chocolate bar, (d) a cold-water detergent, (e) overseas holidays.

8. Explain, with examples, the term "marketing communication".

9. Discuss the proposition that marketing communication benefits suppliers at the expense of consumers.

10. Why do so many new products fail?

11. Discuss "the changing role of packaging".

12. What aspects of service are likely to be especially important in (a) television rentals, (b) banking, (c) motor vehicle repairs, (d) the supply of printing services to industrial customers?

13. Discuss the factors that might influence the choice of distribution channels by manufacturers of (a) tiles for use in canteens, kitchens, bathrooms etc., (b) lawnmowers, (c) shoe polish, (d) office machinery.

Index

A. C. Nielsen Co Ltd, 283, 288, 323, 330
A. I. Kearney, 191
Abernathy, W., 237, 238
accelerator, 17, 19
accounting cost, 60, 141
ACORN, 317
advertising, 302, 307–18
  demand for, 307–9
  economies of scale, 303
  as entry barrier, 303
  expenditure, 307, 313
  media, 313–18
  ratio to sales, 28, 312
  supply of, 309–10
  themes, 310–11
Alcoa, 260, 262
Alfa-Romeo, 78, 202
American Brands, 173
American Can, 173, 261
American Motors, 204, 302
Amersham International, 90
Argos, 33
Asda, 287, 288
Assisted Areas, 39, 40, 41
Association of British Travel Agents, 32
Avana, 282
average
  fixed cost, 62, 63, 68, 124
  total cost, 68, 73, 78, 79, 124, 164, 208, 212, 275
  variable cost, 66, 68, 82, 124, 126

Baden-Fuller, C., 282
bank lending, 94
Banks, P., 192
Barnato, M., 99
barometric techniques, 49
barriers to entry, 27, 128, 135, 160, 170, 303
Batchelors, 321
Baumol, W. J., 140, 214
Bayliss, B. T., 253
Beechams, 320
Beesley, W. H., 149
behavioural theory of the firm, 140, 146–8
Bell, D., 142
Betts, R. J., 232
BIC, 249
bidding models, 263–7
Billett and Company, 317
Birds, 321
Black Bolt and Nut Association, 31
BMW, 229, 278
book rate of return, 108
Boots, 29, 200
Boston Consulting Group, 79, 189, 292

Bovril, 303
Bowbrick, P., 258
branding, 302
British Aerospace, 95
British Airways, 36
British American Tobacco, 190
British Franchise Association, 221
British Gas Corporation, 36, 113, 114
British Leyland (BL), 36, 78, 92, 202, 204, 217, 278, 329
British Market Research Bureau, 317
British National Oil Corporation, 38
British Petroleum, 58, 91, 184, 187, 193, 215
British Rail, 33, 95, 233, 287
British Shipbuilders, 114
British Technology Group, 37
Britoil, 38, 95
Brittan, S., 21
Brown, F., 182
Brown, R., 16
Brown, W., 267
Brown and Polson, 321
BTR, 72
Buchanan, J. M., 60
Buckner, H., 325
business cycle, 50
Business Start-up Scheme, 37, 93
buy-response curve, 255, 256, 257
Buzzell, R. D., 292
Byoir, C., 317

Cadburys, 233
capital
  consumption, 9
  gearing, 96–8
  rationing, 110
Carrefour, 283
Caves, R. E., 195
CDC, 78
Cement Makers' Federation, 31
Central Electricity Generating Board, 33, 35
Chamberlin, E. H., 122
Channon, D., 213
characteristics space, 229, 320
Charterhouse Industrial Development, 92
Chiu, J. S. Y., 258
Chloride, 284
choice of production technique, 224
Christopher, M., 249
Chrysler, 302
Churchill, D., 322
Clarke, C. J., 190, 191, 192
Coaker, J. W., 251

cobweb, 159
coincident indicators, 50, 51
Colgate Palmolive, 233, 320
Colley, R., 309
companies,
  joint stock, 89
  private, 89
  public, 90
  small, 92
competition,
  forms, 305–6
  monpolistic, 121, 122, 129, 135
  perfect, 27, 121–7, 155
  policy, 27–34
Competition Act 1980, 33
consumers'
  choice, 135
  expenditure, 34
  welfare, 26
Continental Can, 173
Continental Shelf Act 1964, 38
continuity of supply, 207
co-ordination of decisions/activities, 167, 171–4
cost,
  accounting, 60, 141
  average fixed, 62, 63, 68, 124
  average total, 68, 73, 78, 79, 124, 164, 208, 212, 275
  average variable, 66, 68, 82, 124, 126
  escapable, 81
  of finance (funds), 96–9
  incremental, 81, 82, 274
  marginal, 79, 123, 124, 132, 142, 155
  opportunity, 60, 82, 141, 158, 209, 295
  subjective, 60
  sunk, 81
cost benefit analysis, 114
costs,
  external, 114
  fixed, 62–5
  overhead, 64–5
  semi-variable, 67
  transactions, 209
  variable, 65–7, 209
Courtaulds, 211, 217
credit, 327
Credit for Industry, 92
Crocker National Corporation, 200
Crowther, J., 286
Cunningham, M. T., 251, 253, 325
current assets, 88
cyclical indicators, 51
Cyert, R. M., 140

DAF, 229
Daimler-Benz, 201, 204
Davenport, J. W., 327
Davis, E. W., 91
Dean, J., 254, 281, 289

Deaton, A., 181
decision tree, 235
Delphi technique, 54
demand
  cross elasticity, 272
  income elasticity, 180
  price elasticity, 272
  stability, 304
  trend, 180
demand curve, 111, 122, 128, 129, 131, 133, 144, 247
  kinked, 131, 132, 143
de-mergers, 217
depreciation, 67
  charge, 63, 64
  methods, 64
  provisions, 67, 89
Development Areas, 39
diffusion, 224, 226, 227
diminishing returns, 125
Director General of Fair Trading, 29, 33, 34, 326
Dirlam, J. B., 244, 260, 261, 262
discounted cash flow, 101–7
discounts,
  to distributors, 279, 281, 287
  quantity, 284
diseconomies of scale, 72, 211
Distant Water Vessels Development Association, 31
distribution channels,
  choice, 329–30
  new, 302
  width, 302
diversification, 146, 188, 212–14
  and growth, 214
  and joint ventures, 217
  motives, 213
  strategy, 212
Dolby, 219
Dunlop, 295
Du Pont, 261, 290

Eassie, R., 257
econometric models, 50–5
economies of scale, 27, 28, 29, 35, 69–77, 165, 168, 193, 247, 275, 303
Economist Intelligence Unit, 283
Edelman, F., 267
Electra Risk Capital, 93
Employment Act 1980, 37
Employment and Training Act 1981, 40
ENI, 58
equal product curve, 124, 225, 226
equilibrium, 148–50
  national income, 10, 12, 14
  output, 127, 128, 129
  price, 127, 129
Equity Capital for Industry, 92
escapable cost, 81

INDEX

European Agricultural Guidance and Guarantee Fund, 42
European Coal and Steel Community, 40
European Economic Community, 41–2, 297
European Investment Bank, 42
European Regional Development Fund, 42
European Social Fund, 40, 41
expansion (integration)
  horizontal, 188, 211–12
  vertical, 188, 208–11
expenditure,
  consumers', 3, 4
  final, 3, 8, 9
  flows, 3
  government, 15
  increase, 14, 18
  investment, 3, 4, 88
experience (learning) effect, 78, 79, 290
Export Credits Guarantee Department, 327
exports, 3, 7
  pricing, 277–8
  ratios, 7
external benefits and costs, 114
extrapolation, 47–9
Exxon, 192, 216

Fair Trading Act 1973, 28, 29, 30, 31, 34
Fiat, 78, 193, 202, 203, 221
final expenditure, 3, 8, 9
Finance Corporation for Industry, 92
Finance for Industry, 92
financial economies of scale, 71
Fine Fare, 283
Fisons, 239
fixed costs, 62–5
Flavell, R. B., 297
Florence, P. S., 139
Food and Drugs Act 1955, 38
Ford, 204, 229
Ford, D., 220
Ford, G. T., 252
Foxall, G. R., 230, 309, 323, 324
franchising, 221
Friedman, M., 21
Froggatt, J. D., 277
Fujitshu, 78
Fulop, C., 310, 311, 318, 320, 321
funds,
  cost, 96–9
  flow, 88
  sources, 89–95
  uses, 87–9

G. Ruddle & Co, 219, 282
Gabor, A., 253, 255, 259
Gale, B. T., 292
gearing, 96–8
GEC, 72
General Electric, 173, 220

General Mills, 261
General Motors, 171, 192, 262
generics, 283
GKN, 29, 218
Glaxo, 29
Goodyear, 262
government
  consumption, 36
  expenditure, 15
Granger, C. W. J., 253, 255, 259
Great Universal Stores, 218
gross
  domestic product, 9
  national product, 9
growth
  and diversification, 214
  maximisation, 140
  as objective, 139, 145

Habitat, 200
Harris International Marketing, 288
Hay, D. A., 87, 98, 142, 208, 223
Haynes, W. W., 271, 300
Heidensohn, K., 142
Heinz, 282, 311, 321
Hitachi, 193
Honda, 78, 202
horizontal expansion (integration), 188, 211–12
Houthakker, H., 52
Hovell, P. S., 277
Humphreys, G., 265
Hunt, H. G., 277
Huster, A. P., 210
hypothetical shopping situation, 255, 258

IBM, 252, 295
ICI, 217, 237
ICL, 37
Imperial Tobacco, 190, 303
import ratios, 7
imports, 9
income elasticity of demand, 180
incremental
  analysis, 105
  cost, 81, 82, 274
  revenue, 81, 274
Industrial and Commercial Finance Corporation, 92
Industrial Development Certificate, 40
Industrial Market Research Ltd, 277
industrial policy, 36–9
Industrial Reorganisation Corporation, 37
Industrial Training Boards, 40
Industry Act 1972, 36, 39
Industry Act 1975, 36
inflation, 19
information agreements, 172
innovation, 226, 227
  customer as initiator, 230

INDEX

defensive, 231
factors affecting success, 236–9
major, 228
minor, 228
offensive, 228
process, 224
product, 224
unsatisfactory rate, 26
Institute of Fiscal Studies, 278
Institute of Public Relations, 320
interest rates, 16
internal rate of return, 102, 103, 104, 105, 106
International Stores, 283
investment,
direct foreign, 194
expenditure, 3, 4, 88
investment appraisal,
applications, 109–10
discounting methods, 100–7
in public sector, 112–15
non-discouinting methods, 107–9
uncertainty, 99
isocost curve, 225, 226
isoquant, 124

J. & P. Coates, 77
Jaques, E., 267
Jarrett, M., 92
Johnson, P. S., 68, 69
joint
stock companies, 89
ventures/ownership, 77, 196, 217
Jones, R., 135
Joseph Lucas, 231, 281, 284

Kaplan, A. D. H., 244, 260, 261, 262
Kelly, J. P., 251
Kennecott, 163, 216
Kenny-Levick, C., 250
Keynes, J. M., 14
Kindahl, J. K., 131
kinked demand curve, 131, 132, 143
Klein, H. E., 57, 58, 59
Kotler, P., 318
Koutsoyiannis, A., 305
Krausher, P., 57
Krystol, I., 142

lagging indicators, 50, 51
Laker Airways, 292
Lamb, C. W., 290
Lancaster, K. J., 182
Lanzillotti, R. F., 244, 260, 261, 262
Layton, C., 231
leading indicators, 50, 51
learning, 148
effect, 78, 79, 290
Leibenstein, H., 73, 142
Lever Bros, 77, 232, 318
licensing, 38, 197, 219, 231

Liggett and Myers, 173
linear programming, 82, 311
Linneman, R. E., 57, 58, 59
Lintas, 187
Livesey, F., 16, 250
London Brick Co, 30
Loan Guarantee Scheme, 37, 93
Lowes, B., 329

McEwan, F., 311
Maclean, I., 330
Macmillan Committee, 92
Madill, J., 322
Magrill, C., 329
managerial
economies of scale, 72
utility, 140, 146
manpower policy, 40–1
Manpower Services Commission, 41
Mansfield, E., 236
March, J. G., 140
marginal
cost, 79, 123, 124, 132, 142, 155
product, 124
revenue, 123, 132, 142, 155
Mark, J., 182
market
evaluation, 56
information, 330
Market Entry Guarantee Scheme, 36
market sharing agreements, 172
marketing
economies of scale, 70
research, 223
markets
development and protection, 302
sub-division, 275–87
Marks and Spencers, 207, 282
Marris, R., 140, 145, 214
Matsushita-JVC, 237
Maunder, W. P. J., 302, 303
maximisation
growth, 140
managerial utility, 140, 146
profit, 123, 130, 135, 138, 140, 141
sales revenue, 140, 142–5
media, 314–18
planning and selection, 311
Medicines Act, 1968, 38
Meeks, G., 28
Mercedes-Benz, 326
mergers, 28, 29
trans-European, 215
merit goods, 26
Merrett, A. J., 107
Metal Box, 286
Metcalf, D., 41
Midland Bank, 199
Miller, M. H., 98
minimum efficient (economic) scale, 76, 77
Minkes, A. L., 230

INDEX

Mobil, 216
Modigliani, F., 98
money supply, 16
monopolistic competition, 121, 122, 129, 135
monopoly, 27, 121, 122, 128, 135
 profits, 128, 135
Monopoly (and Mergers) Commission, 28, 29, 33, 70, 281, 284, 286, 288
Monopoly and Mergers Act 1965, 28, 214
Monroe, K. B., 258
Montgomery Ward, 216
Morgan, A., 319
Morita, A., 237
Morris, D. J., 87, 98, 142, 208, 223
Moss, S., 208, 304, 305
Mothercare, 300
Multidivisional (M-form) enterprise/ organisation, 73, 198
multinational enterprises, 192–8, 199, 297
 direct foreign investment, 194
 patterns of control, 197
 strategy formulation, 192
 transfer pricing, 297–8
multiplier, 17, 19

Naprstek, K., 262
National Bus Co, 217
National Coal Board, 36, 95, 214, 232
National Economic Development Council, 108, 113
National Enterprise Board, 36, 37, 92
National Health Service, 30
national income, 8–14
National Research and Development Corporation, 37
National Steel, 261
nationalisation, 35–6
nationalised industries, 94–5, 113–14
natural rate of unemployment, 21, 22
Net Book Agreement, 31
net present value analysis, 102–7
new issue market, 90
new products, 320–3
 failures, 322
 introduction, 320
 surveys, 55
 timing, 323
Newbould, G. D., 28
Nissan, 196, 202
Northern Foods, 282
Nottingham Manufacturing, 282

O'Brien, D. P., 135
offer for sale, 90, 91, 92
 by tender, 90, 91
Office of Fair Trading, 28, 32, 33, 172
Oi, W. Y., 210
oligopoly, 121, 122, 130–5
open market, 155–9
opportunity cost, 60, 82, 141, 158, 209, 295

organisational slack, 141, 147, 171
overhead costs, 64–5
own labels, 282
Oxenfeldt, A. R., 269, 275, 279

Packaging, 302, 323–5
 as marketing communication, 323
 and product life cycle, 324
Park Bros, 284
Parker Pen Co, 249, 254
Pass, C., 244, 305
Patents Act 1977, 34
Paton and Baldwin, 71
payback method of investment appraisal, 107
Penrose, E., 146, 213
perfect competition, 27, 121–7, 155
Peugot, 78, 203
Philip Morris, 190
Phillips curve, 21, 22, 23
Piercy, N., 277, 278
Pierson, B. J., 182
Pilkingtons, 219, 228
Pindyck, R. S., 51
planning gap, 188
Post Office, 35, 95, 113, 214, 317
Prais, S. J., 139
Pratten, C. F., 76
Prestel, 317
Presto, 283
price
 agreements, 172
 awareness, 253
 basic, 243, 244
 delivered, 276
 differentials, 272, 274
 discrimination, 259, 274
 elasticity of demand, 272
 equilibrium, 127, 129
 experimentation, 253, 258
 ex-works, 275
 floor, 156
 as indicator of quality, 258
 leadership, 28, 172, 262
 legal constraints, 279
 and purchasing decisions, 249–52
 penetration, 289–90
 and marketing mix, 246–9
 sensitivity, 253
 skimming, 289–90
 target, 163, 164, 165, 167
 umbrella, 291
 war, 167
price-last-paid curve, 257
price-minus costing, 171
prices and incomes policy, 19, 20
pricing,
 in bid situations, 262–7
 discretion, 212, 260
 and experience effect, 290
 exports, 277, 278

INDEX

mature products, 292
objectives, 244–6
to other manufacturers, 284
parallel, 28
pioneer products, 289
policies, 165–6, 260–2
and product life cycle, 288–93
product line, 293–6
products in decline, 293
promotional, 287–8
rule-of-thumb, 173
seasonal, 163, 164
transfer, 296–8
private
companies, 89
placing, 90, 91, 92
process
diffusion, 224
innovation, 224
Proctor and Gamble, 148, 233
product,
change, 224, 227
cycle model, 193
development, 302
differentiation, 135, 171, 183, 246, 247
innovation, 224
life cycle, 288–93
new, 320–3
portfolio analysis, 189
resource matrix, 190
product analysis pricing, 267
profit(s),
exports, 277
maximisation, 123, 130, 135, 138, 140, 141
monopoly, 128, 135
normal, 123
stable, 212, 215
supernormal, 129, 130
target, 164
Pryke, R., 36
public
companies, 90
issue by prospectus, 90, 91
relations, 320
purchasing economies of scale, 70

Quinton Hazell, 284

Radcliffe Committee, 92
Ratchford, B. T., 252
rate of return method of investment appraisal, 108
rationalisation, 37
RCA, 266
Reekie, W. D., 232, 307, 308, 309, 311, 312, 320
Regional Development Grants, 39, 196
Regional Selective Assistance, 39, 196
regional policy, 39–40
regression analysis, 50

Reid, G. C., 132
Renault, 78, 193, 203, 204
required rate of return, 114
Resale Prices Act 1964, 32
research and development, 28, 29, 223, 234
as investment decision, 227
portfolio selection, 232
strategic objectives, 228
supplier-customer co-operation, 230
resource portfolio matrix, 191
Restrictive Practices Court, 30, 32
Restrictive Trade Practices Act 1956, 30
retained earnings, 87, 89, 98
revenue
incremental, 81, 274
marginal, 123, 132, 142, 155
Reynolds, 173
Richardson, G. B., 135
rights issue, 90
Rines, M., 57, 324, 330
risk reduction, 71
Robinson, J., 122
Robinson, N., 142
Rolls Royce, 36, 92, 236
Rosenbloom, R., 237, 238
Rosendale, P. B., 277
Rothwell, R., 236
Rubinfeld, D. L., 52
Ryan, C., 220

Saab, 203, 230
Said, H. A., 305
Sainsburys, 72, 282, 287
sales
growth models, 54
promotions, 318
revenue maximisation, 140, 142–5
satisficing, 147
scale
coefficient, 76
factor, 78
of organisation, 61, 64, 124, 158
Scanlon, B., 190, 191
scenario analysis, 57–9
Scherer, F. M., 173, 231
scrip (bonus) issue, 91
Selection Trust, 216
semi-variable costs, 67
Shaw, R. W., 311
Shaw, S. A., 311
Shell, 192
Shepherd, W. G., 143
Shipley, D., 245
Shwayder Bros, 294
Silberston, Z. A., 76
simulated shopping situations, 56, 255, 258
Skillcentres (government training centres), 40
small companies/firms, 37, 92
Smith, A., 171
Smith, H., 326

INDEX

Smith, R. A., 172
Sohio, 216
Sony, 193, 237
sources of funds, 87, 89–95
Sowter, A. P., 259
Sparkes, J. R., 329
Special Development Areas, 39
stability of sales, 207
Stigler, G. J., 131
Stock Exchange, 90, 91
   listing, 91
Stocks, 208
Stout, R. G., 258
strategic planning process, 179–92
strategic search, 188
strengths–weaknesses profile, 185
strikes, 72
sub-division of markets by
   functional role of customer, 279
   personal characteristics of purchaser, 287
   space, 275
   time, 278
subjective cost, 60
substitution, 84, 181, 293
Suckling, C., 237
Sultan, R. G. M., 292
sunk cost, 81
Suntook, F., 277
supply curve, 111, 126, 127, 128, 155, 158, 159
surveys of
   companies' expectations, 53
   expert opinion, 54
   new products, 55
   purchasers' intentions, 53
   sales force, 54
Sutton, C. J., 187, 208, 209, 214, 233, 234, 236
Swift & Co, 260
Sykes, A., 107
Symons, L., 267, 268

T. I. Raleigh, 33
target
   price, 163, 164, 165, 167
   profit, 164
Target Group Index, 217
taxation, 16
Taylor, L., 52
technical
   change, 224, 225, 226
   economies of scale, 69, 75
technically efficient frontier, 224, 225
technology life cycle, 220
Tesco, 282, 283, 286, 288
test
   discount rate, 113
   marketing, 56
Theodore, R. N., 324
Thomas, R. B., 232
Thomas Tait & Sons, 199

Thorn-EMI, 220
time-series analysis, 48
Training Opportunities Scheme, 40, 41
transactions costs, 209
transfer
   payments, 15
   pricing, 296–8
trend projection, 47–9
Tullis Russell, 199
Turner and Newall, 30

Udell, J., 305
uncertainty, 138, 148, 208, 304
   and investment appraisal, 95
   in R & D, 234
unemployment, 21, 22
Unigate, 303
Unilever, 187
unincorporated businesses, 89
Union Carbide, 261
unitary (U-form) enterprise/organisation, 73, 198
United Drapery Stores, 218
Unlisted Securities Market, 91, 92
uses of funds, 86–9

variable costs, 65–7, 209
Venture Capital Scheme, 93
Vernon, I. R., 290
Vernon, R., 193
vertical
   integration, 188, 208–11
   relationships, 206–11
Viota, 282
Virts, J. R., 238
Volkswagen, 78, 193, 202, 203, 204, 326
Volvo, 78, 203, 204, 229

W. H. Smith, 71
Wagner, S., 236
Walker, A. W., 262
Walls, 303
Walters, D., 54
Water Tube Boilers Association, 31
Waterson, M. J., 312
Weston, F. J., 238
Wheatley, J. J., 258
Whyte, J. G., 251, 253
Wiggins Teape, 199
Williamson, O. E., 140, 146
Wilson Committee, 91, 93
Wipac, 284
Woodside, A. G., 327
Wright, M., 92

X-inefficiency, 73, 142, 171

Yeomans, K. A., 91
Youth Opportunities Programme, 41
Youth Training Scheme, 41